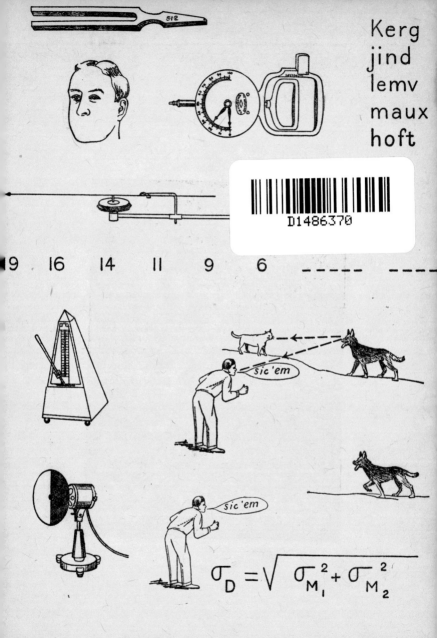

Great Experiments
in
Psychology

THE CENTURY PSYCHOLOGY SERIES
RICHARD M. ELLIOTT, *Editor*

GREAT EXPERIMENTS IN PSYCHOLOGY

Revised and Enlarged Edition

BY

HENRY E. GARRETT

Associate Professor of Psychology
Columbia University

D. APPLETON-CENTURY COMPANY

INCORPORATED

NEW YORK   LONDON

PREFACE TO THE REVISED EDITION

This book differs in at least two ways from its predecessor. About 100 pages of new material have been added, and much of the original text has been rewritten, revised, and reinterpreted. The plan followed in the first edition has been retained; namely, that of beginning with some fundamental psychological problem and bringing the experimental attack upon it up-to-date. Titles of chapters have also been kept. Some of the chapters have been considerably changed and several completely rewritten, while others are less extensively altered. One new chapter, that on personality, has been added. Those sections dealing with intelligence, learning, individual differences, Gestalt psychology, and physiological psychology have been changed the most; those dealing with psychophysics and reaction time have been changed the least. Bibliographies by chapters have been added for those who wish to refer to the literature directly.

I suspect that this book will continue to find its chief use as a second book in the general and experimental courses. For many beginning students it will probably be their chief, and perhaps only, acquaintance with the experimental foundations of psychology. For the more interested students it may well serve as an introduction to and stimulator of further reading.

I am grateful to the many colleagues who have contributed to this revision. Dr. R. M. Elliott, editor of The Century Psychology Series, read the book in manuscript and made many constructive suggestions. The following colleagues read one or more chapters or contributed expert opinion in their special fields: R. S. Woodworth, A. T. Poffenberger, C. Landis, G. W. Hartmann, F. S. Keller, M. Trawick, and T. W. Reese. M. Duane Bown rendered indispensable aid throughout the preparation of the manuscript.

HENRY E. GARRETT.

Columbia University

EDITOR'S INTRODUCTION TO THE FIRST EDITION

Is there in the college curriculum any subject in which it is more easy to interest the student, and more difficult to instruct him, than psychology? At present the student is usually taught first what is known in psychological science (factual content, as in the typical beginning course), second how it has been found out (experimental methods and laboratory), and third how to discover something himself (research). The student's contacts with these three kinds of opportunity are step-wise, one after the other.

This procedure is unjustified traditionalism. The honors student should be treated as a graduate student, less competent perhaps, but recognized as employing the same mental operations of criticism and research. The sophomore or even freshman student should be shown the living methods of psychology, if possible in practice. With or without laboratory facilities to draw upon, the use of a single standard text in the first course is not to be recommended. Habits of skimming, acquired in rapid reading courses in history, literature, and the like, may not affect the study habits of the student when he is up against a mathematics or physics assignment. They do undoubtedly tend to keep him from taking a ten-page psychology assignment seriously.

There has long been need for a *supplementary* text like the present one, stressing experimental methods, giving the student some idea of how psychological facts have been discovered, who the men are who have contributed to the upbuilding of psychology, and what problems await immediate solution.

Dr. Garrett's book, used in parallel with a text of standard content, will punctuate with question-marks the stores of knowledge so authoritatively displayed and will soften the rigidity of the system—behavioristic, experiential, organismic, or what not—which we force upon the unsuspecting and all too gullible beginner. In its pages psychology appears to the student as a live, growing enterprise with a personal history and with a future to which it is not at all impossible to contribute.

R. M. E.

CONTENTS

Contents

Contents

Contents

CHAPTER 8

KÖHLER'S EXPERIMENTS IN PERCEPTION AND LEARNING
AND THEIR IMPORTANCE FOR GESTALT PSYCHOLOGY

CHAPTER 9

THORNDIKE'S AND WOODWORTH'S EXPERIMENTS ON THE
TRANSFER OF TRAINING AND THEIR INFLUENCE UPON
THE DOCTRINE OF FORMAL DISCIPLINE

CHAPTER 10

EBBINGHAUS'S STUDIES IN MEMORY AND FORGETTING

Contents

CHAPTER II

WATSON'S EXPERIMENTAL STUDIES OF THE BEHAVIOR OF THE HUMAN INFANT

CHAPTER 12

EXPERIMENTAL STUDIES OF THE EMOTIONS: THE WORK OF CANNON AND OTHERS

Contents

CHAPTER 13

VISUAL AND AUDITORY PERCEPTION: THE WORK OF HELMHOLTZ AND OTHERS

CHAPTER 14

CATTELL'S STUDIES IN THE MEASUREMENT OF REACTION TIME

Contents

ILLUSTRATIONS

FIGURES

Figures

Figures

Great Experiments
in
Psychology

Chapter 1

BINET'S SCALE FOR MEASURING GENERAL INTELLIGENCE

I. THE BEGINNING OF THE MOVEMENT FOR MEASURING INTELLIGENCE

In 1904 the French Minister of Public Instruction appointed a commission of physicians, educators, and scientists to whom he assigned the task of formulating methods and making recommendations for the instruction of feeble-minded children in the public schools of Paris. One member of this commission was the eminent psychologist, Alfred Binet, at that time Director of the Laboratory of Physiological Psychology at the Sorbonne. Binet was born in Nice, France, in 1857, and was educated to be a physician. His interests, however, early directed him into abnormal and child psychology, and it is in the latter field that he is best known. In 1895 Binet founded the journal *L'année Psychologique,* in which a number of his own studies and those of his students are published. As a direct outgrowth of his work as a member of the commission mentioned above, Binet in 1905, with the collaboration of Theophile Simon, published his first rough scale for measuring general intelligence by means of a set of tests. This first scale was followed by an enlarged and revised edition in 1908, and by a third and last revision in 1911, published shortly before Binet's untimely death.

It has often been said—and truly—that the development of the Binet-Simon Scale marks the real beginning of intelligence testing as we know it to-day. But it must not be thought on that account that Binet's scale is merely of historical interest. After thirty years of revision, criticism, discussion, and experimentation, it is to-day still the prototype of the best modern scales for measuring general intelligence, while Binet's conception of intelligence is in remarkably close agreement with the views of present-day psychologists. Less than ten years after the publication of its final revision, the Binet-Simon Scale was being extensively used in America, Canada, England, Australia, New Zealand, South Africa, Belgium, Germany, Switzerland, Italy, Russia, and China, and had been translated into Japanese and Turkish. Such widespread and immediate popularity demonstrates clearly the great need felt for just such a device for measuring intelligence as Binet's tests supplied.

2. THE DEVELOPMENT OF THE BINET-SIMON SCALE

How can we explain the remarkable response to Binet's simple set of tests? Perhaps the best way of answering this question is to consider just how Binet made his scale, how it differed from previous tests, and what it was designed to do. First, let us look at Binet's conception of intelligence, upon which the method and scale were built. Before Binet, mental tests had been devised chiefly with the intention of measuring rather narrow aspects or phases of mental ability, such as rote memory, attention-span, speed and accuracy of perception, discrimination in checking numbers and recognizing forms, speed and accuracy of voluntary movements, sensory acuity, and the like. Binet criticized tests of this sort as being too restricted in scope to be good measures of general ability. To measure intelligence, he said, we must tap the "higher mental faculties," such as reasoning, imagination, judgment, since it is here that differences in intellectual ability are most likely to be manifested. Attention and adaptability, along with good judgment, were for Binet the most important contributors to

ALFRED BINET

(1857–1911)

general intelligence. Intellect, he says, is compounded of "judgment, common sense, initiative, and the ability to adapt oneself." Again, he stresses "insight" into one's own capabilities (notoriously absent in the feeble-minded), the ability readily to adapt one's behavior to a definite end or goal, and persistence in sticking to a task once undertaken. Binet distinctly marked off intelligence from mere information which may be acquired in school or in a cultural environment, although he insisted that the intelligent person, unless deprived of a normal environment by untoward circumstances, will always acquire more information than the unintelligent one.

Binet did not attempt to analyze intellect into its parts and then devise simple tests to measure the elements. On the contrary, he proposed, as a more promising approach, to estimate intelligence by measuring the *combined* effects of attention, imagination, judgment, and reasoning, as shown in the performance of fairly complex tasks. His first scale consisted of thirty carefully selected questions, or problems. These were arranged in a rough order of difficulty which was determined by trying them out on about fifty normal children of different ages. The tests were not grouped according to age level; Binet simply indicated how many tests a normal child of a given age should be expected to pass. In his second scale, that of 1908, the tests were for the first time arranged into age-groups, constituting the first age-scale. This scale contained from four to eight tests for each age-level from three to thirteen. Tests were allotted to specific age-groups in the following manner. Whenever a test was passed by from 60 to 90 per cent of a given age-group, Binet considered it to be a fair test for children of that age. If all or nearly all of his five-year-olds failed in a given test, he regarded it as obviously too hard for children of that age; while if all of his ten-year-olds passed a test successfully it was clearly too easy for that age-group. This method of discovering at what age a given test should be located was somewhat rough, to be sure, but it possessed the virtue of being based upon experimental evidence rather than upon subjective impression.

The 1908 scale is of more than ordinary interest because here for the first time Binet employed the concept of "mental age." A child's mental age (M A), as computed, depends upon the number of tests in the scale which he can pass successfully. If he performs all of the tests assigned to the eight-year-old group, for instance, he is said to have a mental age of 8 years, no matter what his chronological age (C A) may be. If he happens to be five years old chronologically, he is, of course, advanced three years; if eight years old, just normal; and if ten years old, retarded two years. Description of performance in terms of mental age has proved to be extremely useful in mental measurement. For one thing, "age scores" are more easily understood than other kinds of scores by the non-psychologically trained person; and furthermore, such measures permit a quick and meaningful comparison not only of a child's years of mental growth with his years of physical growth, but of one child's mental growth with that of another.

The 1911 scale represents three additional years of work with the 1908 scale and is the final form in which his tests were left by Binet. There are fifty-four tests in the 1911 scale, arranged in age-groups as follows:

Binet's 1911 Scale

Age III.
   1. Points to nose, eyes, and mouth.
   2. Repeats two digits.
   3. Enumerates objects in a picture.
   4. Gives family name.
   5. Repeats a sentence of six syllables.
Age IV.
   1. Gives own sex.
   2. Names key, knife, and penny.

3. Repeats 3 digits.
4. Compares two lines.

Age V.
1. Compares two weights.
2. Copies a square.
3. Repeats a sentence of ten syllables.
4. Counts four pennies.
5. Unites the halves of a divided rectangle.

Age VI.
1. Distinguishes between morning and afternoon.
2. Defines familiar words in terms of use.
3. Copies a diamond.
4. Counts thirteen pennies.
5. Distinguishes pictures of ugly and pretty faces.

Age VII.
1. Shows right hand and left ear.
2. Describes a picture.
3. Executes three commands given simultaneously.
4. Counts the value of six sous, three of which are double.
5. Names four cardinal colors.

Age VIII.
1. Compares two objects from memory.
2. Counts from 20 to 0.
3. Notes omissions from pictures.
4. Gives day and date.
5. Repeats five digits.

Age IX.
1. Gives change from twenty sous.
2. Defines familiar words in terms superior to use.
3. Recognizes all of the (nine) pieces of money.
4. Names the months of the year in order.
5. Answers or comprehends "easy questions."

Age X.
1. Arranges five blocks in order of weight.
2. Copies two drawings from memory.
3. Criticizes absurd statements.
4. Answers or comprehends "difficult questions."
5. Uses three given words in not more than two sentences.

Age XII.
1. Resists suggestion as to length of lines.
2. Composes one sentence containing three given words.

3. Names sixty words in three minutes.
4. Defines three abstract words.
5. Discovers the sense of a disarranged sentence.

Age XV.
1. Repeats seven digits.
2. Finds three rimes for a given word in one minute.
3. Repeats a sentence of twenty-six syllables.
4. Interprets pictures.
5. Interprets given facts.

Adult.
1. Solves the paper-cutting test.
2. Rearranges a triangle in imagination.
3. Gives differences between pairs of abstract terms.
4. Gives three differences between a president and a king.
5. Gives the main thought of a selection which he has heard read.

Of the tests which had appeared in the edition of 1908, several were omitted from Binet's final revision of 1911 as a result of various criticisms. For instance, Binet left out tests which had been found to depend chiefly upon specific information acquired in school, as well as such routine tests of common knowledge as knowing one's age and the days of the week. Several tests which were found to have been misplaced (being either too simple or too difficult) were either eliminated or else shifted up or down in the scale, and several new tests were introduced. In making this last revision, as in preparing his two earlier scales, Binet attempted to include only those tests which were not difficult to administer, were relatively short, covered an extensive range of mental processes, and did not depend directly upon specific information obtained in school. Such, in his opinion, were the requirements of a good intelligence test.

3. REVISIONS OF THE BINET SCALE IN AMERICA

Binet's tests were quickly taken up in America, where they were adapted and revised to fit American children and the conditions of American life. Goddard (1908) was the first to introduce Binet's tests into America. He translated the scale into English, made some changes in the position and wording of certain tests, and used the scale extensively in his work with the feeble-minded at the Vineland Training School in New Jersey. Several later revisions of the Binet Scale have appeared; one by Terman in 1916, a second by Terman and Merrill in 1937, and three by Kuhlmann in 1912, 1922, and 1939. In addition Yerkes, Bridges, and Hardwick (1915) and Herring (1922) have published revisions in which the classification of the tests into age-groups was abandoned in favor of a "point scale" method. In point scales the tests are first arranged in an order of difficulty, and credits or points are then allowed, depending upon the number of tests passed successfully. This point score may then be translated into a Coefficient of Mental Ability, obtained by dividing the child's score by the norm for his age (Yerkes); or it may be put into the more familiar M A or I Q (Herring).

By far the best known, and up to the present most widely used revision of the Binet-Simon Scale is the 1916 revision by L. M. Terman of Stanford University. This scale is known generally as the "Stanford Revision," or often simply as "Stanford-Binet," and is a careful and thorough working-over of the Binet Scale. Terman found that Binet's tests were too few and too difficult at the upper age-levels; that many were misplaced in the scale; and that the instructions for giving the tests were often indefinite. To insure uniformity of procedure in making his revision, one half-year was spent in training examiners to give the tests, and another half-year in supervision of the testing. In all, thirty-one new tests were tried out, the chief experimental group consisting of about 1,000 school children of average social status. As finally drawn up, the Stanford Revision contained ninety tests, thirty-six more than Binet's 1911 Scale. Six tests and several alternates were placed in each age group from three to ten; eight tests were placed at age twelve, six at age fourteen, six at "average adult" level (taken at sixteen), and six at the "'superior adult" level (taken at eighteen). In addition to the mental age score, Terman introduced the expression *intelligence quotient*, or I Q, to express mental development or brightness.* The I Q is simply the ratio of the mental age to the chronological age. For example, a child of eight with an M A of 8 years has an I Q of $\frac{8}{8}$ or 1.00; if the child's M A is 6 years, his I Q is $\frac{6}{8}$ or .75; if his M A is 10, his I Q is $\frac{10}{8}$, or 1.25. The mental age expresses the intellectual *status* of the child, while the I Q tells us how bright or how slow he is relative to the average child, whose I Q is always 1.00, or 100, as it is more commonly written. In the Stanford Revision, each of the six tests within a given age-group counts for two months of mental age (except at ages twelve, fourteen, sixteen, and eighteen, where each test has a greater value in months), so that mental ages of so many years plus so many months may be calculated from the scale.

The child of six years and six months, say, who is strictly average should pass *all* of the tests for the six year level and *below,* and three tests at the seven year level. As it happens, however, a strictly average child rarely exists except in textbooks, and so in almost every case there is some *scatter* in a child's record of passes: that is to say, he fails some of the tests below his true mental age and passes some of those above it. In the end these failures and successes balance each other, so that the normal child of seven years and four months finally comes out with a mental age of seven years and four months, and an I Q of 100. A superior child will, of course, go higher than his actual age, while a retarded child will find tests which he cannot do below his chronological age-group.

In 1937 a new revision of the "old" (1916) Stanford-Binet

* The term *intelligence quotient* was first used by the German psychologist William Stern.

LEWIS M. TERMAN

(Born 1877)

appeared. This new scale embodies the experience of the authors and of many other psychologists as well and is much more comprehensive than the old Stanford-Binet. Among the chief faults of the old revision the following should be mentioned: (1) the tests, and the subjects who served as the "standardization group," were too few at the extremes of the scale; (2) instructions for giving and scoring several of the tests were not precise enough, and some of the test items were particularly susceptible to coaching; (3) the absence of a parallel or equivalent scale made it difficult to retest a child at a later period; (4) various technical faults and inaccuracies had been discovered over the twenty years in which the old test had been used.

The new scale begins at age 2; and from 2 to 5 there are tests at each one-half year level, viz., 2½, 3, 3½, 4, 4½, and 5. At these very low age-levels, an appeal is made to the interests of the very young child by the introduction of tests utilizing brightly colored pictures, beads, blocks, small toys and the like.

Above age 14 there is one set of tests for Average Adult level, and three complete sets of tests for the Superior Adult level. The Average Adult level represents an M A of 15 years, and is really the "ceiling" of the scale. Beyond this level, intelligence in the general population shows so little additional upward trend with age that M A's obtained from the Superior Adult level are to be treated simply as numerical scores and not as true M A's. The location and scoring of the test items are based upon the responses of more than 3,000 children living in eleven states of the Union. These subjects are believed to be more representative of the American child population than were those used in the standardization of the old scale. The two equivalent forms of the new revision are called L and M. Each of these forms contains 129 separate items as against 90 items in the single form of the old revision. The new scale has not had time to be widely used. But its careful construction and its many advantages in comprehensiveness and range make it probable that it will be as popular as the old Stanford-Binet.

In closing this section a word of warning is in order regarding the administration of the Stanford-Binet, or for that matter, of any individual mental scale. Because the tests seem so easy to give, many people mistakenly imagine that they can administer them without previous supervision in test-giving or training in psychology. The unfortunate part of it is that they *can* give these tests after a fashion, but the results will almost certainly be worthless and will usually be downright misleading. Such "testers" forget that the object of the examination is to see whether a child can do certain things under *carefully prescribed conditions,* not whether he can do them when given plenty of time, and often plenty of suggestion and prodding, too, by the examiner. A trained examiner, first of all, knows the tests by heart; he is careful to see that he has the child's confidence, and has stimulated his interest, so that he will do his best; and he gives and scores the tests strictly according to the directions laid down in the manual. A year's graduate study in psychology plus at least six months' practical experience in giving mental tests under supervision is a minimum requirement for a trained examiner.

4. THE GROWTH CURVE OF GENERAL INTELLIGENCE

As indicated in the last section, the Average Adult level in general intelligence is placed by the Terman and Merrill Revision of Stanford-Binet at fifteen years. The view that intelligence matures or reaches the adult level at this relatively early age is generally regarded with surprise not unmixed with suspicion by non-psychologists. Many people will contend that intelligence surely continues to increase well into middle life, and they resent—when they do not deride—the idea that they are no smarter at forty than at fifteen. The confusion here is due in large part to a misunderstanding of what the psychologist means by *intelligence* and by *maturing*. By intelligence, it must be remembered, is meant ready adaptability to new situations, mental alertness, keenness, and ingenuity, and *not* "knowledge" and "experience," which are products of these, and which usually do increase with age—at least beyond fifteen years. Generally speaking, the average father has more general—and more special—knowledge than his fifteen-year-old son; he can do many more things and has wider experience, though he may be no more alert nor readily adaptable (potentially intelligent) in the psychologist's sense. Carefully repeated measurements of the same and of different individuals over a period of years have shown that mental ability (in so far as it is measured by tests) increases rapidly during the early years; then advances more and more slowly as the 'teens are reached, until somewhere between fourteen and sixteen years the average individual does as well as he will do at twenty or thirty years, or ever. At this comparatively early age, most people possess as much natural keenness and sheer native ability, apart from experience, as they will ever have.*

Curves showing the growth of intelligence in bright, average, and dull children are represented in Figure 1. The middle curve shows the course of average, the upper curve of superior, and the lower curve of inferior intellect. Note that average intelligence rises rapidly during the first four or five years; that from five to ten or eleven, growth, while evident, is considerably slower; and that from this point the curve gradually ceases to rise, becoming level somewhere between fourteen and sixteen years. The curve for superior intelligence rises more rapidly and goes higher than the average curve, probably not reaching its level until eighteen years or later. As shown by the lower curve, mental growth in the retarded (those of in-

* See further Chapter 2, pp. 40–43.

ferior intelligence) is distinctly slower than in the normal and superior. Also, in the retarded group mental growth reaches its maximum from two to three years earlier than in the normal, or average, group. Loss in general ability from twenty to forty

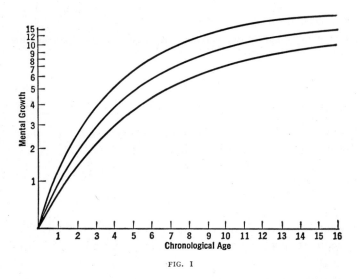

FIG. I

MENTAL GROWTH CURVES FOR SUPERIOR, NORMAL, AND DULL CHILDREN FROM BIRTH TO MATURITY

or forty-five years appears to be relatively slight. In old age general intelligence wanes slowly.*

5. DISTRIBUTION OF INTELLIGENCE

The widespread application of intelligence tests to large numbers of children and adults has established quite clearly the range of intelligence to be expected in the population at large. In statistical language, intelligence is said to be "dis-

* See p. 42.

tributed normally," that is, in accordance with the normal probability curve. Figure 2 shows a normal probability distribution or normal curve. Marked off on it are the percentages of the different grades or degrees of intelligence which might be expected to occur in a very large sample of people.

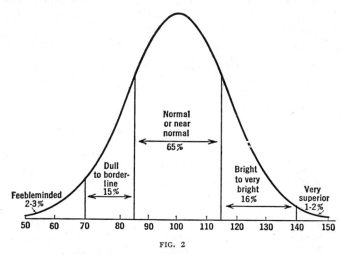

FIG. 2

DISTRIBUTION OF INTELLIGENCE (IQ'S) IN THE GENERAL POPULATION AC-
CORDING TO THE 1937 REVISION OF THE STANFORD-BINET SCALE

A normal distribution of people with respect to any trait, such as height, speed of movement, or general ability, simply means that the majority possess a medium amount of the trait in question; that lesser and lesser amounts are possessed by fewer and fewer individuals; and also that greater and greater amounts are possessed by steadily decreasing numbers. The normal distribution of a human trait or characteristic is well illustrated in the case of height. By far the greater number of men are close to five feet eight inches in height (the average); fewer men will be found two inches taller or two inches shorter than this average; still fewer four inches taller or four inches shorter; while the number of very tall (over seven feet) and very short (under five feet) men is exceedingly small indeed. What is true of height is true also of general intelligence, and probably of all mental traits. In terms of the revised Stanford-Binet tests of intelligence about 65 per cent of the general population are classed as having average or near average intelligence; about 15–16 per cent are somewhat higher and the same per cent somewhat lower than this intermediate group; while roughly 1–2 per cent are very superior and 2–3 per cent are mentally defective. (See Figure 2.)

A more detailed description of intellectual level in terms of I Q may be expressed as follows:

TABLE I

I Q	Classification	%
140 and above	Very superior	1.5
120–139	Superior or very bright	11.0
110–119	Bright	18.0
90–109	Average or normal	48.0
80–89	Dull normal—backward	14.0
70–79	Border-line, very dull	5.0
0–69	Feeble-minded	2.5

The number of feeble-minded in the general population, usually put at between one and three per cent, will depend upon just where the line of demarcation between the normal and the feeble-minded is drawn. Feeble-mindedness is a social and economic as well as a psychological problem. An individual who is judged to be feeble-minded in a complex urban environment, because he is effectively feeble-minded there, may be "normal" (in the sense of being able to get along) in simple rural surroundings. In spite of this qualification, when a generalized statement is called for, the best opinion at present is that individuals below 70 I Q should be considered mentally defective. Three classes of the feeble-minded are generally recognized, idiots, imbeciles, and morons. Idiots, who are the lowest in intellect, have I Q's (when measurable) under 25; and mental ages under three years. Idiots can learn only a few simple words. They cannot learn to wash or dress themselves and must be cared for in an institution or in the home. Imbeciles range in I Q from 25 to about 50, with mental ages of from 3 to 7 years. Imbeciles learn to talk and can even read very simple prose. But they lack foresight and planning ability and can perform only the simplest routine tasks and these under supervision. Morons, the highest level of feeble-mindedness, have I Q's from 50 to 70; their mental ages range from about 8 to 10 years. Morons can often be taught many useful tasks: sewing, washing dishes, house work and simple mechanical jobs. When not under supervision, however, the moron may become a serious social problem. Under the influence of vicious persons the moron boy is likely to steal or commit more serious crimes; while the moron girl is often led into sex delinquency and prostitution.

Worth mentioning in the present connection is a contribution made to theoretical psychology by the Binet and other mental tests. This is the experimental finding that the feeble-minded are not a distinct species separated off from the normal human, as, for instance, animals are separated from man. There is no sharp cleavage between normal and feeble-minded in so far as performance on intelligence tests is concerned, but rather a gradual progression from one to the other. The difference between the two groups is *quantitative* rather than *qualitative;* a matter of more available and more complex behavior resources rather than a matter of a different *kind* of intellectual activity.

Because Binet's original tests were constructed with the express purpose of identifying the feeble-minded, this was for a long time regarded as the chief function of the general intelligence test. Probably a good deal of the suspicion with which intelligence tests were (and, to a degree, still are) looked upon is a reflection of this view. The expression "to submit" to an intelligence test describes this attitude exactly. With the growing importance of mental tests as a means of locating superior children who should be rapidly advanced or given special attention, distrust of intelligence measurement is, fortunately, being overcome. Terman's studies of 1,000 children with I Q's of 130 and above has shown that these superior children tend to be above the average in height, weight, and general health, as well as in looks, and social and emotional maturity (see further page 75). This flatly contradicts the old idea—still widely prevalent—that precocious children are poorly adjusted socially, tend to be puny and undersized, and are apt to die at an early age! The parents of the very bright children selected by Terman were for the most part from the professional and semiprofessional classes (80 per cent), only a small fraction (6 per cent) coming from the semi-skilled and laboring classes. One fourth of the children had at least one parent who was a college graduate, while the average schooling of both parents was about twelve grades—twice that of the general adult population. These results indicate that both the heredity and the environment of these bright children were distinctly above average.

6. CRITICISMS OF THE BINET METHOD

Among the criticisms which from time to time have been leveled against the Binet Scale and its revisions, probably the most common is that a child's performance depends more upon his training and social surroundings than upon his native ability.* For this reason, it is said, the child from an educated and cultured home has a distinct advantage over one not so favored. This is quite generally true, provided the cultural gap

* In this connection, read the discussion in Chapter 2, pp. 52–55.

is wide, and the point has never been disputed by psychologists. Native capacity is of little value *per se* unless an environment suitable for development is supplied. For example, an American White child brought up from birth among Eskimos would undoubtedly test as feeble-minded on the Binet Scale, no matter how great his potential ability. Or to take a scarcely less obvious illustration, it is clearly unfair to compare children from the slums of New York City with children from cultured and well-to-do homes. Many experimental studies have brought out clearly the fact that different environments have an effect upon mental age and I Q. Records of adopted children show clearly the effect of good and poor home environment. Adoption into a good (cultured) home may raise a child's I Q 10 points or even more; while adoption into a very poor home may depress the I Q as much as 10 points or more. Cyril Burt, an English psychologist, found decided differences in Binet test performance in favor of children of superior social status in London. The same investigator found also that children from superior schools were on the average one to two years in mental age ahead of those from inferior schools. In the United States children in isolated rural communities may rank considerably below city children in mental age. In one study, younger rural children (7–9 years old) were retarded from one to one and one-half years, while older children (13–15 years old) were retarded by as much as five or even six years. Probably the reason for the greater backwardness of the older children lies in the fact that a poor social-economic status—even when it remains substantially the same—becomes progressively more restrictive as children grow older. Results like these emphasize concretely the importance of considering the child's environment in interpreting his mental test rating or judging his mental development.

Binet was fully aware that his tests did not measure innate ability completely divorced from the influence of environment.

He consistently held that a comparison of the mental ages of two children was valid only when both had had approximately the same schooling and the same common background of experience. But when these conditions are satisfied, he considered test ratings fair measures of comparative ability on the reasonable assumption that normal children will be exposed to much the same facts, and hence will acquire much the same information. Binet's tests, it must be remembered, were constructed with the express purpose of reducing to a minimum the influences of special training. Unless, therefore, differences in social and economic status are great or the deprivation due to lack of normal contact with the environment is serious, mental ages are close estimates of "real" ability. To be sure, responses in the test make use of verbal expressions which are clearly learned. But the abilities required to see relations, interpret meanings (in a picture, for instance), give sensible definitions, detect absurdities or incongruities, and comprehend social and other situations, demand thought, reasoning, and judgment—and these are the important indices of ability. In short, although the Binet Scale and its revisions draw heavily upon language, they demand a high degree of sagacity, cleverness, and mental alertness, rather than the ability simply to reproduce parrot-like facts learned by rote.

Another criticism sometimes brought against the Binet tests is that they fail to detect character defects, such as bad temper, laziness, and abnormal sex habits, which are as important as intellect in daily living. Also, it is sometimes charged that they fail to discover exceptional gifts in music, art or mechanics. The reply to this is that Binet set out to locate the general intellectual level at which the child habitually functions, not to analyze character traits or to discover exceptional aptitudes. At the same time, from careful observation of a child's behavior during an examination the trained psychologist can gain many clues as to emotional social maturity. The timid, insecure child who asks again and again if he is right; the stubborn, negative child who is defiant or aggressive; the spoiled child who gives up and pouts when he cannot get the answer—all of these children reveal their personalities in reacting to test situations.

The mental test record, therefore, is a decidedly valuable asset even when one is interested primarily in problems of delinquency and emotional maladjustment. Time and again juvenile courts and children's clinics have demonstrated an intimate connection between crime and immorality on the one hand, and low-grade intelligence on the other. The method to be followed in dealing with character defects and delinquencies will depend to a large degree upon the intellectual level of the person to be treated. Also, knowing the mental age rating simplifies to a considerable degree the search for causes, even though the problem turns out to be largely an emotional one.

What may be in practice a decided limitation in the value of the Binet score should be mentioned at this point. In striking an average or mean of an individual's capacities, one is prone to forget that abilities are rarely if ever evenly developed, and that in consequence a gross total fails to tell us in what respects our subject is especially good or especially poor. The same situation is met with in every test which gives a single score intended to be taken as indicative of general intellectual level. Practically, it is often far more valuable to know that a child is advanced or above age in ability to handle numbers, say, or in knowledge of words and word relations, or in retentivity, than to know that his I Q is 90 or 100 or 120. Vocational or educational guidance may then direct the child into those courses of study or that kind of work for which his abilities peculiarly fit him. An experienced psychologist can learn much from a qualitative analysis of a child's performance. Strengths and weaknesses in perception, memory, judgment, language facility, comprehension, etc., may be estimated with

considerable accuracy from the range and character of a
child's response to the individual items of the test. Sometimes
the psychologist supplements the mental age rating with special tests of learning or memory or reasoning, or even with
tests of manual dexterity, such as speed and coördination of
movement. These special test scores may be put in the form
of a "psychograph" or profile—a chart whereon the child's
various records are represented by a series of points plotted
above or below the mean line or "norm" for his age-group.
Relative superiorities and inferiorities can be graphically presented by such a method.

An illustration of a psychograph representing the standing
of a ten-year-old boy, A. F., in several selected measures of
ability is given in Figure 3.

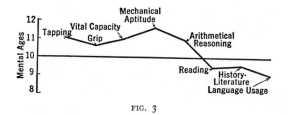

FIG. 3

A PSYCHOGRAPH SHOWING PERFORMANCE ON A VARIETY OF TESTS

This is the record made by a ten-year-old boy, A. F., whose I Q is 104.

It is clear from the chart that A. F. is physically above par
for his age. He is also advanced in arithmetic and in mechanical ability, but lags behind somewhat in language-usage,
history-literature, and reading. Offhand it might seem that this
boy would do well vocationally, in work requiring good physique, manual dexterity, and mathematical and mechanical
knowledge. A further check-up on his interests, ambitions,
financial situation, and personality would, of course, be necessary before venturing a more definite opinion. Interesting use

has been made of the psychograph in representing scores upon tests of musical ability, personality traits, and educational achievement.

A minor limitation of such tests as the Binet lies in the fact that they cannot be used with foreign-born children nor with adults who do not speak English; nor can they be used successfully with the deaf, nor very reliably with those who stutter, stammer, or have some similar language handicap. This general inadequacy is inherent in all tests employing verbal expression and has been remedied to a large extent by the construction of *performance tests*. Such tests require that the examinee fit blocks into a board (form-board tests), reconstruct puzzle pictures, learn mazes, and, in general, perform mental activities which demand ingenuity and insight, with a minimum of language.*

To summarize briefly what has been said in this section, the Binet-Simon Scale and its revisions are valid measures of general intelligence when—and only when—the tests are given and scored in a standard manner; when the subjects come from a normal environment; and when they labor under no special language deficiency. For the best results, individual intelligence tests should be supplemented by careful observation, in order to detect peculiarities or abnormalities which might affect the examinee's record. Whenever possible and practicable, the personal history, medical record, and habits of industry of the subject should be investigated, as well as his social and moral behavior. When the subject is a child, his play habits and the personal traits exhibited in school should be carefully noted.

7. THE INHERITANCE OF INTELLIGENCE

The question of the constancy or stability of an individual's general level of intelligence throughout life is bound up with

* See also page 304.

the prior consideration of whether intelligence is inborn and native, and hence largely if not entirely determined at birth; or whether intelligence is only loosely native in the sense that all behavior is potentially native, and hence is highly susceptible to training. There is considerable evidence in favor of the view that intelligence is inborn—inherited in much the same manner as are physical characteristics.

In the first place, we have the facts of common everyday observation. Bright boys and bright girls tend to grow into bright men and women, while the history of stupid adults reveals more often than otherwise a record of stupidity in childhood. Nearly every one can cite instances from his own experience of dull children, who, in spite of every advantage socially and educationally, have grown into dull and mediocre men and women; while we all know of bright children, who, despite marked disadvantages, have insisted upon remaining bright and becoming successful adults. Among children who grow up in the same community, attend the same school, play together, see the same movies, and, all in all, possess about the same opportunities, some will learn more rapidly and progress faster than others. Such an outcome must be largely the resultant of native differences in endowment.

There are exceptions, of course. Disease, deafness, poor eyesight, unkind treatment, a restricted or vicious environment—all of these serve to complicate the nature-nurture problem. But when such factors are allowed for, the fact still remains that some people are natively better equipped mentally than others.

The biographies of men of genius reveal the fact that exceptional gifts usually appear early in childhood. A famous illustration is the case of Sir Francis Galton, who could read when he was two and one-half years old. The day before his fifth birthday he wrote the following note to his sister: "My dear Adèle, I am 4 years old and can read any English book. I can say all of the Latin substantives and adjectives and active verbs besides 52 lines of Latin poetry. I can cast up any sum in addition and multiply by 2, 3, 4, 5, 6, 8, 10. I can also say the pence table. I can read French a little and I know the clock. Francis Galton. Febuary (sic) 15, 1827." Terman, after studying Galton's biography and later career, estimates that his I Q must have been close to 200. Voltaire began to read at three and at twelve wrote a tragedy. Sir Isaac Newton, as a child, was "constantly occupied during his play hours" in devising all sorts of contrivances and machines, especially water-clocks and kites. At seventeen, Goethe had done extensive reading in German, French, Latin, and Hebrew; he knew the history of the chief European countries in detail; he played the piano and the flute, and was considered a promising art student. According to Cox, who has made a comprehensive study of the childhood of eminent men, Goethe's I Q must have been between 185 and 200. Other illustrations of the precocity shown by great men in childhood abound. Macaulay could read at four, and at eight wrote a "treatise to convert the natives of Malabar to Christianity"; Jonathan Edwards wrote a paper on spiders at twelve which actually increased the scientific knowledge on the subject; Walter Scott (estimated I Q 150) and John Stuart Mill (estimated I Q 190) were child prodigies. The childhood histories of Francis Bacon, Descartes, Spinoza, and many others give early promise of later greatness.

Not all geniuses, however, have been recognized as precocious in youth. Charles Darwin (estimated I Q 135), for instance, was considered rather dull by his teacher, partly, no doubt, because he carried insects and small animals around in his pockets, oftentimes disturbing the serenity of the classroom. Napoleon stood 42nd in his class in military school. Of David Hume it was said by his mother that he was good-natured but "uncommon wakeminded." Thomas A. Edison was usually at the foot of his class in school, and considered "addled" by his teacher; and this despite the fact that he had read Gibbon's *Decline and Fall of the Roman Empire,* Hume's *History of England,* and Burton's *Anatomy of Melancholy* before he was twelve. It is hardly probable that these illustrations are exceptions to the rule, "bright child, bright adult." Many brilliant children are hopelessly misunderstood by their parents as well as by their teachers. Uninterested in what are, to them, the simple facts taught in school, they often neglect their lessons, meanwhile concerning themselves with matters far beyond the capacity or interests of the ordinary child. Bright children, too, are frequently mischievous ("problem cases") because, quickly grasping what is taught, they idle or play instead of dutifully paying attention and carrying out assigned tasks. Intelligence tests are doing much to discover and provide for the exceptionally bright child. Special classes, extra studies, and other expedients of a like nature offer opportunity for initiative and creative endeavor, so that the energy of the bright child is usefully conserved and applied.

To go to the other extreme of the intelligence scale, there is much evidence, from the way in which feeble-mindedness tends to run in families, that intelligence may be native and inherited. To what extent feeble-mindedness is inherited is still a moot question. Authorities estimate that perhaps 80 per cent of all feeble-mindedness is native and inherited, the remainder being due to disease or injury at birth or in early childhood (Penrose, Tredgold). Normal parents who come from families in which there is no mental defect rarely have a feeble-minded child. If one parent is normal and the other feeble-minded, some of the children are likely to be feeble-minded or dull. If both of the parents are feeble-minded, *all* of their children will probably be feeble-minded or at least low-grade.

Many studies have shown that feeble-minded tend to mate

with feeble-minded, thus passing on the defective strain from one generation to the next. But unfortunately these family histories, though interesting and suggestive, do not enable us to separate out the distinctive contributions of heredity and environment. Neither factor remains constant while the other varies. Stupid and ineffective people tend to gravitate to mean surroundings, and superior people to good surroundings —one suspects on the general principle that water seeks its level.

Despite the weaknesses in most studies of family histories, results of such tabulations have value and are often quoted. It seems worth while, therefore, to review one of the best known of these studies, namely, Goddard's study of five generations of the Kallikak family. During the American Revolution, Martin Kallikak (the name is fictitious), a man believed to be of normal mentality, had an illegitimate son by a girl known to be defective mentally. From this son have come 480 descendants. Of these, 143 were judged to be feeble-minded, 46 probably normal, and the rest doubtful. Among the total lot, 36 were illegitimate, 33 were sexually immoral (mostly prostitutes), 24 were drunkards, 3 were epileptics, 82 died in infancy, 3 were criminals, and 8 were keepers of houses of ill-fame. Of this family tree Thorndike remarks that it constitutes "a horrid array of human incompetence." After the Revolution, Martin Kallikak married a normal woman of Quaker stock. Goddard was able to trace 496 descendants of this union, and the records of these offspring furnish an interesting parallel to the other line. All of these legitimate progeny, except possibly two, were normal mentally and morally, and several were evidently of superior intellect. In this group we find lawyers, physicians, governors, professors, and college presidents. Two groups differing more sharply in achievement and social value can scarcely be conceived.

The data of the Kallikak family are striking and dramatic;

but they do not offer conclusive evidence of the inheritance of feeble-mindedness. In the first place, the environments of the two parallel lines did not provide anything approaching equal opportunity. Again, the judgments of feeble-mindedness made by Goddard's field workers were often based upon dubious evidence, amounting to little more than hearsay. Further, the heredity of the two lines was alike as regards the common paternal ancestor, Martin, so that the case for heredity rests entirely upon the maternal lines. The Kallikak study shows what may be expected when initially good and bad strains are placed in good and bad surroundings. Though not so crucial an argument for inheritance as Goddard thought, it is strong nevertheless. Environment could hardly have produced the enormous differences found unless the two family groups had possessed markedly different capacities at the outset.

Better evidence of the influence of heredity in determining the degree of intelligence has come from the study of mental resemblances among members of the same family, and from studies of adopted children. Many studies have shown that twins are more alike than siblings (ordinary brothers and sisters) in traits little affected by training; and also in traits upon which the school concentrates its influence. Leahy, in one of the best controlled recent studies of adopted children, found a considerably higher relationship between the intelligence of children and their own parents than between adopted children and their foster parents. This study is significant because the age of adoption was low (6 months or less), the group large (194), and when examined the children had been in their foster homes long enough (4 to 10 years) for the effect of the home environment to be felt. The degree of resemblance between members of a family in mental traits is as high or higher than their resemblance in physical traits such as height, weight, hair-color, and eye-color. Since the physical resemblances of twins and of brothers and sisters must be due to native factors, it seems that mental resemblances must also have a native basis.

8. THE CONSTANCY OF THE I Q

If intelligence is determined largely by native factors, the I Q—assuming it to be a fair measure of mental ability—should remain constant throughout life. Many studies have demonstrated that the I Q *is* substantially constant over the age-range covered by the Stanford-Binet Scale. But it must always be remembered that even the best mental test is not a perfect measuring instrument, and we cannot expect repeated testings of the same individual on the Stanford-Binet to give exactly the same result. The amount of change which must be allowed for in a test-retest is expressed by the "probable error." In the 1937 Stanford-Binet, the probable error of a calculated I Q is about 3 points. A change in an I Q from 95 to 98 or 92 (or even a greater change) does not imply then, any actual change in a child's mental ability. He is still classified as falling within the normal range. Repetitions of the Stanford-Binet upon the same child after an interval of one year or less will seldom show an I Q variation from its initial value of more than 3 or 4 points. When the time interval between test and retest is longer than a year, variation in I Q may be as much as 5 or even 10 points, but this degree of change is very infrequently observed.*

There are many reasons (besides errors of measurement) why a child's I Q may fluctuate from time to time without leading us to suspect any real change in the child's mental status. It may be of interest to list some of the more important of these factors. (1) *Physical Causes*. These are of

* Several recent studies have contended that the I Q can be increased by proper training to a dramatic degree (refs. 19, 34). The experimental and statistical methods employed in these studies have been sharply challenged by competent authorities, however, and their conclusions cannot be accepted without qualification.

primary concern. On the first test, deafness, poor eyesight, and other sensory defects may pass unnoticed. Malnourished children brought to institutions from bad homes will frequently show marked increase in I Q after a few months of kind treatment, good food, and medical attention, the latter leading, say, to the removal of tonsils and adenoids. (2) *Emotional Causes.* One can hardly expect to get a fair measure of a child's intelligence when the child is badly frightened, angry, or otherwise emotionally disturbed. Children who are badly spoiled, over-indulged, pampered and dependent, also make poor subjects for a mental test. (3) *Examiner.* The "personal equation" of the examiner is extremely important. If an examiner is poorly trained and inexperienced, possesses a harsh voice or peculiarities of physique or appearance, or if he is timid, supercilious, or disagreeable in manner, he will get very little coöperation from many children. It need hardly be said that many a young child has been observed to respond with enthusiasm to a task presented by one examiner, and with indifference or distaste to the same task presented by another. (4) *Testing Conditions.* If (a) the examination room is small, bare, or over-decorated; (b) the temperature too high or too low; (c) the lighting bad or the air stale; (d) interruptions or distractions (opening or shutting doors) frequent, the examination is almost inevitably affected. (5) *Tests.* Only those tests can be expected to yield consistent and valid results from one time to another which, like the Stanford-Binet, (a) have been carefully constructed, (b) have been given to large groups, (c) are made up of test-items which are comparable throughout the scale, and (d) have stable age-norms.

To all of these considerations may be added the matter of general environmental influences, the effect of which has already been stressed. Children raised in isolated communities or under peculiar or restrictive conditions will often show

I Q increases when placed in a normal environment and given fair treatment. And, by the same token, children transferred from good to poor surroundings will show losses in I Q. I Q changes which are the result of drastic alterations in opportunity and stimulation do not contradict the hypothesis that intelligence is fundamentally innate. When neither the child nor the environment has been subjected to radical influences; when the mental test has been adequately administered and scored, the I Q will remain constant.

9. I Q AND SCHOOL SUCCESS

The brightest child is not always the most successful in school. As every one knows, appearance, manner, docility, industry, personality and character definitely influence school grades and often compensate for lack of mental ability. The level of intelligence, however, does set the limit to which a child can go, and a knowledge of his I Q is of great value in educational guidance. The educational expectation of children of different mental levels is as follows:

(a) Children under 70 I Q, when in school at all, remain in the first grade until 10 or 11 years old. A very few may reach the fifth grade by 14 or 15; seldom if ever will a child as dull as this go beyond the fifth grade.

(b) Mentally deficient to dull children (70–85 I Q) will ordinarily be 1–2 years over age for their grade. The eighth grade is the upper limit for most of these children; many will not get beyond the fifth or sixth.

(c) Children with I Q's of 85–115 make up the bulk of the elementary school population. Most of these children will finish elementary school and many high school; but those below 100 I Q will have difficulty in graduating from high school.

(d) Children above 115 I Q are normal or 1–2 years accelerated for their grade. These children are exceptionally good college material. If they possess the necessary personality and character traits, they should be successful in business or professional life.

Several illustrations will show how a knowledge of intelligence level is helpful in educational guidance.*

C.P. Boy, age 10–2; M A, 7–11; I Q 78, border-line, dull. Son of skilled laborer, one of 11 children. Is in third grade but cannot do work. Is capable in games. Will probably never be able to do school work beyond fifth or sixth grade. Except for extreme stubbornness his social development is fairly normal.

G.G. Girl, age 12–4; M A 10–10; I Q 82, dull. From average home. Has had excellent educational advantages and has no physical handicap. Is doing poor work in fifth grade. Appearance, play life, attitude toward other children normal. Will probably never go beyond eighth grade.

M.P. Girl, age 8–10; M A 11–1; I Q 130, superior. Father unusually intelligent house painter. Home above average. M.P. now in fourth grade, marks "excellent." Good health, good social and moral traits. This child will be ready for high school by the age of 12.

E.M. Boy, age 6–11; M A 10; I Q 145, superior. Father university professor. E.M. now 7–8 is in fourth grade. Learned to read by himself at 5, and shortly afterward learned all the capitals of the states in the Union. Entered school in first grade and by the end of the day had been moved up to the fourth grade. Personality and health excellent. E.M. should be ready for college at the age of 15.

By way of summary, it may be asserted with good reason that the Binet-Simon tests and their revisions have amply justified their existence and their widespread use. Their promise for the future is all in the direction of wiser treatment for the incorrigible and inferior child, as well as for the normal and superior, through providing opportunities commensurate with individual ability and fitted to individual needs. Inevitably such a program must lead to better adjustments and increased human happiness.

* Adapted with some abridgement from L. M. Terman.

Chapter 2

ARMY ALPHA AND THE RISE OF GROUP TESTS
FOR MEASURING GENERAL INTELLIGENCE

I. HISTORY OF ARMY ALPHA AND ARMY BETA

The extensive use of intelligence tests in the American army
during the World War, for the purpose of measuring the
ability of large groups of men at the same time, constitutes
psychology's greatest experiment in human engineering. During the years 1917–1918, intelligence examinations were given
to slightly less than 1,750,000 men. As an immediate result of
these tests, about 8,000 men were recommended for discharge
because of inferior intelligence; something like 10,000 were assigned to labor battalions or to other services requiring low-
grade ability; and about 10,000 more were recommended to
be sent to special development battalions for observation and
further training. Nearly one third of the men examined were
unable to read or write, or else did so too poorly to be classed
as literate, and to these was given a special examination prepared for illiterates.

The army mental tests were not, as is sometimes supposed,
a series of questions, puzzles, and other "stunts," thrown together without purpose or design. On the contrary, they were
carefully selected and methodically put together in accordance
with the best scientific principles of test-making then available. A brief outline of the steps leading up to the construction
of a group test for measuring general intelligence, designed
especially for soldiers, will show the care which was exercised.
In April, 1917, a committee was appointed by the American

Psychological Association to which was entrusted the task of preparing an adequate test for measuring the general intellectual level of large groups of men at the same time. This committee consisted of five psychologists who were specialists in the field of mental testing, and was under the direction of Robert M. Yerkes as chairman. All of the material previously used in measuring intelligence was culled over, especially a group test devised by A. S. Otis, which had not at that time been published. The committee decided that a general intelligence examination intended for use with soldiers should, as far as posible, meet certain definite requirements. These, in brief, were as follows: (1) It should as nearly as possible be independent of specific school information, since its aim was to discover a man's *native* ability rather than his degree of formal school training. (2) It should be steeply graded in difficulty, i. e., hard enough to tax the high-grade men, and at the same time easy enough to measure those of lesser ability. (3) Scoring should be simple, rapid, and objective, so that little would be left to the personal judgment of the scorer. (4) It should require a minimum of written answers in order to eliminate speed of writing as an important factor in determining the score. (5) A number of different forms approximately equal in difficulty should be drawn up to prevent coaching on a particular form. In addition to these more formal requirements, an effort was made to utilize material which would be interesting and varied enough to keep the man "on the job." How well these principles were adhered to we shall see in later sections.

After much experimentation and trial, two tests, one for men who could read and write, and one for those who could do neither (or else do so very poorly) were devised. The test for literates was called the Alpha, that for illiterates the Beta, examination. In preliminary trials, Alpha was tried out on elementary and high school children; large groups of students in schools, colleges, and officers' training camps; more than 5,000 enlisted men; and inmates of various institutions for the feeble-minded. The *validity* of the examination, that is, its value as a measure of general intellect, was checked against all available criteria: among the students and the feeble-minded, by such measures of aptitude as school grades, teachers' estimates of ability, and other intelligence tests, such as the Stanford-Binet; among the soldiers, by officers' ratings for ability, rank attained, ability shown in training, previous civilian accomplishments, and the like. The correlations * between the Alpha test and these various criteria ranged from .50 to .95, which means that statistically the test was a reasonably valid measure of general ability as here defined. The Beta test gave returns nearly as good as those obtained with Alpha. The consistency or *reliability* with which Alpha and Beta measure ability proved also to be satisfactory. For example, on taking a second form of Alpha, a man's score will rarely deviate more than four or five points from his first rating, so that an obtained Alpha score may be taken as a stable measure of performance.

2. CONSTRUCTION OF A GROUP INTELLIGENCE TEST

The Army Alpha Intelligence Examination consisted of eight tests which may be described briefly by the following titles: (1) Following Directions; (2) Arithmetic Problems; (3) Practical Judgment; (4) Synonym-Antonym; (5) Disarranged Sentences; (6) Number Series Completion; (7) Analogies; (8) General Information. The items in each of these tests were arranged to be progressively more difficult from the beginning to the end of the test. Time-limits were set for each

* Correlation is a mathematical method of measuring relationship between two sets of test scores or other measures. Correlation coefficients range from + 1.00, or perfect relationship, through .00, just no relationship, down to − 1.00, perfect inverse relationship. A correlation of .50 denotes a fair degree of relationship, one of .95 a very high relationship.

test short enough to prevent any but the very fastest worker from finishing. This precaution is readily appreciated when one considers that the man who finishes a test before time is called is actually unmeasured, as he might have done more had material been available. It is just as true, of course, that the man who scores zero on a test is also unmeasured, as he might have done a very few items, at least, had still easier ones been provided. Five forms of Alpha were constructed, all approximately equal in difficulty.

Just exactly what the Alpha Examination was designed to do will be clearer if we consider the separate tests in somewhat greater detail. In Test (1),* Following Directions, each item was to be marked by the soldier in accordance with certain definite directions given by the examiner. For example, in the second item are nine circles each containing in order a number from 1 to 9. The directions are as follows:

"Attention! Look at 2, where the circles have numbers in them. When I say 'Go,' draw a line from Circle 1 to Circle 4 that will pass *above* Circle 2 and *below* Circle 3. Go!" (Allow not over 5 seconds.)

There are twelve items in this test, the later ones being more difficult than those which come earlier.

Test (2) Arithmetic Problems, consisted of twenty ordinary problems of the "reasoning" or "mental arithmetic" variety. The tenth problem reads as follows:

10. If it takes six men three days to dig a 180-foot drain, how many will dig it in half a day?......Answer (   )
Five minutes are allowed for the entire test.

In Test (3), Practical Judgment, the directions were to indicate the best of three possible answers to a given ques-

* The following illustrations of the different tests are taken from Form 5.

tion by placing an (X) in the "box" before it. Item 7, for example, proposes the following question:

7. Why is wheat better for food than corn? Because
    ☐ it is more nutritious
    ☐ it is more expensive
    ☐ it can be ground finer

Only one and one-half minutes are allowed for this test, which contains sixteen items. It is meant to be a test of practical "common sense."

Test (4), Synonym-Antonym, was designed to gauge ability to apprehend relations of likeness and difference. The ability to comprehend relations of an abstract sort is believed by many psychologists to be highly important in intelligent activity. Items 26 and 36 may be taken as examples of this test:

26. Fallacy-verity ....same—opposite
36. Innuendo-insinuation ....same—opposite

Instructions are to underline "same" if the two words mean the same or nearly the same; otherwise, to underline "opposite." There are forty items in this test, and one and one-half minutes are allowed.

The Disarranged Sentences Test, No. (5), was planned to measure the examinee's ingenuity and cleverness as shown in his ability to rearrange jumbled words into a sentence. To illustrate with items 16 and 21:

16. ninety canal ago built Panama years was the..true—false
21. employ debaters irony never ....true—false

The twenty-four items in this test are answered by drawing a line under "true" or "false." Two minutes are allowed.

Test (6), Number Series Completion, was designed to measure "reasoning" ability. The task set was the completion of given series of numerical arrangements in a logical fashion. The thirteenth and sixteenth items read:

| 11 | 13 | 12 | 14 | 13 | 15 | .... | .... |
| 81 | 27 | 9 | 3 | 1 | 1/3 | .... | .... |

The directions are to write on the dotted lines the two numbers which should come next in the series. There are twenty items in the test, and three minutes are allowed.

Test (7), Analogies, was selected as another test of ability to "reason out" or "see" relations when expressed in verbal form. To illustrate with items 17 and 36:

17. lion—animal :: rose—smell leaf plan thorn
36. tolerate—pain :: welcome—pleasure unwelcome
        friends give ....

The problem is to find the relation between the second and first words, and then underline that one of the four alternatives that is related in the same way to the third word. There are forty items, and a time allowance of three minutes is given.

General Information, Test (8), was included in order to give an estimate of the extent to which the individual has picked up common information from his surroundings. This test has been much criticized on the ground that it draws upon experience and knowledge rather than upon intellectual ability. It proved, nevertheless, to be a fairly adequate intelligence test. If we are justified in assuming at least roughly the same environment for all subjects, it seems reasonable to suppose that those who are mentally alert will garner more information from their surroundings than those who are stupid and dull. Items 21 and 37 from Test (8) will serve as illustrations:

21. The dictaphone is a kind of typewriter multigraph
        phonograph adding machine ....
37. Mauve is the name of a drink color fabric food...

Instructions are to underline that one of the four possible answers which makes the best or "truest" sentence. There are forty items in all, and four minutes are allowed.

After the war a large number of group tests, modeled after Army Alpha, were constructed for use with subjects of different ages. To-day there are intelligence tests designed for pupils in the elementary schools, for students in high school and college, and more generally for adults beyond school age. One of the several revisions of Alpha is probably still the best general test for use with adults who differ greatly in education, occupational status, and cultural background. Examples of tests widely used in schools are: The National Intelligence Test (Grades 3–8); the Otis Group Intelligence Scale (Grades 5–12); the American Council on Education Psychological Examination for College Freshmen. Like Alpha these tests consist of from 5 to 10 sub-tests which differ in content and form. Sub-tests commonly found in group examinations are arithmetic problems, opposites, logical selection and classification of ideas and concepts, common information, analogies, vocabulary, number series completion, and the like. In several of the well-known group tests, the items are not organized into sub-tests but are arranged into a single list following a staggered or cyclic plan—an opposites item, say, recurs at regular intervals in the test. The Otis Self Administering Test is an example of such an omnibus or scrambled test. This examination consists of 75 items arranged in order of difficulty. There are two forms, one for children and one for adults. The "norms" or performance standards for most intelligence tests, together with descriptions, directions for administering, etc., will be found in the manuals accompanying the tests.

Great Experiments in Psychology

The total score on the Army Alpha Examination was obtained by adding together the separate scores on the eight sub-tests. The maximum score possible was 212 points. When a soldier's total score had been found, the next step was to translate this numerical rating into a letter grade as shown in Table II.

TABLE II

SCORE RANGES AND LETTER GRADE EQUIVALENTS ON THE ARMY ALPHA EXAMINATION

Letter rating	A	B	C+	C	C−	D	D − and E
Range of Alpha scores	212–	134–	104–	74–	44–	24–	14–
corresponding	135	105	75	45	25	15	0
Per cent of white soldiers receiving each letter grade	4	8	15	25	24	17	7

The letter grades corresponding to the different score-ranges given in the table were found by drawing up a "distribution" or tabulation of Alpha scores made by a large and representative group. This distribution was then sub-divided into five sections: High scores (A), fairly high (B), average (C+ and C), low (C−), and very low (D, D− and E). Letter designations, therefore, are to be taken as measures of *relative* performance and are not to be confused with *absolute* measures (those taken from a true zero), such as inches and pounds. Any score from 212–135 is given an A rating; any score from 134–105 a B rating, and so on. About 4 per cent of the white soldiers were assigned A ratings, and about 12 per cent A and B ratings, while nearly two thirds (64 per cent) fell into the C+, C, and C− groups. The average score made by White enlisted men was 59 Alpha points, which corresponds to a letter rating of C. The White officers made on the average a score of 139, nearly all of them scoring A or B.

Shortly after the war, several popular writers aroused indignation and some confusion by the unqualified statement that the mental age of the average American soldier was about 14 years. The first reaction of the individual unacquainted with tests and test technology, upon learning that the mental age of the typical soldier was about that of a first-year high school boy, was doubt, derision, or amusement, his attitude depending largely, perhaps, upon his age, education, experience, and sophistication. Among many uncritical people, however, the prevailing attitude was one of uneasiness and even dismay at what was regarded as the precarious outlook for the nation in view of the mental immaturity of a large share of its citizenry.

Such an alarming view, fortunately, is entirely unwarranted; it grew out of a misunderstanding of what the army tests are and of what they really do. Let us look into the method whereby the average mental age of 14 years was obtained. First, the correlation or correspondence between the Alpha scores and the mental ages—as determined by the 1916 Stanford-Binet examination *—of a large group of men was calculated. It was then discovered that the Alpha score made by the average White soldier (C in letter grades) corresponded to a mental age of about 14 years on the Stanford-Binet Scale. The statement of Alpha performance in terms of mental age, then, simply means that the average soldier did about as well on the test as the average fourteen-year-old school child. Certainly there need be nothing alarming, nor even disconcerting, about this finding. Reference to Figure 1, page 12, will show that the rise in the growth curve for normal intelligence from 14 to 16 years is relatively small. This means that the typical White soldier was about two

* See Chapter 1, p. 7.

years below the level set by Terman in the 1916 Stanford
Revision as the point at which intelligence in the average person reaches maturity.* There are several facts which will
account for this apparent deficiency. In the first place, the
schooling of many of the drafted men had ended years before, which put them at a disadvantage when compared with
school-children on a paper and pencil test. Again, it is well
known that specialized training and the routine of adult occupation often play havoc with whatever skill a man may
have had at one time in reading and figuring rapidly.

It should be added further, by way of defense of the soldier, that the Alpha test gave no measure of manual ability
nor of skill in performing mechanical tasks; of ability to
exercise good judgment, and restraint in business relations;
of ability to control one's temper, or to get along on amicable
terms with one's neighbors. Ingenuity, mental alertness, and
the ability to solve problems involving language and numbers with ease and despatch, i. e., to deal with "ideas," are
undeniably important; and these capacities are clearly measured by the Alpha test. But skill in abstract thinking and in
dealing with ideas does not exhaust the gamut of human
achievement; and so, all in all, we need not be greatly per-
turbed that the average soldier had a mental age of only 14
years as measured on the Stanford-Binet Scale.

4. INTELLIGENCE AND AGE

Results from Army Alpha throw light upon a problem important from both the social and economic points of view,
that is, the problem of whether general intelligence changes
with age. We have seen in Chapter 1 that according to
the best available evidence mental growth in the average person (as measured by the 1937 Stanford-Binet Scale) reaches
its maturity at close to 15 years. Since the age-scale or Binet

* In the 1937 Stanford Revision this point is 15 years (see p. 9).

type of test is adapted primarily for use with children, group tests are especially valuable in studies of changes in intelligence among adults. From the late 'teens well on into maturity and old age, general intelligence as measured by average scores on group tests shows a gradual but steady decline. This may be seen in the table below which gives the median * scores by decades of army officers upon Alpha:

TABLE III

Age-groups	21–30	31–40	41–50	51–60
Median score on Army Alpha	145	133	125	120

This same result was obtained in a more comprehensive study in which the Otis Self-Administering Test of Mental Ability was used. The experimental group consisted of 823 persons (both men and women) ranging in age from 7 to 94 years. Figure 4 gives the changes in test score from about 10 to 90 years. Note that the loss is gradual from 20 to about 40, after which the average test score shows a more pronounced falling off.

While some of the loss in test score with age is undoubtedly attributable to the inevitable "slowing up" of physiological and physical function, this is probably not the sole explanation. In the first place there is the matter of selection. Among older adults there is greater variation in education and background than among younger adults; and the older people are more specialized in knowledge and interests. Older groups, therefore, are not as adequate "cross sections" of the later age-levels as younger groups are of earlier age-levels. Older folk, too, are likely to have more visual and auditory defects, and their health is not as good as younger

* The median score is the middlemost when test scores are arranged in order from lowest to highest. It is thus "typical" of the group.

folk. Furthermore, they are further removed from formal schooling and from the rapid performance of clerical tasks; and hence are usually less coöperative and less interested in undertaking tasks which demand performance under timed conditions.

It is significant that the loss in general mental ability with age as indicated by test score is relatively slight in those

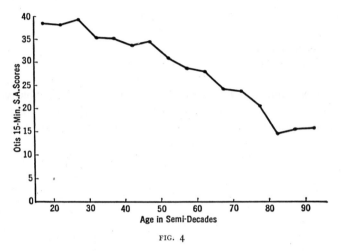

FIG. 4

DECLINE IN INTELLIGENCE TEST SCORES AFTER MATURITY

(From Miles & Miles, 1932.)

tests depending upon previous knowledge and information and relatively large in tests demanding quickness and versatility. When the Alpha sub-tests are studied separately, for example, those depending upon mental alertness show a much greater loss with age than those requiring information, vocabulary and background knowledge. Loss in score with age is also decidedly variable, many older people being far more able than those who are much younger. Statistics on the intellectual productivity of eminent men show that the greatest output of authors, inventors and scientists is between the ages of 25 and 40 years. The ages at which masterpieces are most often produced lie between 40 and 50 years. But many eminent men have done brilliant work long past this age. Bismarck was in office at 75; Gladstone was prime minister of Great Britain at 85; Edison was still taking out patents on inventions at 80; Titian painted some of his best works after 70; and there are many others.

Another fact worth comment here is that the higher the educational level attained in youth, the smaller the loss in mental test score with age. This probably means that the greater the native ability to begin with, the more slowly does it decline with the passing years. The well educated man has more interests than the poorly trained, surrounds himself with a more stimulating environment, and develops more resources within himself. All of these serve to keep up enthusiasm and prevent mental stagnation as the physical activities wane.

5. INTELLIGENCE AND OCCUPATIONAL LEVEL

Since all of the men inducted into the army were required to give their former civil occupations, important data regarding the comparative intelligence of different occupational groups may be gleaned from the army records. In the groups scoring A and B on the tests, we find the professions, for the most part, the civil engineers, mechanical engineers, physicians, lawyers, teachers, and business executives. In the C+ group were men who described themselves in civil life as stenographers, bookkeepers, clerks, photographers, and workers at skilled trades. In the C group were carpenters, policemen, tailors, butchers, printers, farmers, and small storekeepers. Store clerks, cooks, fishermen, firemen, barbers, and day laborers made up the lowest groups (C— and D).

Another way of studying the relationship between intelligence and occupation is to compare the intelligence test ratings of children whose fathers are engaged in different occupational pursuits. Table IV gives the average I Q's of children classified according to their fathers' occupational status. These data are especially valuable because they are based upon results obtained by administering the 1937 Stanford-Binet individually to nearly 3,000 children care-

TABLE IV

MEAN I Q's OF 2,757 CHILDREN CLASSIFIED ACCORDING TO THEIR FATHERS' OCCUPATIONS

(From Terman, L. M., and Merrill, M. A., *Measuring Intelligence,* 1937, pp. 14 and 48.)

Fathers' Occupational Level	*Children's Mean I Q*
I. Professional	116.2
II. Semi-professional and managerial	111.9
III. Clerical, skilled trades, retail business	107.5
IV. Semi-skilled, minor clerical and business	105.0
V. Slightly skilled and unskilled	97.2
VI. Rural owners	95.1

fully chosen to be representative of the general population of American youth. Note that these results closely parallel those obtained with Army Alpha. As the demand for specialized training and education in the fathers increases, there is a corresponding rise in the mean I Q's of their children. Between the lowest and highest occupational levels there is roughly a 20-point gap in mean I Q.

It is likely that both native endowment and training operate to produce the I Q differences in Table IV; their relative influences (as is usual) cannot be disentangled. On the one hand, the more intelligent men seek and are able to hold positions in which professional and technical training are needed, and since there is a definite relationship * between intelligence level in parent and offspring, the children of these more intelligent parents tend to be above average in mental test ratings. At the same time, their social and economic status tend to be superior, and so these children get better training and are exposed to a more cultivated and stimulating home environment. On the other hand, the less intelligent men enter occupations requiring less training and educational equipment *because* they are less able intellectually. Their homes will tend to be lacking in the intellectual stimulation characteristic of the better homes; and this will be reflected in the mental test scores of their children.

Common observation and experience, as well as other studies made of the subject, all emphasize the wide differences in mental level among occupational groups. The army tests confirmed these findings. We must not forget, however, that the *range* of intelligence ratings within any given occupational level is so wide that men of high intelligence are found in occupations the average rating for which is low. Early environment, lack of formal education, opportunity, and temperament, as well as many other less tangible influences play highly important roles in determining one's vocation. Such factors should always be considered before judging a man's probable intelligence from his occupation; they discount but do not destroy the importance of the relation disclosed by the army tests between occupation and intelligence.

We have previously commented upon the fact that officers for the most part made much higher Alpha scores than enlisted men. This result was to be expected, as was also the further finding that officers in those branches of the service which require technical training or special preparation rank

---

* The correlation (see p. 76) between intelligence test ratings in parent and offspring is about $+ .50$.

highest in general intelligence. Officers in the Engineering and Artillery Corps, for example, ranked higher than officers in the Machine-Gun and Field Signal Battalions; while these, in turn, made better scores than the officers in the Quartermaster Corps and the Infantry. One rather surprising result was the relatively low average rating of the officers of the Medical Corps. Wide differences in age and training, as well as the methods of military selection, are no doubt responsible to a large extent for this poor showing. It is a well-known fact that the Medical Corps contained some of the ablest and at the same time some of the weakest men in the profession. For this reason an "average intelligence score" is hardly representative of this group.

6. RACIAL DIFFERENCES IN INTELLIGENCE

Owing to the size of the groups and the lack of special selection, the army test data yield the fairest and most unbiased comparison of Negro and White intelligence which we possess. Negro soldiers scored lower than White on the Alpha test, the median score of the White soldier being 59, that of the Northern Negro 39, and that of the Southern Negro 12 (Table V). Since Alpha was a test designed for literates, it

TABLE V

MEDIAN SCORES ON ALPHA AND BETA OF NEGRO AND WHITE SOLDIERS

	Alpha	Beta
White	59	43
Northern Negro	39	32
Southern Negro	12	20

may be argued—and with much reason—that the better educational equipment of the Whites, and not their superior native ability, led to their better showing on Alpha. To some extent, this must be true, but it is hardly the whole story. The educational opportunities of the Negro have been—and still are—poorer than those of the White, especially in the South, and these inequalities must surely be reflected in any test involving language and a knowledge of numbers. Yet when illiterate Whites and Negroes are compared in intelligence, Table V shows the Whites to be still ahead. On the Beta test, for example, which it will be recalled is a non-language examination, the median score of the uneducated White soldier was 43 points, that of the uneducated Northern Negro 32 points, and that of the uneducated Southern Negro 20 points. Unfortunately, the score differences between Negro and White on Army Beta cannot be compared directly with score differences on Alpha, as the two tests are not scored in the same units and 5 points on the one does not mean the same as 5 points on the other. Hence, while it appears at first glance that the Negro did relatively much better on Beta than on Alpha, this does not prove to be true. Study of the scores made by the two groups reveals that not more than 25 per cent of Northern Negroes made scores as high as or higher than the median White soldier whether Beta or Alpha is the test considered; * and that about 5 per cent of Southern Negroes reached the White median on Alpha as against 10 per cent on Beta. Thus, while the Negro performed slightly better on Beta than on Alpha, he lags behind the White to about the same extent whether the comparison is in terms of a language or a non-language test. Because the overlapping † of scores in the two racial groups is fairly large, however, many Negroes will be found who are more intelligent than many Whites. This is especially

* Fifty per cent of the White soldiers reach or exceed their median score since by definition the median lies in the middle of the score range. Hence about one-half as many Negroes reach this score as Whites.

† "Overlapping" describes how many of a given group reach or exceed the median of another group.

true where the selection of Negroes is stringent, as in the case of officer material. For instance, while only 40 per cent of Negro officers made A or B ratings on Alpha as against 80 per cent of White officers, only 12 per cent of the White draft achieved A or B ratings.

The Northern Negro was superior to the Southern both on Alpha and Beta. It is impossible to say how much of this superiority comes from better native ability and how much from better educational equipment. One opinion often advanced is that the more intelligent and ambitious Negroes move to a Northern state where better educational and working conditions may presumably be found. If this view is true, the Northern Negro is superior to the Southern on tests of intelligence because of better native ability. A contrary opinion holds that it is the shiftless and unstable Negro unable to settle down and get along who migrates North, and that better training and better opportunities—not better intellect —account for the superiority of Northern over Southern Negroes. While good arguments can be made for both views, little definite information exists to support either. In one study planned to throw light on this question, the school records of 562 Negro school children, whose parents had moved North from three Southern cities, were examined to see if these children of migrants had done better or poorer school work at home than those children left behind. It turned out that the migrating children were about equal in school achievement to those who remained; so that as far as it goes this finding supports the environmental hypothesis rather than the notion of selective migration of the more intelligent. Unfortunately, however, the data of this study are meager and the indices in terms of which achievement was determined are so rough that only the most tentative conclusion is warranted.

Another study of the intelligence of migrating Negroes—

somewhat more adequate as to data and method—may be reviewed before leaving this topic. Small groups of Negro children who had lived in New York City for varying periods were given a battery of intelligence and performance tests.* The idea was to see whether test scores would improve with length of residence in New York. A slight but in most cases not significant † increase in average score was found with longer residence, which may be the result of greater confidence and growing familiarity with New York City schools. On the best measure of intelligence, the Stanford-Binet (1916), the latest arrivals (in New York less than a year) had an average I Q of 81.4 as compared with the average I Q of 87.3 of the Negro children born in New York. On the whole the migrating Negro children were probably as intelligent as the Northern-born Negro children; and this result, on the hypothesis that Northern Negroes are more intelligent than Southern, supports the theory of selective migration. Again, however, our conclusion must be tentative as the data are not extensive.

One point should be stressed in conclusion. It must be remembered that the mental test differences cited apply to Negro-White groups as we find them, not to groups in which environmental factors have been equated. That the Negro would test lower than the White under equal social conditions we do not know; that he does test lower under conditions in which we find him is a demonstrated fact.

7. NATIONAL-RACIAL DIFFERENCES IN INTELLIGENCE

An interesting comparison of the intelligence ratings of various nationalities may be obtained from the scores made

---

* These were The National Intelligence Test, the Stanford-Binet, the Paper Form Board, and Pintner-Paterson Scale.

† Statistically speaking, a significant increase is a real increase, i. e., one not attributable to chance fluctuations.

by foreign-born men who were drafted into the American army. The intelligence scores of these national groups may be expressed in terms of a "combined scale"—a scale made up of the eight Alpha tests, the Stanford-Binet tests, and four tests from Beta. The maximum score on the "combined scale" was 25 points. The average scores of the men who were born in various foreign countries, together with the number of men in each group, is given in Table VI.

TABLE VI

Country of Birth	Number of Men	Mean Intelligence Score
England	411	14.87
Scotland	146	14.34
Holland	140	14.32
Germany	308	13.88
Denmark	325	13.69
Canada	972	13.66
Sweden	691	13.30
Norway	611	12.98
Belgium	129	12.79
Ireland	658	12.32
Austria	301	12.27
Turkey	423	12.02
Greece	572	11.90
Russia	2,340	11.34
Italy	4,009	11.01
Poland	382	10.74

It is apparent from the table that men born in northern European countries rank consistently higher than men born in southern European countries, though the differences are slight. These variations in the average scores of different national groups have led to acrimonious discussions and to some ill feeling. On the one hand are the supporters of the theory of "Nordic superiority" who hold that the Nordics (mostly northern Europeans) constitute a group distinct racially from the Alpines (mostly middle Europeans) and the Mediterraneans (mostly southern Europeans). The Nordics, their champions insist, are more intelligent than the Alpines who, in turn excel the Mediterraneans, and they point to the results of the intelligence tests as experimental evidence of this fact.

Arguing on the other side, the opponents of the Nordic claim explain the variations in intelligence test score as due mainly if not entirely to differences in language, customs, training, and educational background. The high standing of the English and Scotch are to be taken, they argue, as concrete evidence of the influence of the language factor. Moreover, while disputing the actuality of the threefold racial division into Nordics, Alpines, and Mediterraneans, they hold that even if such a classification were authentic, we still have no idea how representative of each country (or each race) our small samples are. This last opinion is probably true, as our immigrants have rarely been samplings from the same social and intellectual strata of the various countries from which they come. While the fact remains, therefore, that Nordics excelled Alpines and Alpines Mediterraneans on the army tests, the explanation of such differences in terms of innate ability *alone* is certainly untenable.

Interesting evidence of the apparent decline in intelligence of American immigration over the last quarter-century may be gleaned from the army test results. For instance, those immigrants who had lived more than twenty years in this country scored higher on the "combined scale" than those who had lived here from ten to twenty years. These latter individuals, furthermore, scored higher than the very recent arrivals—those with less than five years' residence. Either we must conclude that our immigration has become steadily less and less intelligent, or take the view that foreign-born men long exposed to American customs, language, and ways of life are enabled thereby to make higher scores on a general intelligence test than men who, by and large, are equally intelligent but have been here a shorter time. The question is not easy to settle. As is well known, our earlier immigrants were drawn mainly from northern European countries, Germany, the British Isles, and Scandinavia, and are generally and popularly believed to have been an exceptionally sturdy stock. Later, American immigration came largely from southern Europe, and there is some evidence that the influx from these countries has not been from the most desirable elements of the native population. Southern Europeans scored lower in general on the "combined scale" than northern Europeans, and their scores were lower on the non-language as well as on the language parts of the test. We have pointed out above that these differences are scarcely significant, but at least they are hardly in favor of the lower groups. It seems probable, then, that our immigration has actually declined somewhat in intelligence. But the many unknown factors at work, such as differences in ability to understand and use the English language, inadequate or different educational preparation, unfamiliarity with American social customs, resulting in hesitation and timidity, prevent us from drawing any definite conclusions from the army test results as they stand.

8. INTELLIGENCE AND SCHOOLING

In Section 5 it was indicated that a soldier's intelligence test score is related to his amount of schooling. The degree of this relationship will depend upon many factors and is often difficult to determine. Some psychologists hold that intelligence tests are little more than measures of scholastic achievement; others, that they measure, to a high degree, native ability. The following table in which are given the median Alpha scores made by officers and enlisted men who had completed, respectively, four or less school grades, five to eight school grades, high school and college may serve to throw some light on this question.

TABLE VII

Median Alpha Scores for Given Amounts of Education

Group	0 to 4 grades	5 to 8 grades	High school	College
White officers	112.5	107.0	131.1	143.2
White soldiers (native-born)	22.0	51.1	92.1	117.8
White soldiers (foreign-born)	21.4	47.2	72.4	91.9
Negro soldiers (Northern)	17.0	37.2	71.2	90.5
Negro soldiers (Southern)	7.2	16.3	45.7	63.8

Striking evidence of the importance of education to success in the Alpha test is seen in the fact that the median scores of all groups (with a single exception) increase regularly with increases in schooling. In fact, the general rule would seem to be, the more the schooling, the better the intelligence score. This might seem to dispose of Alpha as a measure of anything but school training did we not have equally striking evidence of the influence of mental alertness on Alpha score. The officers, for instance, score consistently higher than the native-born White soldiers for each grade of education, while the latter group, in turn, regularly exceeds the other three groups. At each educational level the order of Alpha score is: officers, native-born Whites, foreign-born Whites, Northern Negroes, and Southern Negroes. These regular and consistent differences in Alpha performance, for a *constant amount of schooling,* bear significant testimony to the part played by native ability.

In this connection a comparison designed to test specifically this matter of the influence of schooling on Alpha may be cited. The median Alpha score made by the group of 660 officers *none* of whom had gone beyond the eighth grade was compared with the median Alpha score of 14,000 White soldiers, *all* of whom had gone *beyond* the eighth grade. The officers' median score was 107, that of the enlisted men 97— a difference of ten points in favor of the *less* educated officer group. This result has often been taken as a conclusive demonstration that native ability and not education is the "crucial" factor in determining an Alpha score. While this is probably true, nevertheless when the officers who had completed five to eight grades are compared with White soldiers of the *same* educational status (see Table VII), the difference is fifty-six points in favor of the officer group! Presumably, then, lack of education *reduced* the superiority of the first officer group from 56 points to 10 points.

Such comparisons as these lead inevitably to but one conclusion, namely, that the more able men made the highest Alpha scores and also, generally, had the most schooling. This is doubtless the result to be expected when we remember that education is in itself a highly selective process; that the stupid and unintelligent person does not get through school except rarely, and then, perhaps, not by reason of his own ability. A study of the school records of 80,000 White recruits showed that of every 1,000 who entered first grade, 830 reached grade 5, 490 grade 8, 95 graduated from high school and 10 graduated from college. No doubt there were many reasons, economic and otherwise, for this enormous elimination; but certainly the most powerful was the inability to do the work of the school satisfactorily, with resulting discouragement and loss of interest.

The discovery that the more extensive the education the higher the Alpha score is not, therefore, proof positive that Alpha is a measure of school information and not a test of intelligence. Individuals who have completed high school and college are by virtue of that accomplishment highly selected as to intellect, and hence should be expected to score high on any valid measure of intelligence. Again, we must remember that the educational demands made by the Alpha test are not excessive. Granted a common-school education and ordinary acquaintance with current American life—which was true of the majority of the men who took the Alpha test in the army—a man's score will be principally a measure of his ability to learn and to profit by experience. No intelligence test can ever hope to measure "raw brain-power," and it would be of little value if it could; for intellect, by any reasonable definition, can be measured only as it expresses itself in the activities and tasks of everyday life. For men of high intelligence but meager education—owing to no fault of their own—as well as for those who through misfortune or untoward circumstances have been deprived of a normal environment, the Alpha test is admittedly an unfair measure of ability. This simply means that *any* test score must always be interpreted with due regard for obvious handicaps, limitations and exceptional circumstances.

9. ALPHA IN THE COLLEGES

Immediately after the war, the Army Alpha test was given to hundreds of students in our colleges and universities. A comparison of the scores made by college students with those made by soldiers will prove interesting in view of the discussion in Section 8. The median Alpha scores made by college freshmen from many institutions fall between 130 and 140; this compares favorably with the median Alpha score of 139 made by the White officers, but is enormously higher than the 59 made by the average White soldier. Within the departments of a university, rather distinctive variations in Alpha score appear. In one large university, for instance, the post-graduate students scored highest (median 157), followed by medicine (142), law (142), and engineering (141). Somewhat lower in the scale were the students in education, agriculture, pharmacy, and dentistry. These differences in score must be mostly the result of differences in native ability plus differences in maturity and selection, since the minimum schooling necessary for Alpha is substantially constant throughout.

If a candidate for college has an Alpha score below 100 points (120 for the better colleges), he will have an extremely hard time of it in college. Sometimes, of course, a student who scores not much over 100 points may "get by" in college, while another who scores much higher may be dropped because of poor scholarship. But these upsets, when they occur, can generally be traced to greater persistence, determination, and hard work on the part of those students who are average or below average in intellect; and to distractions, outside interests, laziness, or character defects in those able students who are eliminated. It is true, of course, that success in college does not depend wholly upon general intelligence, but we may be sure that intellectual ability is by far the most influential factor. The marked correlation (.50–.65) between scholarship and the more discriminative and better-constructed group intelligence examinations, such as the Thorndike Intelligence Examination for High School Graduates and the Psychological Examination of the American Council on Education, serve to demonstrate experimentally the close relation between general intelligence and school achievement.

The army tests were the model for a host of group tests designed to measure general intellectual ability. Many of these are now being widely used in our schools and colleges as a means of selecting the more promising material and for the purpose of classifying students in accordance with their ability. More and more, too, intelligence tests are being introduced into business and industry for the purpose of diagnosis and selection. Many workers throughout the country are devoting their energies to the problem of increasing the validity and the accuracy of existing examinations and to the construction of new instruments. Every indication is that intelligence testing has come to stay, and we may be certain that the future of the movement is a bright one.

Chapter 3

GALTON AND THE MEASUREMENT OF INDIVIDUAL DIFFERENCES

I. THE BEGINNING OF INTEREST IN INDIVIDUAL DIFFERENCES

The eminent English scientist, Francis Galton (1822–1911) is probably best known to psychologists as a pioneer student of heredity and as the first investigator to apply statistical methods systematically to the problem of individual and group differences in mental traits. Galton was not a psychologist in the professional sense. He never held an academic position, nor did he confine himself to work upon problems primarily psychological. His interests were wide and varied. According to Terman he showed the marks of genius in early childhood and his later versatility, originality, and active interest in problems of all sorts bear out this early promise. Galton was the founder of the eugenics movement; he established one of the very first laboratories (in 1884) wherein mental and physical tests—mostly of the sensory-motor sort—could be taken for a small fee; he invented or devised various instruments for measuring sensory acuity (e. g., the Galton Whistle); he introduced the rating scale and questionnaire methods later so widely used; and he initiated and fostered the statistical study of individual differences.

Galton's work influenced and was influenced by psychological research in other countries. In 1894 the German psychiatrist Kraepelin established a psychological laboratory for the examination of mental patients in connection with his clinic and hospital. Instead of a vague and general description of symptoms, Kraepelin insisted upon precise measurement, the use of objective "tests" and the importance of measuring deviations from normal behavior. Kraepelin was interested in the magnitude, the range, and the meaning of individual differences. Reaction time, the speed and character of verbal association, memory, perception, sensory acuity, discrimination, and fatigue were among the activities and performances measured in his laboratory. William Stern was another eminent German pioneer in the field of individual differences. Stern's book on differential psychology, first published in 1900, has since appeared in several editions. Stern dealt with differences among people in various psychological traits, from simple sensory capacities to the more complex mental and emotional characteristics. The differences found among various racial and cultural groups as well as between occupational and social levels were analyzed and evaluated.

Under Binet's influence, differential psychology in France was mainly concerned with the measurement of complex activities and in the development of intelligence tests (Chap. 1). Binet's approach differed from the German and English in its objectives and in the kind of tests used in measuring psychological functions. Both movements, however, grew out of a common interest in the likenesses and differences exhibited by individuals, and in the reasons for these variations.

Mental testing in the United States is a direct outgrowth of the work upon individual differences. One of the leaders in this field was J. McKeen Cattell, a student of Galton and a pioneer both in the development of experimental psychology and of mental testing. Beginning in 1894 and for several years thereafter, Cattell administered a series of mental and physical tests to Columbia College freshmen. The relationships among these tests proved to be slight, giving experimental support to the then current theory that abilities are essentially specific in nature. Cattell's tests included among others, strength of grip, rate of movement, perception of differences in weights, reaction time to sound, speed of color naming, bisection of a 50-cm. line, and auditory memory span. These tests, which are patterned after those used by Galton, furnish an interesting contrast to Binet's tests given on pp. 4–6.

Other pioneer psychologists in America were interested in differential psychology. At the Chicago Exposition in 1893, Joseph Jastrow administered tests—much like those of Cattell—to interested volunteer subjects. Two years earlier (1891), Münsterburg had employed tests of controlled association, judgment and memory in studies of school children. Gilbert as early as 1893 carried out a fairly extensive investigation of sex differences, of the relation of physical and mental traits, and of growth changes in mental ability. In Gilbert's study, the "general mental ability" of some 1,200 school children was estimated by their teachers, and these estimates compared with scores on 8 tests of sensory and motor functions, reaction time, and suggestibility. A slight relationship was found between estimated intelligence and memory, and a fairly marked relationship between intelligence and reaction. Steady improvement was noted in the scores on all tests up to puberty.

The field of differential psychology includes a large number of problems dealing with the variations and diversities among individuals and groups. In a broad sense, all individual differences may be thought of as the joint product of heredity and environment, or, more simply, of nature and nurture. Under nature belong such biological factors as immediate ancestry, race, sex, and age; under nurture all of

FRANCIS GALTON

(1822–1911)

the social, educational, cultural, and other extrinsic agencies which shape and fashion the individual from birth until death. It is the task of differential psychology to evaluate—as far as possible—these two groups of influences.

2. THE NATURE OF INDIVIDUAL DIFFERENCES

In common parlance, we often speak of human traits as though they could occur in an "all-or-none" fashion. Thus, a pupil is described as bright or dull; a girl as pretty or ugly; a politician as honest or dishonest. Perhaps a third or inter-- mediate category (for example, average) may be admitted, but quite frequently only two sharply opposed groupings are employed. Again, we often speak of a person as the "kind of man" who would—or would not—do this or that. In part, this inveterate tendency to pigeon-hole people with respect to physical and mental traits may be little more than a lazy method of avoiding more precise description. And in part it may be simply a matter of convenience. Definite classification with respect to traits becomes of interest to psychologists when it expresses the belief—admittedly or by implication—in "types," or in large natural groupings into which many people fall.

Belief in psychological as well as in body (constitutional) types, has had a long history. In an early study of mental imagery, Galton investigated the presence and amount of imagery, and somewhat incidentally the question of "im-agery types." Galton used his now famous "breakfast table" questionnaire. Each of his subjects was asked to call up a picture of his breakfast table as it appeared in the morning; and to report whether the objects seemed well-defined, nat-ural, and comparable in vividness with the actual objects. Many of Galton's subjects were scholarly men, who to his surprise reported an almost total lack of images. Other sub-jects reported that the objects on the table appeared in retrospect to be as real as though they were actually present before the eyes. Galton accounts for the feeble imagery of scientific men in the following way: "My own conclusion is, that an over-ready perception of sharp mental pictures is antagonistic to the acquirement of habits of highly-generalised and abstract thought, especially when the steps of reasoning are carried on by words as symbols, and that if the faculty of seeing the pictures was ever possessed by men who think hard, it is very apt to be lost by disuse" (ref. 10).

Interestingly enough, Galton's work offered no evidence of distinct imagery types, though it is sometimes credited with so doing. As a matter of fact, Galton reported that instead of a "visual type," say, he found a gradation in the clearness of visual imagery from vivid to faint. Several investigators who followed Galton took their work to indicate the existence of "imagery types," and widely popularized the notion. The *visile* who is strong in visual imagery but weak or totally lacking in other kinds; the *audile* who is especially strong in auditory imagery; and the *motile,* strong in motor or kinaesthetic imagery, are the types most often cited. Later work, such as that of Betts, who used an expanded form of Galton's questionnaire, cast serious doubt upon the existence of any "pure" imagery types. Betts found "mixed" imagery to be the most usual, the "pure" visual-minded, auditory-minded, or motor-minded individual being rare if he exists at all.

The discovery that the "mixed" type of imagery is the most common falls in line with other work upon individual differences. Careful measurements of physical and mental traits in large groups of children and adults have given results diametrically opposed to the notion of types. We do not find measures occurring in "bunches" or constellations; nor do we find individuals spread evenly over the whole scale. Instead, the usual result is for many individuals to fall at the middle of the scale, and for relatively few to score either very high or very low. Two illustrations of the way in which human traits are distributed are provided in Figures 5 and 6. These two graphs represent the distribution of brain weights for 416 adult males, and the scores made on a

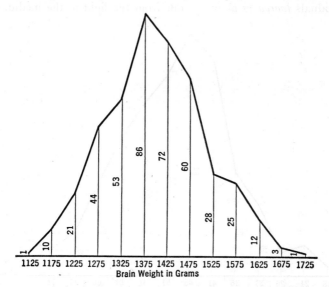

FIG. 5

DISTRIBUTION OF BRAIN WEIGHTS OF 416 MALE ADULTS

(After R. Pearl, 1930, p. 316.)

vocabulary test by 360 11-year-old boys. The two figures are constructed in the same way. To illustrate with Figure 5, brain weights ranging from light to heavy * are laid off on the horizontal axis or base-line. Above each weight-point is then marked off, on successive vertical lines, the *number* of individuals having that particular brain weight. A graph or

* These values actually represent the midpoints of intervals along the base-line.

"curve" has been drawn through the tops of these vertical lines. From the figure it appears that only one man in the group had a brain weight of 1,125 gms while 86 had brain weights centering around 1,375 gms. The number of individuals *increases* as we go out from the light to the medium

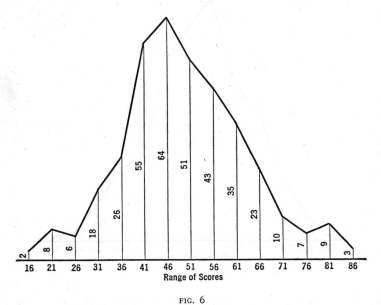

FIG. 6

DISTRIBUTION OF SCORES ON A VOCABULARY TEST MADE BY 360 ELEVEN-YEAR-OLD BOYS

(After Gansl, 1939, p. 27.)

brains; and *decreases* as we go from the medium to the heavy brains. This same arrangement of values may be seen in Figure 6. The "typical" boy with a score of 46 is much more numerous than either the exceptionally poor (score 16) or the exceptionally able boy (score 86).

The distributions of a very large number of human traits

follow the same general form shown in Figures 5 and 6. Both of these graphs approximate closely the "normal probability curve" shown in Chapter 1, p. 13, to illustrate the theoretical distribution of intelligence in the general population. To be sure not all traits in all groups follow the ideal normal curve. The group may be small, heterogeneous, or specially selected (e. g., all feeble-minded adults, or made up of groups of different ages); the test may be poorly suited to the group (too easy or too hard); a trait or character may not occur in such a way as to provide a symmetrical distribution. But when groups are large, representative and carefully measured, so many traits have been found to approximate the normal distribution that this ideal curve is generally used in describing individual differences. When a trait is normally distributed, clearly we cannot speak of "types." Every one then possesses *some,* at least, of the ability under study; and the gradation as we go from small to large amounts is regular and without breaks.

3. CORRELATION IN THE STUDY OF INDIVIDUAL DIFFERENCES

Suppose we have given two tests—one of memory span and one of hand-eye coördination—to a group of 12-year-old boys. Will the boy who ranks high in memory span rank high, medium, or low in hand-eye coördination? If boys hold the *same* order in the two tests the "correlation" between the two abilities is said to be "high"; if standing in the first test has no relation to standing in the second, the correlation is negligible or zero. The method of correlation is a valuable technique in the study of individual differences. From the correlation we can discover which traits and abilities vary together or show correspondence; to what degree individual differences in a variety of measures tend to be consistently maintained; and to what extent related persons, fathers, sons, brothers, sisters, possess traits in the same amount.

The fundamental notions underlying correlation were developed by Galton who used the method in his studies of the inheritance of traits. To Galton belongs the credit of having first shown that quantitative relationships between abilities can be calculated, and of having stimulated interest in such relationships.

Extent of relationship is expressed by the coefficient of correlation—a ratio denoted by the letter r. This coefficient may vary from 1.00 (perfect relationship) through .00 (no relationship) down to -1.00 (perfect inverse relationship). Its meaning may be most simply demonstrated, perhaps, with the help of such a diagram as that shown in Figure 7. These data, taken from Galton's *Natural Inheritance* (1889), page 208, represents graphically the relationship between the heights of "mid-parents" and their adult offspring. Galton obtained the mid-parent heights by multiplying the mother's height by 1.08 and averaging this figure with the height of the father. The same correction was also applied to the heights of the female offspring in order to give the lesser female heights equal weight with those of the males. Each mid-parent is counted separately with each offspring (of which there were often several); hence the table shows the total number of offspring (928). The average height for both mid-parents and offspring is close to 68¼ inches, and the horizontal and vertical lines drawn through the diagram have been located at these points in the two distributions of height. To illustrate how a "two-way diagram" or correlation table is made up note the entry 34 at the center of the diagram. This entry is opposite the 68.5 inch entry in the mid-parent column of heights and below the 68.2 inch entry in the offspring row of heights. This means that these 34 adult offspring with an average height of 68.2 inches possessed

Heights of Adult Children in Inches

Height of Mid-Parents in Inches	Below 61.7	62.2	63.2	64.2	65.2	66.2	67.2	68.2	69.2	70.2	71.2	72.2	73.2	Above 73.7	Total Number of Adult Offspring
Above 72.5												1	3		4
72.5								1	2	1	2	7	2	4	19
71.5					1	3	4	3	5	10	4	9	2	2	43
70.5			1		2	1	3	12	18	14	7	4	3	3	68
69.5			1	16	4	17	27	20	33	25	20	11	4	5	183
68.5			7	14	14	25	31	34	48	21	18	4	3		219
67.5	1		5	12	19	36	38	28	38	19	11	4			211
66.5	1		3	6		17	17	14	13	4	2	1			78
65.5	1	3	9	5	7	11	11	7	7	5					66
64.5	1	3	4	2		5	5	1	2						23
Below	1	1	2	4	1	2	2		1						14
Totals	5	7	32	59	48	117	138	120	167	99	64	41	17	14	928

parents whose average height was 68.5 inches. The other entries are to be interpreted in the same way. Each offspring has been classified in two ways:—with respect to his own height and his parents' height. It is clear from Figure 7 that the entries tend to be clustered in the upper right hand and the lower left hand sections of the diagram. This means that, in general, tall parents tend to have tall children, and short parents tend to have short children. In other words, the heights of parents and offspring are related; and this tendency of the two groups to vary together is expressed by a correlation coefficient or r of .45. The calculation of r is somewhat involved, and is described in detail in textbooks dealing with statistical method. The mathematical derivation of r was made by Karl Pearson, an eminent British biometrician. Since Galton's time, literally hundreds of correlations have been calculated, and the relationships of most physical and mental traits are now well established. In a general way correlations above .60 are considered "high"; those from .60 to about .30 are "marked" or "moderate"; those from .30 to .00 are "low" or negligible. Negative correlations (whose values are to be interpreted in the same way as positive correlation) imply that large amounts of the one trait accompany small amounts of the other—as when degree of skill or accuracy in a performance correlates *negatively* with number of errors committed.

The data in Figure 7 may be used to demonstrate another important discovery made by Galton. Table VIII shows the median (approximately the average) heights of offspring for given mid-parent heights. Note that the offspring of very tall parents—those 72.5 inches, say—tend to be slightly *below* their parents in height; and this discrepancy holds on down to the mean or average height. Below the mean, offspring tend to be *above* their parents in height (see last column of Table VIII). This tendency of the

Table VIII

Tendency for Adult Offspring to "Regress" toward the Mean Adult Height

(From Fig. 7)

Height of Mid-Parents	Median Height of Offspring for Given Mid-Parent Height	Difference
72.5 inches	72.2 inches	.3
71.5 "	69.9 "	1.6
70.5 "	69.5 "	1.0
69.5 "	68.9 "	.6
68.5 "	68.2 "	.3
67.5 "	67.6 "	— .1
66.5 "	67.2 "	— .7
65.5 "	66.7 "	— 1.2
64.5 "	65.8 "	— 1.3

heights of offspring to vary *away* from the heights of their parents and back toward the mean height of the *entire group* (parents and offspring) was called by Galton the *law of filial regression*. This "law" is the expression of a natural tendency which protects the race from extremes. Unless some such principle operated—if tall parents had still taller children, and short parents still shorter offspring—we should soon have a race of giants on the one hand and of dwarfs on the other. The *law of filial regression* holds in a general way for mental traits as well as for physical characters. Its operation is seen in the relatively infrequent appearance of freaks at either extreme of a distribution of physical or mental traits.

4. NATURE AND NURTURE IN THE STUDY OF INDIVIDUAL DIFFERENCES

The relative importance of nature and nurture in determining individual differences is an old and much discussed question. Opinion has shifted back and forth from belief in the all-importance of heredity to confidence in the greater potency of environment. A good part—perhaps a major part —of the disagreement here has arisen from a failure properly to define terms. Heredity and environment are not to be thought of as "forces" which operate separately and independently, though many differences among individuals seem attributable primarily to one or the other influence. The color of a child's eyes and hair, his height, weight, and physique are considered to be native or inborn characteristics; while his "mother tongue," e. g., English or French, since it depends upon the country in which he was brought up, is held to be a product of environment. But the distinction here, while apparent, is not as clear-cut as it seems at first glance. Even physical attributes such as hair and eye color, height and weight, are affected by climate, diet, and disease; and, without the elaborate structure of the throat and vocal cords, speech of any sort is impossible. In neither case is nature or nurture exclusively responsible. Every young animal or human child is born with certain skeletal and muscular structures, as well as with a repertory of movements (many highly coördinated) which are native and inherited. But this equipment would be of little value unless shaped by learning and experience. Intrinsic factors such as immediate ancestry, sex, race always operate in some definite environmental setting. If behavior were arranged on a scale of complexity, from a simple reflex to the most complex literary and scientific achievements, there would be no point where heredity leaves off completely and environment takes over. In any given act, whether it be spelling a word, throwing a baseball, or building a bridge, both native constitution and specific training enter. In short, both groups of influences are indispensable to growth and both must be studied by those who wish to understand individual differences.

Galton was much interested in the problem of the relative importance of nature and nurture. In his study of imagery, already referred to on p. 61, he concluded that the absence of imagery is largely a result of one's training and manner of thinking and working. Galton found considerable evidence that amount of imagery is, at least in part, hereditary. Thus, he discovered that imagery tends to run in families; is stronger in women than in men; is stronger in younger than in older persons. Imagery, according to Galton, is not necessarily correlated with eminence as a painter or imaginative writer. Great individual differences exist in the *kind* and *amount* of imagery.

Galton early attacked the question of the inheritance of conspicuous ability or talent. In the first statistical study of the influence of immediate ancestry upon achievement, Galton selected for study 977 eminent British men, each of whom he judged would rank as one man in 4,000 in ability. These selections were based upon a survey of the man's accomplishments, upon his biography, and upon all other available information. Among those included in the 977 were judges, statesmen, prime ministers of England from around 1768 to 1868, commanders, literary and scientific men, poets, artists, and clergymen. Galton's method was to determine whether these men had more eminent relatives—fathers, brothers, sons, uncles, and others—than would be expected of 977 men selected at random from the general population. His findings showed that his selected group of 977 had a total population of close relatives just as eminent as they were themselves which included 89 fathers, 114 brothers, 129 sons, or 332 in all, against a probable, or expected, number of only 1. Moreover, this same group had 203 equally eminent grandfathers, grandsons, uncles, and nephews, as against a probable number of 3. The probabilities of 1 and 3 here stated mean that the statistical chances are 1 and 3, respectively, that any unselected group of 977 men will have eminent relatives up to Galton's standard of 1 in 4,000. In another study of the inheritance of artistic ability, Galton found that in thirty families wherein both parents were artistic, 64 per cent of the children were artistic, while in 150 families wherein neither parent was artistic, only 21 per cent of the offspring showed artistic ability. Other studies of related individuals revealed a strong tendency for traits to be found in a like degree in parents and offspring. Galton took these data to imply the great superiority of heredity over environment. Even the best environment, he contended, is unable to raise a man to a position of eminence unless he possesses natural gifts of a high order.

The statistical studies begun by Galton were extended and increased in scope by Karl Pearson, Galton's disciple and, from 1911 to 1936, Galton Professor of Eugenics at the University of London. In one typical study by Pearson 2,000 brothers and sisters were rated by their teachers for intelligence, vivacity, conscientiousness, popularity, temper, self-consciousness, assertiveness and handwriting. In each of these characteristics, except handwriting and temper, the individual rated was described simply as falling into the upper or lower group with respect to the given trait. Correlations for all eight traits averaged .52 between brother and brother, .51 between sister and sister, and .52 between brother and sister. Pearson had found that the correlation between such attributes as eye-color, hair-color, height, and length of fore-arm, over which environment can have little if any effect, also averaged from .50 to .55 for siblings (i. e., brothers and sisters). From these results he argued that since the relationship of physical traits must be due to heredity, and since these characteristics are no more highly related than mental traits, the correlation of the latter must also be basically the result of hereditary influences. He writes (ref. 32,* p. 156):

* See Bibliography at end of book.

"We are forced, I think literally forced, to the conclusion that the physical and psychical characters in man are inherited within broad lines in the same manner and with the same intensity."

In spite of the weight of these statistical studies because of the eminence of their authors, several difficulties arise to prevent our accepting their results as incontrovertible evidence for the predominant influence of heredity over environment upon achievement. The first and most obvious difficulty is the error of unfair selection or bias. Galton's choice of eminent men was almost inevitably affected by subjective factors such as personal bias and preferences as well as by the relatively greater accessibility of data on some men than on others. It is extremely doubtful whether eminence as a statesman, in which political and social conditions play so large a rôle, can be equated to eminence as an artist or as a man of science. Again, it is also doubtful whether a man's true worth can be correctly judged from the length of his biography or from what his contemporaries think of him. And it is unnecessary to add that we do not know just what part social factors and family tradition, wealth, education, and opportunity played in determining the eminence of Galton's selected group. The error of unfair selection is almost certainly present, too, in Pearson's ratings. For one thing, the teachers who did the rating knew that the investigation was designed to discover whether children of the same parents resemble each other, and hence they were very likely looking for resemblances more often than not. Moreover, pairs of siblings were rated against each other rather than separately on *all* the traits, thus giving ample opportunity for likes and dislikes to come into play. Finally, Pearson's classification of traits into only two categories was extremely rough, making large errors highly probable.

Still another difficulty regularly arises in studies wherein the questionnaire method is used, or ratings are required. This is the so-called "halo" effect, which means simply that when an individual is rated for intelligence, say, and then for a number of other traits, such, for instance, as reliability, honesty, and courtesy, it is next to impossible to prevent his first rating or ratings from unduly influencing the others. An oft-quoted illustration of halo is given by Rugg. He cites the case of an American officer in the World War who, although one of the most intelligent men in his group as measured by Army Alpha, was regularly rated low for intelligence by his fellow-officers because he was so thoroughly disliked. Suggestion, inertia, misunderstanding, the vagueness of the traits to be rated, not to mention prejudice and envy, are influential forces in producing a halo effect. Beside the unknown amount of halo in Pearson's ratings, it seems evident too that such characteristics as temper, popularity, vivacity, and handwriting must depend to a large degree upon health, home conditions, training and degree of stimulation. It is impossible, then, to say just how much Pearson's fraternal correlation of .50 in mental traits is the result of native and how much of environmental factors.

5. FURTHER STUDIES OF NATURE AND NURTURE

While this early work was subject to many limitations, later studies strongly suggest that Pearson was probably right in emphasizing the greater potency of heredity over environment. One of the most extensive of recent investigations bearing on this topic is Terman's study of gifted children, mentioned elsewhere (p. 16) as evidence that intelligence is inherited. It will be remembered that a gifted child in Terman's sense means a child with an I Q of 130 or above. In Terman's main experimental group of 644 children, seventy-three families contributed two gifted children, and nine families contributed three or more. The number of families in which two bright children were found was more than 1,200 times the number which chance alone would allow. Nearly one fourth of the members of the Hall of Fame were related to these children, while many of their parents and near relatives hold or have held major political offices, college presidencies, professorships, and important business positions. Follow-up studies show that these bright youngsters have maintained their superior status in comparison with average children.

So much for the power of heredity. On the side of environment, we find that these gifted children came, in general, from superior homes. Income level was considerably above that of the average American home; the educational level of the parents was high; and the divorce rate low. It is impossible to define precisely the contributions of heredity and environment in the making of a bright child. It can be argued that intelligent parents have intelligent children and make good homes; and that good environment leads to superior achievement. On biological grounds the argument for heredity appears to be stronger. If one cannot "make a silk purse out of a sow's ear," neither can one make a genius out of an average child. A not unfair analogy is that of an automobile engine. Good oil and careful handling will undoubtedly make a cheaply built engine run better, but even the best oil and the most careful handling cannot make it perform like a first-class engine.

Many careful investigations have attempted to disentangle the specific contributions of nature and nurture to achievement. A few of these will be reviewed. H. E. Jones has reported a study of 105 families containing 317 children, all of whom were born and reared in rural sections of New England. The general intelligence of parents and offspring was measured by the Army Alpha, that of the younger children by the Stanford Revision of the Binet tests. The sample selected for study was particularly good, since environmental conditions, education, home training, amusements, and church influences were closely similar for all members of the group. Moreover, all of the individuals tested were native-born Whites of old American (mostly British) stock and only English was spoken in their homes. Correlation between the intelligence test scores of brothers and sisters was found by Jones to be .49; of father and child, .51; and of mother and child, .55. These results are very similar—almost identical in fact—with those of Pearson. Working with a group of more than 1,000 siblings, all high school students, Thorndike reports a correlation of .60 between sibling scores on a battery of tests designed to measure general ability. Thorndike remarks that if Pearson's coefficient of .52 for sibling resemblance in physical traits is accepted as giving the undiluted native or inherited resemblance, then the effect of the environment is to raise the sibling correlation for mental ability from .52 to .60. Provided that .52 really represents true native resemblance, this result assigns an exceedingly meager influence to environment.

Two studies bearing upon the influences of immediate ancestry and nurture should be mentioned before leaving this topic. The first deals chiefly with the influence of *environment* upon the intelligence of children. It was conducted by F. N. Freeman, K. J. Holzinger, and others at the University of Chicago. The second deals with the relative effects of *nature and nurture* upon intelligence. It was carried out by Barbara S. Burks at Stanford University under the general supervision of L. M. Terman. Both studies make use of foster children, and accept the Stanford Revision as their standard measure of general intelligence. Foster children were selected for study because their heredity is usually poor and the foster homes to which they go are better than their own homes. This gives the investigator an opportunity to find out whether superior environment will operate to increase I Q. In the Chicago study it was found that children who were tested on being placed in foster homes had gained on the average *seven points* in I Q when retested after about four years of residence. Children placed in superior homes (the status of the home was measured by rating devices) gained about ten points in I Q; those in below-average homes, about five points. The Stanford study found an average gain of five to six points in I Q as a result of residence in good foster homes. Both of these studies agree, therefore, that an average home environment may raise the I Q five to six points, while a superior home may increase it still more. Unfortunately this conclusion is not entirely sure, owing to many uncontrolled factors which enter into the choice of a foster child, uncertainty as to the parentage of many of the foster children, and the difficulty in determining with exactitude the cultural status of the foster home. The weight of evidence, however, inclines to the conclusion that environment has remarkably little effect upon general intelligence.

6. THE STUDY OF TWINS

The most direct way of evaluating the influence of immediate ancestry is through the study of twins, since twins represent the nearest approach to identical heredity. Here again Galton was the pioneer. In an early study he gives an interesting narrative account of his study of twin resemblance. Galton collected data on about eighty pairs of twins from teachers, friends, parents, and the twins themselves. These reports are in the nature of stories, anecdotes, and the like, for the most part stressing the prevalent idea that twins are much more alike in mental characteristics than siblings. Galton's records have little scientific validity, in spite of their historical interest, as reports collected from untrained observers are invariably colored by all sorts of temperamental and emotional inferences. It should be noted, however, that Galton did distinguish between fraternal and non-fraternal twins. Fraternal or non-identical twins are the result of multiple births and develop from two fertilized ova. They may be both of the same sex or of opposite sex. Non-fraternal or identical twins are probably developed from a single ovum and are always of the same sex. Their resemblance is striking, and it is often difficult to tell them apart.

Thorndike's 1905 study was the first quantitative investigation of mental resemblance in twins. He measured fifty pairs of twins on six mental tests, comparing the correlation beween their scores with the correlation of siblings on the same tests. The correlation for the twins ranged from .73 to .85 with a mean at .77, while the coefficients for siblings averaged around .30. Thorndike next divided his twins into younger twins (nine to eleven years) and older twins (twelve to fourteen years) and computed correlations among his six tests for the two groups separately. The average coefficient for the younger twins was .83, for the older twins .70, indicating that older twins are no more alike than younger twins in the functions measured by the tests. Thorndike argues that if resemblances between twin-pairs in mental ability are the result of common training and common surroundings in school and home, the older twins should be more alike than the younger, especially in those traits much influenced by training. Since his results showed the opposite to be true, he concludes that the evidence decidedly favors heredity as the cause of twin resemblance.

Many careful studies of twins have been made since Thorndike's pioneer investigation, with more cases, better technique, and better tests; but the results are not far different from his findings. Merriman found the correlation between I Q (Stanford-Binet) for forty-seven twins five to nine years old to be .81; for fifty-eight twins ten to sixteen years old, .76. Lauterbach with twenty-one measures and 212 twin pairs, found like-sex twins (probably non-fraternal or identical) to be more alike in both physical and mental characteristics than unlike-sex twins (probably fraternal or non-identical), the latter being scarcely more alike than siblings. The average correlation for seven mental tests for like-sex twins was .67, for unlike-sex twins .41. Hildreth, using many measurements, found the average correlation between twins to be approximately .75, between siblings about .50. Leahy, whose study has already been mentioned (p. 26), obtained an average correlation of .51 between child and own parents and an average correlation of .22 between child and foster parents' intelligence. McNemar set out to discover whether identical twins are more alike than fraternal twins in certain motor skills, and whether practice will increase or decrease twin resemblance. In five motor tasks, the identical twins were much more alike than the fraternal, the average correlation being .47 for fraternal, and .83 for identical twins. Continued practice in the five motor tasks led to a somewhat closer resemblance between fraternal twins (increase in correlation). But the fraternal twins remained less alike than the identical twins even after practice.

All in all, these studies of twins indicate definitely that (1) twins are more alike than siblings; and (2) identical twins are more alike than non-identical. The difference between the correlations for mental traits of around .50 (for siblings) and .75 (for twins) may be reasonably attributed to the more nearly identical inheritance of the twin-pairs.

To summarize briefly what has been said in the last three sections, it may be repeated that most careful investigators are convinced that native factors are more potent than environmental in fixing the initial amount of an individual's aptitudes and the extent to which these may be developed. But no one disputes the fact that no matter how great a child's potential ability, it cannot express itself adequately when such environmental factors as cruel treatment, and restrictive and circumscribed social contacts are present.

7. SEX DIFFERENCES

Competent investigators who have studied the question of differences in ability between the sexes are convinced that on the whole such differences are small; and that, when they exist, they are probably to be attributed to a complex of temperamental and social factors rather than to innate or hereditary differences in capacity for achievement. The very different training given men and women until recent times; the attitude of conservative men and women toward women entering business or the professions; the traditional idea of what constitutes a man's work and of what constitutes a woman's work—all of these factors have so colored the whole question of sex differences in mental capacity that an unbiased conclusion is extremely hard to reach.

One of the earliest studies of sex differences in ability was conducted by Helen Thompson at the University of Chicago in 1903. A variety of tests were employed, including measures of motor ability, sensory acuity and discrimination, and intellectual ability, the whole battery requiring between fifteen and twenty hours to administer. The subjects were twenty-five men and twenty-five women college undergraduates, between the ages of twenty and twenty-five years with a few exceptions. The results of these tests may be summarized briefly as follows: In motor tests of speed and accuracy of movement, except in speed and accuracy of sorting cards according to color, the men did slightly better than the women; in sensory tests of smell, taste, pitch discrimination, and accuracy in judging weights, there were no differences; in tests of rote memory, the women were slightly better than the men; in quickness in solving "ingenuity" problems, the men were slightly ahead. It must be emphasized that in nearly every case the overlapping was great and the differences extremely small, most of them being unreliable. In short, the differences *within* either group were very much greater than the differences *between* typical members of the two groups: the gap between a high-ranking man and a low-ranking man was much greater than the gap between the average man and the average woman. Thompson's groups were highly selected, and their small size limits the general applicability of her findings.

Pearson in his study of the resemblances of sibs, mentioned before, had brothers and sisters rated by their teachers for such attributes as athletic aptitude, intelligence, shyness, good temper, and conscientiousness. As already pointed out, Pearson's results are open to the errors of bias and misunderstanding likely to affect all ratings. But despite this fact their trend is probably indicative of marked differences between brothers and sisters. According to Pearson's findings, boys are more athletic than girls, more noisy, more self-conscious, and quicker-tempered; girls are more inclined to be shy and are more conscientious. Boys and girls were about equally intelligent as judged by their teachers.

Hundreds of studies of sex differences have been made for all sorts of traits since these early studies.* It would be impossible—and in many cases not worth while—to describe all of them even briefly. In general, differences reported between the sexes have been small and often contradictory. We shall try to summarize what appear to be the major and more reliable findings under the following heads: differences in physical characteristics; differences in sensory traits; differences in motor and mechanical abilities; differences in mental and emotional traits. It must always be remembered that when one sex is said to be "better" in some performance

* For a comprehensive review, see ref. 1 in the Bibliography.

than the other, the meaning intended is better "on the average." In all traits there is at least some overlapping of male and female performances.

1. *Sex Differences in Physical Traits*. Until puberty at least, girls are more advanced than boys of the same age in height, weight, dentition, and anatomical and physiological maturity. The brain of the female is smaller than that of the male, but, in proportion to the weight of the body, is heavier. Women have a faster heartbeat than men, and their simple reflexes are usually quicker. Men have larger muscles than women, and excel them in feats of endurance and physical strength.

2. *Sex Differences in Sensory Traits*. Tests in this field have usually given small differences and often contradictory results. There are probably no real differences between women and men in visual and auditory acuity and discrimination. Women are consistently faster than men in discriminating differences among colors and in quickness of perception. Men judge differences in weight somewhat better than women and endure pain better.

3. *Sex Differences in Motor and Mechanical Traits*. Women are consistently faster than men in cancellation tests. There are no real differences in simple motor functions such as tapping and tracing. Boys are nearly always better than girls in performance tests of a manipulative sort, in form-board tests, and in tracing mazes. They are also superior in tests of mechanical construction, mechanical aptitude, and knowledge of mechanical things. Much of this difference is undoubtedly the result of training and the early cultivation of very different interests. Boys are given mechanical toys and bicycles, girls dolls and fancy wearing apparel, and such things soon come to be identified as belonging peculiarly to one sex.

4. *Sex Differences in Mental and Emotional Traits*. Most studies agree in reporting women as better than men in

nearly all tests of memory. Girls almost always do better than boys on vocabulary tests, as well as on tests involving language usage and verbal association. Terman found girls slightly better than boys on the Stanford-Binet at each age up to fourteen, a result which may be due to the large verbal content of the test. Boys are consistently better in tests involving numbers and spatial concepts (of a geometric sort), and in arithmetical reasoning tests. Men usually do better than women on general information tests, owing partly no doubt to their greater opportunity for contacts in their business and professional lives. In group intelligence tests there are no reliable differences in favor of either sex; the superiority of high school boys over high school girls sometimes reported is probably to be explained by the fact that high school boys form a more highly selected group than high school girls. If stupid boys drop out of school earlier and more often than stupid girls, the boys who survive to high school will be, on the average, somewhat better than girls in school work. Girls usually make higher school marks than boys. This has been explained as due to the slower physical development of the boys, to the greater docility of the girls, and to various temperamental factors. After selecting his potential geniuses, Terman found that 54.7 per cent were boys and 45.3 per cent girls. The occurrence of more very bright boys than very bright girls has been commented upon by several investigators, and has been attributed by some to the reputed greater variability of the male sex in mental traits. Greater variability in males would mean that men range higher (and of course lower, too) on a scale of intellectual ability even when the average man and the average woman are about equally endowed. Greater variability would perhaps account for the greater number of male geniuses, and for the greater achievement of men in general. This is a very neat explanation, but since many competent investigators dispute the evidence for greater variability in the male, the issue is by no means settled.

Studies of sex differences in emotional and temperamental traits have given few definite and consistent results. Women are reported to be more interested in persons and personal problems, men in activities and mechanical things. Girls excel boys in tests of moral knowledge and social attitudes, but are no more honest in tests of cheating or deceit. Studies of sex differences in free association indicate a tendency for women's associations to run to personal ornament and to concrete and individual problems; men's associations to business relations, money-making, and general and abstract matters. Differences in conversation and in preferences for books and pictures reflect so many things besides the sex of the person observed that any differences found are scarcely to be attributed to sex alone. Women have been reported to be more impulsive than men, more introverted, less given to exercising foresight; but such statements are little more than unsupported opinions.

Many studies of sex differences are open to one or more of the following criticisms: (1) samples are small and are selected by different criteria; (2) the tests used to measure abilities are unreliable statistically, and the meaning of their scores is uncertain; (3) overlapping of the groups compared is often ignored and only the average difference stressed; (4) the fact that girls are relatively more mature physically than boys of the same age is not taken into account. The only general conclusions that one may draw with regard to comparative mental ability from the mass of available data is that women are *usually* better in tests of language, verbal usage, vocabulary, and memory; that men are *usually* better in tests of arithmetical reasoning, in performance and manipulative tests, and in the ability to deal with spatial concepts of a geometric sort. Whatever the considerations are (and conceivably they could be many) which guide parents and educators in planning separate courses of study for boys and girls, the assumption of marked differences in mental ability between the sexes need play no important rôle in them.

8. RACIAL DIFFERENCES

The study of individual differences arising from remote ancestry or race is complicated even more than the question of sex differences by prejudice, bias, preconceived notions of superiority and inferiority, and special pleading. There is difficulty, too, in defining just what is meant by a "race," because of the free admixture which has gone on all over the world. Some anthropologists hold that the White peoples of Europe can be divided into three large racial groups, Nordic, Alpine, and Mediterranean, on the basis of differences in eye-color and hair-color, stature, head shape, and other anatomical characteristics. If this classification is accepted then almost every national group is a compound of all three of these strains. The modern British, for instance, are Scandinavian Nordic, Norman-French Alpine, and Old Celtic Mediterranean, the dominant strain depending upon the section of the country selected for study. The modern Germans and Italians are almost as mixed a people as the British, the German being largely Nordic and Alpine, the Italian Alpine and Mediterranean. Probably the Swedes represent as pure a strain as any, being very largely Nordic.

Opinions on race differences vary greatly. On the one hand we find a firm belief in the native superiority of certain groups (usually including our own); on the other hand we find the view that there are really no hereditary racial differences—such diversities as appear being the result of wide variations in culture, kind of education and training, traditions and customs, relative isolation from other groups, and climatic and geographical factors. Galton was a firm believer in race differences in native capacity; and it was to improve his own race that he initiated the eugenics movement in 1883. Galton concluded, as a result of his observations and study of the history and accomplishments of the different races, reports of travelers, and other data, that the Negro is two grades in mental capacity below the modern Englishman, who in turn is two grades below the ancient Athenian Greek. Galton's scale of intellectual ability contained sixteen steps and ranged from very high to extremely low capacity.

Both Galton's conclusion and his scale have been criticized, the latter on the ground that it is arbitrary and subjective, the former on the ground that it is not justifiable to compare races on the basis of the number of famous men produced, or in terms of apparent progress. For one thing, it is hard to define progress, and for another, social and climatic conditions and geographical locations cannot be equated. Granted the force of these objections, it would seem nevertheless that *wide* variations in accomplishment and in the building-up of an ordered civilized life must go beyond the effects produced by environment and culture. Probably no one would contend seriously that the Australian Bushman has shown the same capacity for achievement as have the present inhabitants of that country, or that Eskimos have shown the same aptitude for scientific invention as have, say, the modern Germans. In other words, Galton's contention that there are native differences in intellectual capacity between races far removed from each other on a scale of accomplishment would certainly seem to be justified. As Thorndike aptly remarks (ref. 39, p. 221): "Common observation of the African and European, for example, decides that the latter is superior in intellect, enterprise, and self-reliance . . . two races need not be equally gifted because each is equally well adapted to its environment, if the second race has by superior enterprise sought out or created a more exacting but also more remunerative environment. . . . The Bushman may count all that he needs to count, but to put oneself in a position that needs algebra and calculus may itself be a symptom of superiority. . . . The very fact that a certain test seems unfair to the Bushman may be evidence of his inferiority."

Wide divergences in culture and attainment between races are not so difficult to explain. The real trouble arises in deciding to what *causes* we may attribute small and variable differences in mental measurements between two racial groups. So far, there is no way of isolating native factors from those of training and environment, and it may well be that no method of doing this satisfactorily will ever be found. Differences in language offer a considerable obstacle, as do tests which mean one thing to one group and another and different thing to another group. Culture and convention—habits of thought and action and manner of living—vary widely, and their influences are next to impossible to evaluate. This is well illustrated by Boas's example of an Italian child who in a picture-completion test put a crucifix over the door of a house from which the chimney was missing.* In this child's experience a crucifix was more necessary to a house than a chimney; and hence his response, in view of his background, was an intelligent one, albeit "wrong" from the point of view of the test.

Hundreds of studies have been made in an effort to evaluate the influence of racial extraction upon achievement. Without attempting to discuss more than a fraction of these, we shall try in the next few paragraphs to give those results which seem to be most reliably established. Studies of primitive peoples, as in the pioneer study of Woodworth made at the St. Louis Exposition in 1904, indicate that these races do

---

* Picture-completion tests are drawings in which something left out is to be added by the child.

not differ markedly from the modern White European or American in keenness of vision, in hearing, in sensitivity to pain and pressure, or in delicacy of skin and muscle senses. Form-board tests (see pp. 303–305), designed to gauge intellectual activity of a simple and rudimentary sort, brought out no reliable differences between Whites and many less cultured folk such as Eskimos, Indians, Filipinos, and Senegalese. But the Negrito and Pygmy (African tribes of small stature and extremely low culture) did no better than low-grade or even imbecile Whites. Since the feeble-minded White differs least from the normal in physical characteristics and motor abilities and most in language and verbal usage (represented by the stock tests of general intelligence), this result makes it appear probable that the intellectual gap between the civilized White and these primitive folk is a distinct and wide one.

In America a great many studies have been made of the performance of the Negro on mental tests, and as a result of these the inferiority of the Negro to the White in mental ability has been frequently asserted. It is extremely hard, however, to tell how much of the Negro's apparent inferiority should be attributed to his lower social status, usually inferior training, and lack of opportunity for wide contacts. The fact that the Negro soldier scored on the average lower than the White on both language and non-language tests has been discussed elsewhere and some of the difficulties in accepting this finding at face value have been indicated (pp. 46–49). Mayo, in an early study of Negro high school students in New York City, found that on the average they remained in school longer than the White; they averaged about seven months older than White students judged to be of approximately the same social status; and they were somewhat inferior in school work, only about 30 per cent doing as well as or better than the average White student. Mayo's

Negro students were more stringently selected than his White students, as only the more ambitious and able Negroes remained in high school. Hence the inferiority of the Negroes is probably even greater than his figures indicate. Ferguson administered a number of mental tests to White and Negro students in three Southern cities, in an effort to study abilities less complicated by social factors than are school marks. On these tests the Negroes turned in performances about three-fourths as good as those of the Whites. When classified roughly as to skin-color, those Negroes with apparently the highest degree of White blood approximated most closely to the White norms.

In an interesting study of very young children, McGraw tested 68 White and 60 Negro babies from two to eleven months old by means of the Vienna "Babytests" described on p. 302. This study is important because the extreme youth of these children excludes many social and environmental factors difficult or impossible to equate. The White babies did better than the Negro on the mental tests at each month level, with, however, considerable overlapping. The fact that even at this early age the White children test higher strongly suggests heredity as the cause of differences in mental ability. However, this conclusion is weakened by the fact that the Negroes were not so well developed physically as the Whites nor so well nourished. In studies of older children A. H. Arlitt and D. Sunne have found fairly consistent differences in mental performance in favor of the Whites over the Negroes about as large as those of Ferguson and Mayo. Arlitt stresses particularly the necessity for taking account of social status. When White and Negro children are really equated for social status the superiority of the White is much reduced. Within the White group there was a gap in I Q of thirty-three points between those children from very superior and those from very inferior social surroundings. This is a wider intellectual gap than that between Whites and Negroes, but it must be noted that even the "inferior" and "very inferior" Whites are slightly ahead of the Negroes.

On the whole it is hard to see how selection or variations in social status can account for *all* of the differences found in these studies, although it might very well account for a part. The Negro comes out consistently below the White norms on tests designed to gauge mental ability. Whether these differences are chiefly native or chiefly environmental, we cannot at present say, but a reasonable view is that native differences play some part. This does not alter the fact, of course, that as shown by the overlapping of test scores, many Negroes stand higher than Whites.

There have been a few studies of temperamental differences between Negroes and Whites. In one study McFadden and Dashiell found small and unreliable differences on the Downey Will-Temperament Test, a test designed to measure temperamental and impulsive traits. Crane attempted to compare experimentally the fear reactions of Negroes and Whites in a laboratory situation. His test consisted in measuring the ability to inhibit the withdrawal of the hand from between two uprights when a weight appeared to be falling upon it. Although each subject had been told that no harm would come to him, many were unable, despite this assurance, to keep from pulling the hand away. Crane found among the Whites fewer complete withdrawals on the first trial than among the Negroes; but a greater *tendency* to withdraw on subsequent trials as shown by small tentative movements, twitchings of the arm muscles, and sudden catchings of the breath. He concludes that Negroes are given to sudden and complete impulsive reactions which are over and done with; that Whites are less liable to react violently than Negroes, but are unable to inhibit their reactions entirely.

Various studies of the American Indian and the Mexican

indicate that these groups generally score lower than the White on both verbal and non-verbal tests. There is fairly reliable evidence that mixed-blood Indians are superior to full-bloods, just as mulattos are in general superior in mental test performances to pure Negroes. A part, at least, of the Indians' inferiority in mental tests has been shown by Klineberg to be temperamental, the result of a very different attitude toward life, as well as of different ideas of what is important and valuable. Indians, for instance, while much slower than White children on Klineberg's tests (mostly form-board performance tests) were consistently more accurate, the need for speed having no appeal to them. Orientals, Japanese and Chinese, who have been tested in America are little, if at all, inferior to the native Whites, given equal opportunity for education and contacts with American life.

The comparative showings of various European national groups on the army "combined scale" has been presented elsewhere (p. 50). The results of another study of groups of European origin are given in Table IX. Nearly 5,000 school children from 5 to 18 years old, all offspring of immigrant parents, were given three group intelligence tests * which included both language and non-language items. The results in Table IX are for children grouped according to the nationality of their parents. Scores are expressed in average I Q's. While the differences in Table IX are quite small for adjacent groups, the range is large from the highest to the lowest. Of the seven highest groups, two are predominantly Nordic (English and Swedes); two are Alpine (Germans and Lithuanians); two are Alpine and Mediterranean (Polish and Russian Jews); and one is Mediterranean (Irish). Of the seven lowest groups, one is Nordic (British Canadian); three are Alpine (Russian, Polish and French Canadian); three are

* These tests were the Pintner-Cunningham Primary Test, Dearborn Test A and Dearborn Test C.

TABLE IX

AVERAGE I Q's OF CHILDREN OF IMMIGRANT GROUPS

Nationality	No.	Av. I Q
Polish Jews	75	102.8
Swedes	232	102.1
English	213	100.7
Russian Jews	627	99.5
Germans	190	98.5
Lithuanians	468	97.4
Irish	214	95.9
British Canadians	115	93.8
Russians	90	90.0
Poles	227	89.6
Greeks	270	87.6
Italians	350	85.8
French Canadians	243	85.3
Portuguese	671	82.7

Mediterranean (Greeks, Italians, Portuguese). Many studies of the children of foreign-born parents in New York City and elsewhere agree fairly well that Italian and Polish children born in the United States test consistently below the native-born White, and that the Jewish child is not far below and is often considerably above the performance of the native White. In his main group of gifted children (see p. 16), Terman found that about 10 per cent were of Jewish extraction—nearly twice the number to be expected from the proportion of Jews in the cities covered by his survey. The largest per cent of Terman's group was of British and Scotch extraction, the percentage of Latin blood being very low. This finding agrees in the main with the army results, but again we cannot be sure that Terman's selections represent samplings from the same intellectual strata of the foreign countries from which the forbears of these children came.

The differences found among national groups would seem to be more sensibly explained by selection, differences in training, language, educational background and culture, than by differences in native ability. This conclusion is further supported by the results from a study in which six performance tests were administered to groups of boys ten to twelve years old in France, Germany and Italy. Although the Nordic boys were again slightly ahead of the Alpine and Mediterranean, the differences are small and non-significant. The differences between nationalities of the same race (e. g., German Nordic and French Nordic) and the differences between city dwelling and country dwelling children were far greater than differences between purely racial classifications. In short, differences in intelligence between national groups seem to be extremely small as compared to differences within these groups.

9. SUMMARY ON RACIAL DIFFERENCES

Probably the most salutary impression which a reader can carry away from a survey of the studies of racial groups is a better appreciation of the difficulties encountered, and of the practical impossibility of isolating a resultant effect which can definitely be attributed to racial origin alone. We stress again differences in language, in customs, in culture, in attitude, in schooling, and in social, economic, and geographic conditions. Also, the difficulty in securing comparable samples and in evaluating the meaning of test differences cannot be overemphasized. It is possible that true differences between races as such will never be found, but only differences between groups of somewhat different racial composition. Future workers will do well to avoid broad inferences from unreliable tests, from tests which measure narrow functions, and from very small groups.

Though much remains to be done, the study of individual differences has progressed far beyond Galton's pioneer work. However, it was Galton's invention and use of statistical techniques and his genius in seeing problems that gave the impetus and showed the way. To quote E. G. Boring, Galton was "the father (in large part) of mental measurement of individual differences with respect to traits . . . and the originator of the questionnaire and the theory of eugenics." As a pioneer in these and other fields, Galton's place in the history of science is assured.

Chapter 4

THE EXPERIMENTAL APPROACH TO THE STUDY OF PERSONALITY

I. THE DEFINITION AND MEANING OF PERSONALITY

The experimental investigation of personality has lagged behind the study of such psychological functions as perception, memory, or learning. There are several reasons for this. In the first place, personality is one of those omnibus terms which mean many things to many people. Memory, on the contrary, is better defined, and its phenomena are more readily isolated and controlled. Secondly, even if we agree upon a working definition of personality, it does not follow that we can agree upon the relative importance of the various personality traits. Professional schools, for instance, try to select applicants who are well prepared scholastically and able mentally—and who in addition possess "good personalities." A good personality, as the term is here used, embraces behavior activities ranging all of the way from moral and character traits like honesty and self-reliance, to pleasant social habits like courtesy and good manners. In a follow-up study of gifted children made twenty years after their initial selection by intelligence tests, Terman concluded that above an "I.Q. level of 140, adult success is largely determined by such factors as social adjustment, emotional stability, and drive to accomplish." All of us recognize the worth of personality traits in our everyday judgments. In fact, more often than not, we attribute the success of a physician, statesman, store keeper, or garage mechanic to initiative, hard work, and good disposition rather

95

than to good intelligence or superior training. But in such judgments seldom do we try to identify—in a given case—the personality variable upon which success depends.

In spite of the wide variety of usages, one finds upon examination considerable agreement as to the basic facts connoted by the term personality. For one thing, personality is thought of as distinct from intelligence and as closely identified with social ease and emotional balance—that is, with how one affects people and how one is affected by them. Again, what stamps an individual as a "personality" is the *organization* of his habits, attitudes, and traits rather than the mere existence of certain characteristic behavior. Just as the geographical relationships of a man's features serve to make his face peculiarily his own, so the ways in which his traits *interact* render an individual's behavior unique. In short, personality is revealed in the distinctive ways in which an individual behaves in everyday life situations.

2. FACTORS IN PERSONALITY

Various factors enter into and condition a personality. Some of these are deep and permanent, others temporary and ephemeral. Take the extent, breadth, and depth of a man's emotional responses; the quickness with which he loses his temper, is irritated or frightened. In so far as the basis for these characteristics is physical and physiological, they are probably inherited. On the other hand, good breeding and the social graces of tactfulness, courtesy, and deference are to a large extent habits which the growing child learns just as he learns arithmetic. Psychologists have suggested many factors which are presumably important in shaping personality. Among these we may select, as of special significance, appearance and physique, intelligence, temperament, and social adaptability.

(1) *Appearance and physique* are undoubtedly influential

in determining one's characteristic behavior. The problem of social adjustment of the handsome, well-proportioned child is very different from that of the ill-favored, weak and puny child. When a student is teased at home or in school slight defects often assume exaggerated importance. Such relatively minor handicaps, for instance, as wearing glasses, or a brace on the teeth, having large hands or feet, may cause real unhappiness. Children become supersensitive, hypercritical and arrogant, or timid and apologetic, depending upon their other traits. The matter of physical fitness becomes more serious in those who are deformed or crippled, or who because of a weak heart or other organic defect cannot take part in normal activities. In such individuals unhappiness and feelings of inadequacy are often intensified and acute.

(2) A person's *mental ability* may greatly affect his social and emotional behavior. The slow and backward child is beaten before he starts and his behavior often has the appearance of desperation. Intense feelings of insecurity—expressing themselves in over-activity or in withdrawal—may develop in the mentally retarded child. And the adult who is dull—and knows it—often shows the same typically resentful behavior. Either he is morose and negative, or he is actively rude and defiant. Education and training adapted to an individual's needs is good mental hygiene in such cases. While the charge that the colleges are ruining a lot of potentially good janitors and truck drivers is perhaps too strong, there is certainly an element of truth in it.

(3) *Temperament* refers to an individual's characteristic emotional responses—the breadth and strength of his reactions and the degree of his self-control. Emotional behavior is rooted in constitutional and physiological make-up and hence is predominantly inborn and inherited. The timid person who is easily cowed and browbeaten; the highly irritable man who loses his temper at the slightest provocation; the erratic

person who is at one time dominating and superior and at another pleasant and agreeable—all have personality difficulties of a temperamental sort. People who lack emotional stability and self-control have trouble in making new friends and in keeping old ones.

(4) Finally, *social adaptability* includes those responses, attitudes and opinions, intellectual, temperamental, and moral which are exhibited in social participation and in social intercourse. Social adaptability depends to a very large extent upon the factors listed above; and to a greater degree than is true of these factors, upon training and environment. It is given a separate heading in order to stress the fundamental importance of behavior in a social setting.

3. IMPRESSIONISTIC METHODS OF STUDYING PERSONALITY

In a general way, attempts to discover and gauge personality traits may be classified as *impressionistic* and as *experimental*. Impressionistic methods are characterized by intuition and enthusiasm rather than by logic. The claims of their supporters are often extravagant and the results, compared with these claims, exceedingly meager. Illustrative of such methods of revealing character and personality are (1) the systems of physiognomy; (2) various schemes dealing with physical types; (3) divination methods, as exemplified in astrology, palmistry and graphology.

(1) *Physiognomy:* This pseudo-science claims to reveal character and personality traits by an examination of bodily—and especially facial—characteristics. The conformation, size and shape of the nose, ears, chin, mouth and face; the texture of the skin, hair and eye color are taken as indices of underlying personality traits. Physiognomy has reached its most elaborate modern development in vocational guidance. Blackford and Newcomb, for example, in their book *The Job, the*

Man, the Boss give detailed directions for interpreting the meaning of various facial indices, quality of the voice, manner of walking, style of clothing and the like.

Phrenology, one of the best-known branches of physiognomy, seeks to read personality traits from the size and shape of the skull. The "mind," according to the phrenologist, is composed of various faculties—intellectual, emotional, and moral; and these hypothetical faculties have definite locations in "centers" within the brain. The relative development of the faculties is determined by observing the depressions and protuberances of the cranium or skull. Phrenology as a system was introduced by the Germans, Gall and Spurzheim, about 1796. The system of Gall and Spurzheim, which is essentially the one still in use to-day, divides the skull into thirty-five faculties which are given such high-sounding names as amativeness, benevolence, calculation, causality and the like.

Physiognomists and phrenologists still appear at fairs and carnivals where they practice their art upon the gullible. But none of these systems of personality analysis has any standing whatever as a scientific theory. There is no evidence of a direct relationship between either intellect or character and facial contours, skin texture, hair color or other physical signs. The strong chin, the beetling brow, the aquiline nose, the high forehead are usually judged to be indicative of desirable personality traits just in so far as they are possessed by our own racial or social group. Modern physiology has completely exploded the phrenological faculties. It is known that the supposed "organs" of reverence, conscientiousness and hope, which were located in the roof of the skull, lie directly above the motor areas which control the movements of the hands and feet. Philoprogenitiveness and inhabitiveness lie just above the brain areas concerned with vision. Every controlled experimental test of the notions of physiognomy and phrenology has refuted their claims. Complete reviews of the experimental evidence have been assembled by Hull, Paterson, and Griffiths.

(2) *Type Theories:* There have been many attempts to relate body form and proportion to temperamental and character traits from Lombroso to the present time. One of the most thorough of these schemes is that of the German psychiatrist, Kretschmer, who proposed a system of parallel physical and psychological types. On the basis of physique, man is classified into three major groups—the tall, slender and (usually) weak; the strong, well-proportioned and vigorous; the short, round, and fat. According to Kretschmer, the first group tends to be reclusive and self-contained and to exhibit shy, timid and unsociable behavior; the third type is inclined toward emotional instability and is subject to uncontrolled and boisterous outbursts, which alternate with moods of melancholy and depression. In the main, the middle type exhibits what is called "normal" behavior.

Kretschmer's constitutional types are determined after a careful and exhaustive series of measurements, and his own work showed a rather remarkable association of physical type and personality traits. Later experimental work has, however, failed to show the close parallelism which Kretschmer claimed, and in consequence his theory has not received wide acceptance among American psychologists. It appears that a wide range of personality traits may be exhibited by any one type, and that various types will show a diversity of behavior trends.

Closely related to the notion of parallel physical and psychological types are the attempts to explain personality traits in terms of the degree of development and functioning of the endocrine or ductless glands. The best known endocrine gland is the thyroid, situated in the neck region close to the windpipe. It has been known for some time that in children the feeble-minded condition known as cretinism is caused by a subnormal secretion of the thyroid gland. An overactive thyroid causes general nervous irritability; an underactive gland may lead to sluggishness and mental dullness. Other important endocrines, about which considerable is known, are the pituitary, the adrenals, and the sex glands. The pituitary gland lies in the middle of the head at the base of the brain. It is known to exercise control over the growth of the individual and over sexual development. The adrenals are situated just above the kidneys and are often called the "glands of action." In intense physical exertion these glands secrete adrenin into the blood stream. This substance stimulates the liver to release more blood sugar, thus speeding up muscular activity and increasing resistance to fatigue. The sex glands are physiologically mature when the boy or girl reaches puberty. Secretions from these glands exercise control over primary sexual development and over secondary sex characteristics as well. These latter include voice changes, body form, muscular growth, hair distribution and other attributes which are distinctively masculine or feminine.

Many enthusiastic endocrinologists have linked up definite personality traits to under- or overactivity of some ductless gland. Shyness, timidity, and feelings of inferiority are said to result from deficient thyroid secretion; aggressiveness, expansiveness, feelings of superiority from an overactive thyroid. Lowered activity of the pituitary is said to produce "moral and intellectual inferiority," compulsions, and pathological lying. Pugnacious and aggressive behavior has been attributed to overactivity of the adrenals; timorous and vacillating conduct to underactivity. These speculations are not yet proven experimentally, but it seems probable that much of scientific value with respect to the physiological basis of personality traits will result from investigations in this field.

(3) *Divination Methods of Judging Personality Traits:* The

pseudo-scientific schemes like palmistry, astrology and graphology rank with physiognomy and phrenology and are on a decidedly lower level than the type theories just described. Palmistry and astrology may be dismissed at once from serious consideration. Both belong in the class of parlor amusements and fortune telling; they represent exploded and discredited efforts to find a Royal Road to the understanding of human nature. If palmists or astrologers could produce evidence of high correlation between the lines of the hand, or being born under certain "signs," and the possession of definite personality traits, some credence might be given to their claims. But quantitative studies will never be made by practitioners of these arts so long as people are willing to spend money without asking for evidence.

Graphology offers more possibilities for the diagnosis of personality traits than do the methods just discussed. Handwriting is actual expressive behavior, not a physical "sign" or static index. We all know that from a person's handwriting we can usually tell whether the writer is a man or a woman, is old or young. We infer, too, from his handwriting something about a person's education and his state of health. Handwriting is so susceptible to practice and training, however, that it is doubtful whether any *specific* information regarding personality traits can be obtained from it alone. Hull and Montgomery studied the relation between upward sloping lines, heavy and fine lines, crossing of *t*'s, method of forming *m*'s, *n*'s, *o*'s and the like, and such traits as ambition, timidity, and forcefulness which according to the graphologists are expressed by these characters. Their results were decidedly negative. Allport's and Vernon's studies have been somewhat more favorable to graphology. Handwriting specimens were successfully matched against photographs, voice records, and character sketches. But the agreement was not close enough to allow prediction except in very general terms (see p. 68).

4. WHY IMPRESSIONISTIC METHODS STILL HAVE VOGUE

Why do systems of character and personality analysis still flourish if there is no substance to their claims? Several answers may be given to this question. In the first place, many people possess little or no scientific training, and hence have no conception of what is meant by a rational world in which, because events have causes, things do not happen by magic, nor simply come out of the blue. Such people make up the naïve, gullible, and mentally immature folk who search for Fountains of Youth, universal panaceas, talismans, and cure-alls; who join esoteric cults and indulge in all sorts of emotional vagaries. Secondly, there is just enough truth in some of these schemes—physiognomy for instance—to make them plausible. Much can obviously be inferred—or shrewdly guessed—about a person's early training, cultural background, habits and education from his appearance, speech, mannerisms, occupation, and interests. The effects of dissipation and disease, of a cross disposition or a friendly one, appear in the face, the conversation, the body carriage, and the gait. One can usually tell from a man's hands whether he is a bookkeeper or a mechanic; from his skin whether he is a rancher or a clerk; from his physique whether he is an athlete or a weakling. But this is quite different from saying that the lines in the hand indicate longevity; that a high forehead means intellect; that a bump on the skull indicates "love of approbation"; or that being born in March rather than in September makes the difference between being a successful or an unsuccessful lawyer. Man is a civilized creature living in a social environment, and as such he reflects in his behavior and physique the experiences through which he has passed. Some of the numerous physiognomic signs will occasionally—by chance alone—be associated with almost every personality trait. But none of these signs is related to or expressive of personality in the same way that a child's performance on an intelligence test is expressive of his ability to do school work successfully.

Still a third reason for the continued popularity of the impressionistic methods lies in the inveterate human tendency to classify. People are judged wholesale as good or bad, moral or immoral, sneaky or forthright, though rarely if ever does one deserve such an unqualified judgment. Classification is a lazy way of avoiding analysis and of persuading ourselves that we have made an intelligent decision. Hasty and unwarranted judgments grow out of the tendency (a) to generalize broadly and with disregard of negative cases; (b) to reason by analogy; and (c) to mistake sequence for causal connection. Thus it is "common knowledge" that red-headed people are quick-tempered; that blonds are fickle; that long-fingered people are artistic; that pretty girls are empty-headed. A truck makes more noise than an expensive passenger car, and hence by analogy the man with the loud voice and energetic manner is more "forceful" than the quiet, unassuming one. Because a friend was told by a palmist that she was going to marry a tall, blond man—and did—fortune-telling is raised to the dignity of an exact science.

The best antidote for the impressionistic methods is the rigorous experimental approach. When a well-controlled experiment yields no evidence for the claims made, the hypothesis must be dropped outright—no matter how plausible or desirable it may be—or altered and again subjected to test.

5. EXPERIMENTAL METHODS IN THE STUDY
OF PERSONALITY

Experimental techniques used in the study of personality include the rating scale, the questionnaire, the objective test, and various laboratory methods. In many instances—perhaps most—all of these methods will find some application in a given investigation. They are described in this section.

1. *The Rating Scale.* It is customary in moral teachings to make a distinction between character and reputation. Character is said to be what we really are, and reputation what people think we are. This rather pious contrast is perhaps more apparent than real. Character is reflected in reputation; and hence for better or worse we are essentially what people say we are. Rating scales are devices for ranking or rating individuals with respect to personality and intellectual traits, skills, occupational efficiency, likes and dislikes, attitudes and interests. Supervisors rate clerks for appearance, intelligence, selling ability, cheerfulness, patience, tact and the like. Teachers rate their pupils for learning ability, study habits, and behavior traits. An illustration of a graphic rating scale planned for use with students is given in Figure 8. Note that the rater places a check somewhere along the line to indicate the degree to which the student—in his judgment—possesses the trait. The descriptive phrases below the line are for the guidance of the rater.

The average individual should be rated in the middle of the line. Most rates err on the side of leniency, however, and tend to place more people above than below the middle point. Training and careful instructions are necessary to correct this error and to make the ratings valid. Another difficulty with rating scales is the "halo effect." Halo shows itself in the tendency of a rater to place a person of whom he has a good opinion high in every trait. To avoid "halo" every subject is rated on each trait in order rather than each subject separately on all traits. Makers of rating scales are careful to select for study characteristics which are objective and readily defined; which are not too broad or too vague; and which can be observed in behavior rather than inferred from conversa-

Name of student...

A. How are you and others affected by his appearance and manner?

Avoided by others	Tolerated by others	Liked by others	Well liked by others	Sought by others	No opportunity to observe

Please record here instances that support your judgment.

B. Does he need constant prodding or does he go ahead with his work without being told?

Needs much prodding in doing ordinary assignments	Needs occasional prodding	Does ordinary assignments of his own accord	Completes suggested supplementary work	Seeks and sets for himself additional tasks	

Please record here instances that support your judgment.

C. Does he get others to do what he wishes?

Probably unable to lead his fellows	Lets others take lead	Sometimes leads in minor affairs	Sometimes leads in important affairs	Displays marked ability to lead his fellows; makes things go	

Please record here instances that support your judgment.

D. How does he control his emotions?

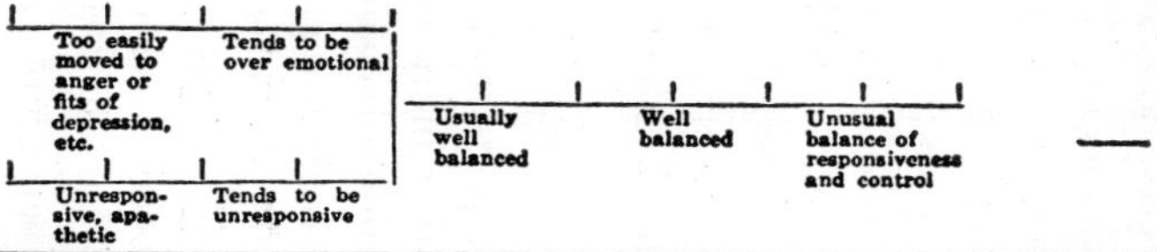

Too easily moved to anger or fits of depression, etc. | Unresponsive, apathetic | Tends to be over emotional | Tends to be unresponsive | Usually well balanced | Well balanced | Unusual balance of responsiveness and control

Please record here instances that support your judgment.

E. Has he a program with definite purposes in terms of which he distributes his time and energy?

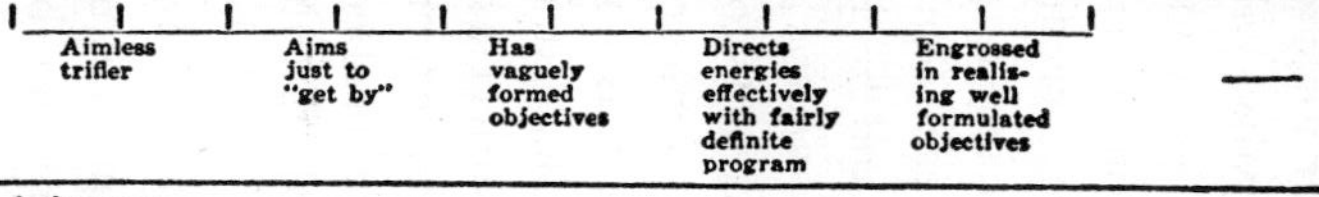

Aimless trifler | Aims just to "get by" | Has vaguely formed objectives | Directs energies effectively with fairly definite program | Engrossed in realising well formulated objectives

Please record here instances that support your judgment.

FIG. 8

GRAPHIC RATING SCALE

(From Bradshaw, *Archives of Psychology*, No. 119 (1930), pp. 44-45.)

tion or hearsay. It is easier to rate a filing clerk for accuracy of work, a teacher for cheerfulness in the classroom, than to rate either for loyalty, value to the organization, or ability as a singer. Psychologists do not put much confidence in a single rating; but the consensus of a group of competent raters has been shown to be exceedingly useful. In some schools pupils are rated on a variety of personality traits year after year. A comparison of these records shows the direction in which the child is growing and his level of maturity.

2. *The Questionnaire.* A questionnaire presents a set of questions or statements to be answered or marked by the subject himself or by someone who knows him well. A questionnaire, unlike a test, is not scored in terms of time or errors or amount done. Instead, it is a systematic report which serves to identify the subject as like or unlike other individuals of the same age-level, sex, or social or occupational background. The questionnaire has been used by psychologists to get data upon (1) personal difficulties or troubles—fears, worries, feelings of inadequacy and the like; (2) attitudes and beliefs; (3) interests in intellectual, mechanical, and social activities, and in sports, vocations, cultural and practical pursuits. Answers to a questionnaire may be categorical—given simply as Yes or No—or varying degrees of assent and dissent may be permitted through providing several alternative replies.

Motivation is especially important in questionnaire studies, as there can be no sure guarantee that a subject is telling the truth. Answers are presumably reliable when the subject feels that an honest reply will aid or be of some advantage to him. Sometimes questionnaires are so constructed that the main purpose of the inquiry is concealed from the subject, who then gives the desired information unwittingly. When the individual report is not very important, and when only group tendencies are desired, anonymity may be resorted to as a means of insuring more nearly honest replies.

3. *The Objective Test and Laboratory Methods.* Most personality tests are really questionnaires though they may resemble mental tests in construction and administration. The George Washington Social Intelligence Test is an interesting example. In this examination, the subject is called upon to give a judgment involving a social situation by marking one of several alternatives; to infer the "mental state" of the speaker from given exclamations and expressions; to decide whether certain descriptions of human behavior in various situations are true or false; to tell which of several possible replies to a given situation is the most humorous. Only one section of this test—that dealing with memory for names and faces—poses a task which is scorable in terms of performance. In the other four parts of the test, answers are scored in accordance with ethical standards set up by society or by a consensus of competent people.

A few tests of personality traits are given and scored like intelligence tests—the Downey tests of Will-Temperament are a good illustration. This ingenious series of exercises purports to measure certain personality traits through simple motor reactions, expressed mostly in handwriting. There are twelve tests in all, arranged into three groups of four each. The separate tests require the subject to mark that one of a series of paired adjectives which best describes himself; to write his name or other phrases as rapidly or as slowly as possible, to practice copying various handwriting models; to write with eyes closed; to write under various distractions. Performance is scored in terms of time and errors. A psychograph or profile (see p. 20) gives the subject's rank in the different tests. A high score in the first four tests is interpreted to mean that the subject is of the "explosive, hair-trigger type"; high scores in the second group of four tests that he is willful, and aggressive; high scores in the last four tests that he is slow, accurate and tenacious. Unfortunately, Downey's tests do not possess very high reliability and the meaning of the separate scores is doubtful. While the author reads more complex motives into her tests than they probably reveal, her method of inferring personality trends from expressive movements has good possibilities (see p. 102).

A number of performance tests of various kinds have been employed in studies of personality traits. Among these may be mentioned reading, drawing, measures of muscular tension, estimation of distance and direction. Even tests of arithmetic and of school information have served as measures of change in attitude or in motivation. The uses to which performance tests have been put in studying personality will be illustrated later in Section 7. In addition to performance tests, various physiological indices have been utilized as indicators of emotional states and of muscular tension (p. 327). Pulse, breathing, blood pressure, and the psychogalvanic reflex are among the measures most commonly employed.

6. THE MEASUREMENT OF PERSONALITY TRAITS

Many adjectives descriptive of behavior represent dimensions of personality along which individuals may be arranged in at least a rough order. It is a matter of common observation that people are more or less cheerful, sympathetic, or irritable; and are rarely totally cheerful *or* gloomy, sympathetic *or* cruel, irritable *or* placid. In the same way emotional difficulties, attitudes, and interests constitute complex dimensions in which people vary greatly. In this section we shall describe some instruments devised to measure these more complex personality traits.

1. *Characteristic Personal Habits and Emotional Attitudes.* The pioneer study in this field is Woodworth's Personal Data Sheet drawn up for use with soldiers during the World War. This so-called "adjustment questionnaire" or Neurotic Inventory contains 116 questions, each of which is

to be answered *Yes* or *No*. The aim of the PD Sheet is to get useful data concerning a person's "maladjustments"—his feelings of insecurity, fears, worries, nervous and mental disturbances. Woodworth's items were taken from authoritative sources and dealt with symptoms reported by men who subsequently had suffered from nervous breakdowns. The selection of questions for the PD Sheet was strictly empirical. Each item was tested for its power to differentiate normals from abnormals—the latter being persons suffering from nervous ailments.

The items of the PD Sheet may be classified roughly into the following categories: *physical symptoms,* e. g., pains, fatigue, incoördinations; *neurotic symptoms,* fears, worries, anxieties, fantasies, chronic depressions, sleep disturbances; *personal reactions* to liquor, tobacco, drugs, sex; *mental symptoms,* vacillations, compulsions, queer feelings about oneself or other people. Sample questions are:

	Yes	No
Do you usually feel strong and well?	Yes	No
Does your heart ever thump in your ears so you cannot sleep?	"	"
Do you have a great many bad headaches?	"	"
Does liquor make you quarrelsome?	"	"
Are you troubled with fears of being crushed in a crowd?	"	"
Does your mind wander badly so that you lose track of what you are doing?	"	"

The PD Sheet has been revised in various ways. It has been added to and subtracted from; a form has been arranged for children and one for adolescents; scoring has been altered to provide for more than two answers (as for example: Yes No ?); and several methods of weighting the answers have been devised. The "trouble score" from a Neurotic Inventory is often valuable in diagnosis as it gives a comprehensive survey of the subject's personal difficulties and real or potential maladjustments. Women report more "neurotic involvement" than men; Jews than Gentiles; freshmen than upper classmen; non-fraternity than fraternity men; delinquents than non-delinquents. While a high score nearly always indicates trouble, it is not always the most serious cases which report the most symptoms. A fairly high score may involve few dangerous symptoms, while a relatively low score may contain some extremely dangerous tendencies. Apparently the neurotic is not only a troubled person, but he is more susceptible to his difficulties than is the more normal person.

Another valuable investigation of a complex personality dimension is Heidbreder's questionnaire dealing with introversion-extroversion. These terms represent the ends of a fairly recognizable behavior dimension. The "typical" introvert, for example, is reclusive and withdrawn and is primarily interested in his own ideas and feelings. The "typical" extrovert, on the other hand, is interested in people and affairs and participates freely in social activities. Samples from this inventory are:

Feels hurt readily; apparently sensitive about remarks or
    actions which have reference to himself.
Blushes frequently; is self-conscious.
Keeps a diary.
Is a poor loser; considerably upset and indisposed after loss
    of competitive game.
Shrinks from actions which demand initiative and nerve.

Instructions are to mark each item + if it is self-descriptive, and — if it is not. In a group of three hundred college students, Heidbreder found an average score which indicates that the "typical" college student is mildly extroverted or better, perhaps, "ambiverted." Most college students exhibit both introverted and extroverted behavior, relatively few falling at the extremes. Good students are more introverted than poor students; women are more introverted than men; and the more introverted tend to have the larger "trouble scores" on the Neurotic Inventory.

A common personality dimension closely related to introversion-extroversion has been called ascendance-submission. Ascendant or submissive behavior may have important implications in vocational guidance; in some kinds of work for instance an aggressive rôle is demanded, while in others a more retiring attitude is more conducive to success. In a questionnaire designed to measure ascendance-submission, subjects are asked—among other things—whether they "usually, occasionally, never" stand up for their rights; take front seats in a theater when by so doing they become conspicuous; like to manage and to take responsibility; feel inferior before superiors. It is interesting to find that students who tend to submissiveness generally make higher grades than the more ascendant.

Aggressiveness is a trait akin to ascendance, the aggressive person being described as characteristically "vigorous, positive, and masterful." Several ingenious tests have been devised to measure this trait. In one test-situation, each subject was required to perform a series of mental additions while gazing fixedly into the eyes of the experimenter who sat facing him. Those subjects rated as the most aggressive shifted their eyes much less often than those rated least aggressive. In other tests requiring addition, aggressive subjects were found to be less affected by distraction, e. g., electric shock while working, presence of a dead snake before the subject, than the less aggressive. In a student group, aggressiveness was positively correlated with effective public speaking and with selling ability.

2. *Attitudes toward Social and Ethical Questions.* Various groups of attitudes which presumably reflect personality trends have been studied by the questionnaire method. One comprehensive series of scales is designed to measure attitudes toward many social, economic, and ethical problems—toward the

church, the movies, the Negro, war, communism, and the like. Samples from the scale designed to measure attitudes toward the movies will provide examples:

Movies are the most important cause of crime.
Movies are good clean entertainment.
Going to a movie is a foolish way to spend your money.
I like the movies as they are because I go to be entertained, not educated.

Subjects are asked to check each statement which they accept or endorse. Scale values or "weights" were determined for each statement from the answers given by an experimental group, the numerical value of the weight denoting the extent to which the statement favors the institution or the question under consideration. In the examples given above, the second statement has a considerably higher rating than the first, and a slightly higher rating than the fourth. Attitude scales have been used to compare groups of different background and training; to measure the effects of instruction and of propaganda; and to study the relations of various attitudes to other factors such as intelligence, personality and socio-economic status.

3. *Vocational Interests.* A valuable practical approach to the study of personality differences is the investigation of the interests shown by groups who are vocationally or culturally unlike. The Vocational Interest Blank designed by Strong is the most extensive survey of occupational interests and of everyday likes and dislikes. The subject who marks the Vocational Interest Blank is asked to express his preferences for a list of occupations, for various school subjects and amusements, and for commonplace activities such as writing letters or decorating a room. The subject must also express an opinion concerning peculiarities of people, his liking for contrasted kinds of work (e. g., indoor vs. outdoor), a judg-

ment of his own abilities and other characteristics. Different scoring keys permit the blank to be evaluated separately for the interests of architect, physician, lawyer, accountant, printer, and many other occupations. An individual's score identifies him as definitely having the interests of a lawyer, say, or as not sure, or as definitely not having the interests of a lawyer.

The Vocational Interest Blank has its chief value in guidance. In one study college seniors who intended to enter law school were rated as having the interests of a lawyer four times as often as students not intending to follow law. The relationships of interest scores in certain fields—chemistry and engineering, for instance—is very high. It has been found, too, that men differ sharply in interests from boys, thus justifying a differentiation of interests in terms of maturity. The interests of men of fifty-five are more mature in the sense of being more largely concerned with social service, education, business and political affairs than are the interests of boys of fifteen.

7. SYSTEMATIC EXPERIMENTAL STUDIES OF PERSONALITY

A number of investigations have been concerned with the identification and measurement of the variables in personality, and with the relations and meaning of personality traits. The studies summarized in this section are representative of the work being done in this difficult field.

1. *Hartshorne's and May's Studies of Honesty.* This is one of the most careful and detailed studies of a personality dimension. Hartshorne and May set out to discover what variables accompany or perhaps determine honest behavior; and whether a general trait of honesty may be said to exist. Is an "honest man" generally honest, or is he honest simply in the rather restricted areas in which we observe him?

Several thousand children mostly in grades 5 to 8 constituted the experimental sample. Test situations in which cheating or deceptive behavior could take place were devised and set up in the classroom, in the athletic field, and in "parlor" games—i. e., out of school social situations. In the classroom, tests of arithmetic, word knowledge, reading, and spelling among others were administered under close supervision, and under "dishonest" conditions, that is, under conditions in which cheating could readily take place. Children were sometimes allowed to correct their own test papers (the scores under honest conditions first having been recorded without the child's knowledge); and again, having determined the "honest maximum" for a test, scores above this level were taken as *prima facie* evidence of deception.

Several ingenious tests took "improbable achievement" as evidence of cheating. To illustrate, in one part of the study an athletic contest was arranged in which chinning the bar, broad jumping, breathing into a spirometer, and strength of grip tests were featured. It is well known that with the hand dynamometer—an instrument which measures hand strength in terms of the maximum squeeze—fatigue sets in rapidly after the first few trials. If a secret record is made of the first three trials and the child then encouraged to practice on his own and report his subsequent trials, any large increase beyond the initial scores is highly improbable—and hence evidence of cheating. The same holds true of breathing capacity and of the other motor tests—marked improvement after a certain point practically never occurs.

The "improbable achievement" technique was also introduced into some parlor games. It is highly improbable that a blindfolded child will pin the tail unerringly on a donkey when told to approach the figure from some distance away. If a child succeeds he is suspected of having peeped under the bandage, followed the lines on the floor, or made use of other cues unfairly. In other parlor games, objects of various sorts including a certain number of dimes were passed out to the children who were told to deposit their "gifts" in a box in another room. As no *apparent* check was made on whether the child did as he was told, retention of the dime seemed to him attractively feasible.

Hartshorne's and May's study yielded many interesting results. Older children cheated more than younger; emotionally unstable more than normal; retarded children more than unretarded. There was a high correlation between honest behavior and intelligence and between honesty and social and economic status. Attendance at Sunday school and religious instruction had little influence upon honesty when socioeconomic factors were ruled out. The morale of the classroom was important. Under some teachers practically none of the children cheated; under other teachers practically all of them did.

From the very low relationships among their tests, Hartshorne and May concluded that there is no general trait of honesty. This is perhaps their most important single conclusion and it has far reaching implications. If honesty is reducible to a congeries of fairly specific habits, there is little meaning to the designation an "honest man." The best training in honest behavior that the teacher can provide is the cultivation of specific honest habits—teaching the ideal of honesty is of little value. Hartshorne's and May's conclusion has been criticized on several counts. It is a well recognized fact that children do not have the same standards of honesty as adults and that they are not motivated by the same considerations. School is often a game in which the pupil is pitted against the teacher; and cheating under such conditions is regarded as a clever and praiseworthy accomplishment and in no sense a violation of the rules of good sportsmanship. Rivalry, competition, desire to please, and varying degrees of effort undoubtedly entered into Hartshorne's and May's tests.

Such factors may well have overweighted the "honesty component" which the tests were designed to assay. Low relations among the tests would then reflect a multiplicity of motives—some working at cross purposes—rather than the absence of a single trait. Common observation and the consistency found in studies of attitudes make it seem likely that honesty is more generalized than this study would indicate. Certainly everyday transactions are predicated on the notion that honest behavior is predictable; that in "honest people" honest behavior is more probable than deception.

2. *Allport's and Vernon's Studies of Expressive Movements.* These authors were interested in the degree to which expressive movements are consistent or harmonious within the individual, and what such movements mean in terms of related personality variables. Expressive movements were defined as characteristic motor acts such as handwriting, speed of reading, drawing and counting; speed of walking and strolling; accuracy in the estimation of sizes, distances, and angles; strength of grip, speed of tapping, muscular tensions and the like. In addition to the objective tests, ratings were obtained from judges as to fluency of speech, intensity of voice, rapidity, smoothness, and rhythm in gesticulation and movement.

Repetition of the test situations showed considerable consistency in the specific ways in which an individual expresses himself. In addition, the relationships among the different tests were positive and rather marked, while the tests were closely enough related to the ratings to indicate surprising agreement between these judgments and the subjects' actual performances. Knowing the speed, tempo and rhythm of *some* of an individual's activities, one can usually predict quite well what characteristics other expressive acts will show. Even when consistency is not evident, Allport and Vernon believe there may still be underlying agreement or "congruence." That is, the same fundamental motive or drive may run through activities which on the surface appear to be contradictory.

In an interesting series of studies of handwriting, Allport and Vernon found that skilled graphologists could match handwriting specimens and thumb-nail sketches of a person considerably better than chance. These experiments indicate that handwriting may be more expressive or more revealing of personality than most of us have believed, though nothing like so accurate an index as the professional graphologist has claimed. Handwriting may be suggestive of aggressiveness, timidity, impulsiveness, or sensitiveness, but it is not an index which "he who runs may read."

3. *The Rorschach Test.* The Rorschach "test" is a technique devised by the Swiss psychiatrist, Hermann Rorschach, and used by him as an aid to the better understanding of the personality difficulties of his patients. The test situations make use of ten irregular ink blots which stand out against a white background. Five of the blots are in black and grey and five contain color—red, yellow, blue and green. In administering the test, the subject is given one card at a time; he is allowed to look at the blot from any direction as long as he likes; and is told to give all of the associations and meanings which are suggested to him by the ink blot. To illustrate, one patient suffering from schizophrenia (shut-in, extremely introverted condition) gave the following responses to Card #1: "It resembles a butterfly with some sort of feelers on it and protruding eyes; a lizard's tail; a double body . . . made of two materials . . . the outside is transparent so you can see the inner; the open parts don't fit in . . . yes, they do; and those are wings, they're attached in three places." Using a detailed scoring procedure, the examiner classifies the subject's responses into categories for form quality, detail, wholeness, originality, color, movement, and the like. From an analysis

of the replies, the dominant personality trends of the subject are then inferred. Common, unoriginal responses and those involving animals are interpreted to mean low intelligence; whole responses, good form and movement, high intelligence. Shut-in and introverted personalities give many detailed responses; emotionally unstable many color responses.

Several criticisms have been leveled against the Rorschach method. It has been said that the test lacks objectivity in its administration and scoring; that norms are scanty or nonexistent; that interpretation is intuitive and without experimental verification. In spite of these valid objections, the diagnosis of mental disease by the Rorschach has often been strikingly confirmed by later clinical findings. Insight, too, into the personality difficulties of delinquents and the feebleminded has been afforded. While too much has probably been claimed for the Rorschach by enthusiasts, in the hands of a trained examiner it is undoubtedly valuable.

4. *Terman's and Miles's Studies of Masculinity and Femininity*. This study is an extremely thorough investigation of sex differences in personality trends, attitudes, and interests. By means of a test of over 400 items, these psychologists arrive at a masculinity-femininity index which locates an individual along a hypothetical continuum ranging from intensely masculine to intensely feminine. The test has seven parts dealing respectively with (1) word association, (2) ink blot association, (3) information, (4) emotional and ethical attitudes, (5) interests, likes and dislikes, (6) opinions, mostly about people, (7) introversion-extroversion. A response is scored + if it is typically masculine, — if it is typically feminine. To associate *meat* with *tender* is masculine, to associate *kind* or *loving* with *tender* is feminine; reading detective stories, liking chemistry, wanting to be a forest ranger are masculine interests, while reading poetry, liking dramatics, and wanting to be a social worker are feminine interests. The

diagnostic value of an item—whether it is indicative of the masculine or the feminine attitude—was determined by comparing the responses obtained from many male and female groups. Hundreds of subjects, children and adults, in school and out, as well as athletes, various occupational groups, delinquents and homosexuals were examined in the process of standardizing the test.

The authors find that males are in general more extroverted than females, less sentimental, more interested in tools, machines and business. Females are more introverted, more sympathetic, and more emotional than males; more interested in occupations requiring personal service. This contrast in masculine and feminine activities and interests follows the traditional pattern and is not surprising. Of more interest is the finding that the scores made by men and women of culture and education differ very little. This suggests that the so-called "typical" male-female differences are more marked as we go down the social and economic scale. A rather interesting verification of the scale is the fact that male homosexuals have strongly feminine scores.

5. *Murray's Explorations in Personality*. These exhaustive studies represent an attempt to obtain a coherent picture of individual personality. Personality is analyzed in terms of *needs* which may be *viscerogenic* (internal, like hunger or thirst) or *psychogenic* (largely external, like seeking prestige or insecurity). The psychogenic needs, though closely related to the viscerogenic, are conceived to stem principally from the social pressures in the environment. Behavior is analyzed in terms of these needs into various categories which are studied as separate dimensions or in terms of their interrelations.

On the whole the approach is more intuitive and psychoanalytical than experimental, though many objective measurements are made. As the first step in the analysis, each subject was interviewed by the five members of a Diagnostic Council, each of whom rated him on forty traits. The subject wrote an autobiography, and answered three questionnaires covering personal data ("troubles"), his emotional and social attitudes and interests. His sex history was then examined by a psychiatrist and he was put through some twenty tests and experiments. There were fifty-one subjects—all Harvard College students—about one-fourth of whom gave thirty-six hours to the investigation.

The dominant needs of an individual—both the verbally expressed and the unexpressed (unconscious or latent)—were diagnosed in the main from fantasies and free associations stimulated by various word lists, stories, poems, pictures. Some of these test situations should be described in a little detail. In one test—called the esthetic appreciation test—the subject was asked to pass upon the artistic merits of ten poems and ten pictures representing a variety of subject-matter. Fundamental attitudes as well as taste and insight were presumably revealed by his replies. Another test measured the "level of aspiration" defined as the level of performance in a familiar task (for example, printing words with a hand-print set) which the subject set for himself and attempted to reach. Tendency to repress unpleasant experiences was ascertained by seeing whether the subject forgot more readily those jigsaw puzzles at which he had failed than those at which he had succeeded.

Two tests situations were especially novel and revealing of personality trends. In the first, the thematic apperception test, the subject was asked to interpret or tell a story about each of a set of pictures; in the second, the dramatic productions test, the subject was asked to arrange a group of small toy figures so as to depict a dramatic scene. Both tests proved to be enlightening indirect methods of obtaining evidence regarding the subject's inner needs and in throwing light upon

The Study of Personality

the environmental and social difficulties facing him. One subject, for example, who had lived through persecution and other cruelties as a child obviously "projected" this background into his replies. In one of the pictures presented to each subject the figure of a boy is seen huddled on the floor against a couch. His head is bowed on his right arm, and beside him on the floor is an object which resembles a revolver. Of this picture, our subject said:

"Some trouble has occurred. Some one he loved has shot herself. Probably it is his mother. She may have done it out of poverty. He, being fairly grown up, sees the misery of it all and would like to shoot himself. But he is young and braces up after a while. For some time he lives in misery—the first few months thinking of death."

The idea that people reveal or reflect their thoughts, experiences, attitudes, and emotions in their spontaneous creations is the basis of the "projective method" of which the dramatic productions test is an example. This method has been successfully used with children, by L. B. Murphy in studies of sympathetic behavior and by Moreno in studies of social adjustments in child society. In Moreno's view, personality traits are revealed by choice of friends, and in spontaneous dramatic play in which "real" (but concealed) motives have a chance to express themselves.

Its scope and tremendous detail make it difficult to evaluate the work of Murray and his colleagues in a brief space. In favor of the intuitive approach to personality analysis, it may be said that the case study material offered is decidedly informative. It seems likely that almost everyone would be benefited by such a personality analysis as Murray's techniques make possible. On the other hand, the method is time consuming, requires a highly trained personnel, is unstandardized, and hence is difficult to repeat. The results obtained, however, show the possibilities inherent in the psychoanalytical approach and what may be expected if and when intuitive insights are brought under laboratory control.

Chapter 5

PAVLOV AND THE CONDITIONED REFLEX

I. THE CONDITIONED REFLEX

The researches of the great Russian scientist, Ivan Pavlov, on the conditioned reflex date roughly from the year 1904, when Pavlov was awarded the Nobel prize in medicine. Pavlov's early results were published only in Russian, and hence for some time they were little known to scientists of other countries. When finally they began to be available they were seized upon with avidity in America, especially by those younger psychologists who were dissatisfied with the introspective psychology then widely current. Here at last, it seemed to many, was the foundation upon which could be constructed a straightforward and naturalistic description of human nature. So it happened that Pavlov's method and his findings became the mainstay of behaviorism, the modern revolt against introspective psychology, and are to-day still the chief scientific weapon of the strictly objective psychologist. In addition, however, and happily, Pavlov's researches have broad and important implications for general psychology as well. They have, for instance, thrown much light upon the mechanics of learning and habit-formation, and have led to an ingenious explanation of the age-old problem of sleep. Besides, Pavlov and his students have succeeded in producing abnormal mental states in animals akin to those widespread modern nervous ailments called neuroses, which are thought by many physicians and sociologists to be largely a by-product of present-day intense and complex civilization. Until his death in 1936, at the age of eighty-seven, this remarkable man, the son of an obscure peasant priest, enthusiastically carried on his work aided by a devoted group of students and followers. Experimental reports from his laboratory are eagerly awaited and are read by scientific men the world over.

Pavlov's researches began with a well-known and frequently observed fact. Every one of us has seen the saliva drip from a dog's mouth as he waits in eager anticipation for his food. Probably most of us, too, have felt our mouths "water" at the sight or odor of appetizing food. Originally, i. e., in young animals or very young children, saliva does not flow until food is actually taken into the mouth: it is an automatic and purely reflexive glandular reaction, the adequate stimulus being food-in-the-mouth. In time, however, as we all know, the sight or the odor of food alone is able to initiate the saliva flow. Such a reflexive act, brought about by a situation other than its original, and biologically adequate, stimulus is a "conditioned reflex." The associated stimulus—the sight or odor of food—is called the conditioned stimulus, and the response to the conditioned or substitute stimulus is the conditioned reflex. The scheme is better shown, perhaps, in Figure 9.

Call A the biologically adequate or unconditioned stimulus for the reflex A_1; and let B represent the biologically adequate stimulus for B_1. If B becomes an effective stimulus for the reflex A_1, B is the substitute stimulus and $B \rightarrow A_1$ is the conditioned reflex. To illustrate, think of A as a clap of thunder which leads to A_1, a startle or fear response, B (lightning) leads to the mild response B_1 (blinking). Now if B accompanies A, as it usually does, B may lead to A_1 and the fear response follow the flash of lightning. Theoretically, all of our native or reflexive activities are capable of being conditioned. The salivary reflex is particularly well adapted for experiment, however, because responses to other than the original stimulus

IVAN P. PAVLOV

(1849–1936)

(i. e., food) can be accurately ascertained and their strength measured by noting the amount of saliva secreted.

The conditioned reflex has been widely employed in modern textbooks on psychology to explain how we acquire new responses. But it would be a mistake to conclude that the conditioned reflex or conditioned response (C R)* is a new term, or that it represents a new explanatory principle in psychology. In reality the idea of "conditioning" is distinctly old, and is clearly implicit in the time-honored laws of association by

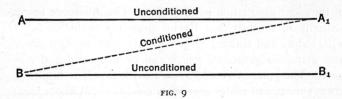

FIG. 9

SIMPLE SCHEME TO SHOW THE MECHANISM OF A CONDITIONED REFLEX

similarity, contrast, and contiguity in space and time. Essentially what the laws of association attempted to explain was how one idea or thought grows out of, or is connected with, or substitutes for, another. As early as 1690, John Locke in his *Essay Concerning Human Understanding* gave illustrations to show how individual peculiarities, likes, and dislikes can be explained on the principle of association or conditioning. Locke also applied his explanatory principle of the association of ideas to the learning of language by children. He wrote: "If we will observe how children learn languages, we shall find that to make them understand what the names of simple ideas, or substances, stand for, people ordinarily show them the things whereof they would have them have the idea;

---

*C R stands for *conditioned response.* This is a more general term than *conditioned reflex* because the term *reflex* is restricted to simple innate forms of behavior.

and then repeat to them the name that stands for it, as white, sweet, milk, sugar, cat, dog." Much later William James (Vol. I, p. 566) stated the law of contiguity, to which the other laws of association may be reduced, in the following passage: "When two elementary brain processes have been active together or in immediate succession, one of them on recurring, tends to propagate its excitement into the other." This is substantially the same principle as that of "conditioning."

If the idea of the conditioned response is by no means new, how, one may ask, does the work of Pavlov differ from that of the older association psychologists? The difference lies essentially in the fact that Pavlov dealt not with "ideas," or with habits and learned responses, but with sensory stimuli and glandular responses which can be measured and compared. The great merit of Pavlov's method is that results are always measured under controlled conditions. Without measurement there can be, ordinarily, no definiteness, no accuracy, and no objective fact. Without definiteness, accuracy, and objective fact there can be no science.

In the following sections we shall first describe Pavlov's work with the conditioned reflex. The broader aspects of conditioning and the role of the C R in learning will then be discussed.

2. PAVLOV'S METHOD

In his studies of the conditioned reflex, Pavlov worked almost entirely with dogs and with the salivary reflex. Implicit in all of his work is the notion that everything the dog learns from puppyhood on is a result of the association of certain events (which happen to occur at the same time) with the biologically adequate stimulus to some native response, such as withdrawing, struggling, eating, sex behavior, or the like. What the dog can learn, i. e., what stimuli can be conditioned, how fast he learns, and how rapidly he forgets, is studied by measuring the saliva flow under rigidly controlled conditions. Pavlov chose to work with the salivary reflex mainly because the strength—or the degree—of a response, and not simply its occurrence or non-occurrence can be determined from the *amount* of saliva secreted. Besides, the salivary glands form a simple organ and not a composite one

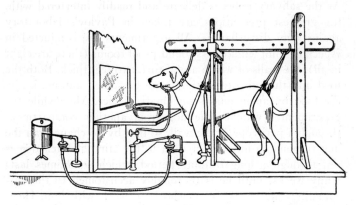

FIG. 10

DIAGRAM TO ILLUSTRATE PAVLOV'S METHOD OF ESTABLISHING A CONDITIONED
SALIVARY REFLEX

The unconditioned stimulus (food) is presented automatically in the small dish through the window. At the same time, or prior to this, the conditioned stimulus, e. g., the ringing of a bell, is given. The saliva which flows from the dog's mouth is collected in the graduated glass receptacle. As the saliva flows into the receptacle, it strikes a small disc which depresses the lever just in front of the animal. This downward movement is transmitted to the lever behind the screen, and an automatic tracing is thus secured upon a smoked drum or kymograph. The kymographic record tells the experimenter how many drops of saliva have been secreted and how regular the flow has been. (From Yerkes and Morgulis, 1909.)

consisting of several muscles; there are no tonic reflexes present to interfere with or complicate the experimental control; and the response, a secretion, can be measured with great precision in units as small as one tenth of a drop.

Pavlov's method of measuring the saliva flow is relatively simple. By means of a small incision, a fistula or opening is made in the dog's cheek through which a glass tube is inserted into the opening of one of the salivary glands, i. e., either the parotid, or the submaxillary. The saliva which drips from the tube is collected and measured in finely graduated containers. As the salivary reflex is delicate and readily interfered with, the greatest precautions are taken in Pavlov's laboratory against any disturbances. All experiments are conducted in especially built windowless sound-proof rooms (there are eight in all), the walls of which are of turf, two feet thick. Both the food and the substitute stimuli are presented automatically, the food by an ingenious pneumatic device. Meanwhile the experimenter watches the dog from another compartment through a periscope in the wall, so that by no chance can the dog respond to him rather than to the stimuli. Each dog is put through a long training period, which sometimes lasts many weeks, until he is thoroughly accustomed to the surroundings and to the man who is to work with him. He is taught to stand upon a small table in the experimental room on which he is secured by a collar and other restraining but not uncomfortable bonds. It is reported that the dogs look forward with every appearance of eagerness to the experiment, jump upon the table without command and place themselves in the correct position for the experiment. A diagram of the laboratory set-up is shown in Figure 10.

3. HOW CONDITIONED REFLEXES ARE ESTABLISHED

The simplest technique in conditioned reflex experiments is to apply over and over again the conditioned stimulus together with the unconditioned or natural stimulus. In Pavlov's experiments, olfactory, auditory, visual and tactual stimuli are all used as substitute stimuli, food in every case being the unconditioned or adequate stimulus. With the dog standing quietly on the table, a small dish of food is presented, and at the same time a tone, say, or a buzzer is sounded. This is repeated time after time on successive days, the number of joint stimulations averaging from eight to ten per experiment. At the first the saliva flows only to the food plus the sound, but finally, after repeated joint stimulations, usually from twenty to forty, the saliva will begin to flow at the sound

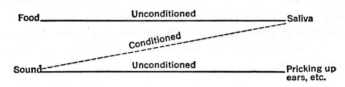

FIG. II

HOW THE SALIVARY SECRETION MAY BE CONDITIONED TO A SOUND STIMULUS

alone. The sound is now a conditioned stimulus for food, and the dog's salivary response is said to be conditioned. Figure 11 will show this more clearly.

Food and sound coming together often enough, the sound gradually becomes an effective stimulus for the salivary flow. Not only auditory stimuli, but olfactory stimuli, such as the odor of camphor; visual stimuli, such as letters and geometrical forms; tactual stimuli, touches or light scratches on the skin—all have been substituted for food and made to produce the saliva flow. In such experiments as these, the dog's brain may be said to have formed a connection between the "new" stimulus (sound) and the response (salivary flow), or to have "learned" that the conditioned stimulus "stands for" the food. Through associations like these, the range of stimuli which may lead to a given simple reflexive act becomes enormously increased. Part, at least, of the learned behavior of both dogs and human beings is acquired through just such simple conditioned reflexes.

4. THE FACTOR OF TIME IN CONDITIONED REFLEXES

The factor of time is important in conditioned reflex experiments. When the conditioned stimulus is given *simultaneously* with the natural stimulus, the conditioned reflex can always be obtained. But if the conditioned stimulus comes for even so short a period as one second *after* the natural stimulus there is ordinarily no conditioned reflex.[*] Krestovnikov, one of Pavlov's associates, carried out 1,000 trials in which the conditioned stimulus—a scratch on the skin—was applied from 1 to 3 seconds *after* the unconditioned stimulus (food) without getting positive results, i. e., saliva flow. Conditioned reflexes may be obtained, however, when the conditioned stimulus is applied *before* the natural stimulus—times as short as one second and as long as five minutes have given positive results. If a conditioned stimulus (e. g., tone or touch) is *continued* until the unconditioned stimulus is applied, the *latent time* [†] is roughly equal to the interval between the application of the conditioned stimulus and the natural one. Thus, if a note is sounded on a horn, and two minutes later food is given, the saliva will not begin to flow, once the conditioned reflex has been established, until the horn has been sounding for two minutes. This is called a "delayed reflex." Apparently, the sound of the horn acts as a *signal* which starts off the dog's nervous machinery—the conditioning process then determines how long the machinery shall run. The longer the interval between conditioned and natural stimulus, the more numerous the applications needed to build in the conditioned reflex.

When the conditioned stimulus is applied *before* the natural stimulus (food), it is not always necessary that it be con-

---

[*] Backward conditioning, though rare, has been accomplished (ref. 11).
[†] The time between the application of the stimulus and the appearance of the conditioned reflex.

tinued until the food is presented. For instance, the conditioned stimulus may first be applied, a pause allowed, and then the food presented. This pause between the conditioned and the natural stimulus may be of considerable length; even three minutes is not unusual. The latent period in these experiments almost exactly equals the period between the application of the substitute stimulus and the food. For example, a note may be sounded once, and two minutes later food given, and this process be repeated many times. Eventually, when the animal is conditioned, saliva will begin to flow just two minutes *after* the sound, at the time when the food ordinarily appeared. This type of delayed response is called a "trace reflex." That the intervening period is not simply one of inactivity is shown by the fact that any extra stimulus (if it be a strong one) which by chance or otherwise is applied during the waiting period will cause a secretion of saliva immediately.* The restraining mechanism at work during this wait is apparently like a delicate balance which is upset by any strong supervening stimulus.

Another phenomenon closely akin to the trace reflex is called simply the "time reflex." If a dog is fed at stated intervals, say every ten minutes, he soon becomes conditioned to this time-interval so that saliva will flow every ten minutes in anticipation, as it were, of the food. It would seem in such cases that some rhythm or periodicity has been established in the nervous system which "sets off" the response at the proper time, much as a "repeater" alarm-clock rings every two minutes or so. Examples of such rhythms or time reflexes in everyday life will at once come to mind. Some people awaken at the same time every morning, oftentimes just before the alarm-clock rings, while many, through vague but unmistakable inner cues, know when their regular lunch-time has arrived without consulting their watches. The fact of peri-

* See also p. 137.

odicity in efficiency during the day—physiological C R's pos·
sibly—seems to be well established.

5. SENSORY DISCRIMINATION IN CONDITIONED REFLEX EXPERIMENTS

Closely bound up with the question of the time relations
between substitute and natural stimulus is that of the degree
of *differentiation* or *selection* possible among various co-acting
stimuli. This is clearly an important problem, for obviously
there must be a high degree of selection and choice among
stimuli. Otherwise, the dog's salivary secretion would be general and uncontrolled, since dogs are continuously being bom-
barded by a multiplicity of sounds, smells, sights, and touches
when eating. How is this selection made, and how fine is a
dog's differentiating ability? Pavlov and his workers have
attacked the problem in many experiments, one of which is
here described. First, two spots A and B on the dog's flank
were selected. The A spot was lightly scratched, and at the
same time food was given. Then B was lightly scratched, but
no food given. After many repetitions and many weeks of
work, A with food, B without food, the point was finally
reached where touching A always gave the salivary reflex, and
touching B never gave it. The negative spot B was then moved
closer and closer to A, in order to study the fineness of discrimination, until the two spots were separated by only a few
millimeters. Still A gave the reflex, while B invariably failed
to give it. Inevitably, however, this very fine differentiation
broke down when a certain point was reached; and this was
true also of other experiments in which auditory and visual
stimuli were used. Whenever the negative stimulus was almost identical with, or very close to, the positive stimulus,
both produced the conditioned reflex, the degree of response
(amount of saliva) in the case of the negative stimulus depending upon its nearness or similarity to the conditioned

stimulus. This phenomenon of spread of stimulation has been called by Pavlov "irradiation." The degree of irradiation can be somewhat reduced by frequently reinforcing the conditioned stimulus: i. e., by again applying the conditioned stimulus together with the unconditioned stimulus (food).

Clear-cut differentiation of stimuli to a high degree has been secured by Pavlov's workers with other than tactual stimuli. Such results throw light upon the extreme sensitivity of the nervous system. Beliakov, for instance, trained his dogs to differentiate between tones of 800, of 812 and of 825 vibrations per second. It was found that one must begin with the least similar (825 vibs.) and proceed to the more similar (812 vibs.) tones in order to secure differentiation from 800, as the reverse procedure failed to give positive results. In other experiments, it was found that the dog could distinguish between metronome beats at the rate of 96 and 100 per second; and in the case of visual stimuli between a circle and an almost circular ellipse (i. e., axes in the relation 7:8).

All of these results were obtained with *simultaneous stimulation*. When there is a time-interval between the conditioned and the natural stimulus, the fineness of discrimination is considerably reduced, being inversely proportional (roughly) to the length of the pause. No high degree of differentiation is possible if the pause between the conditioned and the natural stimulus is long; apparently, irradiation, or spread of stimulation, prevents a clear-cut differentiation from occurring in these delayed responses.

The ability of the brain and nervous system of the dog to differentiate between two closely similar stimuli, sounds, touches, or visual objects, is attributed by Pavlov to an actively restraining neural mechanism called "inhibition." Inhibition is roughly analogous to the braking of an automobile which is gathering too much speed on a hill. This concept is well illustrated by an experiment in which four spots, A1,

A2, A3, and A4, were selected on a dog's flank (Figure 12). When each of these spots was touched, food was given, and this process was continued until all of the spots called out the salivary reflex. These may be called *positive* spots. Another spot, B, in the same region, was next selected and touched

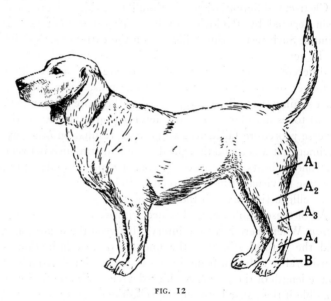

FIG. 12

HOW INHIBITION MAY BE STUDIED

Spots A₁, A₂, A₃, and A₄ are positive spots; B is a negative spot.

again and again, no food being given on these successive stimulations. At first, touches on the B spot led to a saliva flow due to irradiation; but finally, as no food was ever given, the conditioned reflex ceased, and the spot became *negative*. Now, when the negative B was touched and afterwards one of the positive A spots, an interesting result occurred. Spot A4 gave no response, A3 gave about one-half its usual quota of

saliva, while A2 and A1 gave full effect. This highly interesting result is explained by Pavlov as due to the spread of the
inhibiting, or restraining action, set up in the dog's nervous
system. Clearly, the inhibition was related to the distance of
the A spot from the negative B spot. Such "inhibition of an
excitation" is a general fact encountered in all conditioned
reflexes—it occurs with auditory, visual, and olfactory, as well
as with tactual stimuli.

Ordinarily, as we have seen, the negative B spot does not
give a saliva flow. But if when B is touched, a bell or note
is sounded at the same time, the conditioned reflex will at
once appear—saliva will begin to drop as though B were a
positive A spot. This "inhibition of an inhibition" or *disin-
hibition* is fairly common in conditioned reflex experiments,
and has been mentioned before in describing the trace reflex
(p. 133). It will be remembered that the conditioned reflex
does not appear until a given time *after* the substitute stimulus, the exact time depending upon the period originally intervening between the substitute stimulus and the food. During the waiting period the reflex is held in check or inhibited
by the dog's nervous system until the proper time arrives for
releasing the brake. But, as noted above, any strong extraneous stimulus will lift the brake, causing the salivary reflex
to appear. For example, in an experiment conducted by
Anrep, one of Pavlov's students, an irritating odor caused
twenty-eight drops of saliva to flow during a trace reflex;
while on another occasion the buzzing of a fly had the same
disorganizing effect. Perhaps now the reader will better understand the need for sound-proof, windowless rooms, and
for the extreme precautions taken in conditioned reflex work.

If any one of the positive A spots is touched and at the
same time an indifferent spot—one not producing the reflex
—is stimulated, the reflexive response to A will gradually
diminish and finally drop to zero. This blocking of a positive

stimulus by an indifferent one is called a "conditioned inhibition." Blocking may be irradiated to other stimuli. Thus
if A is the positive stimulus, and X the indifferent stimulus, the response may be inhibited not only to A plus X, but
also to A plus X plus Y plus Z. The degree of inhibition—
diminution of saliva flow—depends largely upon the similarity of the added stimuli to the indifferent stimulus X. When
the conditioned reflex is not occasionally reinforced by its
natural stimulus, it soon dies out or becomes extinguished—
fails to produce the salivary flow. This is known as the "extinction" of the conditioned reflex. It usually happens that
the conditioned reflex will function spontaneously again after
a period of extinction, due probably to the fact that the
inhibiting or suppressing stimulus has gradually lost its
force. But reinforcement is often necessary to reinstate it.
There is an interesting analogy between extinction and forgetting. In both phenomena something is lost, following lack
of exercise and the passing of time. But there is also a
marked difference between the two processes. As we have
said above, conditioned reflexes die out unless reinforced
with the natural stimulus, and the exercise of the conditioned
reflex *itself* does not check, but actually aids, the "dying out"
process. Later, the extinguished conditioned reflex spontaneously revives without more ado. Retention of a memory-
lesson is, to be sure, aided by reference back to the printed
page (reinforcement); but unlike the conditioned reflex, recitation or exercise of a memory-lesson checks—does not aid
—forgetting. In fact, exercise is necessary if one is ever to
learn a new task. It appears, therefore, that extinction is a
direct result of a blocking or inhibitory process (in Pavlov's
sense), while forgetting is rather a fading out effect due to
the weakening of associations through interference or lack of
exercise.

6. THE CONDITIONED REFLEX AND EXPERIMENTAL
NEUROSIS

Without doubt, the outstanding finding in Pavlov's experiments on differentiation is the tremendous value of this inhibitory power in the life of the dog. Without his "braking power," the dog would be unable to choose or select. He would respond hit or miss to every stimulation, unimportant as well as important; in short, his existence would be a riotous confusion of events.

What happens when the dog loses his ability to discriminate is clearly shown in a case of "experimental neurosis" produced by Pavlov and his group in a dog. Krestovnikova, one of Pavlov's students, conditioned a dog so that saliva was secreted whenever a circle of light was thrown upon a dark screen. As in previous experiments, the C R was built up by giving the dog food whenever the circle appeared and continuing this combination, food plus circle, until at last saliva flowed to the circle alone. Next the dog was shown a small ellipse again and again, no food ever being given along with it. Eventually, the point was reached when the saliva flowed at the sight of the circle, but never at the sight of the ellipse. To test the dog's differentiating ability, he was now shown larger and more circular ellipses, always without food, until finally he could distinguish—as shown by the appearance of the reflex—between the circle and an ellipse whose axes were in the relation 7:8. This would seem to have been a sufficient feat in itself, but the experimenter was not yet satisfied, and attempted to have her dog distinguish between the circle and an ellipse whose axes were as 8:9—a figure scarcely different from a perfect circle. This task proved to be too much for the dog's inhibitory ability. Saliva flowed first at sight of the ellipse, then at the circle, then at sight of either or both without any distinction. The dog began to whine, barked fiercely at the screen, tore at his restraining apparatus with his teeth, and attempted to jump down from the table. After this experiment the dog was useless as an experimental animal. Saliva would flow at sight of the experimenter, or at sight of the experiment room, or at almost any stimulus. Apparently what had happened was an almost complete collapse of the dog's differentiating ability, due to too great strain being placed upon the brake. When finally the brake gave way, response became general and riotous.

Experimental neurosis had been produced in other animals as well as in the dog. For example, nervous and disorganized behavior appeared in a sheep when (1) the difference between the positive and negative stimuli was *decreased* (as in Pavlov's experiment), and (2) when the *number* of presentations was increased (with shifts back and forth from the positive to the negative stimulus) without decreasing the difference between the stimuli. Electric shock was the unconditioned stimulus and a "defense reaction"—withdrawal by flexion of the foreleg—the reflexive response. Neurotic behavior has also been produced experimentally by the conditioned reflex technique in pigs and in rats. Apparently, the essential element in such behavior when produced by the conditioned reflex method is the clash between mutually incompatible responses. Faced by a dilemma, the animal either reacts violently and without discrimination or refuses to act at all.

A loss of discriminative ability in human beings, as in animals, is often associated with nervous diseases or neuroses. The neurotic individual cannot discriminate between really dangerous and really harmless objects. Hence he is afraid of cats or dark rooms or crossing bridges, or of a thousand and one other things intrinsically harmless. Nor can he choose between really important and really unimportant tasks, and so he is impelled to perform useless acts such as washing his hands ten times a day, touching every other lamp-post, going up the steps two at a time, and the like. Possibly a considerable share of the fatigue characteristic of neurasthenia comes from the large amount of lost motion indulged in.

To be sure, even in normals, conflict and confusion (neurosis) may arise if undue strain is placed upon the discriminatory ability. A little child is allowed to shout and play roughly at one time (is even encouraged and laughed at) and is punished for doing the same thing on another occasion because the mother is tired or "company" is present. Again a child is punished for "lying" but hears his mother tell "social lies" over the 'phone—say she's ill or not in and hence is unable to see an unwanted caller. Many children cannot see the difference between behavior (ostensibly the same) which is sometimes right and sometimes wrong. Unable to fathom such inconsistencies, they are faced by a dilemma as real as that which confronted Pavlov's dog when it was unable to distinguish the ellipse from the circle.

Conflicts due to the interference of competing stimuli often arise in the classroom. Teach a child French and Spanish at the same time, or alternative methods of subtracting or dividing, and for a time at least efficiency in both tasks will be impaired. Although relatively mild, such conflicts are emotionally disturbing and are destructive of morale. Intelligent behavior in the child depends upon a judicious choice and selection from among the many competing stimuli which assail his sense organs. It is the task of the teacher to emphasize those stimuli to which responses should be made, and to prevent needless and wasteful conflicts whenever possible.

7. THE CONDITIONED REFLEX AND SLEEP

One of the most interesting of Pavlov's findings was the discovery that sleep is closely linked up with the inhibitory phenomena which we encountered in the experiments on differentiation and the trace reflex. It will be remembered that in the trace reflex the conditioned salivary flow did not appear until some time after the substitute stimulus had been given. This period depended upon the original time-interval between the substitute stimulus and the natural stimulus. Whenever this delay was one-half minute or more, a peculiar thing happened; the dog became drowsy and often went sound asleep. This even happened in delayed reflexes when the conditioned stimulus was continued through the period intervening between the substitute stimulus and natural stimulus; for example, the dog would fall asleep with the bell or buzzer going loud enough, apparently, to keep a dozen dogs awake. Annoyed by this unforeseen happening, at first Pavlov and his workers tried to get exceptionally lively and active dogs, thinking that the sleep which came so readily might be an individual peculiarity of certain dogs. Even the most active dogs, however, regularly went to sleep, indicating that some general, and not individual, condition was at work. What is the nature of the sleep which occurs in these experiments? It must, said Pavlov, be a condition of general cortical inhibition analogous to, but greater than, the local inhibition or brake effect which we have already discovered in previous experiments. During the waiting period between substitute stimulus and conditioned reflex, the brain and nervous system are actively inhibiting or holding in check the salivary flow. That this must be true is shown by the sudden appearance of the reflex when any strong stimulus comes in to lift the brake. In like manner, when the dog's salivary flow has been positively conditioned to a note of 800 vibrations and negatively conditioned to a note of 812 vibrations, there must again be a delicate balance between the excitation and inhibition of the glandular (motor) response.*

Inhibition is evidently at first a matter of the local negative stimulation of a small sector in the dog's brain. But if this focus of negative stimulation is continued for a fairly long period of time, which happens in the trace reflex, apparently the inhibition gradually spreads over the entire cortex, the dog meanwhile becoming more and more drowsy, until finally it goes to sleep. Normal sleep in man is readily explained after the same fashion as this experimentally induced sleep in the dog. The natural stimulus for sleep is fatigue, which induces first drowsiness (local inhibition) and then sleep (general inhibition). When the brake is lifted—the inhibition removed from the cortex—the sleeper awakens. It is interesting to note how readily sleep as a response is itself conditioned. Ordinarily sleep follows the natural stimulus, fatigue, with which is associated (usually) a comfortable bed, darkness, a certain hour, and quiet. These latter elements in the total situation often become such effective substitute stimuli for sleep that many individuals will fall asleep when in their customary situation, even though not especially fatigued. Again, for many people these associated stimuli become so important that they cannot sleep without them, no matter how tired they may be. Insomnia, according to this view, might be thought of as occasioned by a negative stimulus which represses or inhibits the positive stimuli to sleep. Worry, excitement, fear, and other emotional conditions may readily act as negative stimuli to sleep.

---

* We have already described in Section 5 what happens when too much strain is placed on the brake.

8. THE CONDITIONED REFLEX IN ANIMALS AND CHILDREN

Pavlov's success in conditioning the salivary reflex of the dog has stimulated many investigators, particularly in America, to undertake experiments with the C R. The reflexes which have been most studied are the eye-lid, the pupillary, the flexion (hand or foot withdrawal) and the kneejerk. Except in the case of the pupillary reflex, electric shock is usually the unconditioned stimulus. If a dog's foot is pricked with a pin or given an electric shock, it will be pulled away quickly and involuntarily. By the use of electric shock as unconditioned stimulus, this "withdrawal reflex" of the dog may be so conditioned that sounding a note causes the foot to jump back.

Much work has been done with animals other than the dog; in fact, conditioning experiments have been attempted all the way from protozoa to man. Some of this work is interesting and valuable as showing the possibilities of measuring and comparing the learning processes in the lower animals. Although many of these lower orders are thought of as possessing few activities which can be called mental, we find, nevertheless, that they can often form definite associations. To illustrate, in studying the behavior of the snail, Thompson found that the pressure of a piece of lettuce on the mouth of the snail provoked a chewing movement which did not appear when the pressure was applied to the foot. Here, he thought, is the opportunity of discovering whether the snail is capable of making a connection between pressure on the foot and chewing. To test out this hypothesis, the mouth was repeatedly stimulated with lettuce, causing a chewing movement, and simultaneously with this, pressure was applied to the foot. Continued repetition of these stimuli led to the formation of an association, or a C R: whenever the foot was pressed, the snail began to chew. This learned response was actually retained for four days—not a bad feat of "memory" for a snail! A carefully devised series of experiments on the formation of C R's in fish have been reported from England, with food as the natural or unconditioned stimulus. Fish were conditioned to a number of substitute stimuli such as a slight rise in temperature of the water (as small as .4° C); changes in the salinity of the surrounding water; and to auditory (probably vibratory) and visual intensities.

The C R technique has been employed to study sensory discrimination in animals as well as the retention of simple learned responses. By positively conditioning the saliva flow of a dog to a given tone and negatively conditioning it to other tones, auditory acuity may be accurately determined. Auditory acuity in monkeys has been shown by the conditioned response method to be fairly comparable to that of man. In the experiment with fishes described above, discrimination between one and two sources of light was obtained after differential training—the C Rs being fairly stable. The dog's withdrawal reflex can also be utilized to test for fineness of discrimination between tones. The extinction (p. 138) of a conditioned reflex in rats and its reappearance have been carefully investigated and curves describing the phenomena plotted. In one ingenious experiment, a rat obtained a pellet of food by depressing a bar which released the food. Here the C R itself produced the unconditioned stimulus (food). This form of the C R experiment has been frequently used with children as well as with animals.

There are numerous instances of animal learning which are readily explicable in terms of the C R principle. Performing animals, dogs, horses, elephants and the like, are usually responding to many substitute stimuli, such as the trainer's voice, a movement of his head, or a movement of his hand, all of which have been previously associated over and over again with the desired response. Several illustrations showing how the C R is employed in the training of animals are given in Chapter 7, pp. 197–199.

As children are able to introspect little if any better than animals, the C R method is especially well adapted to the study of their behavior. Krasnogorski, one of Pavlov's students, was the first investigator to study learning in young children by the C R method. He conditioned the salivary reflex in several young children to a variety of stimuli, with a fair degree of success, the sight of food, a bell, sound of a reed pipe, a slight scratch on the skin. As an indication of the amount of saliva secreted, Krasnogorski noted the number of mouth-openings and swallowing movements made by the child. He states that conditioned reflexes can be built up as early as the first year of life; and that almost any stimulus can serve as a substitute stimulus for a reflex motor or secretory activity. An important discovery was that conditioned reflexes break down more readily in normal than in abnormal and feeble-minded children. Apparently the feeble-minded child is less mobile and more mechanical in his associations than is the normal.

In America, Mateer has extended and substantially verified Krasnogorski's work. This investigator worked with more than fifty normal children from about twelve to eighty-nine months of age, and with a half dozen or so feeble-minded children. She studied the formation of the conditioned reflex, its retention over a period, its dying-out or extinction (unlearning), and the ease with which conditioned stimuli could be reassociated. Mateer worked with the salivary reflex, noting the number of swallowings, as did Krasnogorski, but her experiments were much better controlled than his. Conditioned reflexes in normal children were learned and unlearned* in about one-half the number of

* The measure of extinction is the time it takes the conditioned reflex to die out when not reinforced with the natural stimulus.

trials necessary (on the average) for the feeble-minded. Mateer also discovered a substantial relationship between the ease of conditioned reflex formation and mental ability as measured by mental tests. This author regards the conditioned reflex method as especially valuable in work with young children, as it gives a direct measure of native learning ability; and in any case she considers it to be a valuable supplement to other clinical methods.

9. THE CONDITIONED REFLEX IN ADULTS

The problem of the extent to which the reflexes of the human adult may be conditioned has been approached experimentally by many psychologists. Some of the most interesting and valuable work in this field has been done by investigators working with smooth muscle reflexes not ordinarily under conscious control. The possibility of the acquisition of learned movements below the level of conscious awareness has been clearly demonstrated. A few results may be cited. In some early experiments, J. B. Watson, who worked with both children and adults, conditioned the withdrawal of the foot and the withdrawal of the finger. An electric shock was the unconditioned or natural stimulus, while a bell, a buzzer, and a bright light were among the substitute stimuli. Cason conditioned the pupillary reflex (change in size of the pupillary aperture) by ringing a bell each time a beam of light was thrown in the subject's eye. After 400-odd joint stimulations of bell plus light, the pupil dilated at the sound of the bell alone. In one subject, the pupil was even conditioned to contract to the bell—a result which indicates the tremendous possibilities for modification in the human nervous system. Dodge succeeded in obtaining a conditioned lid reflex (wink) to a kneejerk stimulus after many simultaneous presentations of conditioned and natural stimuli. The normal stimulus to the kneejerk is a smart tap on the patellar tendon just below the knee-cap. This stimulus was substituted for the normal stimuli which lead to the protective wink reflex. Much work has been done on variations in the eyelid response during the conditioning process; and comparisons of the response in animals and man have been made.

10. THE CONDITIONED REFLEX AS A PRINCIPLE OF LEARNING

There is, perhaps, no topic in experimental psychology upon which more time and effort have been expended than upon the conditioned reflex. The acquisition of conditioned reflexes by animals, children, and man; the relative ease of conditioning various reflexes; the stability of conditioned reflexes, their extinction and reinforcement; the relation of conventional learning to conditioned reflex experiments; the distinction between natural and conditioned reflexes—all of these aspects of the phenomena of conditioning have been subjected to experimental attack. The C R method appealed to the early behaviorists because it offered the possibility that complex activities could be thought of as composed of simple links forged into more complex patterns. Furthermore, the conditioned reflex seemed to substitute an exact and measurable relationship for explanations in terms of trial-and-error and "satisfyingness" (see Chapter 7). At one time, many psychologists hoped—and the strict objectivists fervently believed—that the conditioned reflex would prove to be the unit or element out of which all habits are built.

Belief in the conditioned reflex as the fundamental unit in all learning is now largely a matter of historical interest. We have seen in this chapter how extremely sensitive are many laboratory-determined conditioned reflexes; how difficult to obtain; how easily interfered with, and how readily lost without reinforcement. It has been pointed out, too, that the characteristics of conditioned reflex learning are different in several respects from learning in which there is active interest and participation by the learner. The active learner picks and chooses among the various alternatives and is guided in his choice by the net-result, in contradistinction to the stereotyped learning characteristic of the conditioned reflex. In fact, much conditioned reflex learning, as in the acquisition of baseless fears, dislikes and preferences is essentially stupid learning. In conditioned reflex experiments in the laboratory many trials under highly controlled conditions are necessary for learning, while oftentimes in actual practice an activity involving many associations may be acquired in a few (even one) experience. The distinction between "extinction" in conditioned reflex learning and ordinary forgetting has already been pointed out.

Learning is not then simply a "long chain of conditioned reflexes" (Pavlov), but is a coöperative enterprise in which the whole organism (animal or man) takes part. Several experiments of Lashley illustrate this point nicely. In one experiment, a monkey was trained to carry out a manipulative habit with its right hand, the left hand meanwhile being partially paralyzed by destruction of the motor areas of the brain controlling left hand movements. Later, the left hand was allowed to recover and the right hand became paralyzed as a result of destruction of the opposite side of the brain. When the monkey was again tested, it was found that almost perfect transfer took place from the now paralyzed right hand to the untrained (and recovered) left hand which had never taken part in the task. In another experiment, a brightness discrimination habit, in which only one eye was used, was found to transfer to the untrained eye, although the same retinal elements were not stimulated on the second occasion. In still another experiment, rats trained to jump to a platform when one visual pattern was presented (a cardboard figure showing a black surface and a white edge), were found to respond to somewhat similar visual patterns immediately. The interesting point here is that although the functionally "equivalent stimuli" did not affect the same parts of the retina, the behavior of the rats was the same as to the original stimuli. These experiments offer convincing evidence against the view that a complex habit may be thought of as the end-result of a mechanical addition of conditioned reflexes or of more elementary habits.

Objection to the conditioned reflex as the unit or basis of all learning does not imply that the broader and more inclusive conditioned response (C R) is not a useful, in fact well-nigh indispensable, mechanism for learning theory. Many of the recent textbooks in psychology make wide use of the conditioned response as an explanatory principle in learning and habit formation. In social psychology, gestures, language, and group phenomena; in abnormal psychology, personality and emotional adjustments are explained in terms of the C R. Methods of reconditioning in children and adults in order to eliminate bad habits, personality defects and other conditions, are based essentially upon C R mechanisms.

Leaving for the future the question of ultimate value, let us summarize the present worth of the conditioned reflex for experimental psychology. First of all, the conditioned reflex technique is an important instrument for research in animal psychology. Animals do not give verbal reports nor do they make introspections. But by means of carefully controlled experiments, we can, nevertheless, obtain exact data on learning and relearning, fineness of discrimination of tones, lights, and tactual stimuli. There is no better way of telling whether a dog distinguishes a note of 800 vibs. from one of 812 vibs., say, than by the general method of the conditioned reflex.

In experiments with human beings, the conditioned reflex

method substitutes objective records for verbal report and opinion. This often has decided advantages. It is possible, for instance, to determine whether an individual "senses" stimuli below his threshold by conditioning him to subliminal lights or sounds.* No report is asked for, nor could one be given verbally if desired. Again, we have seen in Mateer's work that normal children differ from abnormal in the ease with which conditioned reflexes are established and lost. The C R method offers possibilities for the measurement of native aptitude apart from training and experience. Other applications have been suggested. Pavlov's contribution to experimental psychology lies in his having provided a precise technique, machine-like in its accuracy and subject directly to laboratory control. The possibilities of the conditioned reflex methods have by no means been exhausted.

* Stimuli which affect the sense organs but which are too faint to be perceived are called "subliminal."

Chapter 6

FRANZ'S AND LASHLEY'S EXPERIMENTAL STUDIES OF THE RÔLE OF THE BRAIN IN LEARNING

I. THE BRAIN IN LEARNED ACTIVITIES

The experimental work of Shepherd I. Franz and Karl S. Lashley offers one of the best examples of the physiological approach to problems of learning and habit-formation. Both of these scientists were trained in physiology as well as in psychology. Franz received the doctor's degree in psychology from Columbia University in 1899, and in 1902 began a series of studies on the rôle of the brain in learning, using cats and monkeys as experimental subjects. For many years he was psychologist at the Government Hospital for the Insane in Washington, where he did much striking work in the reëducation of individuals who had sustained brain injury. Lashley attained the Ph.D. degree at the Johns Hopkins University in 1914. He is the most eminent American worker in the field of physiological psychology.

The main task which Franz and Lashley set for themselves was to determine *what* regions of the brain and *how much* of the brain function in specific learned acts. Their method was to compare the learning ability of animals before and after destruction of certain brain areas by operation; and also to compare the learning ability of "operated" animals with that of normal animals. A group of rats, for example, is trained to thread a maze, the number of trials and the time being recorded; parts of the brain tissue are then removed and after recovery from the operation the animals are re-tested to see to what extent the loss of brain structure will affect their behavior. Or again, animals whose brains have been partially destroyed are trained to escape from a prob-lem box, and their records are compared with those of nor-mal animals.

Operations involving different brain areas have been per-formed upon rats, cats, and monkeys, and the effect of brain loss upon the acquisition of both sensory and motor habits of different degrees of complexity has been investigated. Ex-periments like these have much significance for human learn-ing. The human brain cannot be experimented with directly and it is only in the event of disease or wounds that brain injury can be correlated with loss of mental function. In pathological conditions of the brain, however, complications arising from bodily disease or injury must be seriously con-sidered. Such disturbances may be so extensive that a definite conclusion as to the specific effect of the brain injury itself is hard to reach. This situation does not arise in operative work with animals; parts of the cerebral cortex in a rat, say, can be experimentally destroyed and the resulting effects upon learning behavior directly noted. Moreover, experimentation with animals permits us to observe the rôle of the brain in behavior less complex and more easily controlled than in man.

In many cases the experimental findings from the higher animals, e. g., the apes, can be carried over almost unaltered to human learning, and even in the lower species problems of the physiology of learning are fundamentally the same as in man. In a careful review of the literature on cerebral func-tion, Lashley concludes that while there is undoubtedly greater specialization as we go up the evolutionary scale, the relation of brain areas to learning does not differ markedly in man from that in other mammals.

2. EARLY STUDIES OF BRAIN FUNCTION AND LEARNING

Before considering the experimental work on brain function in animals, let us get as clear a notion as possible of the topography of the brain itself. The brain of the rat, cat, or monkey is much simpler—but is basically similar—to that of man. Hence we can locate the positions of the various

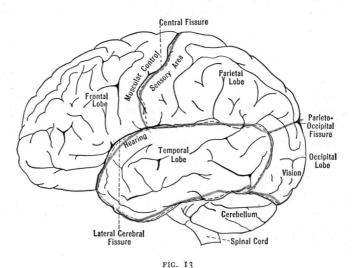

FIG. 13

THE LEFT ASPECT OF THE CEREBRAL CORTEX IN MAN (SCHEMATIC)

structures in the animal brain by reference to Figure 13, which gives a side view of the left hemisphere of the human brain. The frontal "lobes" or areas lie just behind the forehead, while behind the frontals and separated from them by a great fissure are the parietal lobes. The parietals lie under the "roof" of the head. The occipital lobes, concerned primarily with seeing, lie at the back of the head; the temporal lobes, concerned in part with hearing, are just above the

KARL S. LASHLEY

(Born 1890)

temples. The adjoining parts of the parietal and temporal lobes are the great sensory synthesizing and associative areas of the brain, while the frontal lobes constitute the motor organizing and motor discharging centers. The frontal lobes also are believed to be concerned in man with management and restraint of the more primitive impulses.

In his pioneer studies Franz investigated the function of the frontal lobes in the retention of associations formed in learning. His experiments were carried out with cats and monkeys. The cats were first trained to escape from boxes quite similar to those used by Thorndike in his studies of animal learning (see p. 182). These boxes were about twelve inches high, fifteen inches wide, and twenty inches long. The bottom, back, and sides were solid, the front and top covered with three-quarter inch slats. The door was six inches wide by eight inches high, and was hinged at the bottom so that it would fall forward when the latch or other mechanism holding it was released. Three boxes were used. Two could be opened by pushing or knocking against a cord attached in different ways to the door; the third by pressing a button up or down. This third box is shown in Figure 14.

The stimulus to activity was food—meat, fish, or milk—placed just outside of the box. Given a training period of about a week, a normal and hungry cat can learn to escape from boxes such as these in from two to six seconds. After the cat had learned the habit to this high point of efficiency, Franz gave it an anesthetic and operated upon the brain, cutting away both frontal lobes from the rest of the brain structure without, however, removing the severed parts from the skull. After the animal had recovered from the anesthetic and the shock following the operation—which usually required two to three days—it was retested in the box from which it had previously learned to escape. In all three cats used in this experiment the habit of escape, though re-

peatedly tested for, failed to reappear. But the cats still made
impulsive efforts to escape; also they retained old and much-
used habits, such as purring when petted, rubbing against the
experimenter's legs, and responding to being called. When
they were held before a cage of mice, normal emotional re-

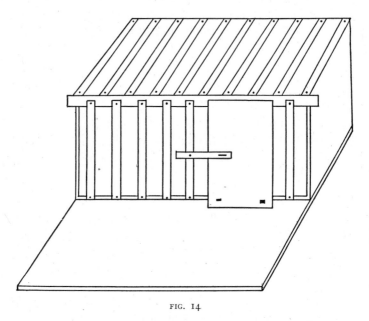

FIG. 14

PUZZLE BOX USED BY FRANZ IN LEARNING EXPERIMENTS WITH CATS

sponses were exhibited, such as increased heart beat, following the mice rapidly with the eyes, and attempts to jump.
Only the *recently acquired habit* of opening the box seemed
to be lost. Franz was careful not to use the results from any
animal in which post-operative infection had set in, and in
every case the cat was later killed and its brain examined to

make sure that the frontals had actually been cut away from the rest of the brain.

The loss of learned responses following extirpation of the frontal lobes holds for monkeys as well as for cats. In his experiments with monkeys, Franz used small animals of the rhesus (short-tail) and the ring-tail variety. Two tasks were arranged, the one opening a food box, and the other obtaining food by completing the so-called hurdle task. The problem set by the food box was to open the door of a small food compartment attached to the cage in which the animal lived. The door of the food box was held by a button much like that in the door of the box in Figure 14. In the hurdle problem the animal had to perform several acts in order, going from one bar to another, crawling through a hole, and so forth, before reaching the food. All of the animals were hungry when placed in the test situations so that active and vigorous behavior was readily obtained.

Six monkeys were used in this experiment. As soon as they had thoroughly learned the habits, parts of their frontal lobes were removed, with the same precautions employed as in the cat experiments. When the monkeys were retested after recovery from the operation, all were found to have lost the trick of opening the food box or of going through the more complex activities of the hurdle. But as in the case of the cats, habits of long standing, such as eating out of the experimenter's hand and jumping upon his shoulder, remained. The monkeys were described as normally active and apparently normal emotionally, screaming and chattering as before the operation.

The conclusion reached in these experiments, namely, that newly formed associations and habits are primarily dependent upon activity of the frontal lobes has encountered objection. In the first place, the shock of the operation (surgical shock) might alone be sufficient to break up the new associations; and secondly, the mere excision of brain tissue in *any* part of the brain (not the frontal lobe particularly) might explain the loss of the habit. To answer these criticisms, Franz performed two control operations. In the one, a cat was trained as before to escape from a box. After the trick was learned, the cat was anesthetized and the skull opened, but no excision of brain tissue was made. The wound was simply closed and bandaged as in the other operations. Twenty-four hours after the operation, this cat was retested and was found to have retained the habit perfectly. Other repetitions of this experiment indicate that surgical shock alone is not sufficient to obliterate new associations.

In the second control test, a cat which had been trained to escape from two boxes was operated on, but this time a portion of the *parietal lobe* instead of the frontal was cut away from the underlying parts of brain tissue. Three days after the operation this animal got out of the box in a little over seven seconds, which was about twice the time required before the operation. Shortly thereafter it reduced its escape time to the former level, showing, apparently, that the associations involved in the habits had not been actually disturbed. Seven weeks later, *one* frontal lobe only in this same cat was excised. Four days after this operation, though extremely slow, the animal was able to do the trick. In another cat which had learned perfectly how to get out of the box, *both* parietal lobes were destroyed. Three days after the operation, this animal performed the trick as well as before. These control experiments indicate clearly (1) that only when *both frontals* are injured are the recently acquired associations lost; and (2) that the loss of the habit cannot be explained as due either to surgical shock resulting from the operation or to mere cutting of the brain tissue.

3. THE VICARIOUS RÔLE OF BRAIN STRUCTURES: RESTITUTION OF FUNCTION

In all of Franz's experiments described so far, the habits and associations lost as the result of frontal injury were of quite recent origin; old and well-established habits persisted. To see whether this would hold true for *highly trained* escape habits, in a second series of experiments Franz trained four monkeys over a much longer period of time until the escape habit was firmly established—almost second nature, so to speak. The frontal lobes of these highly trained animals were then destroyed, and after recovery it was found that the escape habit functioned almost, if not quite, as perfectly as before the operation. In another series of experiments with several cats, the frontals were severed from the rest of the brain *before* the animals had learned to escape from any of the boxes. When these animals were trained later, it was found that they could learn the habits as well as normal cats.

These experiments are interesting and suggestive—they indicate that in an emergency one part of the brain can take over the function of another part vicariously, or by substitution. It seems evident from Franz's results that, in cats and monkeys recently formed complex motor habits are normally carried by the frontal lobes, since the habits are lost when the frontals are removed. But if the habits are well formed, i. e., fairly well mechanized, they persist even when parts of the frontals are lost, being carried on apparently through the agency of other parts of the brain. That these other centers *may* provide a basis for the habit in the first place is indicated by those experiments in which cats whose frontal lobes had been excised *before* training still learned the habit. These findings are opposed to the old idea of specific "learning centers" in the brain which control definite activities.

Such areas, if they actually exist, must be considerably more diffuse, and more loosely organized, than was originally believed.

Several cases of restitution of function taken from Franz's work with human beings are instructive in this connection. These cases are concerned with the reëducation of patients whose brains had been injured by disease or wounds. An aphasic, fifty-seven years old, had recently suffered a paralytic stroke.* His right side was paralyzed, and his language was jumbled and often unintelligible. Many irrelevant words were employed and objects were often named incorrectly. The attempt was made to retrain this patient by having him relearn (1) the names of ten familiar colors; (2) a short stanza of poetry; and (3) the Lord's Prayer. Beginning with an accuracy score of 44 per cent right in naming colors, after three months, in which the trials varied in number from day to day and were sometimes omitted, this man increased his accuracy score to 96 per cent right. Almost the same results were obtained in relearning numbers. An interesting finding here was that the number 5 (probably because of its common use) was most often used spontaneously. In trying to learn poetry—the first stanza of "The Village Blacksmith" was the selection used—the patient read aloud the first one or two lines five times and then tried to recite. Repetition was continued until reproduction was perfect, whereupon the next few lines were attempted, and so on. After five days of work the patient was able to repeat six lines of the selection sufficiently well to indicate that he was gradually learning it. The Lord's Prayer, formerly well known to this patient, was correctly given after twenty-five readings spaced over three

---

* Aphasia is the loss of ability to understand spoken or written language (sensory type); or the loss of the ability to say the correct word to express one's thought (motor type). Aphasia is, in general, the result of injury to the associative areas of the cortex, most often, probably, in the frontal and temporal lobes.

days. A post-mortem examination of this man's brain (he died of pneumonia shortly after the experiments described) showed considerable destruction in the lower part of the cortex, i. e., in the temporal lobes. Franz points out that the slow but steady reëducation of this man suggests the possibility of the reëstablishment of old brain connections or the opening-up of new ones. This seems reasonable in the light of the experimental work on animals which has been described.

A second case illustrates the powerfully stimulating effect of positive suggestion. In this instance the patient was an ex-soldier, a young man who had been struck by a high-explosive shell. The result of his injuries was paralysis of face, arm, and leg on one side. This condition had persisted for nine months. This man entered the examination room hobbling on a cane. At once he was ordered sharply by the examiner to put down his cane and take a seat in a chair some twelve feet away. Although he insisted at first that he couldn't walk without a cane, upon being told that the examiner was quite sure that he could, he laid the cane aside and awkwardly, but unassisted, walked to the chair. Here the authority and the prestige of the examiner proved to be a sufficiently emphatic stimulus to reinstate a partly lost function. Either the old nerve connections conducted under "pressure" or other and new connections substituted for them.

The effect of a strong incentive or an emotional stimulus in making a patient "forget" his disabilities is well illustrated in the case of another partially paralyzed man who had walked with a cane for nineteen years. During a baseball game this individual hit the ball, and in great excitement, without pausing to get his cane, ran quickly to first base, beating out the throw. It is significant that in spite of this achievement he then demanded his cane, saying that he couldn't walk without it. In many cases of this sort it seems likely that old pathways in the brain and nervous system are still partially intact, or that others are able to substitute for them. The patient's attitude is often the controlling factor in stirring these connections into life. If the suggestions are strong enough, or if the patient's interests can be sufficiently aroused, the strengthened motivation may lead to recovery of the lost skills. In some instances, strong emotional incentives—anger or fear, say—may be necessary in order to provoke into activity long dormant functions. Apparently re-education depends more upon the emotional impetus and the will-to-do than upon the degree of physical handicap to be overcome.

4. THE BRAIN IN BRIGHTNESS DISCRIMINATION

Lashley's work, like that of Franz, was directed toward discovering the effect of brain-destruction upon specific learned acts. In one series of experiments a group of white rats was trained in a very simple sensory habit of brightness discrimination. The problem box used (Yerkes Discrimination Box, shown in Figure 15) contains two alleyways, either of which can be illuminated by a transparent screen placed at the far end of the box. When the rat takes the lighted side, it is admitted to the food compartment through a small door; when it takes the dark side it receives no food, but instead gets a shock through an electric grill placed on the floor of the alley. The light can be shifted from the left to the right alley irregularly so that the animals cannot form a place habit. About 100 trials are required for a rat to fix the association between the illuminated alley and food. Training was continued at the rate of ten trials per day until thirty consecutive errorless trials were obtained. After one group of animals had learned the habit perfectly, various amounts of the occipital lobes of both cerebral hemispheres were destroyed by operation, and after recovery from the operation the rats were tested for retention. *All* of these animals upon

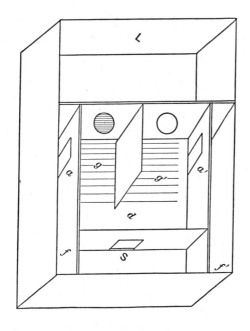

FIG. 15

BOX USED FOR TRAINING IN BRIGHTNESS DISCRIMINATION

The animal is started at S and passes to *d*, where a choice is offered of an illuminated and a dark alley. These alleys lead across electric grills (*g, g'*) through trapdoors of light celluloid (*a, a'*) to the food compartments (*f, f'*). In training, the door on the dark side is locked and the grill charged. The illumination is shifted irregularly from side to side by a movable screen in the light-box (L). In use the entire box is covered except for an observation hood above *d*. (From Lashley, 1929.)

recovery from the operation were found to have lost the brightness discrimination habit. But with practice they were able to reacquire it, the number of trials needed being roughly proportional to the *extent,* but independent of the location, of occipital lobe destruction. The correlation between percentage of cortex destroyed and retardation in learning the brightness discrimination habit was .45.

Another group of animals untrained in brightness discrimination was *first* subjected to brain operations which involved different *one-thirds* of the occipital cortex. These rats were then tested to see how long it would take them to acquire the habit. The results of these tests are quite convincing. Those rats whose brains had been injured *before* opportunity to learn the brightness discrimination had been given acquired the habit just as quickly as did the uninjured animals. This experiment and the one just described seem to establish (1) that the occipital lobes are ordinarily active in brightness discrimination, but that (2) no part of these regions is necessary for it, as various parts—up to a critical limit, i. e., 50 per cent—can apparently take over the function. It also seems clear that (3) brightness discrimination must be related to the activity of the *whole* occipital lobe rather than to any specific part, since the habit is weakened by the extent of injury but is independent of the point where it occurs.

In still another group of rats trained in the brightness discrimination habit the parietal brain areas were destroyed by operation. Upon being retested, these animals, although considerably slower than before, in no case showed complete loss of the habit. This result suggests that the occipital areas were the regions originally concerned in learning this activity. We have already seen, however, that when parts of the occipital lobe were destroyed before training, the rats were still able to learn the brightness discrimination habit as well as normal animals. This led Lashley to propose the following query: *Is there any particular area of the brain which takes over the functions of the injured occipital parts?* To answer this question, he destroyed various parts of the occipital lobes in twelve rats and trained them until they had learned the brightness discrimination habit up to his standard. A second operation was then performed on the same rats, various regions of the remaining parts of the cortex being destroyed. Each operation injured about one-third of the still intact cortex, the injuries sampling the remaining area in such a way as to cover (when all twelve rats are considered) the entire two hemispheres. In no animal was *all* of the brain cortex destroyed, as complete decortication has not as yet been successfully performed in the rat. These twice-operated animals were then retested for retention of the brightness discrimination habit, with the result that none was found to have lost it.

This last experiment forces us to the important conclusion that apparently *any* part of the brain cortex is able to take over the brightness discrimination habit in the absence of those areas whose function it normally is. Since the entire cortex was not removed in any animal used in these tests, it is uncertain whether *some* cortical tissue is not necessary for the retention of the brightness discrimination habit. But after occipital injury no specific area is needed to carry on the habit vicariously. One possible explanation of this phenomenon is that subcortical centers * take over the functions of the injured cortex. This would seem probable in view of the widely held opinion that habits and skills acquired through cortical activity (i. e., by conscious effort)—when thoroughly automatized—will be short-circuited to subcortical levels. But Lashley's work offers no evidence in support of this view. In one experiment, rats were overtrained by 1,200 trials, that is, by more than 10 times the number necessary to es-

---

* Subcortical centers are structures in the older and more primitive brain-stem which are overlaid by the cerebrum and cerebellum.

tablish the brightness discrimination habit. In these animals the brightness habit had surely become highly automatic. After cortical destruction, however, these rats did not relearn any more readily than rats which had received normal training. Lashley writes: "There is no indication that subcortical nuclei have taken over any part of the reaction, even sufficient to facilitate learning." If subcortical centers do not take over the function of the injured parts of the cortex, there must be reorganization or substitution in the remaining intact cortex.

These results which have been quoted from Lashley's work are quite securely established. More than 150 rats were used as experimental subjects, and there were adequate controls, so that the results cannot be attributed to surgical shock or to actual blindness in the animals. Post-mortem examinations to verify the extent of the lesions were also made.

5. BRAIN FUNCTION IN MOTOR HABITS

In another series of experiments, Lashley studied the effects of brain injury upon the learning and retention of a motor habit. Animals were first trained to secure food in the problem box shown in Figure 16. In this box, called the double platform box, it is necessary for the animal to depress platforms *a* and *b* in the fixed order *a—b* in order to open the door, *d*, which leads to the food compartment. These platforms are about four by two inches and are raised one inch from the floor; a slight pressure is sufficient to depress either of them. This task requires a more complex motor response than that needed in the inclined plane box used in earlier experiments by Franz and Lashley. In the inclined plane box, the animal had to climb upon the food compartment (a small box placed within the cage) and depress one small platform in order to open the door of the food box. In the double platform box, *two* platforms instead of one had to be depressed and in the right order.

Nineteen rats were trained in the double platform box *after* about one third (from 14 to 50 per cent), of the cere-

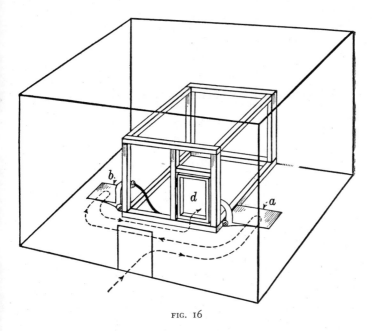

FIG. 16

DOUBLE-PLATFORM BOX USED IN EXPERIMENTS IN LEARNING WITH WHITE RATS

The door *d* is opened when the platforms *a* and *b* are successively pressed down. (From Lashley, 1929.)

bral cortex had been destroyed by operation. These operated animals learned the habit as readily as the normal (control) rats, actually requiring only about three-fifths as much practice, as shown in Table X. This rather remarkable result may be partly explained by the fact that the operated rats showed

TABLE X

THE AVERAGE NUMBER OF TRIALS AND THEIR RANGE FOR
NORMAL AND OPERATED RATS IN LEARNING THE DOUBLE
PLATFORM BOX

(After Lashley, 1920)

Group	Injury	Average No. Trials	Range	No. of Animals	Average Per Cent of Brain-Destruction
1	Normal	142.6	63–204	10	0
2	One hemisphere destroyed ...	87.2	49–141	6	37
3	Occipital injury	68.8	45–107	4	28
4	Parietal injury .	80.0	41–101	5	22
5	Frontal injury .	90.0	90	2	16
6	Fronto-parietal injury	39.0	27–51	2	28
All operated rats		79.0	27–141	19	28

somewhat less distractibility and consequently a smaller
amount of random activity. Animals with brain injuries
jumped over the platforms less often than normal rats, more
often bumping into and eventually depressing them. The task
of opening the door of the food compartment also seemed to
be easier for the injured rats. Lashley found, for instance,
that operated rats slightly paralyzed and with motor disturbances required about 30 per cent less trials than other
operated rats which showed no motor defects. In certain
tasks, therefore, it appears that brain destruction actually
favors quick learning, but it does so by slowing up and
often drastically reducing voluntary activity.

In subsequent experiments rats first trained in the double
platform habit were subjected later on to operations which
destroyed various parts of their frontal and occipital brain
areas. The motor habit, though much disturbed, was not

totally lost as a result of such destruction. This finding suggests that normally the frontal lobes are active in the formation and retention of motor habits. But substitution of function by other areas is immediate and often remarkably effective.

Lashley has checked and extended many of his earlier results on learning and retention in rats. Tests of the learning ability and retention of both motor and sensory habits were made with four mazes of different pattern and with the brightness discrimination box shown in Figure 15. The experimental group was made up of fifty animals, all of which were subjected to brain operations involving from 1.5 per cent to 81 per cent of the total surface area of the cerebrum. A few of the more significant findings in these careful and large scale experiments may be summarized briefly. In substantiation of his earlier work, Lashley found (1) that the capacity to form motor habits (for example, to learn to run mazes) is reduced by brain destruction, the reduction being independent of the place of the injury but roughly proportional to the amount of destruction. The correlations between extent of cortical destruction and retardation in learning ranged from .70 to .80. (2) The more complex the problem set, the greater the effect upon learning produced by *any* given injury. (3) The habit of brightness discrimination is not greatly affected by cerebral lesions even when a considerable amount of the cortex is destroyed. The discrimination of visual forms and patterns such as circles, squares and the like is more affected by cortical lesions than is the brightness habit. (4) Retention of simple motor habits (learning mazes) after forty days is significantly impaired by cerebral injury. The degree of impairment depends chiefly upon the extent of the injury and the initial learning ability of the rat.

6. EQUIPOTENTIALITY AND MASS ACTION OF
THE BRAIN

Perhaps the most far-reaching result of Franz's and Lashley's experimental studies of the brain is their implication that the learning and retention of sensory and motor habits cannot be explained simply in terms of fixed nervous pathways, definite brain structures, or specific synaptic connections. Apparently, complex learned acts draw upon more extensive brain areas and depend more upon the total organization within the cortex than was formerly thought probable. Lashley has used the term "equipotentiality" to designate the capacity of an uninjured part of the brain to take over functions lost by destruction of other areas. Equipotentiality is subject to the law of "mass action"; that is, the efficiency of performance of any complex activity is reduced in proportion to the *amount* of brain injury—the mass of cortex destroyed—but is not dependent upon the integrity of any particular region. Equipotentiality seems to hold in subcortical as well as in cortical destruction. In one experiment, Ghiselli and Brown destroyed various subcortical regions in 45 rats. These animals were inferior to normal rats in learning an 18-unit maze, but no particular subcortical area proved to be indispensable to maze learning.

The brain of the rat is comparatively simple and undifferentiated as compared to that of the monkey or of man. It has been argued, therefore, that Lashley's results cannot be applied to higher species. It is true that to generalize from results obtained with the rat directly to man is fraught with danger. But experimental work with the higher apes, as well as studies of human beings whose brains have been injured by war or disease, have tended to confirm Lashley's theory of equipotentiality and mass action. In a study of the frontal associative areas in the ape, Jacobsen found that the loss of previously learned responses depended upon whether the lesion involved one or both frontal lobes. Further, in a study of monkeys, Jacobsen and Taylor report that the recovery of once learned activities depends upon the amount of injury to the frontal lobes. Complete recovery followed slight lesions; very little recovery followed large lesions. Jacobsen's results indicate that while there is evidence for equipotentiality in the ape's brain, the loss of specific memories (and the retention of others) following lesions of the frontal lobes argues for less mass action in the ape than in the rat. Pike and Chappell, in experimental studies of the effects of brain lesions in cats, report greater specialization of brain structures in cats than Lashley found in rats. These authors stress the importance of organization within the nervous system, and insist that certain structures have definite functions.

The importance of organization in restitution of function after brain injury is well illustrated in an experiment by Klüver. Monkeys were trained to discriminate between pairs of weights, sounds, visual forms and colors. In the method used the animals learned to pull into their cage by strings *one* of a pair of boxes upon which the stimuli to be discriminated were fastened. After the monkeys had learned the trick, the occipital, frontal, and parietal areas in different animals were destroyed by operation. For several weeks following recovery from the operation, the monkeys pulled in the boxes at random, seemingly having forgotten the discrimination habit completely. They were then carefully retrained with a pair of weights and again taught to make a comparison of the resistances offered by the two strings when first one and then the other was pulled. After this training, the animals were able immediately to make correct comparisons of the visual and other stimuli although these discriminations had apparently been completely lost. Training in the basic process of comparing enabled these animals to recover and to utilize lost or forgotten habits which depended upon it. Recovery of function after brain injury would seem, then, to depend upon a reorganization of available responses by training or otherwise as much as or more than upon the *amount* of still intact cortical tissue.

Many studies of the relationship of brain injury to mental disturbances in man give evidence of equipotentiality and mass action. An interesting example is the famous "crow bar" case, reported by Harlow in 1848, in which a laborer lost a large part of the frontal areas of his brain when a crow bar was driven through his head in a blasting accident. According to accounts this man showed little intellectual impairment after recovery, but his temper became more violent and his emotional control was lessened. Evidence of this sort is not, of course, always convincing. After the World War there were many cases in which patients having lost relatively large amounts of brain tissue were reported to have recovered completely. "Complete recovery" seems often to have meant no more than walking across the room and answering a few simple questions. In animal work the same loose statements concerning "normal behavior" are often found. After a brain operation an animal's behavior may appear to be entirely normal to the casual observer, even though careful tests show marked retardation in learning. In fact, the point should be emphasized, that *any* brain injury will affect behavior in some degree.

One of the most striking, and best documented, recent cases showing the effect of loss of brain tissues upon behavior has been described by Brickner. The patient was a successful business man in whom a brain tumor necessitated the removal of large areas of both frontal lobes. The patient apparently showed little loss of intellectual ability as a result of this drastic operation. He was able to remember old experiences and to form new associations; he could, for example, memorize poems, and solve mathematical problems. The patient did, however, show certain marked changes in emotional control and in personality. He was less inhibited and often silly in speech and action; also he became boastful and showed less regard for his friends and his family. In this man it appeared that the intellectual functions of the removed frontal areas were carried on by other parts of the brain. But there was a general loss in emotional control and less regard for social inhibitions.

By way of summary, it should be made clear that the concepts of equipotentiality and mass action do not mean that there is no localization of function in the brain. Certain brain areas have been definitely marked off and their functions are well known. The somesthetic and proprioceptive centers, for instance, are found in the parietal lobes and injury to these regions leads to loss of sensation in specific parts of the body. The motor areas are located in the frontal lobes and injuries here lead to loss of voluntary movements. Brain areas concerned with vision, audition, taste and smell are well established, and studies of *aphasia* have shown articulate speech to be in some way connected with structures in the parietal and temporal lobes. But no center for intelligent behavior or for learning has been localized, and it is in just such complex activities that substitution and transfer of function take place. Associations and learned acts must depend upon much more extensive brain patterns than was formerly thought probable. This may explain why a single operation does not greatly disturb a given pattern, but the greater the injury the greater the likelihood of disturbance. In restitution of function it seems reasonable to surmise that the associations have been reorganized following a break in the anatomical pattern.

It may seem as though we are returning to an older and

less analytic view to say that the brain "functions as a whole," but the work of Franz and Lashley make this view seem more probable than it once appeared to be. The brain, to be sure, is not a sponge, the parts of which are totally undifferentiated. As we have said, localization is an established fact. But our concepts of cortical areas must apparently be modified to allow for wide flexibility, and extended to permit of much functional identity of one part for another. The clinical as well as the experimental evidence indicates that equipotentiality found for the rat's brain holds within broad limits for the brains of cats, monkeys, and men.

7. ELECTROENCEPHALOGRAPHY OR THE STUDY OF "BRAIN WAVES"

The preceding sections have shown that while many functions have been localized within certain cortical areas, the brain itself possesses great adaptability and organizing power. Further evidence that the brain cannot be thought of as an intricate telephone exchange inserted between incoming and outgoing lines, merely waiting to be activated by visual, auditory, tactual and other stimuli, is provided by recent studies of "brain waves." The recording of brain waves is known technically as electroencephalography. The waves themselves are a result of spontaneous activity—much like pulsations or "beats"—within the brain itself. They may be obtained in the following way. First, a pair of electrodes is fastened to the head, one on the forehead the other on the back of the skull (other locations will also work); and these are connected with a kind of radio set containing amplifying vacuum tubes. The continuous electrical pulsations then picked up are recorded by writing points upon a moving strip of paper as "waves" or as up-and-down fluctuations.

These continuous electrical phenomena are classified as

alpha, beta, and delta waves. The alpha rhythms come at the rate of about 10 per second and are fairly regular in form. Beta waves are smaller in amplitude and faster than alphas; their average frequency is around 25 per second. Delta waves —much larger than alphas ordinarily and fairly regular— are quite slow, about 4–6 per second. Alpha waves are known to originate in the cerebral cortex itself while deltas arise in the underlying subcortical structures (the hypothalamus). Alpha and delta waves have been more carefully investigated than have the beta waves.

To the psychologist the question of greatest interest is the correlation of brain wave changes with psychological activities. The surface has hardly been scratched in this field, but already research has yielded much of value. Visual attention to any situation, even shutting and then opening the eyes, depresses the alpha rhythms; holding the eyes closed reinstates alpha activity again. The sound of a buzzer; working on an arithmetic problem; reading a book; carrying out instructions requiring choice, cause the alpha waves to decrease markedly in amplitude and often to disappear altogether. On the other hand, an unexpected question, a ready signal, completion of a task, apparently any sudden change in a person's "mental set," is accompanied by a sudden burst of alpha activity. In general, active attention tends to depress or thin out the alpha waves, while relaxation appears to produce renewed alpha activity. It seems a reasonable guess that the fall in alpha with increase in attention results from a sudden switching of energy from the brain centers and its redirection into muscular and sensory channels.

Decrease in alpha activity is usually accompanied by increase in beta and delta waves. This may be a balancing effect, owing to the fact that these waves and alpha have different origins within the brain; it may arise from the fact that different regions of the cortex have characteristic and different wave activity; and it may be an artifact due to the method of recording.

Other findings about brain waves are of value to the psychologist. In sleep, the alpha rhythm varies markedly and five levels corresponding to stages of sleep have been noted. Drugs, narcotics, changes in temperature and in oxygen supply also lead to characteristic and recognizable changes in brain wave activity. It has proved possible to locate brain tumors by detecting changes in the waves coming from different parts of the brain. Epilepsy and certain of the insanities are known to give distinctive brain wave patterns which should enable the physician eventually to understand these conditions better, to diagnose their severity and predict their progress. Since the delta waves come from the thalamic regions which are known to be active in emotional behavior, the possibility that these may serve as indices of emotional stress or pathological emotional conditions is now being explored.

Interesting studies of brain wave characteristics in hereditary feeble-mindedness have shown that the alpha rhythm becomes more and more normal with increase in mental age. This suggests that the variations in alpha activity found in normal children is a function of differences in mental age rather than of differences in chronological or life age. Much work is now in progress upon the recording and analysis of brain waves. As these phenomena become better understood, their value to psychology and medicine will increase.

Chapter 7

THORNDIKE'S EXPERIMENTS IN PROBLEM-SOLVING BY ANIMALS AND HIS "LAWS" OF LEARNING

I. THORNDIKE'S EXPERIMENTS IN ANIMAL LEARNING

Edward L. Thorndike's studies in animal psychology mark the beginning of the modern laboratory approach to problems of learning and habit formation. Thorndike began his work at Harvard, where as an undergraduate he did several experiments with chicks in the cellar of William James's home. Later, he came to Columbia to work in Cattell's laboratory; and in 1898 he received the doctor's degree in psychology, his dissertation embodying a series of studies under the title *Animal Intelligence: An Experimental Study of the Associative Processes in Animals*. Although he has retained his interest in animal psychology, for the past thirty-five years Thorndike has worked mainly in the field of educational psychology, where he has conducted a large number of important studies.

It must be admitted at once that prior to Thorndike much of the work with animals of such investigators as Lloyd Morgan, Lubbock, and Romanes, can rightly be called experimental even though performed without adequate laboratory control or special apparatus. For the most part, however, writers on animal psychology were contented with anecdotes and with uncontrolled although highly interesting observations of the doings of some pet dog or horse. Many of these accounts are impressionistic and highly colored, with little or no emphasis upon the stupidity shown by most animals. To be sure, animals were rarely credited with the ability to "reason" or "think"—this being usually considered to be exclusively a human accomplishment—but they were regarded as equal to many men, and superior to some, in their ability to form associations and build up habits. That they learned many things through imitation and the use of "ideas" seems not to have been questioned. As we shall see later, Thorndike's studies furnished experimental evidence which called into question these somewhat naïve views.

Although carried out with animal subjects, Thorndike's experiments have broad and important implications for human learning. Certain definite principles, for instance, have emerged from these studies which characterize quite accurately the way in which children and adults form new associations and learn new things. Thorndike's two fundamental laws of learning, the *law of exercise* and the *law of effect,* in spite of criticism and emendation, are still to-day the basis of modern pedagogical theory. And it is highly probable that they will long be regarded as among the most valuable empirical generalizations with which educational psychology must deal.

2. EXPERIMENTS WITH FISH AND CHICKS

Thorndike's experiments dealt with the learning ability of fishes, chickens, cats, dogs, and monkeys. The fishes, a common variety resembling the minnow, were kept in an aquarium measuring four feet by two feet, containing about nine inches of water. These fishes shun sunlight, and one end of the aquarium was covered over to protect them from light; here all food was given, and here the fishes remained most of the time. An experiment consisted in gently forcing a fish from the shady to the sunny end of the tank, by gradually moving across the tank a glass slide placed behind the fish to cut off

EDWARD L. THORNDIKE
(Born 1874)

its retreat. A second glass slide containing a small opening
was then placed between the fish and the shady end of the
tank. The object was to see whether the fish could find the
opening and escape. At the beginning, the fish's behavior,
motivated by its desire to escape from the sunlight, consisted
in swimming up and down the length of the slide, bumping
against it here and there, and looking for a place to get

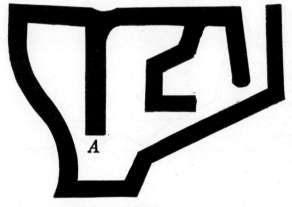

FIG. 17

PEN USED BY THORNDIKE IN STUDYING THE PROCESS OF LEARNING IN CHICKS

through. Eventually it came to the opening and swam
through to the shady section. Upon being replaced in the
same situation again and again, a fish soon indicated clearly
that it had profited by previous experiences, that is to say, it
swam more directly to the opening, with less and less loss of
time and fewer and fewer random movements. This experiment was repeated with a number of fishes, and with slides
containing openings at different points. Always the result was
the same—in every instance the fish ultimately learned the
trick of finding and getting through the opening in the slide.

From this experiment it is clear that learning, in the sense of simple connection-forming, can be experimentally demonstrated in vertebrates rather low in the evolutionary scale.

In his experiments with chicks, Thorndike used a number of pens or mazes, one of which is illustrated in Figure 17. When a chick is placed in section *A* of the maze, there are four possible exits as shown in the drawing. If the opening on

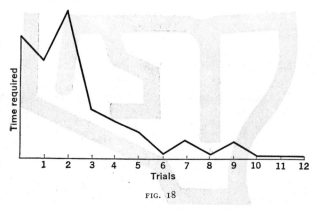

FIG. 18

LEARNING CURVE OF A CHICK

This curve shows the time required in successive trials to escape from the pen shown in Fig. 17. (From Thorndike, *Animal Intelligence,* 1911.)

the extreme right is followed by the chick to the second turn, it leads out of the maze and into an enclosure in which are other chicks and food. The other three exits are blind alleys. The problem is to see how long it will take a chick to select the pathway which will carry him out of the maze. The behavior of a chick when first placed in the pen resembles closely that of a fish which is trying to avoid the sunlight. Taken away from the other chicks and from food, and dropped into the pen at *A,* the chick runs back and forth, in and out of the blind alleys, peeps loudly, tries to jump out of the pen and to squeeze through any available opening. At length "by accident" it picks the right exit and gets out. Put back again and again, for the first few trials the chick's behavior is much as before; soon, however, it begins to eliminate useless movements, such as repeatedly entering the blind alleys, until finally it runs directly to the right exit. A good picture of how a chick learns the trick of escaping from such a pen as the one described is shown in Figure 18. In this figure the separate trials are laid off at equal distances along the horizontal axis, and the time required to escape is laid off on the vertical axis. As shown by the drop in the curve, after five or six trials the chick runs at once to the proper exit.

3. EXPERIMENTS WITH CATS, DOGS, AND MONKEYS

Thorndike's experiments with cats are his best known and most often quoted studies of animal learning. The task set for the cats was to escape from various "puzzle boxes," the general construction of which may be seen from Figure 19, p. 182. These boxes were so designed that escape from them could be effected in a variety of ways: e. g., by turning a button, pulling a string, depressing a lever, or pulling a wire loop. Each of these escape mechanisms, when operated by the animal, released a door which was at once pulled open automatically by a weight attached to it. Only one escape device was employed with the simpler boxes; with the harder ones, two or more separate acts, such as pulling a string and depressing a bar, were required to open the door. An experiment consisted in placing a hungry cat in the box with a small piece of fish or meat lying just outside. This situation usually resulted in immediate activity on the part of the cat. It tried to creep through the slats of the box; clawed at the bars of wire; thrust its paw through any opening large enough; worked vigorously at anything loose or movable, and in general gave a perfect picture of impulsive hit-or-miss effort to escape. In time the animal nearly always succeeded in operating the escape device (hitting the wire noose or turning the button) by accident, and getting out. It was then allowed to eat a bit of fish or meat, and immediately returned to the box for a second trial. During this next trial, and for several trials

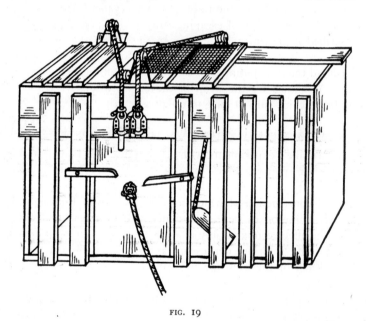

FIG. 19

PUZZLE BOX USED BY THORNDIKE IN LEARNING EXPERIMENTS WITH CATS

thereafter, the cat's plan of attack remained much the same as before; but in succeeding trials its activity became more and more restricted to the button or other escape device, and useless clawings and scratchings were gradually eliminated. Finally the animal, on being placed in the box, went almost at once to the door, worked the mechanism, and escaped.

A cat may make twenty or more trials and require an hour

or so to reach the point where its escape-responses are prompt, sure, and accurate. During this process, improvement is nearly always quite irregular, the escape time seesawing up and down until the act is well learned, whereupon the time becomes fairly regular. A learning curve of the time required in successive trials by one young cat to escape from a box kept

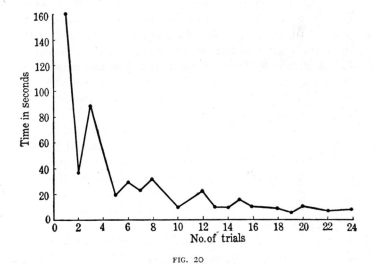

FIG. 20

LEARNING CURVE OF A CAT

The time taken by the cat to escape in successive trials is represented by the height of the curve; the successive trials are laid off along the horizontal base-line. (From Thorndike.)

closed by a single bolt attached to a wire loop is shown in Figure 20.

In the figure the twenty-four separate trials are represented by equal distances laid off along the horizontal axis; and the time in seconds is laid off on the vertical axis. Note the jagged appearance of the learning curve in the earlier trials as the time is first longer and then shorter; and the smoother appearance of the performance line as the cat learns the trick. This graph is fairly typical of animal performance in situations like the one described, and is a good instance of what is generally called "trial-and-error" or "trial-and-success" learning. Such learning begins as a varied hit-or-miss process and continues as such until the successful response is hit upon, as we say, "by accident." After this, elimination of the unsuccessful responses begins, together with a gradual building-in of the successful reactions. The cat whose performance is shown in Figure 20 was evidently learning in a slow and painstaking way to reduce its useless activities. At the same time the successful response of pulling the wire loop was becoming more and more firmly established.

Thorndike's account of how the cat escapes from the puzzle box has become the classical description of animal learning in situations like the one described. It has not escaped criticism by later experimenters, however, who object that cats exhibit much greater ability to think their way out of puzzle boxes than they are given credit for by Thorndike. In one careful experiment, in which Thorndike's boxes and conditions were closely duplicated, the cats' behavior showed much less excitement and "mad scramble" than appeared in Thorndike's cats. Less "random" movement was found and more direction of the escape activity toward specific objects (button, door, and the like). In another experiment with cats and boxes, the escape mechanism was kept standard and the act of escape recorded by a camera operated electrically by the escape mechanism itself. In getting out of this box the method of attack varied from cat to cat, but the behavior of a given cat (once the problem was solved) showed considerable rigidity or stereotypy. Again, there was less "randomness" than was exhibited by Thorndike's cats. These experiments amplify and amend, but do not controvert Thorndike's results. It seems likely that Thorndike overemphasized the aimlessness of his cats' activity and that his animals were frightened and not sufficiently acclimated to the puzzle box situation. Later reviewers, too, have tended to stress the excited and dramatic behavior of Thorndike's younger cats rather than the quieter behavior of his older and tamer cats. On the whole, it appears that trial-and-error is still the best characterization of feline learning in situations where the problem is new, strange, and not closely related to the animal's previous experience.

In some experiments with dogs, Thorndike used puzzle boxes of the same sort as those used with cats. The dogs, like the cats, employed the method of trial-and-error in seeking to escape, but on the whole their learning curves tended to be smoother, indicating better observation, a more planful attack, perhaps, and a somewhat higher level of intelligence. That dogs learn more quickly than cats, and somewhat less quickly than monkeys or raccoons, seems to be the consensus of investigators who have worked with these animals. However, the inferiority of the dog to the raccoon or even the monkey is not certain, since in many of the tests the dog is at a decided disadvantage because his paws cannot so easily manipulate mechanical devices as can the digits of the raccoon or monkey.

Experiments much like those described on dogs and cats were also carried out by Thorndike upon three small South American monkeys. These monkeys were tested to see how readily they could learn to operate simple mechanical devices so as to get into or out of boxes. In addition, they were taught to manipulate a simple mechanism by means of which food could be thrown into their cage. The results of these tests are interesting and quite definite. In almost every instance the monkeys quickly learned the trick—often at an astonishing rate, far surpassing in skill and speed both the dog and the cat. The superiority of the monkey in tests of this sort is probably to be expected, because as Thorndike points out, they have better vision than dogs or cats; and this advantage, plus the fact that they have fingers, would enable them to manipulate simple contrivances more easily than other animals. Beside these natural assets, monkeys are more active and more curious than other animals, and are quicker to play with and manipulate movable objects.

4. DO ANIMALS THINK OR REASON IN SOLVING PROBLEMS?

In spite of the superiority of monkeys over other animals both in speed and permanence of learning, they exhibited, says Thorndike, no real understanding of, nor "insight" into, the problem to be solved. This appeared to be even more nearly true of other animals. In fact, throughout his experiments Thorndike did not find any clear evidence that an animal ever "thinks its way through a problem," i. e., observes relations clearly, uses "ideas," makes inferences and comparisons. This conclusion came out most clearly in a series of experiments involving choice and discrimination. The monkeys had formed the habit of coming down to the bottom of the cage from their accustomed place near the top whenever the experimenter appeared with food. This habit was used to test the monkey's power of discrimination, in the following way. Whenever the experimenter picked up food with his left hand, the monkey was fed; but when he picked it up with his right hand, the monkey was never fed. At another time food was given when taken from a brown pasteboard box, and withheld when taken from a white crockery cover; or food was given at one visual signal (a large letter or geometrical figure), and withheld at another. The problem was to see whether, after having learned to discriminate between the food and the non-food signals, the monkey would get the general idea: *one stimulus means food, the other does not*. Evidence of insight or understanding into the situation might be expected to show itself if, after several discriminations of the kind described, the monkey perceived the relation almost instantly. On the other hand, if there were no clear abstraction of the principle of choice required, the monkey might be expected to take each discrimination as a new task to be solved by trial-and-error. This would, of course, show up in the large number of trials needed for each new task. The results of these tests were not entirely unambiguous, but their general implication seems clear. The monkeys learned some of the discriminations very quickly, but failed to learn others. Apparently they never formed a clear concept of what was essentially involved in *all* of the tasks in terms which they could use in governing their future behavior.

Later experimenters have disagreed with Thorndike's conclusion that monkeys (and other animals also) do not solve problems by reasoning and the use of "ideas." Part, at least, of this disagreement is undoubtedly a matter of definition. If by reasoning one means the free use of symbols—verbal and mathematical formulations—then either animals do not reason, or it would be hard to prove that they do. If, however, by reasoning one simply means the combining into one act (for example, of escape) of habits acquired upon different occasions in the past, then animals certainly do appear to reason. Maier found that white rats trained in two separate motor habits could later combine these experiences into one integrated and successful response, namely, getting food placed behind an obstruction. To be sure, this experiment presents some difficulties in interpretation. One cannot be certain that the habits *were* unrelated, or that the "new" behavior was actually a synthesis of the previous experiences. A somewhat more adequate attack upon the problem of reasoning in animals has been made through use of the *multiple choice method* devised by R. M. Yerkes. The general plan of the multiple choice apparatus is shown in Figure 21. The problem set the animal may best be made clear, perhaps, by an illustration. Suppose, first, that the doors to boxes 1, 2, and 3 are open, and that box 2 contains food. Next, doors 7, 8, and 9 are open and box 8 contains food; or boxes 3, 4, 5, 6, 7 are open and box 5 contains food. The task is to learn

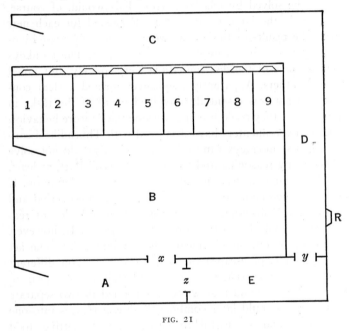

FIG. 21

PLAN OF MULTIPLE CHOICE APPARATUS

The animal is introduced at A, then released into B, the response compartment, and then it enters one of the reaction boxes, numbered from 1 to 9. If the choice is correct, the animal finds food in a cup at the rear of the box, or it may be released into C and D to find food at R. If the choice is incorrect, the animal may be confined for a short time in the box it enters, as punishment. From D the animal enters E to await the next trial. Sliding doors are provided at x, y, z, and at the front and rear of each reaction box. The entire apparatus is about 18 feet wide and 20 feet long. (Modified from Yerkes, p. 5.)

the constant relationship within the different situations. If the animal apprehends the principle or sees the relations involved (food = middle door) it readily solves the problems. Other problems investigated by the multiple choice method are those in which the food box is (1) at the right or left end of the series; (2) is second from the left or right; (3) is alternately at the left or the right end. Discrimination and abstraction of a high order are demanded by the hard problems. Comparative studies of various species have shown the monkey and the ape to be far superior to the rat and to most birds in ability to solve problems of the sort described.

The literally tremendous advantage over animals given to man by virtue of his possession of language is clearly shown in multiple choice problems. Once the principle of choice is discovered, one need only say "second from left" silently or aloud when the next combination of boxes is presented—trial-and-error is immediately ruled out. The advantage of language comes out clearly also in another well-known laboratory experiment—that involving "delayed reactions." The plan of an apparatus used in delayed reaction study is shown in Figure 22. When the animal is released from compartment E (which has glass at the front and on the sides), it learns, after a number of trials, that the lighted box contains food. The box selected for lighting varies, of course, in random order from trial to trial. The food in the lighted box furnishes the positive incentive for learning; a weak electric shock, which the animal gets before the unlighted doors, is the negative incentive. After an animal has learned the association (lighted box = food) it is placed in E and the light flashed as before in one of the three boxes. Then the light is turned off, the animal meanwhile being restrained for varying intervals in E before being released. The purpose of the delay is to see how long the animal can be held and still find the right box. Since the reaction cannot be to a stimulus which is present, it must be to some stimulus-substitute, an "idea" or other memory cue, perhaps a muscle- or postural-set. Comparative studies of the maximum period of delay, which is followed by success, have been made of white rats, cats, dogs, raccoons, monkeys, and apes. Conflicting results

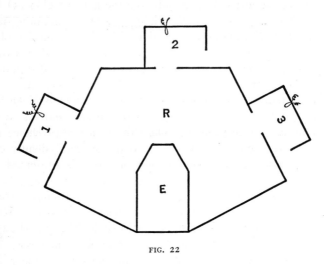

FIG. 22

PLAN OF DELAYED-RESPONSE APPARATUS

The animal is released from E into R, the response compartment, and then enters one of the reaction boxes, number 1, 2, and 3. These are lighted at the rear. (Modified from Hunter, p. 24.)

are reported owing in part, no doubt, to variations in experimental set-up. In several experiments, for instance, the food itself is the signal instead of the light; there is no training period in which the animal learns that light "means" food. Apes and monkeys can react successfully after longer periods of delay than can cats, dogs, or rats; but the white rat makes a surprisingly good showing as compared with dogs and cats.

The delayed reaction technique has been successfully used in similar experiments with young children.

One interesting finding in delayed reaction experiments is the importance of body and head orientation to rats and dogs. After the light has flashed, these animals tend to keep the body or head oriented (pointed) toward the box in which the light was last seen. When released, the animal then simply "follows its nose" to the food box—no memory cue is needed. If the animal's "position set" is disturbed—when the animal, while waiting, is turned around or forced to move—it is often still able to make correct choices, though at first it is much confused.

In summary, it can be said that whether or not one believes that animals solve problems by reasoning or the free use of ideas depends upon how one defines "reasoning" and "ideas." It seems clear that apes and monkeys—and even lower species, such as the rat, cat, and dog—are able to solve problems which demand a fairly high degree of abstraction, ability to discover relations, and the persistence of memory impressions. That animals make use of symbols or think with the aid of language as men do is highly improbable, but almost impossible either to prove or disprove.

5. DO ANIMALS SOLVE PROBLEMS BY "INSIGHT"?

Another line of evidence cited by Thorndike which is opposed to the thesis that animals think or reason is the fact that few sudden drops occur in the learning curves of his cats, dogs, and monkeys. Sudden drops show that the learner has got the point—seen the connections or relations—and henceforth may be expected to solve the problem correctly whenever the situation presents itself. Instead of this sudden insight, what Thorndike found was a gradual sloughing-off of excess and useless movements (see Figures 18 and 20), with no clear evidence that the animal observed how he got out or made use of these observations in future trials.

Thorndike's view that animals learn almost if not entirely by hit-or-miss methods, and have very little insight into the problem at hand, has been attacked by the German-American psychologist, Koffka, who belongs to the school of Gestalt psychology.* Köhler, another member of the Gestalt school, in his studies of learning in the chimpanzee, found many instances of quick learning which, he says, indicate that the ape suddenly grasped the relations involved in the problem. According to Thorndike, such quick learning (which presumably involves insight) is to be expected only when the task is "very simple, very obvious, and very clearly defined"; whenever the problem is at all complex, the animal's behavior, he thinks, may be fairly described as "stupid." In Koffka's view, on the contrary, the animal exhibits insight or intelligence whenever it is possible for it to grasp the problem; stupid errors, he says, occur when the task seems simple to us, but is almost surely not simple to the cat or chick. Koffka argues further that Thorndike's puzzle boxes set before the animals tasks so difficult (for the animal) that trial-and-error learning could be the only possible method of attack. In spite of the difficulty involved in these tasks, Koffka points out instances in Thorndike's own data when sudden vertical drops occur in the learning curve and these, he thinks, indicate insight into the problem.

It is probable that Thorndike overemphasized the stupidity of the animal attack upon a problem, partly, no doubt, because of the kind of problems which he set his animals. And it is equally probable that Köhler found insight in his apes because of the kind of problem which he set. Köhler's chimpanzees were assigned very different tasks from those required of Thorndike's monkeys and cats, and for this rea-

* See Chapter 8.

son the two sets of results are not directly comparable. For one thing, the chimpanzees were given much freedom, while Thorndike's animals were nearly always confined. Examples of the kind of tasks Köhler set the chimpanzees were (1) securing a banana suspended from the ceiling of a cage by piling up boxes one on another; (2) reaching for and pulling into the cage a banana placed outside by ingeniously hooking together two sticks. Many other tasks involved ropes, sticks, and the piling-up of boxes.* In such situations sudden learning might very well take place, if the animals are intelligent to begin with (as Köhler's chimpanzees undoubtedly were) and if the task is not too different from the kind of things which the animals habitually do. Again, *all* of the learning is not shown in the fluctuations of the learning curve. A sudden drop in the curve may be preceded by a long trial-and-error process, which is not represented in the curve, as when a man suddenly "sees the point" of a problem because of a long and varied experience with similar problems. The chimpanzee who suddenly does a trick which he could not do before has not necessarily seen through it in a sudden burst of comprehension. Many tentative trials and errors not shown in the learning curve and not seen by the experimenter may precede the solution.

6. DO ANIMALS USE IMITATION IN SOLVING PROBLEMS?

Before considering the experimental evidence for and against imitation in animals, it will be well to have clearly in mind just what is meant by the term. Suppose dog *A* barks and sets out after a passing cat, and is followed immediately by dog *B* who also barks and chases the cat. Is *B* imitating *A*? The proud owner of *A* will probably say yes, although it is more likely that *B* is simply responding to the same stimulus (moving-cat) as is *A*. Imitation is present

* See Chapter 8.

when a person or animal performs an act which is stimulated or instigated by observing similar behavior in another person or animal. To be genuine imitation must satisfy the following criteria: (1) the act to be imitated must be novel and unfamiliar, and not already part of the imitator's repertory; (2) the imitative behavior must follow immediately upon observation without evidence of trial-and-error behavior; (3) the imitative behavior must be a recognizable copy of the observed behavior. When learning occurs promptly under these conditions, the process may be fairly described as imitation.

Thorndike's statement that his animals gave little evidence of learning through imitation provokes astonishment and protest from many owners of pets. Yet his results point directly to this conclusion. When a cat, for instance, which had not learned to get out of a puzzle box was allowed to observe another trained cat, it made no difference whatever in the first cat's behavior. Nor did it make any difference when an untrained cat was placed in the box with a trained cat and allowed to escape when the second cat opened the door of the cage. The untrained cat still used the old hit-or-miss method as before; there was not the slightest evidence that learning had been speeded up through imitation. This same result was obtained in similar experiments with dogs and chicks. Even monkeys who had failed in their efforts to operate some simple mechanism were unable to do it after having seen a monkey or the experimenter do the trick many times. In one case a monkey was shown fifteen consecutive times how to open a box which contained food (the door was held shut by a simple lever). At the end of this training period, the monkey's efforts did not differ essentially from his previous attempts before tuition. In summing up his observations on imitation, Thorndike wrote: "Nothing in my experience with these animals, then, favors the hypothesis that they have any general ability to learn to do things from seeing others do them."

One may well inquire—if these observations are accepted —why monkeys are so generally believed to be accomplished imitators. Thorndike's answer is that monkeys, being active, curious, and possessed of a repertoire of movements much like ours, will inevitably do many things which seem almost human. He writes, "If you put two toothpicks on a dish, take one and put it in your mouth, a monkey will do the same, not because he profits by your example, but because he instinctively puts nearly all small objects in his mouth. Because of their general activity, their instinctive impulses to grab, drop, bite, rub, carry, move about, turn over, etc., any novel object within their reach, their constant movement and assumption of all sorts of postures, the monkeys perform many acts like our own and simulate imitation to a far greater extent than other mammals."

Recent studies of imitation in monkeys have questioned the sweeping character of Thorndike's findings. In one careful study of imitation in the monkey, two cages were placed side by side. In one cage was a monkey which had been trained to do various tasks: pulling a chain hanging down in front of the panel; opening a door in the panel by turning a knob; pushing down two latches and opening the door, and the like. In the other cage was an untrained monkey. Care was taken to give the untrained animal a clear view of the trained, as these investigators believed that Thorndike's animals were not given sufficient opportunity to observe the act to be copied. Now if the untrained monkey copied the trained one successfully within the one minute interval allowed— without fumbling or trial-and-error—imitation was judged to have taken place. In 70 per cent of the tasks set, the act was successfully performed—often within a few seconds. Contrary to Thorndike's results, these experiments indicate, therefore, that—under carefully controlled conditions—the monkey *is* capable of a high degree of imitative behavior. But a really favorable opportunity to imitate must be provided.

7. FIVE PRINCIPLES OF LEARNING

Thorndike has laid down five principles which serve to characterize animal learning as he observed it. These are as follows:

1. *Multiple response,* or varied reaction to the same external situation. This means that the animal brings to bear all of the instinctive and learned responses of which it is capable when faced by a new problem which it does not fully understand. It is the principle of trial-and-error learning.

2. *Set, Attitude, or Disposition.* Set, or attitude, is the internal "drive" or condition which predisposes the animal to a particular kind of behavior rather than some other kind. A hungry cat, for example, will try to escape from a puzzle box if food is outside, but a well-fed cat is usually content to remain quiet, unless much frightened or disturbed.

3. *Partial or Piecemeal Activity.* As learning proceeds, the animal gradually eliminates useless and unsuccessful movements and confines its activities to those objects or details which have hitherto proved to be of value. From a random and aimless activity, effort becomes more restricted, partial, and piecemeal.

4. *Assimilation or analogy* means that an animal when put into a new and strange situation will draw upon those activities which have proved successful in like or somewhat like situations.

5. *Associative Shifting.* This principle is the same as that of the "conditioned response." It means that, in time, the animal will shift its response from the general situation, box or maze, to some element or detail of the total which possesses value, or from the original stimulus to some fact as-

scciated with it. Ordinary animal tricks by the score furnish illustrations of this principle. The cat taught first to come when a saucer of milk is held in the hand will after a few times respond to the sight of the empty saucer or to the person who does the feeding. In like manner a dog or monkey can be taught to sit up and beg when a command only is given. It is said that bears are taught to dance to music by being placed upon hot grills while music is played. Shifting of response from one stimulus to another, or from the total situation to some part of it, enormously expands the animal's range of responses. This increase in range of response is of fundamental importance in human as well as in animal learning (p. 131).

One of the most striking instances of seemingly intelligent learning in an animal, which is explainable in terms of associative shifting, is that of the famous German horse, Clever Hans. Hans, a five-year-old horse, was trained by his owner Herr von Osten to answer questions and solve problems. A letter system was constructed on a numbered chart to enable Hans to give his replies; if the letter m, for example, occurred in the fourth vertical column and the second horizontal row of the chart, four taps with the left hoof and two with the right meant m. In solving numerical problems, taps with the right hoof meant units and taps with the left hoof meant tens. Thus 53 was represented by five taps with the left hoof and three with the right. By means of these methods, Hans was able to demonstrate his ability to solve problems and answer questions ordinarily requiring considerable intelligence. The wide interest aroused in Hans's performance led finally to his being examined at successive times by two commissions. A psychologist on the second commission named Pfungst apparently solved the mystery of Hans's answers. He showed that the horse responded to involuntary "cues" or signals given by his trainer, such as slight (approving) movements of the head, changes in facial expression, and the like. Thus if the answer to a problem were 68, Hans would count rapidly with his left hoof until some small (and almost certainly unintentional) signal from his trainer warned him to stop and begin with the other hoof. The trainer, therefore, was himself the substitute stimulus to which the clever horse responded.

Hans was later acquired by another owner and became one of the group of famous Elberfeld horses. One of these horses, an Arabian named Mohammed, was reputed to be able to extract square and cube roots besides performing the simpler arithmetic operations of addition, subtraction, multiplication, and division. No satisfactory proof seems to have been brought forward to show that these horses were responding to cues, but such seems undoubtedly to have been the case. For one thing, these horses learned too quickly to justify the explanation that they had any real understanding of the problem; they took no longer to solve hard problems than easy ones; often they would begin tapping without even glancing at the problem set up before them. Again, the kind of mistakes made were not those of an intelligent calculator; common errors were reversals of figures such as 36 for 63, or errors of one unit such as 26 for 25. These errors might easily happen if the horse temporarily confused the left and right hoof or failed to stop tapping quite soon enough. All of the evidence, then, is emphatically against the opinion that performances of clever animals really indicate mathematical genius or intelligence of a high order. Such "stunts" do show, however, that animals are extremely clever in picking up very slight cues and signals not readily observed by onlookers, who, of course, are not usually watching out for them.

All of the principles outlined in this section apply with but little modification to human learning. When placed in a totally new situation or faced by a complex and little-understood problem, the behavior of a man will differ very little from that of a dog, cat, or monkey. His activity at first is largely of the trial-and-error type, as he draws upon the reservoir of his past experiences for a possible solution of his immediate difficulty. Multiple response growing out of some set or disposition finally passes over into piecemeal activity, as certain features of the problem offer greater hope of success than others. Associative shifting (conditioned response) is common in human learning. Many illustrations come to mind: a young man has an unreasonable distaste for orange juice because it has at some time in the past been used as a "disguise" for castor oil; a child is fearful of the dark after having heard fantastic ghost stories; a college student cannot listen to hymns because of their association with his mother's funeral. Teaching a child that C A T "means" a small furry animal, and that notes on a chart "stand for" keys on a piano, are examples of associative shifting.

A good illustration of human learning in situations which are roughly analogous to Thorndike's puzzle boxes is found in some experiments with difficult Chinese ring puzzles. Learning curves for these puzzles look very much like those of Thorndike's cats, dogs, and chicks; but instead of the irregular rise and fall observed in animal learning curves, sudden drops are frequent. These, according to the subjects' reports, occurred when conscious analysis took place or when insight was reached into the mechanical features or principles of the puzzle.

There is a distinct gap between the things which men and animals *can* learn and the *rates* at which they acquire new habits. Very soon in the course of human learning, often at the very beginning, men begin to use verbal formulations. Alternatives are accepted or rejected symbolically, rather than by concrete trial-and-error; principles are perceived and applied; insight into the problem is gained. The ability to formulate general principles, evolve concepts, and educe abstract relations would seem to be strictly a human accomplishment.

8. LAWS OF LEARNING: THE "LAW" OF EXERCISE

Out of his experiments with animals grew Thorndike's two fundamental laws of learning, *the law of exercise* and *the law of effect.* These "laws" developed logically from the traditional laws of association (p. 127). The law of exercise, which is often called the law of habit formation, has two parts, one of which is the complement of the other. The first part, *the law of use,* may be stated simply as follows: When a given situation is frequently followed by a certain response or group of responses, the bond or linkage between stimulus and response becomes stronger through the exercise so obtained. The law of use is clearly shown in the learning curves of Figures 18 and 20. When once it has learned the knack of escaping from the box or pen, the movements of the chick or the cat become faster and smoother as they are more and more often repeated.

The opposite of the law of use is the law of disuse: When a given situation is rarely followed by a certain response, the association between the stimulus and this response is weakened, its degree of weakness depending upon the amount of neglect. For instance, the tendency to enter a blind alleyway —strong at the beginning of the learning period—becomes progressively weaker through the cumulative effect of disuse.

Numerous applications of the law of exercise to human learning will at once come to mind. Learning to skate, to drive an automobile, or to run a typewriter consists in getting the right movements in their proper sequence *first,* and then rehearsing them until they run off rapidly, smoothly, and accurately. This is true also of verbal learning. In order to learn well a French vocabulary, a poem, or a set of mathematical formulas, it is necessary to repeat (i. e., exercise) the elements of the task in their right order regularly and often.

Thorndike's formulation of the law of exercise has been criticized by many psychologists as being too mechanical, and as not giving adequate consideration to other factors in the situation—motives, interests, special training and the like. Studies of *incidental memory,* that is, memory for things and events not specifically attended to, have shown how little one may really know about many things constantly around him. A man looks at his watch many times a day, but cannot tell (when asked) whether the numerals on the watch face are Roman or Arabic; many people cannot report at all accurately the color or size of a paper dollar, or the number or color of the license plates on their cars; others cannot even describe their cars with fair accuracy. The school room offers much evidence of the ineffectiveness of mere repetition. The story is often told of the boy who had formed the bad habit of saying "I have went." In order to correct this habit, he was required by his teacher to remain after school and write "I have gone" 100 times. Having completed his task and finding the teacher gone, he left the following note: "I have written 'I have gone' 100 times and since you are not here, I have went home." This boy evidently did not see any connection between *writing* "I have gone" as a chore and *saying* "I have gone"; and the exercise without this understanding had been of no value. Pupils do not learn when they are uninterested in school work, and when they fail to see any relationship between arithmetic and history as taught in the school and business and political conditions as found in the everyday world. The examples given above—and many more might be cited—demonstrate clearly that mere frequency of the stimulus-response connection is not in and of itself sufficient to produce learning.

The law of exercise has recently been subjected to a rigorous series of experimental tests by Thorndike. "Exercise" is now best regarded as a principle which describes how *skill* is acquired under certain conditions, rather than as a "cause" of learning. Conditions for efficient learning include active effort on the part of the learner, interest, feelings of satisfaction, and belief in the appropriateness and value of the task.

Under the law of exercise belong several sub-laws or corollaries which readily follow from it. These are the principles of *frequency, recency,* and *vividness.* The *"law" of frequency* emphasizes the cumulative effect of repetition or repeated effort. Improvement in a given function is usually fairly rapid at first. Sooner or later, however, the "physiological limit" is reached, beyond which additional repetitions have little beneficial effect. This is as true of learning poetry or the multiplication table as it is of learning to skate or dance; continued application is necessary up to a certain point, but after that it is probably of little value (p. 266). The principle of frequency must be interpreted with due regard for the limitations listed above under the law of exercise.

The *"law" of recency* refers to the commonly observed fact that performances recently learned or practised are smoother and less subject to error than those unpractised for some time. Most busy adults have completely forgotten the algebra and Latin learned in high school or college (unless they happen to be teachers!); but they remember the necessary details of their business or profession. The negative side of the law of recency is covered by the law of disuse. Activities once learned but not recently practised tend to deteriorate with the passing of time.

The *"law" of vividness or intensity* means that active and interested activity is more beneficial than passive and perfunctory repetition. If the learner sets out vigorously and with determination to learn a given task, if he has, as William James puts it, "the will to learn," he will progress more rapidly than if he simply sits passively, hoping that somehow the desired information will sink in. The law of vividness will explain why a boy learns his Scout Manual and the fine points of baseball more quickly than he learns to play the piano or recite his Sunday-school lesson.

All of these principles of learning are illustrated in modern advertising. Over and over again (frequency and recency) by newspaper, magazine, radio, and flashing electric sign (vividness), we are told about the merits of some particular cigarette or tooth-paste. As a result of this bombardment, most of us have become familiar with the names and slogans of many articles and "brands" and this very familiarity predisposes us to the purchase of these products. In the school room, the operation of these laws may be readily observed. For example, there is drill and repetition (frequency); constant review and recitation (recency); and finally, the attempt is made to relate the subject-matter of mathematics or literature in as many ways as possible to the everyday needs and interests of the student (vividness).

9. THE LAW OF EFFECT

The *law of effect* may be stated most simply, perhaps, as follows: When a response or series of responses leads to success or to a satisfying state of affairs, the connection between the situation and this response is strengthened, while other responses not so satisfying (i. e., annoying) are weakened and hence rendered less probable of recurrence. The law of effect is really prior to the law of exercise, since it explains *how* the successful response came to be selected in the first place. This is clearly evident in the instances of animal learning which we have cited. When a cat, for example, in learning to escape from a puzzle box, makes a variety of responses most of which are useless, one might expect from the law of exercise alone that *all* of these responses would be equally bound up with the situation "trying to escape from the puzzle box." Hence, all would tend to be repeated. Instead of this, however, the successful response, namely, pulling the loop or turning the button of the cage, soon gets the upper hand, while the useless responses are dropped out. Reference should be made again to Figures 18 and 20. Note how the escape of the cat or chick becomes faster and smoother as the animal goes more and more promptly to the proper exit. The successful response—that is to say, the one which leads to food or comrades—once having been made, exercise soon enables it to supplant the unsuccessful reactions. Suppose that five cats have been taught to come to the call "kitty, kitty." Now suppose that later on, upon being called, cat no. 1 is given some fish and is petted; cat no. 2 is petted only; cat no. 3 is totally disregarded; cat no. 4 is sprinkled with water; and cat no. 5 is doused heavily with water. What will happen the next time these cats are called? Prediction is easy. Cat no. 1 will come quickly and promptly when called; cat no. 2 will probably come, but not so promptly; cat no. 3 may come, also, but still less promptly; cat no. 4 may try it once more, but if sprinkled again will surely give it up; cat no. 5 will not only fail to come, but (if he is a normal cat) will run in the opposite direction. Here the end-effect—what happens to the cat—is the primary factor in guiding behavior.

Thorndike's law of effect has not escaped criticism at the hands of other experimenters. The most frequent objection seems to hinge on the difficulty in seeing just how the satisfaction which comes *after* the successful response could possibly work backward so as to "stamp in" this one response or make it more probable than some other. This problem is really *the* fundamental problem of learning, since it deals with the basic question of why we retain some responses and lose others. It has excited investigators for thirty years or more, and has been subjected to analysis from many points of view. A practical explanation of many instances of learning is that the successful response (the one which is retained) and the resulting satisfaction occur together, or so nearly together that they are essentially parts of the same process. The successful movements and the satisfaction which they bring are so closely associated—in time or place or through their relatively greater intensity—that the successful movement comes to "mean" or "stand for" the satisfying effect. The substitution of one response for another and the linking-up of the second or substitute response with the original situation through repetition is the familiar principle of associative shifting or conditioned response. In many cases, therefore, the conditioned response and the laws of effect and exercise are really two ways of describing the same phenomena.

10. SUMMARY ON THE LAWS OF EXERCISE AND EFFECT

If satisfying states are taken to mean those which lead to positive approach-behavior, and annoying states are those which predispose to avoidance and retreat, the law of effect would seem to be adequate to explain nearly all learning as we find it in a practical and understandable way, i. e., to explain why some responses are retained and some are not. If the results of our behavior are pain, punishment, social disapproval, regret, and failure, the acts which lead to such annoying states are not repeated by the normal person. On the other hand, responses which bring food, comfort, kindly treatment, praise, and success will be repeated and through repetition (exercise) become more rapid and more certain. In those cases in which learning takes place although apparently not followed by satisfaction, but even by indifference or actual annoyance, it may be true that behavior of the opposite sort would be still more dissatisfying. The boy who dutifully practises his music lesson, often has an ulterior motive which is not wholly inconsistent with the law of effect. And it is probable, too, that the life of a martyr is not entirely devoid of psychological rewards.

It often happens, of course, that the end-result, i. e., the effect, while providing self-satisfaction to the individual concerned, is actually injurious, or is socially disapproved or morally hurtful. Numerous examples could be brought forward to illustrate this situation. If a baby is fed or caressed whenever it cries; if the small boy is given money or candy whenever he whines or teases; and if the bully is applauded and feared by the other members of his group, such unfortunate behavior, because satisfying to the individual concerned, will tend to persist. To change or alter it, the end-effect must be made unsatisfying. Social disapproval, the withholding of something valued or desired by the child, mild punishment, or the substitution of new interests at once satisfying and more healthful, are common methods employed. Prizes, medals, the honor-roll, and other forms of approbation are some of the traditional ways in which the school has utilized the law of effect. The modern school has attempted to make the results of industry and application seem worth while in themselves to the child. To reach this end, it strives to get the desired responses and then through active and vigorous exercise to build them in. This is the fundamental problem in the psychology of learning, and it involves essentially the laws of exercise and effect.

Chapter 8

KÖHLER'S EXPERIMENTS IN PERCEPTION AND LEARNING AND THEIR IMPORTANCE FOR GESTALT PSYCHOLOGY

I. THE MEANING OF GESTALT PSYCHOLOGY

The point of view and method of interpretation represented under the name Gestalt psychology, had its rise in Germany as recently as 1912. Max Wertheimer is generally credited with being the founder of the movement in Germany, but Kurt Koffka, formerly of the University of Giessen, and Wolfgang Köhler and Kurt Lewin, formerly of Berlin, through academic appointments in this country have become the principal champions of the Gestalt viewpoint in America.

Perhaps the simplest way of describing just what this school of psychology stands for is to indicate first what it is not. "The psychologist," says Titchener, "seeks, first of all, to analyze mental experience ('consciousness') into its simplest components." "The rule, or measuring rod, which the behaviorist puts in front of him," says Watson, "always is: Can I describe this bit of behavior I see in terms of stimulus and response?" To both of these programs, Gestalt psychologists stand strongly opposed. It is bad psychology, they say, to contend that the complex behavior of men or of animals can be explained genetically as an accumulation of specific S-R bonds—the so-called "bundle hypothesis." And it is equally invalid, they hold, to apply strict analysis to complex sensory data with the expectation of finding some fundamental psychological "atom" out of which experience is built. To the Gestalt psychologist sensory elements appear only after careful and somewhat "unnatural" introspection. The *real* data of experience are organized and extended wholes, never mosaics; we do not encounter specific elements either in consciousness or in behavior. And so instead of the world being to the infant "a big, blooming, buzzing confusion" (William James) from which here and there bits must be laboriously picked out and tied together by the process of association, even for the very young child, there is—according to this view—a certain degree of orderly arrangement in sensory data to which he may respond without previous learning. Later on adults react not to specific stimuli but to tha pattern or total organization of objects around them. These Gestalten or configurations, as the word has been translated, are the true "mental elements." For this reason, Gestalt psychology studies the organization of these unitary experiences; how they come about; what "laws" govern their changes; and upon what factors they depend.

2. STUDIES OF VISUAL PERCEPTION

The first problem attacked by the Gestalt psychologists was that of how we perceive apparent movement. All of us know that when pictures which differ slightly follow each other in rapid succession we see *movement*—not a series of separate and distinct "stills." This common observation was the basis of Wertheimer's classical experiments on apparent movement. The principle of these experiments will be made clearer by an illustration (Fig. 23). Suppose that through a vertical aperture light is thrown at short regular intervals upon a screen in a darkened room, thus producing a series of flashing white lines against a black background. Now, if a second beam of light is projected through a second aperture,

Courtesy of Clark University Press

WOLFGANG KÖHLER

(Born 1887)

slightly to the *right* of the first, and somewhat later in time, logically it would seem, we should see first one and then the other of *two* parallel lines, the one to the right of the other. When the time interval between the first line and the second line is relatively *long,* this is exactly what we do see. But a very different result *may* be obtained. If the timing is car-

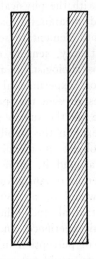

FIG. 23

TO ILLUSTRATE THE PHI-PHENOMENON

fully adjusted, the observer sees not *two* lines, but a single line oscillating or "jumping" from side to side. The addition of the second line changes greatly the stimulus-value of the first. Instead of a simple addition of stimuli, what we perceive is a complex fusion which cannot be analyzed into two separate lines.

The appearance (under these conditions) of movement for which there is no physical basis was called by Wertheimer the *phi*-phenomenon.* *Phi* illustrates what is meant by perceptual Gestalten. From the Gestalt viewpoint, the value of this phenomenon lies in the fact that it shows our perception of apparent movement to be an unique and unanalyzable experience, not a rubber-stamp impression of nature. It is evident, say the Gestaltists, that our experiences do not correspond point-for-point with the physical stimuli. Rather they fall into coherent and meaningful patterns which cannot readily be separated into elementary sensations and images. According to Gestalt theory, sensory elements are not the units with which the psychologist can most profitably work.

It is likely that most experimental psychologists would now agree with the Gestalt view that perceptions are "whole experiences" which are not the sum of their parts. But they would be inclined to explain the stability and constancy of our perceptions of an object (its meaning) by the variety of associations built up around it, rather than by appeal to some principle of inherent organization. Thus, one's visual perception of a rose would be attributed to a complex of associated olfactory, tactual and other stimulations, plus personal and emotional experiences and verbal descriptions. With this explanation of perception in terms of association the Gestalt psychologists would not concur. They deny that objects and events have meaning for the observer only in so far as he is able to bring past experience to bear upon them. On the contrary, they insist that all experiences have form, pattern, and meaning because their elements "come" organized. And they point to the fact that except perhaps in disease and some forms of insanity, no psychological experience is ever totally unorganized.

This inherent organization of experience is illustrated,

* Wertheimer's experiments on the *phi*-phenomenon have been repeated by several investigators under various conditions. His essential results have been substantiated.

Köhler thinks, in those cases wherein persons born blind later acquire sight. It is to be noted, he says, that while such individuals do not recognize geometrical forms, e. g., squares and circles, *as such,* they do *understand* the question when asked what a given form is. This must mean, according to Köhler, that organizations and arrangements of the visual field are present even though the stimulus situations are not yet tagged with verbal symbols (with names). An adult born blind, whose sight has been restored, is able to identify a coin lying on his palm. He may call the coin a quarter, perhaps inaccurately, but he distinguishes the coin as being something apart from his hand.

The visual field is chaotic, relatively speaking, when there are serious brain lesions or diseased conditions in the optical centers of the brain, so that only separate bits can be grasped visually at one time. Köhler cites a study made by Gelb and Goldstein of a patient suffering from brain injury. This man had learned to rely upon motor and kinesthetic experiences to piece out his visual data. When his name was written in large letters, and presented to him, he would perceive the first few letters as a group and then guess the remainder from the context and from the amount of movement needed to span the whole name. But if several lines were drawn across his name, as shown in Figure 24, the patient could no longer see the letters as a *name.* Since he did not see his name as an organized perceptual unit, the lines drawn in over the letters were mixed indiscriminately with the letters. What the patient saw was a single confused pattern—not two separate and independent groupings—one of lines *and* the other of letters. Nothing was added from other parts of the field to give the letters complete organization and in consequence no Gestalt (name) appeared.

Perhaps it should be said at this point that while some primitive form-sense (inborn perceptual Gestalts) *may* exist apart from experience, such an assumption is not necessary to explain the facts of perception. The retina furnishes an area upon which objects are spread out in two dimensions. To the spatial cues from this source, other sensory experiences add associations which lend meaning to our perceptions. Certain experiments have shown that learning is at least as important as native factors in judgment of distance and depth (see Chapter 13). And learning certainly gives meaning and value

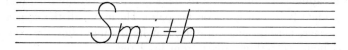

FIG. 24

TO ILLUSTRATE THE EXPERIMENT OF GELB AND GOLDSTEIN

to our understanding of the objects themselves. Basic "native" Gestalts may, of course, exist. But they must still be accounted hypothetical rather than proven facts.

3. SOME PRINCIPLES GOVERNING THE FORMATION OF PERCEPTUAL GESTALTS

To the Gestalt psychologist, the distinction between "figure" and "ground" is decidedly important in the psychology of perception. Every Gestalt exists as a figure *against* a more general, and usually vaguer, background. In auditory perception, for example, a melody is heard against a background of silence or against a vague mixture of miscellaneous noises. And in the same way, every visual configuration, a sunset or a prize-fight, is projected against a larger and less clearly defined background.

The figure-ground relationship has been carefully studied in the sphere of visual perception. Ambiguous figures in which figure and ground are interchangeable serve to define most clearly the distinction between these two factors. Figure 25 shows an ambiguous geometrical construction. Note that the four-pointed "cross," the one composed of radii, "stands out" rather easily as a Gestalt against the concentric circles which form the ground. Now interchange figure and ground by fixating intently upon the circles, and note that the arcs

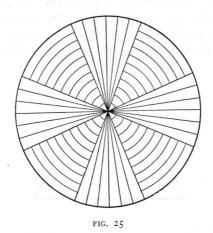

FIG. 25

AN AMBIGUOUS FIGURE TO ILLUSTRATE FIGURE-GROUND RELATIONSHIP

(From Koffka.)

in the *new* figure, again a four-pointed "cross," are *true* arcs, i. e., cut-off sections of circumferences, whereas before they were visible parts of unbroken circles. The circles behave differently depending upon whether they are in the figure or in the ground. Following the lead of Rubin, Gestalt psychologists have developed other characteristic differences which they believe serve to distinguish figure and ground. The figure is more clearly formed than the ground, (i. e., has better structure) and is more resistant to change; is more vivid; holds its color better; is more solid and more substantial.

Koffka illustrates the principles of figure-ground relationship in the following way. Look, he says, through a stereoscope at a slide which to the one eye presents a solid blue, and to the other a circle made up of alternate blue and yellow sectors. The yellow "slices" easily stand out against the blue ground in the single figure which results; but the blue sectors have a hard time of it as "figure" against a yellow background, being overwhelmed by the surrounding blue.

The drawing in Figure 26 illustrates another principle stressed by the Gestalt psychologists, namely, that of "clos-

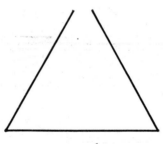

FIG. 26

THE FIGURE IS SEEN AS A COMPLETED TRIANGLE, AN ILLUSTRATION OF CLOSURE.

ure." The figure is seen at once to be a triangle, although it has only two true angles. Our drawing, to be sure, is not closed; but the direction that closure will take is so clearly indicated that reaction is immediate and undisturbed. Had this figure been exposed for a fraction of a second on a screen, the opening would not have been perceived at all. Another illustration of the phenomenon of closure is given in Figure 27. If one gazes intently at the staircase it suddenly turns upside down and becomes a staircase viewed from underneath or a piece of overhanging masonry. When the "new" figure leaps into view closure is said to have taken place. The puzzle pictures for children in which one searches through a maze of lines for a man's face (which suddenly appears) illustrates the same phenomenon. The meaningful figure, when it emerges, is seen as a totality and not piece-meal. In the interval during which one is seeking for a solu-

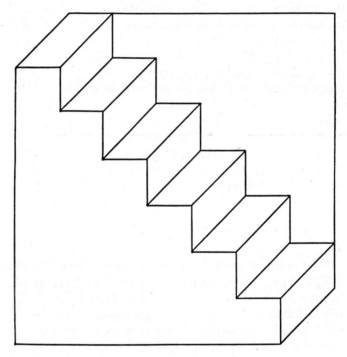

FIG. 27

THE AMBIGUOUS STAIRCASE FIGURE, ILLUSTRATING CLOSURE

tion—before closure—there is decided discomfort and even tension and nervousness.

The explanation of closure given by the Gestalt psychologists is that, first of all, there is an inherent tendency toward "form" and meaning in all of our perceptions. Furthermore, this tendency is so strong that when the external situation is incomplete or confused we strive to complete it and are dissatisfied until we do. Closure is a special case of the "law of Prägnanz" (usually translated "pregnance"). According to this law, every experience (perceptual or otherwise) tends to complete itself and to become as "good as possible." Thus, our perceptions of the drawings in Figures 26 and 27 exhibit a decided tendency to arrive at a condition of maximum simplicity. Closure and the law of Prägnanz are used by Gestalt psychologists as explanatory principles in learning as well as in perception. Thus, the solution of a problem or the attainment of a goal brings closure and ends the active search of the learner.

4. LEARNING FROM THE VIEWPOINT OF GESTALT PSYCHOLOGY

The Gestalt psychologists have not confined themselves to studies of perception, but have extended their methods and interpretations into other areas. Particularly in studies of animal learning, they have many experiments to their credit which are of value whether interpreted according to Gestalt principles or not. To many psychologists these experiments seem more substantial and less artificial, perhaps, than much of the perception work. As illustrative of the Gestalt attack upon learning, several experiments of Köhler will be described.

The question whether in learning we respond to specific stimuli in the environment (strict S-R bonds) or to the *relations* among such stimuli is of practical as well as theoretical concern. In 1915 Köhler attempted to answer this question in the following interesting experiment. First he trained two hens (birds which are generally notorious for their lack of intelligence) to expect food from the darker only of two papers (one dark and one light) glued side by side on

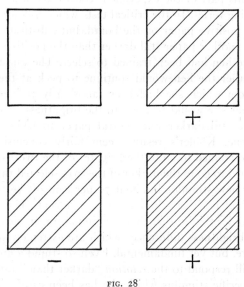

FIG. 28

TO ILLUSTRATF KÖHLER'S EXPERIMENT

a wooden board (see Fig. 28). The hen was placed in a wire coop on one side of which apertures were so arranged that the fowl could easily thrust its head out to peck grain from the paper-covered board next to the coop. Grain was scattered in equal amounts upon both papers. Whenever the hen pecked at the grain upon the dark or positive paper she was allowed to eat, but whenever she pecked at the grain upon the light or negative paper, she was at once shooed away.

After 400 to 600 trials in which the positions of the positive and negative papers were frequently interchanged to prevent any association by the fowl of the positive stimulus with the right or left side, the hen at last learned to select the positive and to avoid the negative stimulus with great regularity. This part of the experiment constitutes what is called the training series. In the critical tests which followed Köhler kept the positive paper on the board, but substituted for the negative another paper still darker than the positive stimulus which the hen had been trained to select. The question now was whether the hen would continue to peck at the *specific* paper from which she had been laboriously trained to eat, or whether she would respond to the brightness *relation* and select the still darker but neutral paper to which she had never gone. Köhler's results seem fairly conclusive. Four hens, two trained to go to the brighter of the two papers and two trained to go to the darker of the two, selected the neutral paper or new stimulus in about 70 per cent of the trials and the original positive stimulus in 30 per cent. These results show, Köhler thinks, that there are in nature simple organizations of brightness differences which are extremely primitive, to be sure, but yet fundamental. Even so stupid a creature as a hen will respond to the *relation* "darker than," rather than to the specific stimulus which she has been carefully trained to select.

Köhler repeated this experiment with chimpanzees and also with a three-year-old child. The child was allowed to learn by the method of trial-and-error that only the brighter of two colored boxes contained candy. Forty-five trials were necessary in order to establish this differential response to the point where no errors were made, i. e., the brighter was always chosen. In the critical tests which followed, a new and still brighter box was presented with the old positive stimulus, the negative darker box now being removed. Köh-

ler reports that in this series the child "invariably" took the
new bright box, instead of the one in which it had formerly
found candy. This again is good evidence, he says, that human beings react toward situations as *related wholes,* and
not to bits or portions of the environment.

Köhler's ape experiments—which are perhaps his best
known—were conducted during the years 1913–1917, upon
the small island of Tenerife, located in the Canary Islands, a
short distance off the African coast. Here a colony of chimpanzees was established, and owing to the isolated and trop-
ical nature of the country, experiments could be carried on
under conditions closely resembling those of the animal's native habitat. In one experiment a chimpanzee was not fed in
the morning as usual, but instead his food was fastened to
the roof of his cage and a box thrown casually upon the floor
of the cage some distance from the point where the fruit
hung suspended. The ape had never used a box as an implement, and hence ignored it completely. He could easily
have reached the fruit, however, by pulling the box under the
fruit and climbing upon it. The animal spent many hours in
unsuccessful effort, trying to reach the fruit by jumping up
toward it, climbing up the walls, and the like. Finally the
experimenter dragged the box over beneath the suspended
fruit, stepped upon it, reached up and touched the banana.
He then got down and placed the box some distance away.
Almost immediately the chimpanzee pulled the box over under the fruit, climbed upon it, and pulled down the food. A
variation of this experiment was tried by Köhler with another ape which he considered particularly stupid. This animal had often seen other chimpanzees use boxes as platforms
from which to reach food, but he had never actually done
the trick himself. To see whether he had learned from his
fellows what to do when put into a situation requiring the
employment of a box as a platform, Köhler fastened a ba-

nana to the roof of his cage, threw in a box, and left the
animal to his own devices. The ape's subsequent behavior is
quite enlightening as a demonstration of how hopeless the
solution of even a simple problem may be unless the relations involved are clearly apprehended. This monkey at once
ran to the box, but instead of dragging it under the fruit, he
either climbed upon it and jumped up, or else climbed upon
the box, hopped down, and quickly ran over to jump up from
the ground under the fruit.

This experiment, says Köhler, shows how necessary for
learning it is to see the situation involving the task as a whole
or in its entirety. The first ape did not connect box and
fruit until the relation was demonstrated to him by the experimenter. Once the relation was perceived, the box ceased
to be simply a box and became an implement—something to
be used in getting fruit. More technically speaking, at the instant this relation was seen, the Gestalt was formed. The
stupid ape, it appears, knew that the box and jumping up
were both involved in the task of getting the fruit, but that
was as far as his analysis went. Had the connections ground-
box-fruit been made in their proper sequence, the situation
would have been organized at once, and the grouping would
have become meaningful. But this last Gestalt was never
formed by the stupid ape; instead there were for him two
separate groupings, box-jumping-up and jumping-up-fruit.

5. OTHER EXPERIMENTS ON LEARNING AND
MOTIVATION

In another series of experiments Köhler attempted to see
whether Sultan, apparently his most intelligent chimpanzee,
could combine two sticks into one useful implement. The
sticks were two hollow bamboo rods, the one being enough
smaller than the other so that it could be fitted easily into
the end of the larger to form a single long stick (see Fig.

29). All of the animals had frequently used single sticks to pull in bananas and other fruit placed outside of the bars of their cages. But none had been given the task of joining two

FIG. 29

A CHIMPANZEE FITTING A SMALL STICK INTO THE BORE OF A LARGER ONE

(Adapted from Köhler's *The Mentality of Apes.*)

sticks into a single one and using the resulting long stick as an implement with which to pull in fruit.

The set-up of the experiment was as follows. The chimpanzee was put into a cage in which were two sticks, and several pieces of fruit were placed outside of the bars too far away to be reached by either stick alone, but within easy reach of the joined stick. Judged in the light of this rather simple situation, the animal's behavior seems incredibly stupid to human eyes. First, he tried to reach the fruit with one stick and then with the other. This failing, he next pushed one stick out as far as possible, and then with the second stick pushed the first one on until it finally touched the fruit. This actual contact, Köhler notes, seemed to give the animal great satisfaction, but it didn't give him the fruit! At last, as the animal seemed no closer to a solution than at the start, the experimenter gave him a hint by sticking one finger into the opening of the larger stick directly before his eyes. But this cue failed to help any, and after an hour or so of futile effort, the ape apparently lost interest and gave up the task as hopeless. He continued to play with the two sticks, however, and after some manipulation, holding the one stick in the left hand and the other in the right, he accidentally got them together as shown in Figure 29. The first connections were loose, so that the sticks frequently fell apart, but the animal persisted, with great eagerness pulling in not only all of the fruit, but all other small moveable objects, such as stones and sticks, within reaching distance. On the following day, after some desultory pushing of the one stick by the other (repetition of the old useless behavior), Sultan quickly joined the two and got the fruit.

This experiment, as interpreted by Gestalt principles, shows again the growth of elements, at first unconnected, into an organized whole. Until the ape perceived the two sticks as capable of forming a single unit in the situation, reaching-the-food, no Gestalt appeared. When the two sticks became one implement, however, a new pattern was at once formed. Many illustrations of the growth of such patterns or Gestalts are cited by Köhler. A box will often be employed as a platform for reaching fruit if it is in close proximity to the fruit;

but not if it is in a far corner of the cage. A stick will be used to pull in fruit from the outside of the bars if it is close enough to where the fruit is lying to "get into the same picture" with it, but not if it is at some distance, or is only potentially present as in the branch of a tree which has been thrown into the cage.

The point made by the Gestaltists is that, to be used as an implement, the box or the stick must exist in an organized visual field, the relations of whose parts are perceived. Learning, according to this view, is not then a bundle of specifically acquired stimulus-response bonds. When the relations involved are quickly grasped, i. e., when the animal almost at once gets the whole picture of connections and mutual implications, as, for instance, climb-on-box-to-get-fruit, it is said to have "insight." A situation is experienced without insight when its various parts are seen as parts having no dependence or orderly arrangement. Insight into a problem, then, involves seeing the problem with its various implications as all of one piece.

A series of interesting investigations in the general field of motivation has been carried out by Kurt Lewin and his students. Lewin, whose work has been principally in child psychology, has made many contributions both to the theoretical and experimental aspects of Gestalt theory. In one study made under Lewin's direction, Zeigarnik investigated the difference between the retention of finished and unfinished tasks. Nearly 200 subjects, including both adults and children, were given from 18 to 22 fairly simple problems such as solving match-stick puzzles, writing names of cities beginning with L and the like. In one-half of the tasks, the subjects were interrupted by the experimenter before completion of the task; in the other half they were allowed to finish. Later, the subjects were required to write down all of the tasks which they could recall. If the interrupted and completed tasks had been retained about equally well, the ratio IR/CR (where IR = number of interrupted tasks, and CR = number of completed tasks) would closely approximate 1.00. Actually, the ratios for the different groups of subjects were nearer 2.00 than 1.00—showing the unfinished tasks to be much more clearly remembered than the finished. In other variations of the experiment, Zeigarnik interrupted the subjects at different stages in their solutions. She found retention of tasks, broken toward the end or in the middle, to be much greater than the retention of tasks interrupted at or near the beginning.

The greater retention of unfinished than of finished tasks is explained by Zeigarnik as an instance of closure. The finished task is a completed Gestalt—the goal has been attained, tensions relieved, and relaxation obtained. The unfinished task, on the other hand, leaves the individual unsatisfied and often irritated. No closure has taken place. The "need" to complete a task once begun is shown, according to Gestalt theory, by the subject's disturbance on being interrupted and his willingness to resume as soon as opportunity is provided.

To the non-Gestalt psychologist the greater vividness of the unfinished tasks in recall is an illustration of the tendency shown by many activities—unfinished as well as finished—to "perseverate" after removal of the stimulus. Catchy tunes tend to run in the head; interesting happenings, unsolved or disturbing problems, spontaneously recur over and over again. Apparently physiological activity often continues for a considerable period of time *after* the subject's active response has ceased. Such activity may be greater for unfinished than for finished tasks.

Besides building up a thoroughgoing experimental basis for their theoretical concepts, the Gestalt psychologists have advanced cogent and searching criticisms of other methods and points of view. Köhler's criticism of the methods employed in many animal learning experiments is noteworthy. In learning problems of the "choice reaction" type, the animal is trained to go to one stimulus, a red light, say, and to avoid another stimulus, a green light, by being fed when it chooses the one and shocked when it takes the other. In such experiments, Köhler points out, instead of giving the animal an electric shock in the feet when it responds to the negative stimulus it would be much more logical from the point of view of the animal's own experience to have the negative stimulus do something to the animal—move forward or frighten it in some way. Not only would this be closer to the natural situation for the animal, but the connection between reward and the one stimulus, and punishment and the other, would be much more obvious and sensible. The latter situation, Köhler thinks, would furnish a good Gestalt; the former, which is traditional in animal experimentation, a poor one, since it is well-nigh impossible for the animal to organize into one situation punishment-in-feet-for-taking-the-wrong-light. As noted in Chapter 7, p. 192, both Köhler and Koffka have criticized the animal experiments of Thorndike on much the same ground. The animals in these experiments, they say, were forced to learn by trial-and-error, since there was no possible way—in the light of their experience—by which they could organize such acts as opening a latch or pulling a loop into the situation getting-out-of-a-box-and-getting-food. Much of the so-called stupid learning of animals, Köhler believes, results from the setting of almost impossible tasks for the animal, tasks which cannot *readily* be organized into a meaningful pattern, if they can be so organized at all.

6. STUDIES IN GESTALT THEORY IN AMERICA

The work of the Gestalt psychologists, most of which has been done in Germany, has inspired American psychologists to undertake investigations to verify or to extend the German work. Much of what has been done in the field of perception and learning is technical and difficult to describe simply or in brief space. Several studies will serve however as illustrations of the kind of work being done. De Silva has investigated the factors determining apparent visual movement such as is represented by Wertheimer's *phi*-phenomenon (p. 210). Gestaltists argue that the apparent movement which occurs in the *phi* is a clear-cut demonstration that configurations are non-additive. Actual movements and illusions of movements, they hold, are fundamentally the same, the latter being limiting cases of the former. To some extent De Silva substantiates this viewpoint. The perception of real or actual movement, however, he finds to depend upon speed or velocity; while the perception of apparent movement is conditioned by the separation in space of the stimuli and by their degree of intensity. De Silva especially emphasizes the subjective factors present in the perception of apparent movement. Hulin has studied apparent tactual movement by applying two pressure points upon the skin of the forearm. These tactual stimuli were applied sometimes together and sometimes as much as .3 sec. apart; spatially, they were separated in eight steps from 5 to 150 mms. Hulin's subjects were instructed to report when they experienced apparent movement from one point to the other. About 30 per cent of the 13,500 judgments given by seven observers indicated the experience of apparent movement, i. e., configurations in the tactual field. Apparently, tactual *phi* are dependent upon definite temporal and spatial relations among the stimuli. Not all tactual Gestalts, of course, need be illustrations of the *phi*-phenomenon. *Phi* is somewhat harder to observe in the cutaneous sense than in the visual, but it is found there.

An interesting investigation, growing out of Köhler's work

with chimpanzees, is the study by A. Alpert of the rôle of insight in the learning of very young children. Forty-four nursery school children ranging in age from nineteen to forty-nine months were subjects. Situations closely resembling the problems set by Köhler for his apes were devised. For example, a toy was placed on a shelf out of reach and a box or chair left near by; if the child used the box or chair as an implement—stood upon it—the toy could be secured. Again a toy would be placed outside of the bars of a playpen and a stick left handy near by with which the desired object could be fished in. Sometimes this problem was complicated by providing two sticks and a toy—a short stick, which was too short itself to reach the toy, but which could be used in raking in the long stick, and a long stick with which the toy could be fished in. The question in these experiments was whether the child would show the same sudden insight into the task as was exhibited by several of Köhler's apes. Alpert discovered what she called "immediate insight"—a quick, sure solution—more often than Köhler found it for his apes. In many cases, however, insight came gradually or partially, preceded by what seemed to be a certain amount of fumbling trial-and-error. It is impossible to say just how much tentative trial-and-error preceded this "immediate insight," but on the whole it was probably more often present than not. If comparisons between species are valid—which is doubtful—the young children were more intelligent in their solutions than the chimpanzees.

Köhler's experiment on relational learning in hens, described on p. 218, has been repeated by Taylor with conflicting results. Köhler was interested, as we have indicated, in refuting Thorndike's theory that learning consists in the establishment of specific S-R bonds; and in showing instead that the hens responded to the relationship "brighter than." Taylor trained his hens using black, grey, and white surfaces;

and to speed learning, gave an electric shock to the hens that pecked from the "wrong" surface. In his critical test, 82 per cent of the responses were to the *specific* shade to which the hen had been trained to respond positively—not to the brightness relation. Taylor suggests that Köhler's hens may not have been sufficiently trained to guarantee responses to the specific stimulus; and that it is a question whether hens can really distinguish the slight brightness differences which Köhler used. In the light of Taylor's experiment, Köhler's results appear to be less conclusive than he thought. It is only fair to say, however, that the transpositional type of learning exhibited by Köhler's hens has been demonstrated with other animals and for a variety of stimuli.

7. PRESENT STATUS OF GESTALT PSYCHOLOGY

Gestalt psychology has been presented by its champions with vigor and enthusiasm, but it has not, as yet, won many outright adherents in America. Objection has been raised to its theoretical assumptions rather than to its experimental procedures. It has been urged, for instance, that the term Gestalt conveys nothing essentially new. Perception has long been regarded by non-Gestalt psychologists as a unified response or as a "combining activity." Few if any would care to argue that perception consists in a mechanical photographic registration; or in an accumulation of specific S-R bonds "bundled" together into a meaningful whole. When the Gestaltists attack the mechanical theory of learning or the "bundle hypothesis" they are in reality demolishing a not very strongly defended point of view.

Non-Gestaltists agree that Gestalt psychologists have contributed notably to our better understanding of perception. But they hold that their contribution has been in the nature of a refinement of understanding and a better distribution of emphasis than in the discovery of essentially new facts. The distinction between figure and ground, for instance, is not especially original. The well-known phenomena exhibited in binocular rivalry * and in the ambiguous figures show how a detail can stand out against a background at one instant and become a part of it later on. It should be said, however, that the Gestaltists have carried the study of the figure-ground relation and the laws governing it much further than have other workers.

In the field of learning, criticism has been leveled at the term *insight*. The contention is that this word is descriptive, but that it adds nothing in the way of fundamental explanation. Apparently there are two ways of defining insight. One is to make the term purely descriptive of some end-result. A child operates a new mechanical toy quickly and deftly, with clear understanding of its function, and we say he shows insight. Used in this way, the term is neat and unambiguous and would be objected to by no one.† The second definition makes insight an explanatory principle like trial-and-error or the conditioned response—a person learns "by insight." The Gestaltists seem often to mix these usages, sometimes employing the term descriptively, sometimes as an explanatory principle. It is the latter usage which is hard for non-Gestaltists to accept, since there is a certain mystical or intuitive flavor about it.

Insight, according to Gestalt psychology, appears when a man or an animal fully grasps the principles involved in a task or sees the proper relationships forthwith. It has been picturesquely called a "click" or "A-ha" experience. But as indicated elsewhere, it is very difficult to know just how

* Binocular rivalry occurs when two dissimilar pictures are placed in a stereoscope. The result is a competition or rivalry between the two, first the one and then the other picture being suppressed.

† Note that in psychiatry a person is said to possess insight when he realizes that his behavior is abnormal. An insane man lacks insight—at least part of the time.

much trial-and-error learning has preceded the flash of understanding. It may be that this is always the case, provided
the learning is closely analyzed. In hard and little-compre-
hended tasks, we know that both men and animals resort to
hit-or-miss learning until "by chance" the successful move or
act is performed. In simpler problems, of course, there is
usually a marked reduction of random activity, and oftentimes the sudden appearance of insight. This also happens
in activities in which the individual is able to bring to bear
information or knowledge from previous and somewhat similar situations. It would seem plausible, then, that insight,
genetically looked at, may well be the end-result of a
much reduced trial-and-error period. The previous tentative
trials exist, to be sure, but are not represented in the particular learning curve under scrutiny, prior to the appearance
of insight. It has been pointed out elsewhere (p. 192) that
the insight shown by Köhler's apes was clearly a function,
in part at least, of the tasks set the animals. When the
learner is well acquainted with the facts of the situation so
that a solution (reorganization) comes swiftly, insight would
seem to be the correct term to apply.

On the whole, the doctrine of insight, with its emphasis
upon understanding and generalization, has had a salutary
effect upon pedagogy and educational theory. Stress is no
longer laid upon a strict frequency theory of learning nor
upon the all-importance of simple drill and mechanical repetition. Thorndike's present formulation of the law of exercise, for example (p. 200), minimizes the value of exercise
per se as an important factor in learning. Emphasis upon insight has apparently been of aid, too, in leading teachers to
strive for the emergence of broad principles with a consequent better transfer to other situations.

The notion of insight fares better as a broad generalization than as a guiding principle in practical learning situa-

tions. Suppose that a class in arithmetic is being taught long division. What advice, exactly, would the Gestalt psychologist give the teacher? According to Wheeler, a leading American exponent of Gestalt psychology, an act is learned "when the stimulus-pattern in which the goal figured presented relationships on the learner's level of insight, that is, fitted his level of maturation" (ref. 17, p. 317). Presumably, the teacher would be told to set a goal—praise, an honor-roll, a promise of more interesting tasks—and then wait patiently for the child's insight to develop. Such insight might be expected if and when the child possessed the requisite physical and mental maturity. But until such time, it would appear that the teacher must employ the time-honored principles of association and habit formation. In other words insight must be given an opportunity to function; it cannot be expected to spring forth without effort on the part of the learner.

Criticism has sometimes been made also of Köhler's animal work on the score that the experimenter's presence on various occasions during an experiment, constituted an uncontrolled factor. Animals are quick to pick up cues from an entirely innocent experimenter, as has often been shown in the cases of horses and dogs which calculate or perform other supposedly "intellectual" feats that turn out upon investigation to be anything but "intellectual" (see pp. 197–198). Again, the results of many Gestalt experiments are not statistically well established. In the experiment quoted on page 218, for instance, the hens responded to the relation of brightness in 70 per cent of the trials. Although this result makes the relational response more probable than the specifically learned one, it is not sufficient to establish it with certainty.

———

In the preceding sections we have sketched in brief outline the point of view and some of the experimental findings of the Gestalt psychologists and have given, as well, some of the more obvious criticisms which have been directed against this new school. Whether psychologists agree with the Gestalters' viewpoint or not, most of them are agreed as to the intrinsic value of their experimental work. As a fresh and vigorous movement with emphasis upon experiment, Gestalt psychology will probably play an important rôle in the development of some branches of psychology.

Chapter 9

THORNDIKE'S AND WOODWORTH'S EXPERIMENTS ON THE TRANSFER OF TRAINING AND THEIR INFLUENCE UPON THE DOCTRINE OF FORMAL DISCIPLINE

I. FORMAL DISCIPLINE AND FACULTY PSYCHOLOGY

The doctrine of formal discipline is the time-honored view that by hard study and application the fiber of the mind becomes toughened like a muscle; and that, as a direct result, one's "powers" of attention, memory, reasoning, and the like are markedly strengthened and increased. Advocates of this belief will contend that a boy's "reasoning ability," if thoroughly trained by the solving of numerous originals in geometry for example, is thereby better prepared to handle the knotty problems of business and professional life later on. In other words, the transfer of training from one activity to another, or the spread of improvement, is conceived to be broad and general. Opposed to the concept of general mind training inherent in the idea of formal discipline is the view that transfer of acquired skill or special training is relatively specific and narrow; that training, for example, in the duties of a department store salesman will carry over or benefit another activity or pursuit only in so far as there is a similarity of method or material between the two. For many years a controversy, which is still very much alive, has raged between these two opposing views.

Historically, the doctrine of formal discipline owes its origin and its present-day survival to two well-entrenched beliefs. The first is the view that mind is made up of numerous distinct powers or faculties—the so-called "faculty psychology"; the second is the idea that discipline is the essential function and even the main duty of education. According to the extreme form of faculty psychology, mind is analogous to an intricate machine, the various parts of which correspond to the faculties of observation, memory, reasoning, judgment, volition, and the like. Experiences are the raw material fed into this mind-machine; here they are weighed and estimated by the faculty of judgment, arranged in logical sequence by the faculty of reasoning, and stored away by the faculty of memory. With training and long practice the mind takes on strength, agility, and quickness, and these characteristics are generally exhibited in all sorts of situations.

The second belief, that of the disciplinary function of education, grows directly out of faculty psychology. It is deeply rooted, too, in the moralistic view that whatever is difficult, by virtue of that fact alone, is valuable in the training of the child's mind. This view is still widely prevalent to-day among school people, although it is showing some signs of weakening. It has long been a tradition that among school studies Latin and mathematics are especially valuable in training the powers of concentration, reasoning, and precision. It is interesting to trace the growth of this belief in the disciplinary value of Latin. For many years Latin was taught as a very necessary subject for priests and men of learning; later on it was studied for its cultural value in contrast to the often despised language of the common people. To-day, when its chief use seems to be in furnishing inscriptions for monuments and in decorating college diplomas, its value has become largely disciplinary. Thus, its value in disciplining the mind seems to have grown greater and greater as its utility became less and less. Much the same thing is true of

Photograph by Bachrach

ROBERT S. WOODWORTH

(Born 1869)

certain branches of mathematics. Thousands of high school boys and girls study geometry to-day, although an almost negligible per cent of them will ever use it in later life. Its retention in the curriculum is based upon its alleged value in training the mind in precision, in judgment, and in logical reasoning.

As we noted above, the view is still widespread among educators that an individual has a mind which possesses certain powers, and that these can be trained and disciplined only by hard and not always interesting tasks. The following quotations, some of which are quite recent, will show how strong and orthodox is the belief in the superior disciplinary value of certain subjects. This doctrine, it must be remembered, is based implicitly, if not explicitly, upon the faculty psychology.

"The study of the Latin language itself does eminently discipline the faculties and secure to a greater degree than that of the other subjects we have discussed, the formation and growth of those mental qualities which are the best preparation for the business of life—whether that business is to consist in making fresh mental acquisitions or in directing the powers thus strengthened and matured, to professional and other pursuits."—*Lectures on Education*, by Joseph Payne, Vol. I, page 260.

"The most valuable thing in the way of discipline which comes from the study of a foreign language is its influence in improving the pupil's command of his own. Of course this means the improvement in general judgment and discrimination which is evinced by a finer linguistic sense."—*Methods of Teaching the Modern Languages*, by E. H. Babbitt, page 126.

The value of the study of German "lies in the scientific study of the language itself, in the consequent training of the reasoning, of the powers of observation, comparison and synthesis; in short, in the upbuilding and strengthening of the scientific intellect."—*Methods of Teaching Modern Languages,* by Calvin Thomas, page 26.

"We speak of the disciplinary studies . . . having in our thought the mathematics of arithmetic, elementary algebra, and geometry, the Latin-Greek texts and grammars, the elements of English, or of French or of German. . . . The mind takes fiber, facility, strength, adaptability, certainty of touch from handling them, when the teacher knows his art and their power. The college . . . should give . . . elasticity of faculty and breadth of vision, so that they shall have a surplus of mind to expend."—Woodrow Wilson, in *Science,* November 7, 1902.

"A knowledge of a foreign language contributes in an unusual degree to the making of internationally minded, broad thinking, intellectually resourceful and contented citizens." —B. Q. Morgan, *The Place of Modern Foreign Languages in the American High School,* School and Society, Feb. 28, 1928.

"Specifically, Latin and Greek become effective as educational instruments in at least seven ways:

By training in the essentials of scientific method: observation, comparison, generalization;

By making our own language intelligible and developing the power of expression;

By bringing the mind into contact with literature in elemental forms;

By giving insight into basic civilization;

By cultivating the constructive imagination;

By clarifying moral ideals, and stimulating right conduct;

By furnishing means of recreation."—F. W. Kelsey, *Latin and Greek in American Education,* New York: Macmillan, 1921, page 21.

"Every great study is not only an end in itself, but also a means of creating and sustaining a lofty habit of mind; and this purpose should be kept always in view throughout the teaching and learning of mathematics."—Bertrand Russell, *Mysticism and Logic,* New York: Longmans, 1921, page 64.

"I believe that education has been getting worse in this country. It is trying to spread out and teach too much—a smattering of everything. We will live to see the time when there will again be more emphasis on mental discipline, on toughening the fibers of the mind, on subjects that make the mind tackle a hard problem and work it through to an accurate conclusion.

"If you go through high school and college taking easy courses you are not cheating anyone but yourself. Put into your curriculum some hard courses—some courses that may have no relation to the work that you will do after but will exercise your mind, so that you can stand competition in the office or profession where you will eventually have to battle for a living."—Bruce Barton, 16th Annual Convention of CSPA, Saturday, March 16, 1940.

2. EVIDENCE AGAINST THE FACULTY PSYCHOLOGY

The modern view of mental organization holds, in opposition to the faculty doctrine, that what we loosely call "mind" consists of numerous more or less closely connected behavior tendencies, and that transfer of improvement as a result of special training takes place almost exclusively among related activities. Activities may be related through similarities in form or in procedure and method, or through identities in content or material. A knowledge of Latin will undoubtedly aid one to learn Spanish more easily, while a knowledge of mathematics is indispensable in engineering or physics. Moreover, experience gained as a consulting chemist with one concern will usually enable a man the more easily to perform his professional duties with another firm. Added to this fairly specific transfer, there is almost certainly a general carry-over growing out of such broad factors as a common language, definite rules of study, habits of neatness, care, and thoroughness, quickness in reading and writing, and the like. Attitudes, motives and drives may also be general to a considerable degree.

The evidence against formal discipline and the faculty psychology comes (1) from everyday observation, (2) from physiology, and chiefly (3) from experiment. In the first place, we all believe in a certain amount of transfer—but in a certain amount only. The able lawyer is made a judge, and the active young executive becomes a general manager. But the engineer is not made health officer, nor is a minister or physician put in charge of building bridges. In other words, common sense tells us that special training cannot possibly prepare a man for all sorts of vocations nor make him an expert in all branches of knowledge. In fact, striking instances of the opposite are found. All too often the eminent scientist gives opinions on theology which are simply banal, while the highly trained mathematician is rarely more logical or rational in selecting an automobile than is his less gifted neighbor. In other words, there is little evidence from everyday life of general mind training.

The pseudo-science of phrenology is closely related to faculty psychology on the physiological side. Phrenology taught that the different faculties of the mind have "seats" in specific parts of the brain, and that their respective developments can be estimated from the "bumps" or prominences on the skull. Phrenology is no longer taken seriously by scientific men, but, like palmistry and astrology, has descended to the level of a parlor amusement. Physiologists who have studied the brain and the nervous system have found no evidence of nerve centers corresponding to the alleged phrenological faculties. They have been able to map out on the cortex general sensory and motor areas, a visual area, an auditory area, and an area for taste and smell. But no centers for such faculties as judgment, observation, volition, fear-of-the-Devil, or concentration have ever been found. To the present-day psychologist the term *concentration,* for instance, instead of meaning a power or faculty, is simply a name to describe responses which are alike in being marked by a high degree of intensity. Such responses may fall into many categories, from concentration upon a symphony to concentration upon a boxing match. In short, what a man "concentrates" upon is dependent upon his age, education, special interests, and training, not upon a mysterious "power of concentration" which exists *per se*.

The experimental attack upon the question of general *versus* specific transfer of improvement has been made by psychologists interested in the theoretical problem of mental organization as well as by those interested in the educational aspects of the transfer problem. Upon both of these questions the laboratory studies of transfer have thrown much light.

3. FIRST EXPERIMENTAL ATTACKS UPON THE PROBLEM OF TRANSFER OF TRAINING

The first experiment dealing with the problem of transfer seems to have been made by William James in about 1890. James measured the time required by himself and four students to memorize selections from the poems of Victor Hugo and Tennyson before and after training with other passages of poetry, for example, lines from *Paradise Lost*. After memorizing a given passage, each subject spent a varying time up to a month attempting to train his memory with other selections, after which he again memorized passages from the original material. On these final tests, three of the subjects showed slight improvement over their first records, but the other two were slightly worse than before training. This experiment of James was inadequate in method and inconclusive in result, but it possesses historical significance, since it started the experimental attack upon the problem of the extent of transfer through special practice. A later and better controlled series of experiments upon the general topic of memory training was carried out by W. F. Dearborn. Dearborn set out to discover whether the memorizing of lists of nonsense syllables and of meaningful material (e. g., vocabulary lists and poetry) would improve one's memory for numbers, letters, words, prose and poetry. The extent of transfer —i. e., the improvement in memorizing *after* practice—varied from zero to about 50 per cent. The degree of transfer was not as great, however, as the improvement shown in learning the material upon which the subjects *specifically* practiced. Dearborn writes: "The results indicate that a considerable part of the improvement found must be attributed to direct practice in the test series, and not to any 'spread' of improvement from the practice series proper."

The most significant of the early attacks on the problem of transfer was a series of three studies by E. L. Thorndike and R. S. Woodworth. These experiments furnished the first really exact and quantitative evidence against the doctrine of formal discipline. In order to get material which was not too familiar, the tasks were drawn from the field of discrimination and perception. The influence of the training received in one kind of perception upon efficiency in other related activities was investigated by giving training to five or six subjects in (1) estimating the areas of various geometric figures, the lengths of lines, value of weights, and so forth; and (2) observing designated words or letters on a printed page. In the first series of experiments—those on sensory and perceptual discrimination—Thorndike and Woodworth trained their subjects to estimate the areas of rectangles and other geometrical figures. *Before* the training or practice period, and *again afterward*, the subjects were tested for their accuracy in estimating the areas of other figures, e. g., rectangles, circles, triangles, and trapezoids. Some of these figures were different in shape but similar in size to those of the training period, others similar in shape but different in size, and still others different in both size and shape. From the records before and after practice, the effect of the intervening training period upon the accuracy of discrimination was determined. If we let IT = initial test; TP = training period; and FT = the final test, we can represent the experiment diagrammatically as follows:

IT—TP—FT

During the training period (TP) of the principal discrimination experiment, the subjects practiced in estimating the areas of rectangles from 10 to 100 square centimeters in size, in every case carefully checking the accuracy of their results until they had acquired marked proficiency at this task. The improvement—as measured by tests given before and after this training period—made in estimating areas of the *same size* as these rectangles, but of *different shape,* was about 44 per cent as large as the improvement shown in the TP, namely, in estimating areas *different* in size but of the *same* shape. When the subjects were tested with figures of the *same* shape but somewhat *larger* in size (e. g., rectangles of 140 to 300 square centimeters) than those used in the training series, the improvement was only 30 per cent as great as in the TP. Very probably this low figure is partly a result of confusion and interference due to the similarity in shape of the rectangles in the two series. For areas different in shape and larger in size (140 to 400 square centimeters), the improvement in accuracy was 52 per cent as great as in the training series.

Thorndike and Woodworth next trained their subjects in estimating the lengths of lines .5 to 1.5 inches long until an improvement of about 25 per cent was noted. This training period produced little or no improvement in the estimation of lines six to twelve inches long as shown by tests given before and after the practice period. Nor did the training with six-inch to twelve-inch lines lead to any improvement in estimating lines fifteen to twenty-four inches long.

In another sensory field, that of tactual and kinesthetic

discrimination, improvement to about the same degree as with geometrical figures was noted as a result of previous training in closely similar functions. The subjects were tested this time for their accuracy in estimating weights of 120 to 1,800 grams. They were then trained in estimating weights from 20 to 120 grams; and retested with the first set of weights in order to measure the effect of the intervening practice period. The improvement in the FT over the IT was about 40 per cent of that improvement which appeared in the TP alone, indicating that transfer, while evident, was by no means considerable.

Thorndike's and Woodworth's second series of experiments, those with language, are especially valuable because of their implications for educational practice; that is, because they parallel fairly closely the kind of work done in school from which much transfer has been confidently expected. In these experiments, which dealt with the perception of words and letters, the training period consisted in the rapid cancellation of every word on a printed page containing both *e* and *s*. *Before* and *after* this training, the subjects were tested for their ability to perceive and cancel words containing *a* and *t, s* and *p, l* and *o,* and the like. In another experiment the subjects were tested for their ability to perceive and cancel certain parts of speech, e. g., verbs and adjectives, as well as words of a certain length, and misspelled words. They were then trained in like material and again retested. Improvement in finding and canceling two letters—as shown by tests given before and after training—was about 25 per cent as great as the accuracy achieved in the training period itself. Efficiency in finding and marking verbs and prepositions was improved from 20 to 25 per cent in speed, and often three times as much in accuracy, as a result of training with analogous material. But although the ability to perceive and mark other parts of speech as a result of this training in some instances showed an increase in speed, there was often a great decrease in accuracy. Here again interference rather than transfer of improvement seems to have been the rule.

The result of Thorndike's and Woodworth's experiments indicated that even in performances superficially alike there may often be not only comparatively little transfer of improvement, but instead considerable interference or negative transfer. Such transfer as appeared our authors attribute to the carry-over of specific methods and rules of procedure, or to similarity in the trained and tested material. One subject, for example, discovered in himself a tendency to overestimate small areas, and allowed for this in his later judgments. Another found that too much interest in the subject-matter of the selection canceled slowed him up, and that too close attention to the particular letters canceled led to interference when other letters were marked. In general, attitudes of confidence, familiarity with the task, and improvement in methods of attack seem also to have been transferred.

Thorndike's and Woodworth's experiments delivered a broadside against formal discipline—at least in its extreme form—from which it never fully recovered. Their findings gave little encouragement to the belief in a general observational ability; or in a faculty of perception which, once trained, raises thereafter the whole level of performance in such abilities. On the contrary, these experiments suggested strongly that the *amount* of transfer from one activity to another depends chiefly upon the degree of community between the two. The dozens of experiments on transfer carried out since—although differing in method of attack and in activity selected for study—have on the whole corroborated Thorndike's and Woodworth's findings. The transfer effect of practice has proved to be far from general and is, for the most part, confined to related capacities. Such a result is, of course, diametrically opposed to the idea of formal discipline.

4. TRANSFER EXPERIMENTS IN MAZE LEARNING

The greatest degree of transfer seems to be found in studies of animal maze learning, the least in studies of the disciplinary or transfer value of school subjects. Typical investigations from each of these fields will be cited in this and the next sections. A careful and well controlled study of transfer in maze learning (in which both rats and humans were subjects) was carried out at the University of Chicago by Webb. Webb employed six square mazes as learning problems for his animals. In order definitely to favor positive transfer, two of these mazes, A and B, were closely similar as to turns and blind alleys, while the other four, C, D, E, and F, were dissimilar in this respect in order to favor negative transfer. When a group of rats had learned maze A, transfer was measured by seeing how much more quickly these trained rats could learn the other mazes than comparable control groups which had had no previous practice in A. Records were kept in terms of number of trials, errors made, and time required to learn. In every instance, there was positive transfer from maze A to the other five mazes, the greatest carry-over being from maze A to maze B wherein the patterns were *most similar*. The effect of practice was shown in a decided tendency to enter blind alleys less frequently. Increase in the efficiency of learning the other mazes as a result of practice in A varied from 19 to 77 per cent for the trials required; from 20 to 95 per cent for errors; and from 29 to 90 per cent for time. The greatest transfer occurred in the first five trials with the second maze. Substantially the same result, i.e., consistently positive transfer, was found for human subjects, who were trained with four pencil mazes.

Positive results in this experiment are probably to be attributed to the fact that mazes require the learning of fairly simple motor habits. Even the most dissimilar mazes are more alike than are the learning tasks ordinarily confronting rats or human beings outside of the laboratory. The fact that transfer of practice is concentrated mainly in the first five trials on the second maze is especially significant. It suggests that what is carried over from maze A to the other mazes is a *general familiarity* with the task to be learned, plus feelings of confidence, perhaps, which enable the learner (rat or human being) to get off to a "running start." Transfer even from maze A to maze B, however, fell considerably below 100 per cent, the average carry-over being about 82 per cent.

The positive transfer found in this experiment was corroborated by Wiltbank who repeated and extended Webb's work, using different mazes. An interesting result reported by Wiltbank is that there is little transfer *except* to a maze which is unfamiliar or only slightly learned. Different groups of rats were given 0, 2, 4, 8 or 16 trials in maze 1. They then learned maze 2 *completely,* after which maze 1 was completely learned. Table XI shows that when the first maze

TABLE XI

Number of Trials in 1st Maze before Learning 2nd Maze	Saving in Total		
	Trials	Errors	Time
0	43	61	53
2	45	55	19
4	33	− 5	− 8
8	22	− 33	− 32
16	− 11	− 43	24

is unknown or slightly known (0–2 trials) there is a large saving in trials, errors, and time as a result of learning a second maze. When the first maze is fairly well known (8–16 trials), there is little transfer from a second maze: —in fact, negative transfer or *interference* is more likely than

246 Great Experiments in Psychology

positive transfer. The appearance of negative transfer means that the carry-over even from one simple motor habit to another may prove to be a hindrance rather than a help. The problem, then, is not simply one of transfer *versus* no transfer; but of transfer *versus* no transfer plus interference!

5. TRANSFER EXPERIMENTS IN SCHOOL LEARNING

Probably because the advocates of formal discipline have so vociferously defended the training value of Latin, many experimenters have appeared to be especially eager to test the claims for this subject. Several studies have been made of the transfer effect of Latin. In one of these the gains in English vocabulary during the first year of high school, made by 717 Latin pupils, were compared with the gains in vocabulary made by 677 non-Latin pupils. Two vocabulary tests were administered, at the beginning and at the end of the school year; the first consisted of twenty-five English words derived from Latin words frequently occurring in high school Latin, and the second of twenty-five words derived from Anglo-Saxon and Greek sources. The gains made by the pupils upon the words of Latin and non-Latin origin are shown in Table XII.

TABLE XII

VOCABULARY GAINS DURING FIRST YEAR OF HIGH SCHOOL OF 717 LATIN PUPILS AND 677 NON-LATIN PUPILS UPON (A) 25 WORDS DERIVED FROM LATIN AND (B) 25 WORDS DERIVED FROM ANGLO-SAXON AND GREEK SOURCES

	Latin Derivatives	Non-Latin Derivatives
717 Latin pupils	5.5	1.2
677 Non-Latin pupils	2.0	1.4
	3.5	— 0.2

The Latin pupils improved more than did the non-Latins in their knowledge of English words of Latin origin; but on the non-Latin words neither group showed significant improvement. The study of Latin evidently made the student better acquainted with certain English words derived from Latin. But apparently it did not develop any "general language ability" which operated to improve the students' vocabulary for words of non-Latin origin.

It is interesting to see to what extent method of teaching affects the transfer value of a school subject. In one experiment the gains in English vocabulary made by four groups were compared. The four classes included a class in English conventionally taught; a class in English taught with emphasis upon word study; a class in Latin conventionally taught, and a class in Latin taught with special reference to word meanings and derivations. The children in the four groups were approximately equated for general intelligence by means of group tests. Gains in English vocabulary made by the various groups are shown in Table XIII:

TABLE XIII

COMPARATIVE GAINS IN ENGLISH VOCABULARY OVER ONE YEAR MADE BY FOUR GROUPS DIFFERENTLY TAUGHT

	Gain
Latin with word study	10.7
English with word study	8.5
Latin, conventionally taught	6.7
English, conventionally taught	6.0

When attention was *specifically* directed toward derivatives and word meanings, Latin "transferred" to English vocabulary—being slightly more effective than English. When there was no especial emphasis upon word study, there was little difference between Latin and English, neither being very effective.

The most extensive study of the transfer value of various school subjects was carried out by Thorndike in 1924. This experiment meets the criticism often leveled (correctly) against laboratory experiments on transfer (1) that training is too brief and (2) that the functions studied are too narrow for comparison to be made with the training given in school or life. Thorndike investigated the effect upon intellectual achievement of a year's work in several high school subjects, such as Latin, mathematics, and history. The subjects were 8,564 high school students in grades 9, 10, and 11. As a preliminary or initial test (IT) all pupils were given Form A of the *Tests of Selective and Relational Thinking,* published by the Institute of Educational Research, Teachers College, Columbia University.* After one year of school work these students were given Form B of the same examination as a final test (FT). The two forms A and B are equivalent, being of approximately equal difficulty. The training period (TP) was supplied by one regular year of schooling in from four to five studies. The gain in final score over initial score (FT—IT) was taken to be a joint product of growth *plus* the improvement or transfer effect of the subjects studied. To separate out the differential effect of each school subject, Thorndike employed the following plan. All pupils whose programs included, let us say, English, geometry, history, and Latin were matched for initial score in Form A with pupils whose programs included English, geometry, history, and some other subject than Latin, say physics. These two groups, being equal in initial ability, and having taken the same subjects throughout the year, except for

---

* This "battery" included those tests usually found in group tests of general intelligence, e. g., arithmetic, opposites, number series completion, analogies, sentence completion, etc. There were fifteen tests in all.

Latin in one group and physics in the other, any difference in gain upon Form B, at the end of the year would be the result, presumably, of the differential or transfer effect of the two compared subjects. To cite an example, if the average gain in the final test of the Latin Group is 25 points, and the average gain of the Physics Group 15 points, then since the two groups were equal at the start, the training effect from Latin is, on the average, ten points greater than that from physics. The transfer effect of the other school studies was calculated in the same way. The amount which each contributed to the final score was computed by balancing programs alike except for the one variable study in each case. Of course, various combinations of studies had to be made owing to the wide diversity of programs, so that the task of determining differential gains was by no means so simple as our illustration might suggest. The example given will serve, however, as a much simplified description of the method. To determine the carry-over value of a study as against simple growth effects during the year, equated groups with programs containing studies ABCD, for instance, and studies ABCDX were compared. This gives the effect of study X against non-X, the growth period being the same for both groups of students.

The results of this extensive investigation were later checked in another study of 5,000 pupils. The implications of these two experiments for formal discipline are extremely important, and the specific findings are probably at variance with what many of us might have been led to expect. Table XIV summarizes the results for more than 13,000 pupils. As far as the different studies are concerned, mathematics, proved to have the greatest training effect, with the social sciences, civics, economics and the like a close second. Latin is inferior to mathematics and science, about equal to French, and superior to sewing, stenography, manual training, and

TABLE XIV

RELATIVE VALUE OF A YEAR'S TRAINING IN VARIOUS HIGH
SCHOOL SUBJECTS IN INCREASING "ABILITY TO THINK"

Subject Groups	Weighted Average Differences (Relative Influence)
1. Algebra, geometry, trigonometry, etc. ..	2.99
2. Civics, economics, psychology, sociology	2.89
3. Physics, chemistry, general science	2.71
4. Arithmetic and bookkeeping	2.60
5. Physical training	.83
6. Latin, French	.79
7. Cooking, sewing, stenography	— .14
8. Biology, zoölogy, botany	— .15
9. Dramatic art	— .48

dramatic art. In general, these last-named studies show a slight negative transfer—a *loss* in final score rather than a gain. Clearly the traditional view that Latin is the subject *par excellence* for training one to reason or think is not borne out by these findings.

Fairly consistent differences appeared as between school subjects, but the transfer effect of even the best subjects was astonishingly small. The gain made by a pupil during the year apparently depends far more upon his native ability (as shown by a high initial score on Form A) than upon the transfer value of a particular study. This is clearly shown by the fact that the *highest* 1 per cent in initial general ability gained about twenty points in the final test after a year's work in high school, while the *lowest* 1 per cent gained only one and one-half points. This gain was irrespective of the subjects studied. In commenting upon these results Thorndike writes:

"The expectation of any large differences in general improvement of the mind from one study rather than another seems doomed to disappointment. The chief reason why good thinkers seem superficially to have been made such by having taken certain school studies, is that good thinkers have taken such studies, becoming better by the inherent tendency of the good to gain more than the poor from any study. When the good thinkers studied Greek and Latin, these studies seemed to make good thinking. Now that the good thinkers study Physics and Trigonometry, these seem to make good thinkers. If the abler pupils should all study Physical Education and Dramatic Art, these subjects would seem to make good thinkers. These were, indeed, a large fraction of the program of studies for the best thinkers the world has produced, the Athenian Greeks. After positive correlation of gain with initial ability is allowed for, the balance in favor of any study is certainly not large. Disciplinary values may be real and deserve weight in the curriculum, but the weights should be reasonable."

Thorndike's findings uncovered a common fallacy into which many staunch defenders of the disciplinary subjects (especially the defenders of Latin and mathematics) fall. This is the fallacy of *selection*. Because more classical students than non-classical go to college, take honors, make Phi Beta Kappa, and later appear in "Who's Who," superior achievement is taken to be a *result* of classical training. The fact is overlooked that it is the more intelligent students who take Latin and mathematics; and it is likely that this intellectual superiority leads to later achievement rather than the classical training itself. Given high intelligence to begin with, almost any kind of training is effective, as Thorndike's results showed.

6. THEORIES OF TRANSFER: SUMMARY AND CONCLUSIONS

The present-day opinion of psychologists on the problem of transfer of training may be summarized as follows: improvement in one function, as a result of the exercise of another, depends (1) upon the identity of elements or components (to be found both in the material and method) between the activities being measured; or (2) upon the carry-over of attitudes or methods or techniques of attack which are generalized. Both of these descriptions of the mechanism of transfer, it need hardly be said, are directly opposed to the faculty notion of mental organization. The first view is substantially that of Thorndike and Woodworth stated above; the second, that of "generalized experience," was first advanced by Judd and is sometimes taken to be an alternative—and opposed—explanation of transfer. It is doubtful, however, whether there is any fundamental opposition between the two theories, though there is a difference in emphasis. The value of Latin as an aid in learning French depends upon the "identical elements" in the two languages, as well as upon the similarity in general form and syntax which they possess in common with English. Common attitudes and techniques are best abstracted from a variety of experiences when there are common bonds running through them all. The most common bond is language; others are everyday information, similarity of method or procedure, and plan of attack. Such connections as these supply the identical elements as well as the more abstract principles upon which transfer depends.

Some psychologists have objected to the notion of transfer through identical elements. They hold that such a view over-emphasizes the mechanical linkages among overlapping habits, and does not take sufficient account of the intelligent co-operation of the individual, his interests, motivation, and drives. Allport comments, apropos the theory of identical elements, that it is perhaps only the young child and the mentally undeveloped who must be taught in terms of specific habits because not capable of generalizing. Part of the trouble here lies in the use of the term "element." Undoubtedly, any theory which deals with "elements," thought of literally and perhaps atomistically as numerous and shifting bits of behavior (like grains of sand), is much too narrow to cover a great many cases of transfer. The man with a "chip on his shoulder" sees insults in many apparently innocuous situations; the religious fanatic interprets even disasters in pious phrases; the "100 per cent American" sees any opposition to his view as evidence of subversive activity; the incurable optimist always sees the "silver lining" no matter how tarnished it may be. In each of these illustrations, it is evident that the "identical components" or linkages are supplied by the emotionally colored glasses of the subject— though there may be other common elements as well. Besides motivation and strong emotional interests, superior intelligence makes for transfer (as we have seen, p. 250) by supplying relations and analogies as well as general principles of attack. Emphasis upon common elements, especially in teaching, also aids transfer (p. 247). In short, the identical elements or common bonds may be supplied by the behaving person as well as by the situation. Viewed thus broadly, there is no contradiction between a theory of identical elements and a view which sees transfer as dependent upon the personality organization of the behaving individual.

A summary of studies of transfer of training is presented in Table XV. This table and the results of many investigations justify the conclusions which follow.

(1) *Some* transfer of training is the rule rather than the exception.

(2) The degree of transfer depends upon the *amount* and *kind* of training; teaching specifically for transfer enhances the carry-over effect.

(3) Transfer depends upon native intelligence and upon the development of techniques and methods.

(4) Transfer may depend upon a unifying motive or drive.

(5) While some school subjects have greater transfer value than others, the transfer effect of none is very large.

TABLE XV

RESULTS OF TRANSFER EXPERIMENTS FROM 1890 TO 1927
(After Orata)

Finding	Number of Investigations			
	Laboratory Experiments	Classroom Experiments	Total	Per Cent
Finds considerable transfer	18	14	32	32
Finds appreciable transfer .	23	26	49	49
Find very little transfer ...	1	7	8	8
Finds no transfer	1	1	2	2
Claims transfer, but no data given	1	0	1	1
Claims no transfer, but no data given	1	1	2	2
Claims no transfer, but faulty calculation	0	2	2	2
Finds transference and interference	8	0	8	8
Finds interference only ...	3	0	3	3
Grand Total	56	51	107	108
Duplication	8	0	8	8
Net Total	48	51	99	100

7. THE EXPERIMENTAL TECHNIQUE IN TRANSFER EXPERIMENTS

Many of the early experiments on the transfer value of practice were faulty because of the experimenter's failure to check the results obtained from special training against the results secured from a *control group*. A control group, which takes the initial test and the final test, but not the training, enables one to separate out, from the transfer effect due to special training, the carry-over due to mere repetition of the final test. The control group technique—often called the *method of matched groups*—is so generally employed to-day in transfer experiments, as well as in many other experimental problems in psychology, that it seems worth while for us to consider it in some detail. The first step in the method of matched groups is to equate the two (or more) groups employed on the basis of one or more variable factors, such, for example, as age, sex, or general intelligence. Often the groups are equated in terms of the specific function, e. g., memory or reaction time, upon which the influence of the experimental factor or EF (in transfer experiments this is special practice) is to be studied. In equating groups, the usual method is to match or pair off the subjects so that the two groups will have the same or nearly the same average initial score (IT) and the same variability around this average. After the groups are equated, the EF is applied to one group—the experimental—and at the conclusion of this training period *both* groups are given the final test (FT), which is usually an alternate form of the IT. The difference in gain of the experimental group over the control gives a measure of the effect of the EF, *minus* the practice effect of simply repeating the test. That is to say, the control group enables us to sift out the practice effect due to mere repetition of the IT, from the effect of the EF *plus* the repetition of the IT. We may diagram the whole process simply as follows:

$$\text{Experimental group: IT—EF—FT} = C_1$$
$$\text{Control group: IT————FT} = C_2$$
$$C_1 - C_2 = \text{the effect of the EF}$$

An experiment by Gates and Taylor illustrates clearly the method of matched groups as applied to transfer problems; it is cited here as a concrete example of the method. The problem was to discover to what extent a simple function, i. e., digit span, could be improved as the result of intensive practice and how permanent such improvement would be. A group of kindergarten children four to six years old were subjects. From this group two equated groups were made up by matching each child with another child as nearly as possible in the following traits: sex, age, mental age, I Q, scholastic maturity as estimated by teachers, memory for digits presented orally, for letters presented orally, for unrelated words presented orally, for geometric figures, for pictures, and for names. How well the two groups were matched may be judged from the following table:

TABLE XVI

	Number	Age	Mental Age	I Q	Memory for Digits	Memory for Letters	Memory for Unrelated Words	Memory for Related Words	Memory for Geometrical Figures	Memory for Pictures	Memory for Names
Experimental group	16	5.1	6.31	122	4.33	3.64	3.86	14.0	4.3	5.3	7.5
Control group	16	5.1	6.35	123	4.33	3.71	4.07	13.7	4.0	5.7	7.0

The experimental factor was intensive practice in immediate memory for digits. For seventy-eight days the children in the experimental group were given daily drill in learning groups of digits, the control group, meanwhile, receiving no training. At the end of the practice period when both groups were retested (FT) for digit span, the practice group had progressed from an average span of 4.33 digits (see Table XVI) to an average of 6.40, a gain of 2.07 digits. Meanwhile the control group had only increased its average from 4.33 to 5.06, a gain of .73 digit. The difference between 2.07 and .73 gives the effect of the intervening practice upon this simple memory function. Gates writes: "In the Stanford-Binet Scale, repeating 4 digits is placed at year 4, and 6 at year 10. The practice group, then, advanced during a period of 4.5 months during which they practiced on 78 days, an amount equal to that which the average untrained child advances in approximately 6 years."

Is this comparatively enormous gain the result of some real improvement in retentivity, or of a stimulated rate of growth of neural connections, or can it be attributed simply to an improvement in the technique of memorizing, better methods and the like? To answer this question, Gates allowed four and a half months to pass, and then retested fourteen members of each group—all that could be located. The result was quite conclusive. On this retest, the average memory span of the practised group was 4.71 digits, that of the control group 4.77 digits: the two groups were again equal as they were at the beginning of the study. Improvement, although quite large immediately after training, had resulted in no permanent benefit. This result indicates clearly that the large increase in score brought about by the seventy-eight days of intensive practice was probably due almost entirely to the acquisition of special techniques, familiarity with the task in hand, adaptation to the examiner's voice and signals, loss of anxiety, better habits of attention, and the devising of simple schemes of grouping, getting combinations, and the like. These techniques, though temporarily highly effective, did not remain as permanent acquisitions.

The method of matched groups has been widely used in numerous psychological problems and has proved to be exceedingly valuable in the study of the effects of various experimental factors. Apart from the EF of special training in transfer experiments, the incentive value of praise and blame, the effects of various drugs upon mental activity, visual versus auditory presentation, and positive versus negative suggestion may be mentioned as a few of the many problems which have been investigated by this method.

Chapter 10

EBBINGHAUS'S STUDIES IN MEMORY AND FORGETTING

I. EBBINGHAUS AND THE INVENTION OF NONSENSE SYLLABLES

The importance to experimental psychology of the memory experiments of Hermann Ebbinghaus lies in the intrinsic value of the work itself as well as in the impetus and inspiration which it gave to literally scores of later investigations. Ebbinghaus was born in 1850 near Bonn, Germany. He attended several German universities, but returned to take his doctor's degree in philosophy at the University of Bonn at the age of twenty-three. For eight years (1886–1894), Ebbinghaus was a professor at the University of Berlin, from which post he went to the University of Breslau. He died in 1909 while in the midst of preparing a third edition of his book *Principles of Psychology*.

In his experimental work on memory, Ebbinghaus was much influenced by Fechner,* from whom, apparently he got the idea of mental measurement. The results of his memory experiments were published in 1885 after several years of interrupted work. They mark the first real attempt to apply precise scientific method to the study of the "higher mental processes." Such phenomena had been regarded as too "subjective," too fleeting, even too personal, perhaps, for exact and quantitative treatment. It is Ebbinghaus's contribution to have shown conclusively that memory products are as amenable to experiment

* For Fechner's work on the measurement of sensation, see Chapter 15.

and to measurement as are any other natural facts with which science deals.

Ebbinghaus devised several valuable methods for measuring memory which can be employed with different kinds of material. In addition, he introduced a new kind of memory material —the so-called *nonsense syllables*—which possess among other advantages the very real one of being relatively free from "ready-made" associations. Nonsense syllables as constructed by Ebbinghaus were meaningless combinations of three letters, each combination consisting of two consonants separated by a vowel or diphthong. Examples are *bap, tox, muk,* and *rif.* Nonsense syllables of four letters, e. g., *nult, rulb, selx,* are often used also, and are perhaps more widely employed in memory experiments at the present time than are those of three letters.

To illustrate the very real advantage of using nonsense syllables in memory experiments, let us suppose that one sets out to measure the memory ability of a small group of educated adults, using as material Lincoln's "Gettysburg Address," or Poe's "Raven." Differences in memory ability will quickly appear, a considerable part of which may be attributed to the varying degrees of acquaintance with the material possessed by the subjects. In fact, probably as much individual variation will result from differences in familiarity as from differences in native ability to learn. One man may be favored because he is already slightly familiar with the selection, or because he is literary in bent and hence accustomed to such memory tasks. Another man may be at a decided disadvantage because he is a mechanical engineer in whose everyday activities literary selections and poems are rarely encountered. This unequal initial state of acquaintanceship and familiarity will always exist for much material when subjects differ greatly in age, education, cultural background, or training; and it is present, but to a somewhat lesser extent, even among children.

It was to overcome these handicaps, and as far as possible to equalize the backgrounds of different subjects so that each might start with a clean "memory slate," that Ebbinghaus invented his nonsense syllables. An equally important advantage of nonsense syllables is that the same individual can be tested under different conditions and at different times with material sufficiently equal in memory value and homogeneous in content to yield closely comparable results. All told, Ebbinghaus constructed about 2,300 nonsense syllables which he employed in the experiments to be described.

2. EBBINGHAUS'S EXPERIMENTS ON MEMORY

The phenomena of memory may be conveniently classified under the heads of (1) fixation, (2) retention, (3) recall, and (4) recognition. Fixation refers to the acquisition process; it is concerned with getting the impression, learning the new activity. Retention is usually thought of in physiological terms (brain traces, neurograms, etc.); it can only be measured indirectly through recall and recognition. Both recall and recognition measure completeness of learning. The distinction between them will appear in the following example. One recalls facts in answer to a general question ("When was the Battle of Waterloo?"); he recognizes the "right" answer as one response out of several possible responses ("Which of these five pictures have you seen before?").

Psychologists have been chiefly concerned with methods of insuring fixation, as responses must first be learned or comprehended before they can be recalled or recognized. Since Ebbinghaus's pioneer work, methods of presentation, techniques of organizing material, and the relation of fixation to recall have been carefully investigated. Ebbinghaus was primarily interested in the problems of fixation and recall. All of his experiments were carried out upon himself as subject and were performed in an extremely careful and highly controlled

HERMANN EBBINGHAUS
(1850–1909)

manner. In each group of experiments, Ebbinghaus proposed a general problem which he attempted to answer by means of specific experiments. These problems may be arranged under the following five heads:

1. What is the relation between the amount of material to be memorized and the time and effort required to learn it? Specifically, what effect does the *length* of a series of nonsense syllables have upon the *rapidity* with which it can be memorized?

2. What is the relation between amount or degree of learning and retention? What effect does the *number of repetitions* of a given series have upon its *retention?*

3. How is *forgetting* related to the time-interval between learning and recall? What effect does the passing of time have upon one's memory for comparable series of nonsense syllables?

4. What effect do *repeated learning* and frequent review have upon one's ability to retain what he has studied?

5. What sort of connections are formed in learning: do they run forward serially from one term to the next following only, or do they skip terms in the forward direction, and even sometimes in the backward direction? What is the relative strength of these different associations, assuming them to be so formed?

These questions may appear at first glance to be pretty closely restricted to nonsense-syllable learning, and hence to be of minor value in clearing up the vexed questions of learning and forgetting so common in everyday life. Closer inspection of Ebbinghaus's work, however, will show that its bearing upon the more complex problems of memory is considerable. Ebbinghaus approached such problems in the only really scientific way, namely, through the use of a rigorously controlled method and of standard material which avoided to a high degree inequalities in initial memory value.

In the following sections we shall consider the five experimental problems, listed above, and show how they were attacked by Ebbinghaus.

3. WHAT IS THE RELATION BETWEEN THE AMOUNT OF MATERIAL TO BE MEMORIZED AND THE TIME AND EFFORT REQUIRED TO LEARN IT?

Common experience tells us that the longer a poem or a prose memory lesson, the harder it is to learn up to the point where it can be repeated "by heart." Will the learning of ten verses of a poem require twice as long, three times as long, or six times as long as the learning of five verses? Probably no one would care to commit himself to a definite arithmetical answer to such a question as this, though doubtless every one would be perfectly certain that the longer selection would take more time. Ebbinghaus attacked this problem in the following way. First, he recorded the time and the number of repetitions necessary for him to learn different lists of seven, ten, twelve, sixteen, twenty-four, and thirty-six nonsense syllables each, up to the point of *one* errorless reproduction. This scheme Ebbinghaus called the "learning method." He then calculated the average time spent on each syllable in the different lists, in order to get a comparative measure of effort. Ebbinghaus's results may be stated in tabular form as follows:

TABLE XVII

Length of Lists	Number of Readings	Time for Lists	Average Time per Syllable
7	1	3 secs.	.4 secs.
10	13	52	5.2
12	17	82	6.8
16	30	196	12.0
24	44	422	17.6
36	55	792	22.0

From this table it is clear that the *time* as well as the *number* of repetitions necessary for learning increases much faster than the length of the list to be learned, and that neither of these measures of memory ability increases in simple arithmetic or geometric progression. There is, relatively speaking, an enormous jump in the number of readings needed as we go from seven to ten syllables; but after this the increase is roughly constant and at the rate of about 50 per cent from each syllable list to the next following. If we disregard the again comparatively large increase in time of learning from the seven-word to the ten-word list, the time increment also is roughly constant and at the rate of about 100 per cent. It is interesting to compare the effort involved in learning twelve, twenty-four, and thirty-six syllables, as these lists are in the ratio 1:2:3. Taking the "average time per syllable" for a list of twelve, i. e., 6.8 seconds per syllable, as our standard, the list of twenty-four syllables requires two and one-half times as much time per syllable as the list of twelve, and the list of thirty-six syllables requires three and two-tenths as much time. The absolute increase is about 11 seconds per syllable, on the average, from twelve to twenty-four syllables and about 5 seconds per syllable from twenty-four to thirty-six; hence it is clearly harder to go from twelve to twenty-four syllables than from twenty-four to thirty-six.

As the memory task increases in length, not only do we get an increase in the number of readings and in the time required —which is to be expected—but a marked increase in the *time per syllable* as well. This suggests that the greater the number of associations required, the greater is the effort which must be expended on each association; and that learning a long list is not, therefore, simply a matter of adding on *more* syllables to a short list. The moral for the practical learner studying a long lesson lies in recognizing the necessity of expending not only more time and effort than in learning a short lesson, but more time and effort per item or unit as well.

A partial explanation of this finding would seem to lie in the need for linking together parts or sections of the longer lists into a coherent whole as well as of tying together the separate syllables or elements. It is highly probable, too, that in the longer lists the later-formed associations serve to confuse and to be confused by those which come earlier; and as a result *all* require better fixation, i. e., more learning. This interference of one set of associations with another set is called *retroactive inhibition* when it extends in the backward direction, and *proactive inhibition* when it extends in the forward direction. Both kinds of confusion have been studied by psychologists, especially the retroactive effects which result when a memory task is followed immediately by other memory tasks. Experimental data show that the confusion effect on recall is greatest when the activity which is interpolated between fixation and recall involves the learning of material closely similar to the original lesson. One is likely, for example, to remember more of a French vocabulary if he studies algebra in the interval between fixation and recall than if he studies Latin in the interpolated interval. There are, of course, many factors which enter into and condition the confusion of one memory lesson with another. Besides similarity, there is the length of interval between fixation and recall; degree of original learning; and ability and previous training of the learner. There is a large body of experimental literature on the subject.

By way of contrast with the data from nonsense material, it is interesting to compare some results got by Ebbinghaus with meaningful subject-matter. In seven tests, each test comprising six stanzas from Byron's "Don Juan," Ebbinghaus found that he required on the average about eight repetitions to reach his standard of one errorless recitation. Each stanza contained about eighty syllables. On the basis of the results given in Table XVII above, Ebbinghaus estimated that he would probably have required about seventy to eighty repetitions to learn eighty nonsense syllables up to his standard of one errorless recitation. A comparison of these figures for meaningful and meaningless material gives us a ratio of 10:1 in favor of the meaningful, and furnishes, in Ebbinghaus's words, "an approximate numerical expression for the extraordinary advantage which the combined ties of meaning, rhythm, rhyme, and a common language give to material to be memorized."

Objection has been raised to Ebbinghaus's standard of learning, namely, the time and the number of repetitions necessary to reach the *first* errorless reproduction. Impetuous subjects, it is said, will attempt to reproduce a list before it has been well learned, and hence run the risk of becoming confused and discouraged; while cautious individuals will study longer than is necessary, and hence tend to "overlearn." This "error of variable standard" can be controlled in a practical way by requiring a subject to attempt reproduction early—but not too early—in his learning, thus making sure that the first errorless recitation is really the first reproduction of which he is capable. With trained subjects little difficulty arises on this account. Probably no one since Ebbinghaus has been better trained or more careful than he; and hence his results are highly reliable, although based upon data from only one person.

4. WHAT IS THE RELATION BETWEEN THE AMOUNT OR DEGREE OF LEARNING AND RETENTION?

The reader will readily understand that the results quoted in the last section are limited in scope, since in every case Ebbinghaus only learned his lists up to the point of one correct reproduction. Ordinarily we memorize to a considerably greater degree than this, and in general the slower the learner, the more often and the more painstakingly does he go over his

task. What is the influence of this "overlearning" * upon retention? Ebbinghaus undertook to answer this question in the
following experiment: He read over lists of *sixteen* syllables
in exactly the same way and at the same rate, except that the
number of readings varied from *eight* to *sixty-four*. This
meant, of course, that some of the lists were overlearned to a
very high degree. Twenty-four hours later he studied these
same lists until he could just recite them once. He then figured
the percentage saved in relearning each list—i. e., he found
how many repetitions *less* were required to relearn than to
learn twenty-four hours before, and what per cent this saving
was of the original learning time. This method of studying
memory was devised by Ebbinghaus and is known as the
"saving method." Following are some of his results based on
several lists:

TABLE XVIII

Number of readings on the first day	8	16	24	32	42	53	64
Per cent saved in relearning the lists 24 hours later	8	15	23	32	45	54	64

Evidently each original repetition brought about a saving of
almost exactly 1 per cent in the relearning necessary on the
following day. The remarkable uniformity of these results
suggest that 100 readings on the first day should logically make
it possible to reproduce a list on the next day without any
additional learning—the saving would be 100 per cent! But
Ebbinghaus found that it was impossible for him to read
through a list 100 times without serious lapses of attention,
fatigue, and drowsiness. This indicates that the regular saving
of 1 per cent for each previous day's reading will eventually
break down as the learner's "physiological limit" is reached;

---

* According to Ebbinghaus's standards, any learning over and above
that necessary to obtain one correct reproduction constituted overlearning.

and that beyond this point further repetitions will be of little or no value.

The clear implication of this experiment is that degree of retention depends directly upon the amount of work done (overlearning), as well as upon the amount to be learned. In memorizing nonsense syllables the strength of the connections formed, as shown by the saving in relearning, is, up to a certain point, roughly proportional to the amount of study. This fact throws light upon the widely held view that the slow learner retains better than the fast learner. Perhaps the truth of the matter is that the slow learner does more overlearning than the fast learner, and hence saves more in relearning. In this connection the following data from Radosavljevich * are of interest. This experimenter compared children with adults in the learning of twelve syllable nonsense lists and the relearning of the same lists after twenty-four hours. His results were as follows:

TABLE XIX

	No. Readings in First Learning	No. Readings Needed to Relearn 24 Hours Later	Per Cent of Saving
Adults	20	6	70
Children	42	7	83

The children took twice as many readings to learn the lists originally, but they saved a considerably larger per cent in relearning than did the adults. Very probably this is what happens in the case of the slow but sure learner, and accounts for his apparent superiority in retention over the rapid learner. For when the *amount* or *degree* of learning is kept constant, the quick learner retains better than the slow learner.

* A later investigator (1907), who repeated much of Ebbinghaus's work using more subjects. See Ladd and Woodworth (ref. 9).

Of the many studies of degree of learning and retention which have followed those of Ebbinghaus, one of the most thorough is that of Luh. This experimenter had ten subjects memorize lists of twelve nonsense syllables to four degrees or stages of completeness: 100 per cent, 150 per cent, 67 per cent, and 33 per cent. In 100 per cent learning each subject memorized his lists up to the point of *one* errorless recitation; in 150 per cent learning he was allowed as many repetitions as in 100 per cent learning plus a bonus of half as many again; in 67 per cent learning he was given two-thirds as many repetitions as in 100 per cent learning; and in 33 per cent learning, one third as many. Retention was tested by three methods: *written reproduction, recognition,* and *reconstruction* (for description, see later p. 274). Luh's results showing the amounts retained after three time-intervals are given in Table XX.

TABLE XX

Memory Method	Amount Retained after Three Time-Intervals		
	4 hours	1 day	2 days
Written reproduction			
150% learning	82%	39%	31%
100%	65	46	40
67%	66	42	25
33%	43	26	14
Recognition			
150% learning	93%	83%	73%
100%	92	78	79
67%	85	74	62
33%	55	46	26
Reconstruction			
150% learning	91%	43%	44%
100%	75	49	44
67%	65	57	32
33%	48	26	20

On the whole these results support Ebbinghaus in so far as they indicate that increasing the repetitions (up to a certain point) leads to better retention. The "diminishing returns" from overlearning, commented upon by Ebbinghaus, are clearly shown in Luh's records, since after intervals of one day and two days better results are obtained from 100 per cent than from 150 per cent learning. However, the loss from overlearning appears much sooner in Luh's than in Ebbinghaus's results. From Table XVII we find that it took Ebbinghaus thirty repetitions to learn sixteen nonsense syllables up to the standard of one correct recitation. If we take thirty-two repetitions by Ebbinghaus (see Table XVIII) as roughly equivalent to Luh's 100 per cent learning, it would seem that Ebbinghaus overlearned his material up to 100 per cent (sixty-four repetitions) without any diminishing return appearing. This same result—a failure to get diminishing returns from overlearning—also appears in the more recent work of Krueger, who checked some of Luh's results. Krueger had 20 subjects learn lists of 12 monosyllabic words (nouns) presented at 2-secs. intervals on a rotating drum apparatus. Degree of learning was varied from 100 per cent learning (no overlearning) up to 200 per cent learning (100 per cent overlearning); and retention was tested after 1, 2, 4, 7, 14, and 28 days. Krueger found that overlearning up to 50 per cent (150 per cent learning) led to an increase in retention almost directly proportional to the additional effort. But no evidence was found of large diminishing returns with overlearning even for the longer periods between learning and recall. Krueger's results, therefore, substantiate Ebbinghaus's and are opposed to Luh's in so far as they indicate little or no harmful effect from excess learning.

It should be pointed out that Luh's findings are not strictly comparable to those of Ebbinghaus or of Krueger. Luh used different methods of presenting his learning material and of measuring memory retention; and his lists were shorter than those of Ebbinghaus—12 vs. 16 nonsense syllables. Again, Luh's results are based upon the average of 10 persons while Ebbinghaus's findings are for himself alone. Krueger's lists were of the same length as those of Luh (viz. 12) but were meaningful words instead of nonsense syllables. Hence a part at least of the apparent discrepancy in their results may be attributed to differences in method and differences in materials.

On the whole, except in the case of nonsense syllables, there is little experimental evidence of memory loss attributable to overlearning. Probably there is a point beyond which the time spent by a student on German grammar or geometrical propositions represents wasted effort. But this lack of return is perhaps due to boredom (i. e., to indifference or loss of interest) and fatigue rather than to the fact that the added study is in itself of no value. Summarizing our positive findings from these experiments, it seems evident that overlearning up to a certain point (to be located experimentally) definitely increases retention.

5. HOW IS FORGETTING RELATED TO THE TIME-INTERVAL BETWEEN LEARNING AND RECALL?

No doubt many of us have had the experience of discovering that a poem memorized long ago, although it cannot be recited now, can be relearned in a much shorter time than a new poem of the same length and the same approximate difficulty. Fortunately, this quicker relearning holds for most of the facts learned in school for which retention appears to be almost zero. Indeed, the ability to "get back" material once learned but now forgotten seems oftentimes to be the only real justification for having learned it at all. It is common experience, too, that the more recently we have studied a topic the fresher it tends to be. Just how is this forgetting related to the passing of time? Do memories dim gradually and progressively, or is a large amount lost comparatively quickly, some details with possibly a vague outline remaining for a longer time? Ebbinghaus attacked this particular problem in what is probably his most important, and is certainly his best-known, experiment. Eight lists of thirteen nonsense syllables each were learned up to the point of *two* errorless recitations. Then, after a lapse of twenty minutes, the lists were again taken up and studied as before until each list could be recited *twice* without error. The actual time saved in relearning was expressed as a *per cent* of the original learning time (the *saving method*). To illustrate the procedure, it took Ebbinghaus on the average about eighteen minutes (1,080 seconds) to learn twelve lists of thirteen nonsense syllables each up to his new standard of two correct reproductions. After a lapse of twenty minutes it required only about eight minutes (498 seconds) for him to relearn the same lists. This means there was a saving of about $^{10}/_{18}$, or 56 per cent *, of the time which Ebbinghaus required to learn the lists originally. Fifty-six per cent measures the retention or the amount which "stuck" over a period of twenty minutes and shows that the forgetting during this time was 100 minus 56, or 44 per cent. Other lists of thirteen syllables were learned by Ebbinghaus in the same manner and relearned again after periods of one hour, nine hours, one day, two days, six days, and thirty-one days. The per cent of saving in each case was calculated after the intervals stated above. In memorizing his lists and then relearning them, Ebbinghaus was careful to distribute his learning so as to prevent any one period being unduly favored by practice. Table XXI summarizes his principal results.

If we draw a graph of these results, laying off the time-intervals between learning and relearning along the baseline and the per cents retained on the vertical axis, we get Ebbinghaus's Curve of Retention (Fig. 30). This graph, which has

---

* This percentage was determined more accurately to be 58 per cent by Ebbinghaus when all of his data were considered.

TABLE XXI

Interval between Learning and Relearning	Percentage of Work Saved (Retention)	Loss Due to Forgetting
20 minutes	58	42
1 hour	44	56
9 hours	36	64
24 hours	34	66
2 days	28	72
6 days	25	75
31 days	21	79

been a classic in psychology for all of fifty years, has the general character of an inverse logarithmic relationship.* It indicates that, after the large initial drop from twenty minutes to two days, forgetting proceeds more and more slowly until there is very little difference between the loss after ten days and after thirty days. Presumably a certain minimum sticks almost indefinitely; and it is just this minimum which tips the balance against the uneducated man and in favor of the educated man long out of school.

Later investigators working with many subjects and with meaningful material as well as with nonsense syllables have obtained results different in some respects from those of Ebbinghaus, but not markedly different. The following table from Radosavljevich gives the records from several subjects both for nonsense syllables and poetry.

In Table XXII, forgetting proceeds at a slower rate than was found by Ebbinghaus, but the general trend of the two experiments is much the same. Radosavljevich's retention curve is less regular than that of Ebbinghaus owing in large part to the extremely poor record after eight hours. This ir-

* Its equation is $b = \dfrac{100k}{(\log t)^c + k}$ in which $b =$ per cent retained, $t =$ time-interval elapsing, and k and c are constants.

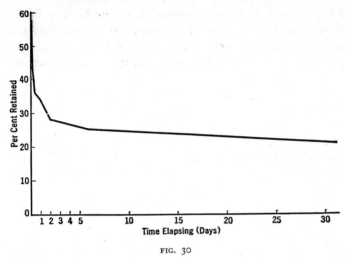

FIG. 30

CURVE OF RETENTION (EBBINGHAUS) FOR NONSENSE SYLLABLES AFTER
VARIOUS TIME INTERVALS

regularity was attributed by Radosavljevich to the unfavor-
able time of day at which the relearning fell—a factor which

TABLE XXII

Interval be-tween Learning and Relearning	Percentage of Retention for Nonsense Syllables	Percentage of Retention for Poetry
5 minutes	98	100
20 minutes	89	96
1 hour	71	78
8 hours	47	58
24 hours	69	78
2 days	61	67
6 days	49	42
14 days	41	30
30 days	20	24
120 days	3	

Ebbinghaus has guarded against in his work. The immediate retention for poetry is, as might have been expected, somewhat better than that for nonsense syllables, though, surprisingly enough, after twenty-four hours the difference between the two is negligible.

The differences between the records of Ebbinghaus and Radosavljevich are attributable, in part at least, to the fact that the latter's subjects probably overlearned their material, since they were neither so well trained nor so uniform in their learning methods as Ebbinghaus. Radosavljevich considered his results to be far superior to those of Ebbinghaus, but it is doubtful whether they actually discredit the earlier work.

Beside the matter of individual differences and overlearning, the retention of nonsense syllables depends to a large extent upon the *method* employed in measuring retention. This has been clearly shown by Luh in an experiment in which five relearning methods were compared: *anticipation, relearning* (or saving), *written reproduction, reconstruction,* and *recognition.* Throughout Luh's work the presentation of nonsense syllables was effected by a rotating drum apparatus which exposed the twelve syllables one at a time through an aperture in a screen. In the *anticipation* method, the subject attempted in his reproduction to anticipate each syllable before it was shown; the *relearning* method is the saving method of Ebbinghaus previously described; in *written reproduction* the subject simply wrote down all of the nonsense syllables which he could remember; in *reconstruction* he was given the twelve syllables, each on a separate slip of paper, and was instructed to rearrange them in the original order of presentation; and in *recognition* he attempted to select from twenty-four syllables the twelve which he had seen. Luh's results are shown in Table XXIII and his retention curves in Figure 31.

The striking fact in Table XXIII is the discrepancy in per-

TABLE XXIII

Method	Percentages Retained after				
	20 mins.	1 hour	4 hours	1 day	2 days
Anticipation	68	50	39	18	10
Relearning (saving) .	75	66	55	52	48
Written reproduction.	88	82	61	39	27
Reconstruction	92	90	75	51	39
Recognition	98	95	93	75	72

centages retained after the five given intervals. Clearly the method employed in recording amounts retained is sufficient in itself to make the losses after various time-intervals decidedly different in size. The hardest method is anticipation, which is almost pure recall, with a minimum of "cues"; the easiest method is recognition, in which the loss after two days is slightly less than the loss after twenty minutes by the anticipation method. This result, namely, that recognition is decidedly easier than recall, has been found by other investigators.

The percentages retained as found by the relearning method are shown in Table XXIV. These are the only data directly comparable to those of Ebbinghaus (see Table XXI), since Ebbinghaus employed only the relearning (i. e., saving) method. A comparison of the percentages saved for four time-intervals as found by Ebbinghaus and Luh is as follows:

TABLE XXIV

	20 mins.	1 hour	1 day	2 days
Ebbinghaus	58%	44%	34%	28%
Luh	75%	66%	52%	48%
Difference	17%	22%	18%	20%

Ebbinghaus's results run regularly from 18 to 20 per cent below those of Luh for comparable time-intervals. Part of

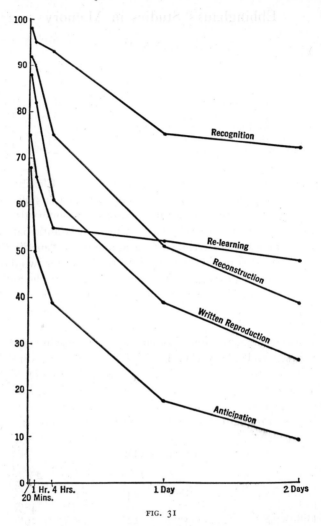

FIG. 31

CURVES OF RETENTION FOR TWELVE NONSENSE SYLLABLES LEARNED BY FIVE
DIFFERENT METHODS

Percentages retained are laid off on the vertical axis; times between learning and relearning on the horizontal axis. (From Luh, 1922.)

this difference is due to the fact that Ebbinghaus learned thirteen nonsense syllables, while Luh's subjects learned only twelve. From Table XVII we know that the addition of two extra syllables (the jump from ten to twelve) increases the number of readings necessary for learning from thirteen to seventeen; hence an increase of one syllable might be expected to have some effect, at least, on the saving from relearning. But the greater part of the difference is undoubtedly due to the method of presentation. Luh's presentation was rigidly controlled, each syllable being shown as an isolated unit so that connections must have been almost 100 per cent in the forward direction. On the other hand, Ebbinghaus's lists, which were spread out before him, offered ample opportunity for backward as well as forward associations and for associations with the list as a whole (see later, p. 282). If learning was easier in Ebbinghaus's procedure than in Luh's, the enforced overlearning of the latter's subjects as compared with Ebbinghaus would inevitably have made forgetting less rapid.

Turning now from the more carefully controlled laboratory experiments on memory retention, let us consider some investigations which have sought to discover the permanence of subject-matter learned in school. Table XXV shows the per cent retention of certain school subjects at the end of the course and after one and two years.

These percentages undoubtedly represent a kind of optimum, as many of the poorer and less interested students presumably dropped out and were not retested, especially after one and two years. It is doubtful whether the per cents recalled of high school algebra and Latin would be as large as shown here for students in general. The slight differences in percentage retained are probably due to differences in initial ability, difficulty of course, effectiveness of instruction and the like rather than to inherent differences in subject matter. On the whole, the students tested showed a retention of about

TABLE XXV

RETENTION OF VARIOUS SCHOOL SUBJECTS AT END OF
COURSE AND AFTER ONE OR TWO YEARS

(From Pressey, p. 393)

Per Cent of Perfect Score on Test Used

	End of Course	After 1 Year	After 2 Years
Botany (college)[1]	.68	.21	.16
Zoölogy (college)[1]	.78	.39	.30
Psychology (college)[1]	.70	.24	.19
Algebra (high school)[2]	.87	.56	...
Latin (high school)[1]	.82	.60	...
Chemistry (high school)[1] ..	.63	.47	.33
History (eighth grade)[3] ...	.71	.56	...
Average	.74	.43	.24

[1] Results based upon objective tests.
[2] Results based upon Regents' examination.
[3] Results based upon essay-type questions.

75 per cent at the end of the course and of about 25 per cent after two years.

Results very much like these were found in a more intensive study of the retention of lecture material by college students after various time intervals. In several groups of subjects, it was found that at the close of a forty-minute lecture students can reproduce on the average about 62 per cent of the material just presented; after three or four days, about 45 per cent is remembered; after one week, 35 per cent; after two weeks, 31 per cent; and after eight weeks, 24 per cent. The retention curve plotted from these data falls off in much the same fashion as that of Ebbinghaus for nonsense syllables: i. e., the loss is rapid at first and progressively slower as time goes on.

Results of much practical importance have been obtained in studies of "school forgetting." Over a summer vacation, elementary school children show an increase in ability to read and a loss in spelling, arithmetic and history. Here the obvious explanation is that children exercise (overlearn?) reading skills in their everyday activities during the summer, but ignore and hence forget the more "scholastic" subjects. This tendency to forget what is not used holds, of course, for adults as well as for children. The physician forgets his poetry, the engineer his history and the business man nearly everything except his economics. The relative "permanence" of material learned by different methods of instruction has been studied exhaustively by educational psychologists.

Since forgetting is much faster during the period immediately following learning, obviously the thing to do is to review early and often. In this way what one has learned will be held, so to speak, above the "memory threshold." It must be kept in mind that Ebbinghaus barely learned his material in the first place. We have found already how enormously retention is affected by overlearning. Therefore, when a memory lesson is exceedingly well learned to begin with, forgetting must proceed at a very much slower rate than that exhibited by Ebbinghaus's curve (see Fig. 30). The effect of repeated learning will be considered in the next section.

6. WHAT EFFECT DO REPEATED LEARNING AND FREQUENT
REVIEW HAVE UPON ONE'S ABILITY TO RETAIN WHAT
ONE STUDIES?

We have seen in the last section that material just barely learned tends to be forgotten very rapidly at first and then more slowly as time goes on. Also, that the amount forgotten depends upon the method of recording retention, as well as upon the labor expended in the original learning, appears clearly in Ebbinghaus's and Luh's results (Tables XVIII and XX). What effect, we may now ask, does repeated learning (review) have upon retention? Ebbinghaus attempted to answer this question in the following experiment. First, series of twelve, twenty-four, and thirty-six nonsense syllables as well as stanzas from Byron's "Don Juan" were learned. These were then relearned at the same hour on six successive days, each time up to the standard of one correct recitation. Table XXVI shows the number of repetitions required at each period and the per cent saved over the first day's record.

TABLE XXVI

No. of Syllables in Series	No. of Repetitions Which (on the Average) Were Necessary for Relearning the Series on Successive Days; also Per Cent Saved on Successive Days over the First Day's Record					
	Days					
	I	II	III	IV	V	VI
12 Number of repetitions	16.5	11	7.5	5	3	2.5
% saved over first day	...	33	55	70	82	85
24 Number of repetitions	44	22.5	12.5	7.5	4.5	3.5
% saved over first day	...	49	72	83	90	92
36 Number of repetitions	55	23	11	7.5	4.5	3.5
% saved over first day	...	58	80	86	92	94
1 stanza "Don Juan" Number of repetitions	7.75	3.75	1.75	.5	0	0
% saved over first day	...	52	77	94	100	100

The important fact in Table XXVI is that the necessary amount of relearning becomes progressively less and less on each succeeding day. In other words, the much exercised or older associations are forgotten more slowly than the less exercised or newer associations. On each succeeding day, Ebbinghaus brought his learning up to the standard of the previous day—one correct recitation. If this means that the associations formed were left in the *same* condition at the end of each day's learning, then logically we should expect the loss to be about the same from one day to the next, no matter how often the learning was repeated. To use an analogy, forgetting according to this view might be conceived of as the running down of a clock which must be rewound to the same point each day in order to bring it back to its original efficiency. So if it took eleven repetitions on the second day to bring the twelve nonsense syllables up to their original strength on the first day, it should take eleven repetitions to bring them up to the same standard on the third day, the fourth day, the fifth, and the sixth. On the contrary, however, we find that the loss due to forgetting became less and less after each learning period. This can mean but one thing, namely, that connections are more strongly established the more often they are exercised. So the multiplication table, the months of the year, and the names and relations of common coins are rarely forgotten except by very old persons or by those suffering from mental disease.

It is interesting to note in Table XXVI that the repetitions, when the learning was repeated at stated intervals, were relatively fewer for the longer lists. This is owing to the fact that many more repetitions were needed originally to fixate the longer series; hence from the beginning the associations in these lists were the more firmly established. The saving, for example, in relearning thirty-six nonsense syllables after twenty-four hours was 58 per cent as against a saving of 33 per cent for twelve nonsense syllables after the same interval. But nearly three and one-half times as many repetitions were needed to learn the longer list in the first place.

An important discovery made by Ebbinghaus in the present connection has to do with the relative value of *distributed* versus *concentrated* learning. Ebbinghaus found that sixty-eight successive readings of a twelve-syllable list made it possible for him to relearn the same list on the following day after only seven repetitions. When his readings were spaced over three days, the same result was not attained until the fourth day—but this time only thirty-eight readings were necessary! In other words, a judicious distribution of effort over three days produced a result which when learning was packed into a single day required *twice* as much labor. The superiority of spaced over massed learning has since been verified by other experiments; more will be said about it in Section 8.

7. WHAT SORT OF CONNECTIONS ARE FORMED IN LEARNING?

Do the connections formed in learning run forward serially from one term to the next following only, or do they skip terms in the forward direction, and even sometimes in the backward direction? What is the relative strength of these different associations, if they can be shown to exist?

In serial learning, it often seems that in addition to simple 1, 2, 3, or *a, b, c* forward associations, other connections are set up in various ways within the material to be learned. In the experiments of Ebbinghaus hitherto described, repetition always proceeded regularly from one syllable to the next following. Hence, it would appear that only serial connections could be made, and that these connections must be formed in the forward direction only. Are there any other associations formed in rote learning?

Ebbinghaus set out to answer this question first by learning lists of sixteen syllables up to the point of one correct recitation, and then twenty-four hours later by learning "derived" lists made up in various ways from the original lists. If we designate the syllables of an original list of numbers, 1, 2, 3 . . . 16, a sample derived list might read:

1, 3, 5, 7, 9, 11, 13, 15, 2, 4, 6, 8, 10, 12, 14, 16.

Such a derived list would clearly benefit from forward asso-

ciations between one term and the next following if such associations had been formed in learning the original list. Also, if
this is true, it should be easier to relearn such a derived list
than an entirely new one. Another derived list might skip two
syllables in the forward direction:

1, 4, 7, 10, 13, 16, 2, 5, 8, 11, 14, 3, 6, 9, 12, 15,

thus giving more remote forward associations a chance to
operate if present. Still other derived lists drawn up by Ebbinghaus skipped three, four, and up to seven intervening syllables.
In addition to lists like these, others were constructed in which
the syllables were reversed in regular order from 16 to 1, or
were simply jumbled up or arranged in chance order. Thus
forward associations, both near and remote, backward associations, and any other incidental connections were given a chance
to operate in the relearning if present in fact.

The average saving in terms of repetitions in learning these
derived lists twenty-four hours after the original lists had
been learned is shown in Table XXVII.

Table XXVII

Saving in relearning original lists unchanged 33%
Saving in learning lists derived by skipping 1 syllable . 11%
                                         2 syllables 7%
                                         3   6%
                                         7   3%
Saving in learning reversed lists 12%
                   reversed lists, 1 syllable skipped .. 5%
                   lists, syllables arranged by chance . .5%

The percentages of saving shown in the table are rather small
in several cases, but they are based upon six or more lists and
are statistically reliable. It seems clear that connections were
actually formed in learning these lists not simply from one
syllable to the next following, but to the second, the third, and
even more remote terms. To quote Ebbinghaus: "As a result

of the repetition of the syllable series, certain connections are
established between each member and all those that follow it.
These connections are revealed by the fact that the syllable
pairs so bound together are recalled to mind more easily and
with the overcoming of less friction than similar pairs which
have not been previously united." The more remote the terms,
the weaker the connection tends to be. Only in the case of derived lists in which the syllables are simply thrown together by
chance or reversed with one syllable skipped is there no real
saving.

An explanation of "backward," "remote forward," and "incidental" associations is *probably* to be found in the learning
method employed by Ebbinghaus rather than in any reversible
neural mechanism. With his lists of nonsense syllables spread
out before him, it was almost impossible for Ebbinghaus to
refrain from glancing backward and forward as he read slowly
through a list. Hence his method might account for the adven-
titious connections which showed up later on in learning the
derived lists. It seems likely that much of the benefit obtained
from overlearning is brought about by a strengthening of the
essential forward associations together with a gradual weakening of indirect and useless connections. With continued repetitions, bonds which might easily cause confusion and interference when learning is imperfect are minimized in favor of the
more necessary direct ones.

8. ECONOMY AND EFFICIENCY IN MEMORIZING

In Section 2 it was pointed out that Ebbinghaus and many
more recent psychologists have been especially interested in
the fixation process because without adequate registration
there can be little effective recall and recognition. One can
probably do little to improve his physiological retentivity
other than to build up his physical and emotional well-being;
apparently some minds are natively more impressionable than

others, just as some sense organs are natively more sensitive than others. Various schemes and methods may be utilized, however, for improving memory-fixation, and for making recall and recognition more efficient. Some of these will be outlined in the present section.

1. *Spaced versus Massed Learning.* When Ebbinghaus massed his learning of nonsense syllables into a single day, he obtained a result (p. 281) which required only one-half as much effort when distributed over three days. The superiority of distributed or spaced learning over concentrated or massed learning appears in laboratory studies as well as in studies of learning in school. Both with respect to amount retained and accuracy of recall, spaced learning of 3-place numbers has proved to be better than massed learning. In an experiment dealing with memory for a prose passage of 1,500 words, it was found that the material was better remembered after four readings spaced one day apart than after four readings in immediate succession. Spaced learning is but little—if any—better than massed learning when the memory lesson is easy— there is little value in repeating an easy task. But spaced learning has a decided advantage over massed when the material is difficult, as it is here that repeated attack is most necessary and most effective. The superiority of distributed learning is due, perhaps, to many factors: (a) when the learning periods are comparatively short, there is less tendency to fall into a rut and repeat errors; (b) frequent review maintains the freshness and recency of the memory task; (c) there is better attention and less boredom when the learning period is not too extended.

The finding that spaced learning is better than massed is important for school practice since it indicates that frequent repetition and review are more effective and more saving of time and labor than learning concentrated into one grand effort. It is sometimes true, of course, that a clever student will be able to "cram" enough of what has been taught during the term to pass the next day's examination. But he will almost surely retain less of the content of the course than his more sagacious brother who has distributed his learning throughout the term. And so in the matter of retention, at least, virtue is rewarded!

2. *Whole versus Part Learning.* When material of any length is to be memorized, it is generally a better plan to study it straight through from beginning to end ("as a whole") than to split it up into bits and learn each part separately. Nonsense syllables as well as poetry and prose are learned more efficiently by the "whole" method; and retention over intervals of time is better. Poetry learned by the whole method, for example, was recalled 160 per cent better at the end of two years than poetry learned by the part method.

The reason why the whole method is better than the part is that in whole learning associations are formed in the order and direction in which the learner wants them to function eventually. It is not necessary as in part learning to "tie together" sections often artificially separated. The whole method would seem, too, to be the more intelligent plan of attack. It is probable that the better students work out some plan of "whole" learning (finding relations and implications) for themselves, while the poorer students waste time on details and unrelated bits of knowledge.

When a lesson is long and difficult, a combination of the whole and part methods is the most efficient mode of attack. The material is first surveyed as an entirety in order to give perspective and provide logical relations in terms of which the ideas presented may be integrated. Intensive study is then directed selectively to those parts of the memory-lesson which are most difficult. Breaking up a long lesson into "natural" divisions prevents the learner from being overwhelmed, and hence emotionally disturbed, by the size of his job.

3. *Active versus Passive Learning.* Closely related to the question of the best distribution of learning effort and plan of attack is that of the value of recitation during the learning itself. If a memory task is studied by first reading it through and then reciting it to oneself, rereading those parts not clearly remembered, again reciting and so on, retention will be better than if one reads and rereads without recitation. Table XXVIII shows the results of an experiment in which both nonsense syllables and meaningful material were employed. The subjects were eighth-grade pupils.

TABLE XXVIII

(From Gates, 1917)

	Nonsense Syllables, Per Cent Remembered:		Five Short Biographies Totaling about 170 Words, Per Cent Remembered:	
	Immediately	After 4 Hours	Immediately	After 4 Hours
All time given to reading	35	15	35	16
⅕ time given to recitation	50	26	37	19
⅖ time given to recitation	54	28	41	25
⅗ time given to recitation	57	37	42	26
⅘ time given to recitation	74	48	42	26

Evidently, recitation is a decided aid to recall, and the more recitation the better the recall.

Students can greatly aid their retention by training themselves in the simple technique of reading, and reciting often, prompting themselves by reference back to the lesson when necessary. The value of self-recitation for recall and recognition lies in the fact that in reciting to himself the learner is reacting actively to the task. This active search for connections and implications is often called the "will to learn," and is most effective in memory work. In reading or listening to a lecture the student is forced into a passive rôle. In self-recitation, instead of sitting quietly hoping that somehow the lesson will record itself photographically upon his "mind," the student aids the recording process (fixation) by taking an active part in it. Writing abstracts of what one has read and discussion of this material with others aids recall by providing richer connections and associations with the material.

4. *Overlearning and Review*. We have seen in Section 4 how "overlearning" (i. e., learning beyond the bare reproduction level) strengthens retention. Frequent and strategically placed reviews also aid recall and recognition. Reference to Figure 30 will show that the loss through forgetting is most rapid at first, becoming slower and slower as time goes on. Retentivity is helped, then, by reviewing early and often; early to catch the first abrupt sag in the retention curve, and often to prevent later and recurring sags. There is much evidence to support this contention. When a 40-minute lecture was followed immediately by a 5-minute review, recall after 2 months was 50 per cent better than when no immediate review was given.

5. *Memory "Training."* Since failure to remember is such a universal complaint, it is small wonder that various systems claiming to "train" or improve one's memory have been devised. All such systems depend essentially upon the building up of associations between the facts to be learned and the facts already known. When the associations formed are meaningful and relevant (when new facts are hung, so to say, upon the peg of some known fact) the system is helpful. But when extraneous and meaningless associations are advised, it often becomes more difficult to remember the system than to learn the lesson in the first place.

There are several techniques for aiding memory which are useful and hence are worth mentioning. (a) In memorizing number series, telephone or street numbers, say, *grouping* is helpful. Stanzas, rules, dates, paragraphs, sections and the like which represent logical groupings should be utilized whenever possible. Often the material will fall into "natural" groups—the succession 25, 35, 45, for instance, is easier than 27, 36, 48. When *rhythm* is added to the grouping, as in music or poetry, recall is still further aided. (b) Attention to *meanings* and the formation of *secondary associations* helps recall and recognition. If one has good visual imagery, one may aid recall of three specific facts by means of a diagram—by thinking of the three as perched upon the apices of a triangle. Or he may rule off a square into smaller squares (in his "mind's eye") and think of each section as a pigeonhole into which an article is placed. Objects and facts which can be related to important happenings in one's life are more likely to be recalled. Thus, a man may remember the age of a neighbor's child whose age is the same as his own child but forget other children's ages; a boy remembers football signals but forgets his algebra assignment; a girl remembers her "date" but forgets to wash the dishes and so on. Meanings are important aids to memory. Dates in history are better remembered as milestones marking off social, political, or economic periods than as times at which a certain battle took place. Interest and utility, by investing many otherwise tedious statistics with meaning, enhance their memory-value. (c) "Crutches" or memory aids are often useful when the facts have no inherent organization in themselves; though many such aids are probably more of a hindrance than a help. A far-fetched association or idea brought in to aid recall may itself be forgotten; and an ambiguous aid though it may itself be recalled may not revive what it is supposed to revive and may even hinder such revival. The well-known doggerel "Thirty days hath September, etc." is helpful only if one can remember the doggerel! The same is true of the verse "In 1492 Columbus sailed the ocean blue," "oysters *r* in season" and many others. Counting on one's fingers may be definitely useful at first, but it becomes a hindrance and a nuisance if persisted in. When crutches work it is because of their novelty and humorous appeal rather than because of their inherent value.

Probably more people, especially older people, complain of their failure to remember names than of any other memory loss. Part of the trouble here may be due to loss of plasticity with age, but the failure to form adequate secondary associations is probably more important. As one gets older the increase in number of acquaintances puts an inevitable burden upon one's memory and the number of friends with the same or nearly the same name makes for confusion.

Failure to remember a name is often due to poor fixation in the first instance—a name may have been mumbled or not clearly heard upon introduction. A hint on how to improve name fixation is provided by those in whose work it is important to remember names and faces. Such persons upon introduction to a stranger repeat the name with some emphasis and find occasion to use it later on. Secondary associations of names with the characteristics of persons will also help, and are carefully noted by many people. One may remember that Mr. Fox has a long, thin face and a prominent nose; that Mr. Johnson is tall and blond; that Miss Redding has red hair; that Mr. Lee is a Southerner and so on. For those whose memory for names is notoriously poor, writing down the names of people one often forgets with brief descriptions of each, age, appearance, occupation, family connections, and outstanding traits, will help. The adult who wishes to improve his memory should heed William James's advice to teachers to treat their pupils "as so many little systems of associating machinery." More and better associations is still the best advice that the psychologist can give the person with poor memory.

9. SUMMARY OF EBBINGHAUS'S WORK

Leaving our digression into the practical application of experimental studies in memory to affairs of everyday life, let us attempt to summarize in a few words Ebbinghaus's chief contributions to experimental psychology. Certainly we must list his (1) introduction and use of quantitative methods in the study of learning and forgetting; (2) measurement of the factors governing fixation, retention, and recall in verbal learning; and (3) invention of nonsense syllables. Ebbinghaus's memory methods are to-day standard procedures in the psychological laboratory. His main results may be accepted substantially as he left them. Of his invention of nonsense syllables Titchener remarks (ref. 18, p. 380) "It is not too much to say that the recourse to nonsense syllables, as a means to the study of association, marks the most considerable advance, in this chapter of psychology, since the time of Aristotle." In short, Hermann Ebbinghaus was the founder of the quantitative study of memory.

Chapter 11

WATSON'S EXPERIMENTAL STUDIES OF THE BEHAVIOR OF THE HUMAN INFANT

I. BEGINNING OF EXPERIMENTAL STUDY OF THE CHILD

Prior to the studies made between 1917 and 1920 by John B. Watson and his co-workers upon the growth and behavior of the human infant, little actual experimental work had been done in this highly interesting field. There were, to be sure, several excellent biographies of individual children, notably those by Darwin and Miss Shinn. But owing to the resistance and the objections of many people, parents in particular, to any "experiments" upon the human young, few systematically controlled observations on the appearance and development of behavior patterns had been made on large numbers of children from which reliable conclusions could be drawn. Watson's pioneer studies, carried out upon many young children at the Harriet Lane Hospital in Baltimore, did much to remedy the neglect of this field and to emphasize the need and importance of further work. A large share of the interest in the study of the young child which we see exhibited so widely to-day in the establishment of institutes of child welfare and nursery schools had its origin in these early experiments of Watson and his students.

While the value of his pioneer work in child psychology is well recognized, Watson is best known to-day not as a child psychologist, but as the "founder" and champion of an objective "school" of psychology known as behaviorism. Watson received the Ph.D. degree from the University of Chicago in 1903 with a dissertation in the field of animal psychology. The next year he went to Johns Hopkins University, where in 1908 he became professor of experimental psychology at the age of thirty years. To Johns Hopkins, Watson brought a strong interest in animal experimentation and a growing belief in the practicability of extending to man the objective methods used with so much success in animal work. One of his primary objects, in fact, in initiating the experiments with children described in this chapter, was to exemplify the value of objective methods in genetic studies of the human young.

Watson's method was to observe infant activity progressively from birth onward; to catalog fundamental reflexive and instinctive tendencies and unlearned emotional expressions; and to discover how early habits develop from "innate" modes of behavior. Careful note was made of the times at which children begin to reach for, manipulate, and handle objects; sit alone, crawl, and walk. What objects and situations babies are afraid of, angered by, and delighted with were also listed, and the genesis of these emotions studied. Information was obtained, not simply by observing behavior, but by arranging situations and trying them out on children as well. Such records have proved to be extremely valuable in giving a picture of the developing human infant, and in enabling us to detect and remedy habit-deficiencies and perverse emotional attachments at an early age. They have furnished also exact and definite data on the old and much-discussed question of whether a person inherits specific fears of animals and objects, or whether such fears are learned. Eventually studies like these will aid the psychologist the better to guide and direct older children toward the kind of education and the kind of vocation for which their talents fit them.

2. MOTOR AND SENSORY DEVELOPMENT IN THE INFANT

The earliest reflex noted by Blanton, who worked under Watson's direction, was sneezing, which may occur even before the so-called birth-cry. Hiccoughing, yawning, and, of course, crying, also appear very shortly after birth. Besides the birth-cry which is apparently reflexive and comes with the first gasping intake of air by the new born infant, Mrs. Blanton differentiated crying due to (1) hunger, (2) injury and rough treatment, and (3) fatigue. It is interesting that the regular flow of tears does not ordinarily appear until the child is about a month old. Sucking which includes tongue, lip, and cheek movements, and is followed by swallowing, can be demonstrated in the first hour after birth. The reflexes of elimination occur shortly after birth, and sometimes even before birth. Smiling, which comes somewhat later—usually not before the fourth or fifth day—is also unlearned behavior. If the baby is comfortable and well fed, smiling may be elicited by light touches on the body, by stroking the skin, or by a gentle rocking. Apparently the child does not *learn* to smile until it is at least one month old. Mary Cover Jones in a study of 365 babies, found that conditioned or learned smiling, i. e., smiling when the experimenter smiles or talks baby-talk, rarely appears before the child is thirty or forty days old. Gesell reports smiling in response to social stimulation at about ninety days.

Careful observation of the new born infant has shown that the first activities of the baby are in the nature of "mass movements," that is, general diffuse bodily shiftings rather than local movements of separate parts—arms and legs. Apparently almost any stimulus will lead to almost any response, although the reaction is strongest at the point of stimulation, spreading out with decreasing intensity to other body parts. Pinching the toe, for example, causes general body activity;

Photograph by Nikolas Muray, New York

JOHN B. WATSON

(Born 1878)

a bright light provokes thrashing movements of the arms and legs as well as eye movements. Local differentiated movements appear as the child grows older. One of the earliest voluntary motor activities to appear is that of grasping (Fig. 32, A). A baby's fingers will readily close upon a stick, pencil, finger, or any small object. Clinging to this like a small monkey, the child can easily be lifted. All but about two per cent of normal children can support their own weight in this way, the time during which they hang suspended varying from a fraction of a second to as long as a minute. This activity, which is apparently unlearned, appears shortly after birth and drops out when the child is about four months old, although it sometimes persists for a longer time. Once having disappeared, it never returns. The late disappearance of this reflex may be an indication of retarded growth; but at just what age the line should be drawn has not as yet been determined definitely. If an experimenter stimulates a new born child by pressing with his finger upon its chin, the coördination of the two arms into a single defense movement at first is diffuse and poor. After four or five days, however, coördinated movements of the two arms appear with fair regularity. Figure 32, B shows the "defense reflex" of a baby to a slight pinch on the inner surface of one knee. Note that the opposite leg is drawn up as though to push away the annoying stimulus.

With the waning of the grasping reflex (at about 5 months) the child begins to reach; this activity involves extending the hands for an object, seizing it, and (usually) carrying it to the mouth. Somewhat later (6 months) the baby begins actively to employ its thumb, which hitherto has been well-nigh useless, in opposition to its other four fingers. Reaching activity is tested for by holding some attractive object, say a stick of candy, directly in front of the child and allowing him to try and get it. If he grasps it, he is allowed to taste or suck it. A 6-months-old baby will reach not only for candy but, in general, for any small object held close by. If the object reached for hurts or gives pain, the child will soon learn not to reach for that particular thing. After several scorches from a candle, for example, the baby, even at an early age, learns to let lighted candles alone when they come within his reach. A somewhat surprising result obtained from this study of reaching is the discovery that the child does not reach for objects more than two feet away. This is quite contrary to the poetic notion that the young child will reach for the moon or for any distant object.

Grasping of objects depends upon hand-eye coördinations; and hence it is important to know when eye movements become coördinated and which movements are first to appear. One method of studying eye movements is to place the baby on its back in a dark room with the head held gently in place by an assistant. Just above the baby's head a perimeter is then placed. This contrivance, which looks like the half of a hoop, carries a small light. The baby's head being the center of the circle of which the perimeter is the semi-circumference, the light when moved is always the same distance from the baby's eyes. Now by moving the light to the right or left, the movements of the child's eyes in following the light can be studied. Watson found that the "roving" movements of the eyes are poorly coördinated at birth. Sherman, who has verified these observations on ninety-six babies ranging from one hour to twelve days old, adds that after thirty to forty hours coördination is fairly good. The first coördinated following movements with true fixation are those in which the baby's eyes turn to the left or right. Somewhat later (after fifty to eighty days) upward and downward movements appear; and the baby when two to three months old is able to follow the light if it is moved in a circle. At about the same age, the baby responds more often to colored than to uncolored objects; and by the age of 6–9 months color preferences become

A

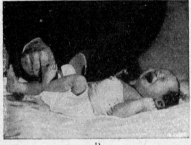

B

FIG. 32

SHOWING SOME INFANT REFLEXES

A is the grasping reflex of a child twelve days old. B shows the defensive reflex of left foot to slight pinch on inner surface of right knee. [From J. B. Watson's *Psychology from the Standpoint of a Behaviorist*, 2nd edition (J. B. Lippincott Company, 1924), Fig. 56.] For another reflex, see Fig. 32, C and D, facing page 298.

marked. Red is the preferred color, followed by yellow and blue. Individual differences in preference for colors appear clearly after about two years. The motor response of blinking, brought about by passing the hand between the child's face and a source of light, occurs at 2–3 months. This reflex is extremely useful in protecting the eye from injury, and belongs to the general class of movements known as "protective reflexes."

An important sign of development in the young child is the ability to sit alone, for, like reaching, it shows that the baby is gradually learning how to use its own body. At three months and a half, says Watson, the infant may sit unsupported for as long as two minutes. M. C. Jones, on the basis of more observations than Watson, puts the first appearance of sitting alone at five months, Gesell at six to eight months. The discrepancy here is apparently the result of setting up different criteria for "sitting alone." By the age of six months the child will sit alone twice as long as at three months, and will play with its toes, pull at its clothing, and strike the bed upon which it is sitting. After sitting alone, the first step in the locomotion series is crawling, from which standing and walking develop. Many infants can support themselves in the standing position, by holding on to some object, as early as the eighth or ninth month. The age at which a child begins to walk depends upon its health, its weight, and whether it has had any frights or injuries from falls. Walking may appear at one year of age or even earlier. After the first step has been taken, actual skill in learning to walk is contingent upon the increase in body strength and growth, as well as upon the praise and encouragement received from the parents. As the sphere of his interests enlarges, the normal child seeks voluntarily to increase his means of getting what he wants.

Tickle the sole of a baby's foot or stroke it gently with the blunt point of a pencil and the big toe will turn upward in a fanning or extension movement, while the other toes are turned down (flexion movement). This reaction, which is entirely unlearned, is called the Babinski reflex, and is found in practically all infants (Fig. 32, C and D). Sherman reports that in 90 per cent of the cases examined by him, extension at the first stimulus was followed quickly by flexion at the next stimulus. He regards the failure of the second movement to appear as evidence of poor functional or neural development. The Babinski reflex usually disappears between the sixth and twelfth months of the child's life. It is of considerable clinical value, since its presence indicates incomplete development of the nervous system. Hence if the reflex persists longer than one year the supposition is that the baby is not developing normally. When found in adults the Babinski reflex is a sign of a pathological or diseased condition.

3. HANDEDNESS IN CHILDREN

As is well known, most adults are right-handed, although a fair minority (perhaps 10 per cent) use the left as the preferred hand. Is the preference for the right hand innate or is it a learned response? The answer to this question is of more than theoretical interest. If handedness is inborn, it is probably safer to let a child use his preferred hand rather than try to change him, because there is some evidence that stammering and emotional disturbances occur when a left-handed child is forced later on to change over to his right hand. But if handedness is a matter of chance or of early habit-formation, then, since most people are right-handed, it would seem best to teach all children from the beginning to use the right hand in preference to the left. Watson investigated this question of handedness in several ways which illustrate so clearly the experimental techniques used in child study that they will be described rather fully.

1. First, a comparison was made of the length of time during

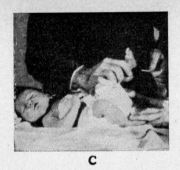

C

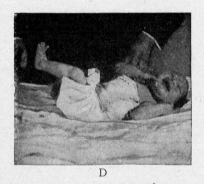

D

FIG. 32 (*continued*)
SHOWING SOME INFANT REFLEXES

C is stimulation for the Babinski reflex. The blunt end of a match is rubbed across the sole of the foot. The result is shown in D. The great toe shows extension, the small toes "fanning or flexion. (This is a very variable reflex so far as pattern is concerned.) [From J. B. Watson's *Psychology from the Standpoint of a Behaviorist,* 2nd edition (J. B. Lippincott Company, 1924), Fig. 56.] For other reflexes, see Fig. 32, A and B, facing page 296.

which twenty very young children could hang from a bar, supporting their own weight either by the right hand alone or by the left hand alone. The tests were begun at birth and continued for the first ten days of the child's life. Results showed that children hang, on the average, as long with the left as with the right hand, i. e., no innate preference in this activity, at least, was apparent (see Fig. 32, A, for illustration).

2. Next the amount of random slashing movements made by the baby with its right and its left arms was measured. The record of such voluntary activity as appeared was kept by means of a small "work adder," a device which when operated caused a notched wheel to revolve in one direction. This wheel wound up a weight attached by a cord to a drum thus giving a record of work performed. One end of the adder cord was fastened to the child's wrist, the other to the weight. Two adders were used so that records from both arms could be taken simultaneously. This experiment, which occupied about five minutes, showed that almost identical amounts of work were done by the right and left arms, thus indicating that neither arm (and neither hand) is favored in gross slashing movements of this kind.

3. In the third test, children from five to twelve months old were examined to see which hand was used first in reaching for objects. Twenty babies were tested once a week, ten to twenty trials being given to each. Generally a stick of candy or a candle served as the test object. This was brought in slowly toward the baby on a level with its eyes, and exactly in the middle line squarely between the baby's two hands. Usually reaching occurred when the object was about two feet away. A careful record was kept of which hand was used for reaching; or, if both hands were used, as sometimes happened, which touched the object first. No marked preference for either hand appeared in this test; sometimes the child used the right and again the left hand more often.

4. As a final test, measurements were made of the length of the right and left forearms, wrists, palms, and fingers. No significant differences were found between the right and left measurements of 100 babies.

These studies of handedness suggest the absence of any inborn preference for either hand. Other studies, however, indicate that—if not inborn—hand preference develops very early. Thus, left-handedness is often marked at one year and may be well established before the age of two years. The origin of handedness in a given child is not definitely known, and hence modern educational practice takes a compromise position with regard to treatment. If the child who shows a strong preference for the left hand finds great difficulty in changing, develops speech disorders, or shows signs of irritability, nervous tension, and unhappiness, he is usually left alone. Changing such a child from left to right hand involves an expenditure in nervous energy which does not justify the result. But children who seem able to change from left to right hand without too great effort—and this is true of most children—are encouraged to shift.

Ours is a right-handed culture. The desire of parents that their children shall not be "different" is of major importance in fitting the growing boy and girl into the right-hand mold. At an early age the boy is taught to shake hands, take off his hat, and write with his right hand; later on he finds that tools, baseball gloves, and golf-clubs favor the right-hander. Convenience and social pressure are usually strong enough to make all but the most stubborn left-handers conform.

4. TESTS OF DEVELOPMENT IN YOUNG CHILDREN

Tests of physiological development and motor control are often used to determine whether a baby is "normal" for his age. Tests for young children are usually grouped into a graded series or scale from which norms or developmental

standards may be calculated. A good illustration of such a
scale is Kuhlman's "Tests of Mental Development." Kuhlman has assembled and standardized 89 tests which cover the
age-range from 4 months to 16 years and beyond. The early
age-tests represent, for the most part, methods of discovering
whether a child possesses the normal reflexes, as well as
the motor, sensory, and language activities characteristic of
children of his age. By the age of 6 months, according to Kuhlman's scale, a child should be able to sit without support one-
half minute or more; to react by turning his head toward the
source of sound when a telegraphic snapper or small bell is
sounded; to reach for objects such as a bell, rattle, colored ball
when dangled before his eyes within reach; to pick up a red
checker by a pincer-like movement using thumb in opposition
to fingers. By the time he is one year old, a child should—
among other things—be able to remove a cloth cover from a
cup or rattle, imitate arm movements, crawl or creep three or
more feet to secure an interesting toy, mark with a pencil on
paper. At two years, the child should obey simple commands
such as "Go bring me the ball"; recognize objects such as a
block, key, watch, doll; name familiar objects seen in a picture, e. g., apple, flower, bird. In accordance with his successes and failures with these tests, the mental age of the baby
can be calculated in much the same way as that of an older
child.

An interesting set of "performance" tests for the young
child is the Merrill-Palmer series of tests drawn up and
standardized by Rachel Stutsman. These tests (there are
ninety-three in all) are grouped into six-month intervals
from eighteen months to six years; that is, the first group of
eleven tests is for children eighteen to twenty-four months old;
the second group (ten tests) for children twenty-four to thirty
months old; and so on. The mental age of the child is calculated from the total number of tests in the series which he is

able to pass. To illustrate the kind of performances called for, the average child of two to two and one-half years is expected to be able to repeat four simple words (e. g., *kitty, ball*); to recognize himself in the mirror; fit sixteen cubes into a box in 125 seconds or less; put pegs into a board; pull a stick attached to a string in toward himself, using one or both hands; arrange four cubes—of different sizes all open at one face—into the form of a "nest," each cube being fitted into the one next larger in size; answer six out of ten simple questions, e. g., "What does a kitty say?" "What is this (chair)?"; cut paper with scissors; and repeat simple word-groups, such as "see the pretty dollie." As is evident, these tests measure the child's ability to recognize and manipulate familiar objects of his environment in a sensible if elementary fashion.

Various other test series or scales have been developed for use with the preschool child. Two of these, the Minnesota Preschool Tests and the Vienna Babytests will be briefly described. The Minnesota scale consists of both language and non-language items; it may be scored to show either verbal or non-verbal development or both (combined scale). The materials employed in the test are interesting to young children and varied enough to cover a wide range of activities. The tests span the age-range from eighteen months to six years, and must be administered by a trained psychologist. The Vienna Babytests, developed by Charlotte Bühler and her assistants, cover the first and second years of life. Four areas of activity are sampled by these tests: (a) bodily control and coördination; (b) mental ability; (c) object manipulation, memory and attentiveness; (d) social development, e. g., smiling when another smiles, actively seeking contacts with people, play, use of toys and the like. No claim is made that a given test samples only *one* of the four fields, but the division is convenient and useful in diagnosis.

Tests of very young children do not have very precise predictive value for later years. This is owing in part, at least, to the real difficulties encountered in testing very young children. A young child's attention is easily distracted and hard to hold once secured. It is hard to get an adequate measure of the shy, timid child, or of the boisterous, spoiled, and stubborn child. Physical condition, fatigue, emotional upsets all make for variability and serve to decrease the significance of a test rating. Even more than with older children, the personality of the examiner is important; and a person unacquainted with children can rarely get coöperation. In spite of these real obstacles to accurate rating of the very young child, measurements made at a later age-level do not often change the child's general classification. Thus while the I Q of an individual child may drop from 160 to 140 between the ages of two and six, or may increase from 70 to 80, the designation of the child as bright or dull remains unchanged. The size of the vocabulary is perhaps the best single index of a young child's later mental level.

Seven simple performance tests, much used with younger children, are shown in Figure 33. These tests all measure, in a general way, the child's muscular development and hand-eye coördination. They gauge, too, his perception of form and shape, and knowledge of common everyday things. The Wallin Peg Boards (A and B) set before the child the task of fitting the six round pegs in A, and the six square pegs in B, into the holes in the board. These are very easy tests and can be done by normal children from eighteen months to two years of age. They are often used as tests of the feeble-minded and the low-grade. The Nest of Cubes Test (C) has been described above. Each cube is to be fitted into the one next larger in size. The average child of two to two and one-half years should do this test in four minutes or less. In D, Pintner's Manikin Test, the child is required to fit the arms, legs, and head pieces, which are separate, onto the trunk to

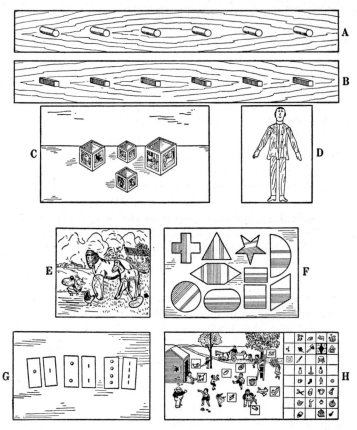

FIG. 33

SOME PERFORMANCE TESTS MUCH USED WITH YOUNG CHILDREN

A and B are Wallin Peg Boards; C is the Nest of Cubes Test; D, Pintner's Manikin Test; E, the Mare and Foal Test; F, the Sequin Form Board; G, the Decroly Button Test; H, the Healy Picture Completion Test, No. 1.

form a man. This test is rarely done correctly by children under eight years of age. The Mare and Foal Test (E) sets the task of fitting certain cut-out pieces into their correct locations. The normal three-year-old takes about five minutes to do this test. The Sequin Form Board Test (F) is the best known of the many form-board tests. The average child of three years can fit the blocks into their proper places in about two minutes.

The Button Test (G) was devised by the Belgian psychologist, Decroly. The six strips are of flannelette, three inches by six inches, and are arranged in pairs. The first pair consists of a strip with a button sewed on it and a second strip in which a button-hole has been worked to fit the button. The next pair of strips contains two buttons and two button-holes, respectively, and the third four buttons and four button-holes. The buttoning and unbuttoning process is first demonstrated to the child, who is then encouraged to try it. A normal child of two and one-half years can usually do one button, a child of three years, two buttons. The Picture Completion Test, No. 1, of Healy (H) is usable with children from about five to twelve years of age. The child is called upon to fill in certain cut-out portions in the picture with appropriate blocks selected from a set supplied by the examiner. There are more blocks than are needed to complete the picture, so that a real choice must be made. The test is first explained and demonstrated to the child. The score is computed from the number of correct placements. Of the tests shown in Figure 33, A, B, C, D, E, F, and G are used in the Merrill-Palmer series; D, E, F, and H are a part of the Pintner-Paterson Scale of Performance Tests.

Gesell, in his studies of pre-school children at the child clinic of Yale University, has devised an extensive schedule of tests and observations to be employed with children from about one month to six years of age. Four fields of behavior activities are sampled: (1) *Motor behavior,* which deals with muscular capacity, coördination, locomotion, and the use of hands and arms; (2) *language,* involving vocalization, word comprehension, speech, and conversation; (3) *personal-social behavior* as exhibited in reactions to persons, initiative, play, social experience, and information; and (4) *adaptive behavior,* concerned with hand-eye coördination, imitation, discrimination, ability to make proper adjustments to a given situation, and sensible control. Gesell's schedule is not a test in the sense of being concerned primarily with determining a score or mental age. It is rather a summary and a diagnosis of the child's developmental status based on physical and psychological examinations as well as upon clinical observation.

5. EMOTIONAL DEVELOPMENT OF THE YOUNG CHILD

As a result of many observations carried out on very young children, Watson reached the conclusion that there are only three fundamental emotions, fear, anger (or rage), and love. These "primary" emotional patterns appear at birth or shortly thereafter. Watson's method of testing for native emotions was to bring the child into the laboratory, present stimuli which are known to produce emotions in adults, and note carefully the child's typical reactions. In every case, an effort was made to describe the emotion in terms of its characteristic pattern, and to define it strictly in terms of the situation which called it out.

What stimuli, for example, will call out the emotion of fear in the very young child? After working with various situations, Watson discovered that *loud noises, painful stimuli,* and the *sudden loss of support* (allowing the child to drop a few inches) cause the infant to recoil, catch its breath, clutch with its hands, and if possible crawl away. These responses constitute the "pattern" of what Watson called a fear-reaction. No other stimuli brought out fear so regularly and definitely; for instance, these very young children were found to have no native fear of the dark, of animals, of people, or of the thousand and one things of which children are supposed to be "naturally" afraid.

To bring out the emotional response of rage or extreme anger Watson found it sufficient to hamper or restrict the infant's movements in some way. If the child's head is held lightly between the hands, or the movements of its arms or legs restrained, it will exhibit the behavior which is called rage. This "pattern" consists in a stiffening of the body, crying or screaming, and struggling to escape. If first attempts are unsuccessful, the child will hold its breath or scream until it becomes blue with rage.

In very young children the emotion of love, as Watson defines it, is characterized by smiling, gurgling, and cooing. Sometimes the child moves its arms and legs rapidly, and sometimes it lies very still, the picture of contentment. The stimuli for love responses are a stroking of the skin, tickling, patting and rocking. When the child becomes older, it will hold out its arms to be taken by the adult.

Other investigators have found that Watson's situations do not *always* lead to fear, anger, or affection as he supposed. For example, some young children show no fear of loud noises or of the threatened loss of support, though most children do. Later research, also, has failed to reveal the definite and clear-cut *patterns* of rage, fear, and love which Watson believed to be the only "primary" emotions. An experiment by Sherman is enlightening on this point. A group of 32 graduate students in psychology were shown motion pictures portraying the reactions of infants to four kinds of stimuli—hunger, sudden dropping through a distance of two or three feet toward a table, restraint of head and face, pricking with a needle. The stimuli themselves were not seen by the observer, as the scenes showing the administration of the stimuli had been deleted from the film, leaving only those showing the child's reactions. Little agreement appeared when the student judges recorded what they thought was the emotional reaction exhibited by the child in each instance. Thirteen observers called the hunger response, anger, seven called it hunger, seven fear, three pain, one grief, and one consternation. Fourteen called the response to dropping anger, only five fear. In another test, a group of medical students and nurses were shown the stimuli which produced the emotional responses being administered, as well as the responses themselves. Judgment under these conditions was much improved, fear being most often named for the dropping responses, anger for restraint, and pain for the needle prick. When the films were arranged so that the infant's emotional behavior was shown preceded by some other stimulus than that which actually produced the emotion, accuracy of judgment was much decreased, suggesting that the observers had based their opinions more on the stimulus situation than on the behavior. No doubt this is generally true for other than laboratory situations. We judge a person's probable emotional state from the expected effect of the stimulus upon him more often than from his overt responses. A given emotion is not revealed by a stereotyped and invariable sequence of movements. While fear may be "typically" characterized by shrinking of some sort, and rage by aggression or attack, the extent and variety of the behavior differs greatly from child to child and for the same child on separate occasions.

6. HOW CHILDREN ACQUIRE FEARS AND OTHER EMOTIONAL ATTITUDES

In searching for situations and objects which might lead to emotional behavior, Watson carried out several tests on older children, i. e., those varying in age from about four months to one year. All of the children examined had been brought up in the hospital and had never seen any of the animals or other objects used in the tests.

First, the child was brought into the laboratory and allowed to sit upon the lap of its mother or an attendant. Various animals were then presented and the baby's reactions noted. When a very lively black cat purred near by, the baby showed no fear; nor did he show any fear of a pigeon, a rabbit, or a white rat. These were all reached for, one baby trying to put the rabbit's ears into her mouth. In addition to the tests in the laboratory, each child was taken to the zoo and allowed to get quite close to the animals. The result was the same as before: not the slightest fear was shown.

These tests are highly interesting and at first sight almost unbelievable. If originally a baby shows fear only when confronted by a loud noise or when threatened with loss of support or when actually injured, how does it come about that older children and many adults are afraid of so many things: the dark, snakes, dogs, bugs, cats, and far more innocuous stimuli? The answer given by Watson is that they have *learned* to fear these things, and that the method by which such fears have been learned is the familiar conditioned response.* A conditioned response, as we know, is behavior called out by some stimulus other than that to which it was originally bound. Strike a dog with a stick and yell "Go away," and it is probable that at a later time the dog will not wait to be struck, but will run when he sees the stick, or even when he hears your voice. This is a simple illustration of a conditioned response. Fear and running away are brought out in the dog by stimuli, sight of the stick or yell, originally powerless to produce these specific reactions. In the same fashion, fear of lightning is often aroused in the young child by the fact that lightning and thunder (loud noise-original stimulus for fear) occur together. Many examples of the same kind are cited elsewhere (see pp. 196–197).

Watson decided to see whether he could build up a con-

* See Chapter 5.

ditioned fear in the laboratory. His subject was a boy, Albert B., eleven months old, and possessed of a stolid and phlegmatic disposition. First, it was determined by actual test that Albert was not in the least afraid of furry animals, such as the rabbit and the white rat. When put within his reach he immediately attempted to grasp them. However, Albert's reaction to a loud noise made by striking a steel bar with a hammer was distinctly one of fear. He would pucker up his lips, throw up his arms; then turn over on his side away from the noise and begin to whimper. The problem which Watson set was this: Can an animal be "substituted" for the loud noise and thus become a fear-object? The experimental set-up was as follows. First, the white rat was presented to Albert. At once he reached for it, and as soon as he touched it, the steel bar just behind the child's head was struck a heavy blow. The fear reaction immediately appeared. The next time the child reached for the rat the noise was repeated, with the same result—fear was distinctly shown. Seven days later the child eyed the rat warily when it was presented, refusing to touch it. When the rat touched the baby's hand, the hand was quickly withdrawn, but the child did not cry. It was clearly apparent, however, that the child, while not quite afraid, was not favorably inclined toward the rat. No fear response at all was shown by Albert toward other objects, such as building blocks, which had not been presented together with the noise. Three more joint presentations of rat plus noise were now given, which were sufficient to produce unmistakable signs of fear when the rat was later presented alone. Two more joint stimulations, and the instant the rat appeared on the scene the baby began to cry and to crawl away as fast as he could. Five days later the child was still afraid of the rat.

In order to discover whether this conditioned fear had spread to other objects, Watson then tested Albert with a rabbit, a dog, a fur coat, and cotton wool. To all of these the child was sharply negative: either he cried or crawled away or both; in every case he refused to play with the objects. None of these things, it must be remembered, had been presented along with the loud noise. Yet because of their similarity, the fear reaction had been "transferred" to all of them. But no fear was exhibited whatsoever to building blocks, the conditioned fear apparently having spread only to furry objects.

Watson did not attempt to build up any rage reactions experimentally, evidently because of the danger involved in dealing with such reactions; nor did he condition any love reactions in the laboratory. Conditioned or learned rage reactions are often encountered, however, as when a child goes into a temper-tantrum or into a screaming fit in order to get candy or some other desired object, or to gain its ends. We are all familiar, too, with the ease with which a child's love reactions can be transferred from mother to nurse or to grandmother, depending upon which one provides food, petting, and comfort.

Research in child psychology has greatly expanded since Watson's pioneer experiments. The present-day worker in the field of child development is essentially interested in the broad aspects of emotional, social, physical, and intellectual growth as these are related to each other and to everyday living. Literally scores of studies have been made of the child in school, his behavior problems, nervous habits, social difficulties and the like. To illustrate, studies of anger in children from seven months to seven years show this emotion to be typically overt, violent and unrestrained in the very young; personal, relative and socially motivated in the older child. Irascibility has been linked with poor health, over-indulgence, over-solicitude, and with hypercritical parental attitudes. Apparently, most fears in young children can be tied up with poor training at home or with lack of good training. In very young children (2–4 years) sympathetic, friendly and co-operative behavior appears, when investigated carefully, to be a consistent and characteristic trait. It increases with chronological age, and with mental development; is about equal for boys and girls; and differs greatly from child to child.

7. METHODS OF BREAKING UNDESIRABLE HABITS

Experiments like those described in the last Section are valuable in showing how useless and even harmful emotional responses may arise to many innocent situations. The discovery of just what causes lie behind such behavior and the formulation of methods of treating and eradicating them is a major problem for the child psychologist. If, working backward, we are able to uncover the reason why a child is afraid of a dog or a dark hallway, or why he is thrown into a tantrum by a seemingly innocent circumstance, we are certainly in a better position to clear the matter up. Much unhappiness could undoubtedly be prevented if harmful habits could be broken up or "reconditioned" in childhood as soon as they appear.

Several experimental studies of various methods of eliminating harmful habits have recently been undertaken, largely as an outgrowth of the work we have described. Among the most interesting of these is the study of unnatural fears in childhood carried out by Mary Cover Jones. About seventy children in all, from three months to seven years old, were the subjects. These children were all being maintained in an institution for the temporary care of children; they were from fairly good homes and were of normal intellect as determined by individual mental examinations. Children who showed marked fear of snakes, rats, rabbits, frogs, "scare" faces (masks), loud sounds, and so on were selected for study. The main object was the removal of these useless and hampering forms of behavior. The following descriptions will serve to illustrate the methods employed.

1. *The Method of Elimination through Disuse.* This method is grounded in the common opinion that a childish fear will gradually wear itself out, if the child is shielded from the fear-inspiring object. This may be true when the interval extends over long periods of time during which the child grows and enlarges his experiences; but it did not work very well in Jones's tests, which extended over several weeks and even months. At best, ignoring a fear, or shielding the child from fear-objects would seem to be a temporary expedient. Fears cannot all be so treated, nor can the child be shielded all of its life.

Disuse is often accomplished through change-of-environment—a method much used in therapy. Thus, an overworked and harried person may be advised to take a trip, the supposition being that upon return the irritating stimuli will be weakened. Change-of-environment is most useful, perhaps, when combined with other devices which seek to change the person's attitude.

2. *The Method of Verbal Appeal.* It is a common assumption of many parents that a child can usually be "reasoned with" or talked out of his fears, of say, snakes or dogs; that by telling stories woven around the fear-object, showing pictures, and the like, the child's curiosity and interest will be sufficiently aroused to overcome his fear. This plan was tried with a five-year-old-girl who exhibited marked fear of a rabbit. Picture-books of "Peter Rabbit," toy rabbits, and stories were used to create interest in real rabbits. At the end of a week of such treatment, however, the child's fear of the real rabbit was as strong as before. Apparently verbal assurances are not sufficient defense against a strong fear urge. Here actions not only speak louder than words, they speak more truthfully.

3. *The Method of Negative Adaptation or Toleration.* Negative adaptation in plain language means that familiarity breeds contempt or at least indifference. The idea behind this method is that the child will finally become "used to" snakes, bugs, or even "ghosts" in a dark room, if such situations are encountered often enough. This assumption seems fairly well founded. In several instances a child, originally very much frightened by a white rat, became at least tolerant, if not exactly friendly, when the animal was often seen around. This method would seem to be valuable if used intelligently—i. e., if the stimulations are not too frequent nor too drastic.

Another form of the negative adaptation method is called the "exhaustion method." A child will often whine and tease for some favor as long as there is some hope of eventual success. If ignored long enough he may finally give up and resort to a more socially acceptable approach. In like manner, an animal on first being confined in a cage will actively and persistently seek to escape. Failing in this, he finally "gives in" and after a time accepts captivity with an appearance of equanimity. The method of exhaustion is based, of course, upon the law of effect (see p. 203). In the case of children, at least, its application is usually more trying upon the "experimenter's" patience than upon the "subject's" emotional make-up. Swift and immediate punishment is often more effective in ending the undesirable behavior than is the "wearing-out" process; and in some cases is more justifiable.

4. *The Method of Repression.* Children's fears are often repressed or temporarily hidden under the surface when they are ridiculed by other children or by adults. Little boys, particularly, of around four or five will often make a brave show, their desire not to be eclipsed or made to feel inferior serving for the time to overcome their real feelings. But the repression of a fear in this way is dangerous business, as the remedy may turn out to be worse than the original ailment. Instead

of being lost, a fear may be more strongly entrenched as a result of social ridicule and teasing.

5. *The Method of Distraction.* This method, much used by mothers in everyday child upbringing, consists in presenting an object or other stimulus so pronouncedly positive in appeal that the child's attention is temporarily, at least, distracted from the fear-object. A child's fear of a frog or rabbit can be somewhat lessened by placing toys and other desirable playthings near the animals. Verbal distractions, too, such as soothings, calling the animal by name, pointing out characteristics of the "bunny" or "hop-toad" prove useful in inducing a child to forget his fear in the new interest. But the presence of an adult (who does the distracting) introduces a variable factor so that it is impossible to tell how much of the child's confidence is due to the reliance and trust which is placed in the protection of the grown-up. In many cases, the fear may be temporarily lightened, however, if not completely overcome.

6. *The Method of Direct Conditioning.* In this method an attempt is made to associate with the fear-object some stimulus which is known to be capable of calling out a strong positive (pleasant) response. The hope is that in time the fear-object will itself bring out a positive rather than a negative reaction. In several experiments, food was used as the positive stimulus-object to overcome a specific fear of animals, e. g., a rabbit. The procedure was to put the rabbit upon the table, on which the child's food had been placed, at a sufficient distance not to interfere with the child's eating, but close enough to keep the animal well in sight. At first the child ate with a wary eye on the rabbit; and for several days this continued with nothing happening. Gradually the animal was moved closer and closer to the food until finally tolerance changed to indifference and even to the positive response of reaching and stroking the rabbit. While very successful in many cases, this method requires the most careful handling. If fear of the animal or other

object is very intense, it may produce a negative response to the food, or such violent crying and screaming as to make the child ill. If care and patience are exercised, however, it would seem to be the most effective method of removing useless and hampering fears.

7. *The Method of Social Stimulation.* There are many cases in which this method may be used successfully. When a child discovers that other children—as well as grown-ups—are not frightened at the sight of dogs, rabbits, bugs, and so on, curiosity and self-assertion are often powerful enough to "overcome" his fear without more ado. To some extent this is true also of adults, unless the fear be deeply ingrained as the result of some intense experience; or else serves some ulterior purpose. Girls, for instance, are no more afraid of small animals and bugs than boys up to the period of adolescence. When the "grown-up" period is reached, girls find that it is considered "feminine" and rather commendable by the young males if they scream and show fright at such objects; and so a fear, partly feigned, is developed. If an adult is in earnest about ridding himself of a foolish and useless fear, the original cause must first be found and a period of reëducation instituted until the fear-stimulus becomes no longer effective.

Of the seven methods outlined in this Section, undoubtedly the most practical are direct conditioning and social stimulation. While sometimes effective alone, verbal appeal, elimination through disuse, negative adaptation, repression, and distraction are probably most valuable when employed together with the other techniques. Which method to employ will depend upon the kind of fear and its intensity, as well as upon the child's general health, intelligence, and environmental background. Work on problems such as these is going on in many laboratories through the country. Watson's studies marked the beginning of the present widespread activity and interest in the problems of the preschool child.

Chapter 12

EXPERIMENTAL STUDIES OF THE EMOTIONS:
THE WORK OF CANNON AND OTHERS

I. PSYCHOLOGICAL THEORIES OF THE EMOTIONS

The experimental study of the emotions offers some of the most fascinating and at the same time most elusive problems for research in psychology. The interest of psychologists in the topic is seen in the number of experimental studies recently made or now in progress; while the difficulties encountered in them are attested to by the diversity in their results. Reasons for this are not hard to find. Emotions tend to dissipate when examined introspectively and to lose color and intensity when recalled. It is not easy, either, to get genuine emotional states under laboratory conditions; and numerous technical difficulties arise when the attempt is made to measure complex physiological changes in order to square these off against the subject's verbal report of his felt emotion. Such obstacles as these, however, have acted as a spur rather than a check to experimental investigation.

The importance of the emotions in behavior has long been recognized by psychologists. But it is only recently that they have come to realize keenly that the success or failure of an individual in his professional or occupational career—and of course in his private life—is contingent upon emotional balance as much as, if not more than, upon intellectual ability. The stimulus to investigation, therefore, has come from practical as well as from theoretical considerations.

What do we mean by an emotional response? How does it

arise? Upon what factors does it depend? Historically, nearly all writers on the subject of emotional states have in some way connected them with the viscera—the heart, stomach, lungs, and other internal organs. The ancient Greek philosophers located the "seat" of the emotions in the heart or abdomen. Such expressions as "hard-hearted," "spleeny," "to eat one's heart out," "bowels of mercy," show the influence of venerable notions which have survived in the common speech of our times.

Several views of the emotions seem to be fairly well defined to-day, despite the existence of variants and modifications. The first of these—the "common-sense" view—regards emotions as being primarily mental or conscious phenomena, followed, to be sure, by organic and circulatory changes, but not dependent upon these. The difference between a man running a race and one running away from a mad dog lies, according to this view, not in the physiological activities of the two men, which are closely alike, but rather in their very diverse mental states. A second view considers an emotion to be the subject's conscious awareness of the organic and physiological processes going on in his own body. This is the famous James-Lange theory of the emotions, proposed by William James in 1884 and independently by the Danish physiologist C. Lange in 1885. In the average man's view, a person cries when he is sorry and laughs when he is happy or joyful: the bodily expression *follows* the sorrow or joy. Commenting upon this common-sense notion, James wrote: "My thesis on the contrary, is that the bodily changes follow directly the *Perception* of the exciting fact, and that our feeling of the same changes as they occur IS the emotion." "We feel sorry," he says, "because we cry, angry because we strike, afraid because we tremble." Partly because of its novelty, and partly because of the authority of its authors, this view of the emotions has exerted much influence upon the thinking of later workers.

WALTER B. CANNON

(Born 1871)

A third view stresses the part played in emotions by visceral and skeletal muscles as well as by glandular changes, but it places considerable emphasis, too, upon the conscious processes involved. Woodworth and Cannon represent this position. An emotion, according to Woodworth, is a "stirred up state of the organism" in which there is an impulse or conscious attitude tending toward some definite activity. First comes the stimulus; then the tendency, impulse or motor set, e. g., to escape or fight, which in turn is followed by physiological changes. The organic components are biologically valuable in that they prepare the animal or man the better to run or fight, as the case may be. Feats of strength and endurance— the run from Marathon to Athens, unbelievable deeds on the football field, heroic actions in the face of danger—all illustrate the value of an emotion in reinforcing the dominant drive and giving impetus to behavior. The factor which, according to this view, marks one emotion off from another is the *set* or *impulse,* which is, in turn, governed by the total situation. Typically, then, emotion *follows* impulse. A man sees a car bearing down on him; he jumps back hastily to the curb, fear surging over him *as* or *after* he jumps. The behavioristic approach represents still a fourth view. Consciousness is completely ignored. We have done all we can scientifically, according to the behaviorist, when we have described the motor and glandular reaction patterns which accompany what we call an emotion. The difference between anger and joy is simply the difference in the way the body reacts. The individual's mental state is of no consequence, at least to the extreme behaviorist, though it may be the basis for a verbal report of how he feels.

2. PROBLEMS AND METHODS IN STUDYING EMOTIONS

From these different, and to some degree contradictory, points of view, various problems involving the physical basis, as well as the isolation and measurement of emotions have been attacked by psychologists. The following groups of problems are fairly typical of the experimental work in this field. Although by no means exhaustive, they will help to center the discussion and make it more concrete. (1) First are those studies which deal with the *physical basis* of emotions and the *physiological changes* in emotional states. What rôle do the brain and the rest of the nervous system play in emotion? Can an emotion exist apart from the bodily changes—flushing of the skin, rapid heart-beat and breathing, clenched fists, and so on—usually associated with it? (2) In another group are experiments which have sought to discover whether emotions can be *measured* by instruments; whether there are any fairly *definite* and *recognizable* emotional patterns; and whether emotions can be differentiated on the basis of the physiological changes corresponding to the subjective emotional states reported by the subject. (3) Still other experiments have been planned to discover whether emotional states are highly correlated, i. e., whether a person who reacts in a highly emotional way to one stimulus will tend to react with equal intensity to other stimuli. (4) Finally, there are the attempts to reach and resolve emotional difficulties (complexes) by ferreting out the cause of the original upset in the subject's history. This list will serve, at least, to illustrate how wide and varied has been the experimental attack upon the subject.

In general, two methods have been employed by psychologists in investigating emotions: *the method of expression* and *the method of impression*. The method of expression is the more widely employed, largely because it is more objective. What it seeks to do is to record and measure the bodily changes which accompany emotional states, putting little or no emphasis upon introspective reports. The method of impression, on the other hand, studies emotions introspectively or, more exactly, retrospectively. The subject, for instance, tells which of two color combinations he prefers, or which of two musical selections has moved him most. Again, after an emotional experience, the subject may be asked to report upon his thoughts and feelings. Were there conflicts, feelings of embarrassment, or anger? When and how did they appear? Sometimes the emphasis is on one method and sometimes on the other, but most experimenters have combined the two, taking objective records wherever possible, and recording, too, the verbal reports or introspections of the subject.

3. THE PHYSICAL BASIS OF EMOTIONS

The question of the extent to which an emotion depends upon its accompanying bodily changes is largely a matter of physiological research, and in consequence the experiments in this field have been performed for the most part by physiologists. One notable experiment is that of Sherrington, the eminent English physiologist. Sherrington transected the spinal cords of a number of dogs in the neck region, thereby severing all connection between the brain and the body organs of the trunk. All sensations from the viscera and the skin were completely destroyed by this operation, only sensations arising from stimulation of face, head, and neck region remaining intact. In spite of this drastic reduction of the animal's source of sensory impressions from its own body and skin, emotions persisted with little or no apparent reduction in intensity. One operated dog, for example, showed marked rage and antipathy toward an attendant. She growled, snarled, and bared her teeth, giving the same picture of anger seen in normal animals. At the same time this animal displayed affectionate behavior toward the person who customarily fed and stroked her. We do not know, of course, whether this animal actually *experienced* an emotion. But these experiments certainly prove that emotional expression *can* take place in the absence of the usual visceral changes.

An interesting feature of Sherrington's experiment was the

retention by a dog of what might be called "disgust" behavior. Normal dogs, Sherrington found, refuse to eat dog meat, no matter how much it is disguised by being mixed with other foods or covered with milk. Always they exhibit disgust and aversion toward it; probably the odor has much to do with this. Sherrington's "spinal dogs," as these operated animals were called, exhibited the same digust when given a bowl containing dog meat, refusing to touch it or to eat it no matter how much they were urged.

Much of the recent work on the nervous and physiological basis of the emotions has been carried on by W. B. Cannon of the Harvard Medical School, and his associates. Cannon has investigated with much thoroughness the rôle of the autonomic nervous system in emotional activity. The autonomic nervous system, as its name implies, is normally active in those functions of the body which involve little or no volition, or knowledge, on the part of the subject. The autonomic nervous system controls the vegetative functions of the body— the activity of the heart, lungs, stomach, and internal glands, as well as circulatory and sweat-gland changes. The two main branches of this system are the thoracico-lumbar or sympathetic (the middle part) and the cranio-sacral (the upper and lower parts). Cannon has found that the sympathetic branch is active in intense or unpleasant emotions such as fear and rage. Its general function in the body is to intensify certain sorts of activity; for example, it increases the heart-beat, raises the blood-pressure, and increases breathing rate. The craniosacral branch, on the other hand, acts as a check and balance to the sympathetic. It inhibits rapid heart-beat, speeds up salivary and gastric secretion (thus aiding digestion), and maintains muscular tonus. During pleasant emotional states —joy, contentment, etc.—the cranio-sacral branch of the autonomic is ascendant over the sympathetic.

In order to discover whether an intact sympathetic is necessary for emotional experiences, Cannon removed the entire sympathetic division of the autonomic nervous system from a number of cats. This operation cut off the source of all sensation from the viscera such as might conceivably be present in fear or rage. After the operation, however, the animals all showed marked signs of anger in the presence of a barking dog; these signs including hissing, growling, retraction of the ears, and baring of the teeth.

This experiment, like that of Sherrington, indicates clearly that body sensations are not *necessary* to emotional states, even though they may be normally present. Other experiments which point in the same direction are those in which powerful drugs have been employed to bring about rapid heart-beat, trembling, blushing of the skin, rapid breathing rate—i. e., all of the changes which ordinarily are found in emotional reactions. Logically it would seem that if an individual's emotion is simply his awareness of such stirred-up states in his own body, he should feel rage or fear when so disturbed by drugs. But this result does not occur. Cannon and his associates have shown in a long series of tests that adrenin (the secretion of the adrenal glands, which lie just above the kidneys) has almost the same effect upon body behavior as violently unpleasant emotions such as intense excitement, fear, and anger. When adrenin is injected into the blood stream of a normal person, the result is a decidedly stirred-up physiological state. But the subject reports no real emotion, rather he states that he feels as though he *might* be afraid without any actual fear. In connection with this finding Cannon has pointed out how *alike* are the bodily or physiological changes in different emotional states, as well as in emotional and non-emotional states such as those resulting from strong muscular exercise, exposure to cold, and the like; and how *unlike* are the conscious states involved. Such observations as these would seem to render the James-Lange theory untenable—at least without some modification. One case of pathological loss of sensation in a human being may be cited before leaving this topic. Dana reports the case of a woman patient, who owing to a fracture of the neck and the resulting spinal cord injury, had suffered complete paralysis of the muscles of the trunk, arms, and legs, and complete loss of sensitivity. This person lived for a year showing little or no change in personality: grief, joy, and affection seemed unaltered. Such a case can hardly be squared with the James-Lange theory.

Cannon has proposed as a substitute for the James-Lange theory the hypothesis that emotions result from the interactivity of the cerebral cortex and the interbrain (thalamic regions). The interbrain, sometimes called the diencephalon is a large mass of gray matter lying just below the cerebral cortex. It is a great sensory receptive center for impulses from the body and is a kind of vestibule for the cortex. Cannon found that when the cortex was entirely removed from a cat, the decorticated animal still showed great emotional excitement ("a sort of sham rage"), which strongly supports the view that rage, and probably other emotions as well, depend upon impulses from the subcortical regions. Following this lead Bard has shown, after some fifty operations on cats in which the cortex and various parts of the brain stem were removed at the same time, that the center for the emotional display of rage is located in the lower *thalamus* (part of the interbrain). According to Cannon's theory, then, at the same time that the thalamus discharges upward into the cortex it also releases motor impulses which produce complex internal changes of a reflex character. In turn sensory reports of these changes in the body are sent back by way of the thalamus and so reinforce or intensify the emotional consciousness. Cannon cites considerable clinical evidence to show that the thalamus is closely connected with emotional or affective experiences. Normally this old and more primitive part of the brain is under inhibition from the cortex; and when it is "released" through disease or injury, there is often an extensive and uncontrolled emotional display (e. g., laughing or crying). The difference between one emotion and another is explained as being due to central (cortical) factors, that is, to the *meaning* which the emotion-arousing stimulus has for the individual. In the one case the stimulus may release fear and the impulse to flee; in another anger and the impulse to strike. The effect of Cannon's theory has been to switch the emphasis in studies of emotion from body changes to brain changes.

4. THE CORRELATION OF PHYSIOLOGICAL CHANGES AND EMOTIONAL STATES

Two experiments planned to find out whether definite emotional "patterns" exist physiologically and can be correlated with reported emotional states will be described in this Section. These studies, the one by Blatz and the other by Landis, are illustrative of the best techniques now available in work of this sort.

Blatz's experiment was concerned with discovering whether there is a definite physiological disturbance corresponding to what we call *fear*. His subjects, about twenty in all, included both men and women. They were told that the purpose of the experiment was the study of heart-rate differences over a fairly long period of time. Each subject was carefully tied in a chair and required to sit alone and blindfolded in a room for about fifteen minutes. During this period cardiac, respiratory, and electrical changes (of the skin) were carefully recorded. The force and regularity of the heart-beat were measured by an electro-cardiograph (a delicate galvanometer) and were recorded on a photographic film. Breathing records, taken by means of an electric pneumograph, were photographed on the same film. Changes in the electrical behavior of the skin, a phenomenon known as the psychogalvanic reflex,* or P G R, were obtained from the galvanometric readings. (See Fig. 34.) After three sittings, Blatz found that his subjects gave consistently normal records, i. e., the slight nervousness and timidity which appeared at first due to the strangeness of the situation had been entirely lost. So much was this so, in fact, that many of the subjects almost fell asleep before the 15 minute period was up. These preliminary records constitute what may be called a *control series*.

The chair used in this experiment was hinged in front so that when suddenly released it would fall over backward, carrying the subject with it. A powerful door-check stopped the fall gradually after the chair had passed through an arc of 60°. At the fourth sitting, Blatz allowed his subject without warning to fall over backward. This backward drop was intended to set up a fear response, so that the records taken at the time would give a physiological picture of the emotion which we subjectively call fear. That the fall really caused fear can hardly be doubted. All of the subjects reported a genuine fear at first, followed later on, oftentimes, by anger or amusement. In addition, they struggled, yelled out, called the ex-

---

* The psychogalvanic reflex requires a word of explanation. If electrodes are attached to two different points on the skin and are connected with a sensitive galvanometer, an electric current (as shown by deflections of the galvanometric needle) will be found to flow between the two points. This current indicates the difference in electrical potential between the two points, and is found to increase markedly during emotional states; hence it is often taken as an index of the intensity of the emotional state. The galvanic deflection is called the psychogalvanic reflex. It is due presumably to changes in sweat-gland secretion. The sweat-glands are controlled by the sympathetic branch of the autonomic nervous system, which, as we have seen (p. 322), is active in intense emotional reactions. The assumption, then, is that fear or anger, say, cause an increased outpouring of sweat secretion; this sweat, in turn, lowers the skin resistance to the electric current, thus giving an increased galvanic deflection.

perimenter by name, and in various ways gave evidence of emotional upset. The effects produced by the fall may be briefly summarized as follows (records were taken before, at the time of, and six minutes after the fall):

1. Breathing was much disturbed. As the chair fell over backward the subjects tended to "catch their breath," and then exhale in short gasps. The fraction $\frac{\text{Inspiration time}}{\text{Expiration time}}$, called the "respiratory ratio," was immediately *increased*. That is to say, the breathing-in became relatively much longer than the breathing-out, the ratio I/E increasing from a normal of about .70 to as high as 4.00.

2. Heart rhythm was irregular. The heart-rate was markedly accelerated at first by as much as twenty beats (from 84 to 104 beats on the average). This initial increase was usually followed by a retardation and then another period of acceleration.

3. In the psychogalvanic reflex there were wide deflections. These began from one-half second to three seconds after the drop and ranged from one to ten units over the scale.

In addition to these organic disturbances, there were also gross muscular movements, struggles to escape, reflex movements, and threshings of the arms and legs, and yelling. In later tests, when the subject expected a fall (having been forewarned), the physiological effects were less intense than when the fall was unexpected. Adaptation was rapid, the second and third falls producing much less upset than the first.

This experiment gives a very definite picture of general physiological disturbance, but there is no pattern or regularity in the response which is constant from person to person or for a given individual. There is too much variability in all of the measures taken to warrant the assumption that we have a clear-cut physiological state which can be confidently labeled "fear" or "terror."

In his experiment, Landis investigated the effects of severe emotional upset upon respiration, blood-pressure, gastro-intestinal activity, and basal metabolism. Respiration, both thoracic (chest) and abdominal, was measured by means of pneumographs. Blood-pressure, which can be best described briefly, perhaps, as the pressure in the arteries resulting from both the force of the heart-beat and arterial tension was obtained by means of a sphygmograph * attached to the upper arm. Gastric contractions were obtained by having the subject swallow a small balloon attached to a rubber tube, so that changes in the size of the balloon resulting from stomach contractions were recorded directly. Rectal contractions were secured by using a similar balloon arrangement placed in the rectum. Basal metabolism (roughly, the amount of carbon dioxide given off in breathing) was obtained by having the subject breathe into a specially designed apparatus. All of these measures of physiological change or variability were recorded simultaneously by means of tambours and writing points upon a moving smoked paper.

Landis used three subjects in this experiment. After normal records had been taken over a period of three weeks, the following schedule was begun. Each subject went without food for forty-eight hours and without sleep for thirty-six hours. At the end of this time an electric shock was administered which was "as much as the subject could bear without struggling," and which lasted until the subject signaled that he could endure the pain no longer. Each subject was then given a stimulant, and records were taken hourly for a five-hour period and daily afterward for five days. Landis's results in brief were as follows:

1. *Basal Metabolism.* Basal rate increased about 30 per cent

---

* This instrument consists essentially of a rubber sleeve attached to the arm. When it is inflated to the point where the flow of blood is cut off, the blood-pressure is measured either graphically or on a scale, by a tube leading off from the inflated sleeve.

on the average (with much variability) during the time of anticipation before the shock; it then fell off rapidly until, after six to eight hours, it was practically normal again. Anger, which occurred occasionally, was accompanied sometimes by an increase and sometimes by a decrease in metabolic rate.

2. *Blood-Pressure.* There was a rapid rise in blood-pressure upon the onset of the shock, together with a rapid and irregular heart-beat. Upon continuation of the stimulus the heart-beat became more regular and the pressure decreased. Landis states that these changes are quite similar to the shock symptoms following a surgical operation.

3. *Respiration.* Breathing was faster and more shallow, with some tendency toward gasping.

4. *Gastric and Rectal Contractions.* The electric shock stimulus had a variable effect on gastric contractions. In one subject gastric contractions were marked, while in another they ceased temporarily. The third subject could not retain the apparatus, and hence gave no record. Rectal contractions ceased in all subjects upon the onset of stimulation.

On the day following the experiment, each subject wrote out an account of his experiences, attitudes, and feelings. All stressed fatigue, nausea, occasional fits of anger, irritability and lack of coördination, with surprisingly little emphasis upon definite feelings of pleasantness or unpleasantness. There was little or no awareness of specific physiological changes, and no agreement as to the specific emotion felt. As in Blatz's experiment, no evidence appeared to indicate that a consistent pattern of physiological changes invariably accompanies a reported emotional state.

The only behavioral pattern which seemed to correspond *regularly* to a given subjective state was that of *surprise*. Surprise is the immediate response to any sudden and intense stimulus; it has been better named, perhaps, the "startle pattern." When studied with the aid of high-speed photography the startle pattern has been found to comprise two main elements: the eye blink and a complex, but identifiable, facial-bodily reaction. These two responses are reflexive and involuntary, and constitute a definite pattern of stereotyped behavior. "Startle" is the only emotional state which fits into the James-Lange definition of an emotion as an *invariable* complex of bodily changes.

5. JUDGING EMOTIONS FROM FACIAL EXPRESSIONS

The earliest attempt to discover experimentally how accurately one can judge the probable emotional state of a person from a photograph is that of Feleky. To each of 100 judges this investigator submitted eighty-six photographs of herself, posed to represent a wide range of emotional states, together with a list of common names for emotions. The judges were instructed to write on a sheet opposite the number of each photograph the emotion which they believed it portrayed. The emotions which were represented ranged from fear, rage, and suspicion to surprise, sympathy, and religious feeling. Perhaps the most striking first impression which one gets from Feleky's data is the wide scatter of emotions attributed to each pose. Closer examination shows, however, that—allowing for synonyms and variations in descriptive names—there is rather remarkable agreement on many of the poses. The following table gives the percentage of times a selected group of posed expressions was judged correctly or nearly correctly:

Pose	Called by Judge	Percentage of Judgments
Happiness	Happiness, mirth	90
Surprise	Surprise, happiness	82
Fear	Fear, suffering, anger	91
Anger	Anger, fear, suffering	73
Disgust	Disgust, contempt	75
Contempt	Contempt, disgust	93

This experiment is limited, of course, in its practical application, since one never strikes and holds a pose when normally upset. It does indicate, however, that we may interpret an individual's emotional state quite accurately from a photograph.

Landis has performed an experiment designed to discover whether reported emotions are accompanied by definite and easily recognized facial expressions. A series of photographs were taken of his subjects while they were undergoing various emotion-producing situations. There were seventeen of these situations in all, several of the more striking being: smelling a bottle containing ammonia, falsely marked lemon; looking at pornographic pictures; decapitating a live rat; severe electrical shock. Twelve women, twelve men, and one boy acted as subjects. In order the better to analyze the kind and amount of movement exhibited by the facial muscle groups, these were traced out upon the face of each subject with burnt cork to make them show up better in the photographs.

The subjects characterized the emotional value of the situations in various ways, by profanity, outcries, and verbal descriptions. Disgust, anger, surprise, and sex excitement were reported often enough to be studied in connection with the photographs of facial expressions taken during these states. After many comparisons Landis writes: "With no verbal report of a given emotion did a muscle, group of muscles, or expression occur with sufficient frequency to be considered characteristic of that emotion. There is no expression typically associated with any verbal report."

Perhaps this negative finding is in part to be explained by the fact that (1) emotional states changed rapidly during the experiment and were often not very genuine—smiling was the most common reaction reported; (2) the photographs were small; and (3) the markings on the face were probably confusing rather than helpful.

A study of children's judgments of posed facial expressions shows that youngsters judge pleasant and fairly simple emotions better than they do unpleasant and more sophisticated states. The pose for laughter was judged correctly 70 per cent of the time at ages 3–4 years, and 100 per cent accurately by age 10. The age-levels at which certain emotions were correctly judged by at least 50 per cent of the children examined are as follows:

Pose	Age
Laughter	below 3 years
Pain	5–6 years
Anger	7 years
Fear-horror	9–10 years
Surprise	11 years
Contempt	above 14 years

Contempt, which was hardest for children, was easy for adults as shown by Feleky's data (p. 330). Failure to name correctly the more "adult" emotions such as contempt, suspicion, jealousy and the like may result from the fact that children have no *names* for these emotions. Hence they are classified simply as pleasant or unpleasant.

6. THE PSYCHOGALVANIC REFLEX

The question is often asked whether the intensities of an individual's emotional states are correlated, i. e., whether the individual who gives an intense fear response to a fear-provoking situation, for instance, tends to react in the same highly emotional way to situations provoking anger, joy, or grief. Several investigators have attempted to answer this question, using the psychogalvanic reflex as an indicator of emotional intensity. The psychogalvanic reflex has been described on p. 326 as an electrical phenomenon which results from a difference in potential between two points on the skin. The electrical response is dependent upon changes in sweat-gland secretion which are, in turn, a result of activity in the sympathetic branch of the autonomic nervous system (p. 322). Since the autonomic nervous system is known to be active in emotional behavior, the psychogalvanic reflex or P G R thus becomes, potentially at least, an index of emotional states.

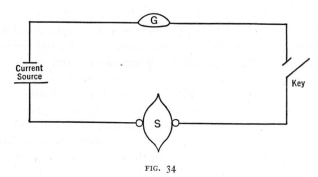

FIG. 34

SIMPLE DIAGRAM TO SHOW HOW THE PSYCHOGALVANIC REFLEX (P G R) MAY
BE MEASURED

G is the galvanometer and S is the subject, who is in circuit with G and with a source of current, usually of two to four volts. When the circuit is closed by the key, there will be an initial galvanometric deflection on the scale (see Fig. 35), which is recorded by the experimenter. When the subject is stimulated, the deflection measured from this point is a measure of the P G R. A Wheatstone bridge is often employed to bring the initial deflection back to zero, so that all P G R's may be taken from this reference point.

A diagram of a simple set-up for securing the galvanic reflex is shown in Figure 34, while in Figure 35 is shown an ordinary D'Arsonval galvanometer. There is considerable reason to doubt that the psychogalvanic reflex is correlated as closely with emotion as has been claimed for it by several experimenters. Body resistance, upon which the psychogalvanic reflex depends, is known to change during the course of the day, while fatigue, deep respiration, and muscular exertion all provoke deflections in the absence of any reported emotion. Emotional states, however, do produce marked psychogalvanic reflexes: and hence in an experiment in which the stimuli have been selected so as to provoke emotional reactions, the extent of the galvanic deflection may be taken as an indicator of *relative* emotional intensity.

In one experiment with the P G R eleven different stimuli were employed, such as pricking the subject with a needle, sounding an automobile "klaxon" horn suddenly, and ringing a bell. All of these, possibly excepting two or three, were calculated to surprise or annoy the subject by arousing anger, pain, or mild fear. The subject's response to each situation was measured by the galvanometric reading. In accordance with the extent of the psychogalvanic response, the thirty subjects were ranked in order of merit for the eleven situations. The correlation or correspondence of these rankings ranged from o or negative (just no relationship) to .80 or more (close relationship), with an average at .58.* In the case of the high correlation of .80, this very close correspondence was almost certainly due to the identity of the two stimuli involved; the first was the sudden sound of an automobile horn, and the second the same stimulus repeated.

This experiment is certainly not conclusive, and within the limits of the laboratory situation it offers no evidence that emotions are highly correlated—that persons tend to be *generally* emotional or unemotional. Other experimenters have found the same tendency toward specificity of emotional reactions. And these experimental findings are substantiated to a considerable degree by everyday experience. A few people may be fairly described as "choleric"—easily disturbed or excited by a variety of stimuli, some relatively mild. Others, more "phlegmatic," react mildly even to intense and demanding stimuli.

* For meaning of correlation, see p. 66.

But these are exceptions. Most people fall in between these two groups and the "generally" excited and "generally" placid constitute small groups which fall at the extremes of an emotional scale. Only when situations are closely alike or the emotions elicited quite similar are intercorrelations high. In a number of situations, for example, *all* designed to provoke surprise or startle, Patterson found agreement between the *intensity* of

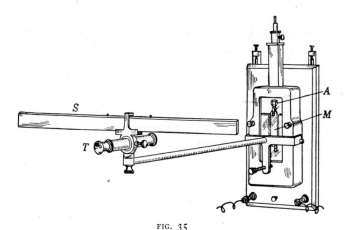

FIG. 35

D'ARSONVAL GALVANOMETER

Changes in the subject's resistance produced by emotional stimuli cause movements of the magnet, M, to which is attached a small mirror, A. As A turns to the right or left, these deflections may be read from the scale, S, by the experimenter, through the telescope T.

the P G R in various situations to be expressed by correlations of from .53 to .88.

The question of what conscious state or states most regularly accompany the P G R has been attacked by Landis and Hunt. These authors refer to the P G R as the G S R (galvanic skin response), a better term, perhaps, because it describes rather than interprets the actual phenomenon. Landis and Hunt presented to their subjects various stimuli intended to arouse amusement, fear, sex emotion, unpleasantness and other emotional states. Each observer was asked to report his subjective feelings or mental state after each response. When reports were tabulated, the P G R was found to be most nearly related to *tensions*—fear, anger, startle, and the like. But the galvanic response occurred under such a wide variety of conditions that it was clearly not an index of any one conscious state.

Cannon has conceived of the sympathetic branch of the nervous system as performing an *emergency* function. When animal or man is confronted by sudden danger, or is trapped and must attack or escape quickly, the sympathetic system "takes over," according to this view, and the organism is "stripped for action." Emotion, then, becomes a "reinforcer" of bodily action—a means of supplying additional energy to the body muscles during the emergency. The experimental connection established between sympathetic activity (via the P G R) and reported conscious emotional states of tension, startle, confusion and the like fits in well with Cannon's "emergency theory" of the emotions.

7. THE ASSOCIATION METHOD IN EMOTIONAL DIFFICULTIES

One of the best illustrations of the method of impression is furnished by the free association test. Used as a means of diagnosing emotional difficulties or complexes, the association test method was first employed by the Swiss psychiatrist Carl Jung. Jung's method was to present to his subject or patient a set of words (usually 100), to each of which he was instructed to give as quickly as possible the first word or first association which occurred to him. The stimulus words were selected to cover a wide range of situations, including many which would presumably have emotional value for the subject. These so-called "critical words" were mixed in with many indifferent or innocuous words. By way of illustration Table XXIX gives a selection of twenty-five critical words from Jung's list. The theory underlying the association method is that extreme timidity, embarrassment, useless fears, anxieties, worries and the like which occur in nervous or neurotic persons, and to a lesser degree in normal persons, center around forgotten and little-understood emotional episodes in the person's life. Those words in the list which revive these occurrences, or "tap" his complexes, should therefore provoke a highly personal or emotional association, accompanied, say, by laughter or blushing. Lengthened reaction time, repetition of the stimulus word, silly or far-fetched answers, or an entire lack of response are interpreted as an attempt to avoid unpleasant associations connected with the stimulus word. Such reactions are called "complex indicators." A complex, as the psychoanalyst uses the term, denotes a group or constellation of ideas centered around some particular episode or theme which possesses emotional significance to the subject. Thus an individual much excited or disturbed over religious matters may have a "religious complex"; other persons are described as having sex complexes, or

Table XXIX

A Selection of Twenty-five Critical Words from Jung's List of 100 Association Words

dead	old
to dance	to beat
sick	to wash
angry	to fear
to swim	brother
pity	false
to die	anxiety
to pray	to kiss
money	bride
despise	pure
unjust	contented
to marry	woman
ridicule	

inferiority complexes, the latter term being used to cover feelings of inadequacy of all kinds.

On the principle of psychological determinism, every reaction is explicable in terms of its antecedents, since all of these are inevitably linked up with it in some way. So it is argued that any word which is tied up in the subject's experience with an original emotional upset will, if followed up, finally lead back to the source of his difficulty. To illustrate, a highly emotional or lengthened response to the word *ridicule* might enable the psychologist to discover by further questioning that the examinee's "touchiness" regarding ridicule grew out of his having a peculiarly shaped nose or a speech impediment. If this defect led others to tease and torment him, feelings of inadequacy, and the misery arising therefrom, might interfere with his normal life. In Table XXIX the words *kiss, bride, pray, ridicule, anxiety,* and the like might conceivably lead to reactions which would in many cases be considered complex indicators.

The validity of a complex indicator as a revealer of emotional stress has been studied in various ways. Checking one indicator against another is perhaps the best procedure; and this method has revealed considerable agreement among certain indicators. Repetition of the stimulus word and misunderstanding of the stimulus word are among the best indicators; long reaction time and irrelevant responses are also good but somewhat less valuable than the first two. Two indicators occurring together are more "diagnostic" than a single indicator. The emotionally toned or critical words differ from one investigation to another and for different subjects, but they are usually concerned with love, anger, injustice, ridicule, pity, danger, and death.

The association method in one form or another has been much used by psychologists. Perhaps the chief objection to association tests as indicators of troublesome and unconventional thoughts is that they may easily prove too much. Nearly every person has frequently been worried about religious matters or sex adjustments, or has felt inferior, and if sufficiently prodded, can probably reveal several "complexes." This is particularly true of the sex life, since society as now organized greatly curbs and limits freedom of expression in such matters.

By far the most extensive use of free association has been made by Kent and Rosanoff in their comparison of the responses given by the normal and the insane. These investigators drew up a list of 100 words, some having probable emotional value, i. e., covering the usual worries and anxieties, and some being presumably indifferent words such as *table, chair, stove.* This list was administered to 1,000 normal and 247 insane adults, the responses to each word being carefully tabulated. Probably the most striking result obtained from this mass of material was the large percentage of "individual" responses given by the insane as compared with the normal. If a person gives a response not duplicated by any one else in the group, it is considered to be an "individual response." The normal group gave about 7 per cent individual responses, the insane group 27 per cent. A large number of individual responses is considered by the authors to be probably indicative of eccentric thinking or other peculiarity; while a large number of "common" responses (those given by others) indicates normality in the sense of conformity to the standards of the group. Each response, together with the frequency of its occurrence, has been tabulated for each of the 100 words in the list. From these tables one can determine how commonplace or how exceptional his associations are.

Frequency tables have also been prepared giving the responses of 1,000 school children, ages 9–12, to 100 stimulus words—90 of these taken from the Kent-Rosanoff list. In general, children's responses are more *concrete* than those of adults. They tend to be in terms of use, or to tell something about the idea expressed by the stimulus word. To the stimulus word "table," for example, 36 per cent of the children answer "eat," while only 5 per cent of adults say "eat," 30 per cent answering "chair." To the stimulus word "man," children reply "work," adults, "woman"; to "soft," the children say "pillow," the adults "hard." *Coördinate* responses (man—woman, table —chair) and *opposites* (dark—light, deep—shallow) are given more often by adults than by children. These differences probably reflect the adult's larger vocabulary, and the tendency for adults to think in abstract terms to a greater degree than children.

8. ATTEMPTS TO DISCOVER GUILT OR DECEPTION

From the experimental point of view, the "detective" use of the free association test is probably the most direct application of the *method of impression*. As its name implies, this method is intended to discover the "real" culprit from among several persons suspected of a "crime." In the psychological laboratory, the "crime" is usually a stunt of some kind through which one person out of several possible candidates is put. It is so arranged that neither the experimenter nor the class knows who is the "guilty" person. The object of the association test is to select this guilty individual from among the several suspects by means of his telltale associations. Usually these responses will be abnormally long or emotionally tinged (accompanied by laughter or embarrassment), or they will bear directly upon the stunt, thus giving the culprit away.

Jung has employed the word-reaction method in the following experiment, which may be used as an illustration. The supervisor of a hospital reported to him the theft of a pocket-book from one of the nurses in her charge. The purse contained a fifty-franc note, one twenty-franc piece, some centimes, a small silver watch-chain, a stencil, and a receipt from Dosenbach's Shoe Shop in Zurich. The purse had been taken from a clothes-closet in which it had been placed by the nurse. Owing to various circumstances which need not be described in detail, suspicion narrowed down to three nurses, all of whom were asked to submit to the association test. The critical words were the name of the robbed nurse, *cupboard, door, open, key, yesterday, banknote, gold, seventy, fifty, twenty, money, watch, pocket-book, chain, silver, to hide, fur, dark reddish leather* (color of the purse), *centimes, stencil, receipt, Dosenbach.* Other words not bearing directly upon the theft but having emotional value were *theft, to take, to steal, suspicion, blame, court, police, to lie, to fear, to discover, to arrest, innocent.* These critical words were distributed among twice as many indifferent words, the total constituting the final test.

To each of the three nurses the test was then given, the response and the time of reaction (in fifths of a second) being taken for each word. The median reaction times of the three nurses, whom we shall designate A, B, and C, to the indifferent and the critical words are given in the following table:

REACTION TIME (FIFTHS OF A SECOND) OF A, B, AND C TO THE INDIFFERENT AND CRITICAL WORDS

	A	*B*	*C*
Indifferent words	10	11	12
Critical words	16	13	15
Difference	6	2	3

Although A's "normal" reaction time—as shown by her responses to the indifferent words—is the shortest of all, she is considerably slower than either B or C in replying to the critical words. This, of course, is evidence, though surely not conclusive, against A. Jung next computed the number of "imperfect reproductions" given by each nurse. An imperfect reproduction or reaction is one which is haltingly or stumblingly given, with repetition or evident emotional upset. Such responses may grow out of an association of strong feeling-tone aroused by the critical word which is carried over to several succeeding responses. The subject, so to speak, becomes "rattled," and gets more flustered as the experiment goes on. The result of this tabulation showed that A gave 65 per cent imperfect reactions, B 56 per cent, and C 30 per cent. The actual responses were distributed as follows:

NUMBER OF IMPERFECT REACTIONS GIVEN TO INDIFFERENT AND CRITICAL WORDS BY A, B, AND C

	A	B	C
Indifferent words	10	12	11
Critical words	19	9	12
Difference	9	3	1

A has an excess of 9 responses to the critical words, B has three, and C has only 1. By this test, then, suspicion again points to A. Still another check was made in terms of the percentage excess for each subject of "complex indicators" given to the critical words, over and above those given to the presumably indifferent stimuli. A's excess is 100 per cent, B's 0, and C's 50 per cent. On the basis of these statistical results and upon careful study of the character of the responses, Jung decided that the greatest suspicion fell on A. Confession by A later on confirmed this judgment.

An experiment of much the same sort was able to find the guilty person in the case of a dormitory theft. Long reaction-time to critical words together with other complex indicators gave indices of "guilt probability."

The *method of expression* has also been used in attempting to discover guilt or deception. Both Marston and Larson have employed changes in blood pressure, as evidence of lying or deception, with much success. Marston believes that a rise in blood pressure of from 8 to 12 millimeters in conjunction with a response to a possibly compromising question is sufficient to indicate that the subject is lying. Larson, who first used the association test method and later the method of direct questioning, has employed blood pressure rises and changes in respiration with success in several cases involving actual crimes. It is probable that blood pressure changes are indicative of deception because the attempt to deceive causes general excitement which in turn raises the blood pressure. Blood pressure, however, is affected by many factors and its use in crime detection is still experimental to a high degree.

Perhaps it need not be pointed out that neither free association nor any of the other so-called "lie-detector" methods such as blood pressure changes and P G R can pick out a guilty person with certainty. Nor can these methods distinguish between one who is guilty and one who is not guilty but possesses guilty knowledge. They may yield valuable information in many cases, however, and are often useful in leading to confession.

9. PRESENT STATUS OF THE STUDY OF EMOTIONS

In the first part of the chapter we outlined four views—representing somewhat different emphases—of what constitutes an emotion. According to the *first* view, an emotion is a mental or conscious phenomenon largely independent of the body changes which are its usual but somewhat incidental accompaniments. In the *second* view, an emotion is considered to be the individual's perception of the sensory changes arising from glandular, muscular, and circulatory reactions in his own body (this is the James-Lange theory). The *third* view regards an emotion as a felt impulse or set toward a certain type of activity plus a mass of sensations resulting from stirred-up body states. The *fourth* view is the behavioristic dictum that an emotion is simply the reaction pattern itself, the conscious state, if admitted at all, being of no consequence.

Let us now attempt to evaluate these views as best we may in the light of the experimental evidence at our disposal. The first view, that an emotion is simply a conscious or mental state, is clearly too narrow. The part played by body changes in preparing the individual to meet danger or some other emotion-producing situation is too real to be ignored. Furthermore, we cannot omit from a treatment of emotional reactions the rôle of the skeletal muscles nor the enormous importance of the glands in emotional states. The second view—that expressed by the James-Lange theory—is largely untenable in view of the experiments of Sherrington and Cannon, though to this theory should go the credit for being the first to recognize the reflexive component in emotion. The fourth view (the extreme behavioristic) seems to most psychologists to involve a distortion and even a suppression of the truth. Certainly experiments carried out with the best techniques now available have failed to find for a given emotion either a definite physiological pattern or a very characteristic behavior response.

This leaves us, finally, the third viewpoint as the most satisfactory, since it provides both for the conscious side of the emotion and for the body changes which accompany it. The "pattern" for an emotion, according to this view, does not lie in the mass of physiological changes, which vary little from one emotion to another, but rather in the *impulse* or *set* of the organism. In fear, for example, the set is to get away—to escape the influence of the stimulus—while in joy the impulse is to continue the influence of the stimulus. Usually the impulse precedes the bodily changes, which are often biologically valuable as preparatory reactions. This view is consistent with the emergency theory of the emotions described on p. 324.

This chapter has tried to show that, as a result of recent experimental attacks, there is now a respectable body of knowledge regarding the emotions. Much is now known about the nervous and physical basis of emotional states; many of the complex physiological, circulatory, and electrical changes accompanying emotions have been measured; and techniques have been developed for investigating the causes of certain abnormal emotional states. Much remains to be done. Future research will further define and differentiate emotions both on the physiological and psychological side. And genetic studies will aid in showing how emotions develop, how they become organized, and, possibly, how they may be better controlled for the benefit both of the individual and of society.

Chapter 13

VISUAL AND AUDITORY PERCEPTION: THE WORK OF HELMHOLTZ AND OTHERS

In the history of experimental psychology, no topic has excited more research, and led to more discussion than that of how we perceive or come to know the positions, relations, and meanings of things around us. The reasons for this interest are clear. Sense impressions lie at the basis of all mental activity, and have an enormous practical importance in everyday life. The two senses best fitted for the perception of objects in space are touch and vision, since both the skin and the retina are spread out spatially in two dimensions. Of these two, vision is easily the most valuable for everyday life. Second only to vision is audition. Seeing and hearing, in fact, are usually called the "higher" senses in contrast to tasting and smelling, the "lower" senses. This distinction is due not so much to the greater complexity of eye and ear, as to the relatively greater value of the sense data derived from them. A man who loses his taste or smell is handicapped to be sure; but such deprivation is not comparable to the loss of sight or of hearing.

In the following sections we shall first describe briefly the physical apparatus concerned in hearing and seeing. Important experimental findings in the field of auditory and visual perception will then be presented.

I. THE AUDITORY APPARATUS

While it is true that in a general way "we hear with our ears," the most indispensable part of the auditory apparatus is the inner ear. The outer ear acts as a collector of sounds, and as a not too efficient ear-trumpet. The middle ear transmits the sound waves which impinge upon the ear drum to the inner ear. From the inner ear nerve impulses pass over the auditory nerve to the brain—and we hear sounds. An important part of the inner ear is a tissue-like structure called the basilar membrane—upon which rest extremely sensitive receiving cells. The basilar membrane, which is often compared to the strings of a piano, is made up of some 24,000 fibers ranging in size from short and thick to long and thin. These fibers and their sensitive cells constitute the essential auditory receptive apparatus.

If one throws a stone into water, concentric rings will surround the splash. These "rings" grow larger and larger as they move out in wave-like form. In the same manner, sound waves arise as vibrations in the air or in any ponderable medium. Most of the sounds we hear result from the back-and-forth movement of air particles. But sound is also transmitted in other ways, as we all know; through metals, through the ground, and through water. The Indian put his ear to the ground to hear distant sounds, and the swimmer knows how loud the clapping of two stones can sound under water.

Sounds differ in pitch, in loudness or intensity, and in timbre or tone quality. Variations and differences in these characteristics enable us to tell quickly, and usually accurately, one voice from another over the telephone—when the voice is the only cue to the person's identity. The pitch of a musical note depends directly upon the vibration rate of the sound producing body—string or resonance chamber (wood-wind instrument). Pitch differences from 25 vibrations per second or less to 20,000 vibrations per second or more can be heard by the human ear. The high squeaky voice and the deep bass rumble differ markedly in pitch as well as in intensity and quality. Loudness or intensity varies with the amplitude or size of the sound waves. Judgments of intensity also depend upon pitch or vibration rate. As a tone dies away, it becomes lower although its vibration rate does not change. High tones, therefore, are said to be "intrinsically" louder than low tones.

Timbre or tone-quality is an important differentiating characteristic; it depends upon the wave composition of the sound. If two tones which have much the same pitch, 256 and 260 vibrations per second, say, are sounded together, *beats* arise— their number depending upon the differences in vibration rate between the two tones. Beats are often heard as disagreeable variations in intensity, and sometimes as rattles or burrs accompanying the tones. When the difference in vibration rate between the two beating tones is 40 or more, the beats disappear and a new low tone or "difference" tone appears as part of the tone complex. Besides difference tones, other tones the vibration rates of which are multiples of the fundamental, also accompany a single tone. The difference between the shrill sharp note of the piccolo, and the rich full note of the violin resides in the number and character of the accompanying "overtones."

The best tests constructed by psychologists for gauging one's "ear for music" or ability to perceive differences in tone are the well-known Seashore tests of musical talent. These tests consist of 6 double disk records which can be played on any standard phonograph. Each record is designed to cover a different aspect of musical aptitude: pitch discrimination, intensity, time, rhythm, consonance, and tonal memory are the characteristics measured. These tests have been carefully constructed and the scoring is objective. In the test for pitch discrimination, for example, a person must decide whether of two tones presented in succession the second is higher or lower than the first. There are 100 comparisons in all ranging from very easy to very difficult. Similarly, the tests of time, intensity, and rhythm demand a judgment by the observer based upon a series of comparisons. The test of consonance is some-

HERMANN LUDWIG F. VON HELMHOLTZ
(1821-1894)

what different from the other tests. The observer is no longer called upon to give a judgment which can be checked against known physical differences in the stimuli. He must, in this test, decide which of two tone combinations is the more pleasant, i. e., shows greater fusion, less harshness and noise effects. The test of tonal memory requires the observer to tell which of two, three, or four tones played in succession has been changed upon a second presentation. Tests like these when used in conjunction with measures of ability to sing and read music are useful in the selection of persons who possess musical talent.

2. HOW SOUNDS ARE LOCATED IN THE ENVIRONMENT

Not only do we identify sounds as the ringing of an alarm clock or the conversation between two friends, but we also locate them somewhere in space. Sound localization, especially in familiar surroundings, is usually immediate and fairly accurate. This is shown by the fact that we are disturbed when we cannot locate a given sound at once. It is hard to see, however, how such a receiving apparatus as the ear can supply exact knowledge of distance and direction. And for this reason, psychologists have spent much time on the problem of how we localize sounds in our environment.

Experiments on sound localization are usually carried out by means of a "sound cage"—a metal circle supported by uprights. Such an apparatus is shown in Figure 36. The subject is seated blindfolded in the center of the circle and sound stimuli—usually neutral sounds like the click or snap of a telegraph snapper—are presented from different points in the cage. The subject locates the position of the sound by pointing or when he has learned the angular divisions on the circle by giving positions in degrees.

Certain definite results have been obtained by use of the sound cage. Sounds to right or left are most sharply distinguished—the difference in relative intensity of the sound as heard by the right and left ear being apparently the primary factor here. Sounds directly ahead or directly behind the observer are localized fairly accurately; better localization is obtained when the observer is allowed to turn his head. Sounds above or below the observer are in general poorly placed. We

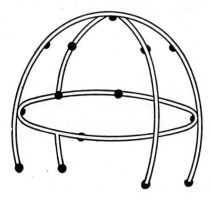

FIG. 36

SOUND CAGE

The horizontal axis is placed at the level of the subject's ears. Stimulus points (black circles) are possible in horizontal, median, and transverse planes and above, below, or at the level of the ears.

all know how difficult it is to locate an airplane—the sound cannot be "anchored" to anything familiar. In ordinary hearing, cues furnished by vision and by past knowledge of the sound (a familiar voice or the opening of a door) are helpful and perhaps crucial in effecting localization. Blind persons depend more upon echo, resonance, and secondary cues than do the seeing. This is shown by the fact that persons deaf or partially deaf in one ear locate sounds more accurately when in the sound cage than do normal people with one ear plugged. One-ear hearing is, however, definitely less efficient than two-ear hearing.

An interesting experiment has been made in which sounds entering the two ears were interchanged. Tubes fitted into the two ears were carried over the head to a trumpet or receiving horn just over the opposite ear. In this way each ear got the stimulus which would ordinarily have affected the other ear. The observer wore this instrument (called a pseudophone) an hour or so a day for two weeks and then all day for three days. At first there was general confusion. A horse would be seen trotting along a street and the sound of his hoofs would come from the opposite direction. A person coming through a door would be heard from the opposite side of the room. When the eyes were closed the reversed localization persisted without improvement throughout the experiment. When the eyes were open, however, correct placement of sounds was never completely lost and got steadily better as the experiment proceeded. More and more the visual cues dominated the auditory, so that by the end of the experiment the observer was localizing fairly well. When the pseudophone was removed the return to normal localization was immediate.

3. THEORIES OF HOW WE HEAR

Several theories have been proposed to explain the various phenomena of hearing. The oldest and best known is the resonance or "piano" theory of the great German scientist, Hermann von Helmholtz (1821–1894). This theory holds that the long and short fibers of the basilar membrane pick up different sound waves like the strings of a piano. The vibrating membrane agitates the sensitive cells resting upon it, and these in turn pass the effects of the stimulus on to the auditory nerve. Differences in length and in thickness of the basilar membrane fibers enable us to distinguish sounds of different vibration rate, and hence to hear high, low, and intermediate tones.

Another theory, called the frequency or "telephone" theory, suggests that the basilar membrane vibrates as a whole rather than by parts. Nerve impulses thus set up are thought to preserve faithfully the sound waves so that their vibration frequency is exactly reproduced in the brain center. Instead of a complex tone being analyzed into its parts in the ear itself, as the piano theory supposes, the telephone theory holds that analysis takes place in the brain.

Recent experiments have modified the telephone theory. In one careful experiment, Wever and Bray exposed (under anesthesia) the auditory nerve of a cat from the point where it leaves the inner ear to where it enters the brain-stem. When a tone of known composition was sounded at the cat's ear, it was discovered that the sound came through the auditory nerve without loss or change in vibration frequency. Thus it might seem that the frequency rate of a sound is accurately conveyed to the brain as the telephone theory supposes. But further objection has been offered to the telephone theory on the ground that the auditory nerve cannot transmit the vibration rates of very high tones. Nerves do not carry more than 1,000 impulses per second and the upper limit of human hearing is around 20,000 vibrations per second. To meet this difficulty Wever and Bray have proposed the "volley theory," an interesting and ingenious modification of the telephone theory.

According to the volley theory the separate nerve fibers respond differentially to the successive sound waves set up when a note is heard. To illustrate, suppose a tone of 10,000 vibrations is received in the ear. Instead of each single nerve fiber responding to each vibration, according to this theory nerve fiber #1 responds, say, to every *tenth* vibration, beginning with the first—e. g., 1, 11, 21, 31, 41, etc. In like manner, nerve fiber #2 responds to every tenth vibration, e. g., 2, 12, 22, 32, 42, etc. Nerve fiber #3 responds to every tenth vibration, 3, 13, 23, 33, etc. In this way the nerve fibers discharge by groups or squads instead of all at once. No fiber carries more than 1,000 impulses per second, but all together carry 10,000 vibrations per second without "over-loading" the nerve.

While no theory fully accounts for all of the facts of hearing, the three theories described above are the most comprehensive. Much experimental work is still being done.

4. VISUAL PERCEPTION OF DISTANCE AND DEPTH

The immediate stimuli to visual perception are light-rays which reach the two retinas (the inner surfaces of the eyes) by way of an aperture called the pupil. Figure 37 gives a simple schematic representation of the mechanics of this process. Although the retina is a slightly concave surface, a two-dimensional "field," yet, as we all know, our perceptions of distance, depth, and motion are given in three dimensions. How, we may ask, is this possible? Why aren't the objects of our experience—houses, trees, and people—spread out before us as though pinned upon a large flat board parallel to our retinas? This has been a hotly debated question in psychology, and many of the experimental data on the subject go back to the researches of Helmholtz. Beside numerous studies dealing with the physiology of the eye and the physics of optics, Helmholtz accumulated many data of direct psychological interest upon the question of space perception. It is largely upon such data that the *empirical theory* of space perception is based. This theory holds that our knowledge of distance and depth is built up largely, if not entirely, through the mutual coöperation and checkup of vision, touch, and locomotion. The *nativistic* theory, on the other hand, explains facts in three dimensions as natively given and unlearned. Many data can be marshaled to support each of these theories. Probably most psychologists to-day are inclined to accept the empirical view

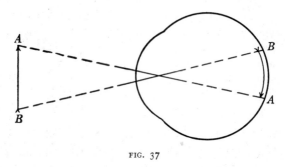

FIG. 37

HOW THE IMAGE OF AN OBJECT AB IS FOCUSED ON THE RETINA

with the reservation that there must be a substantial framework to visual perception which is natively given.

5. HOW WE SEE OBJECTS IN THREE DIMENSIONS

The invention of the reflecting stereoscope by Wheatstone in 1833 permitted a direct experimental attack upon the problem of how we see objects in three dimensions. Wheatstone's stereoscope was a scientifically accurate instrument, but somewhat clumsy and impracticable for ordinary work. It has been generally displaced by the refracting stereoscope invented by David Brewster somewhat later (*circa* 1843). Essentially, the stereoscope is an optical instrument by means of which two plane pictures may be presented, the one to the right eye and the other to the left, to give a single fused picture in three dimensions. This striking result follows from the fact that man is a two-eyed animal. His eyes are separated spatially, so that when they are focused upon a common object, each eye views it from a slightly different position. In other words, two pictures are presented in binocular vision, and it is the fusion of these two which gives us our visual perception of three dimensions.

Simple stereoscopic effects may be obtained in the following way: Hold a pen and a pencil straight out in front of the face, about one foot away, and a little to the left of an imaginary line passing through the nose. Now move the pencil slightly to the right of the pen and about two inches away from the face. Close the right eye and draw on a sheet of paper the two objects as they appear to the left (open) eye. Now close the left eye and draw the two objects as they appear to the right eye. It will be sufficient to represent the two objects simply by straight lines. Your picture should now

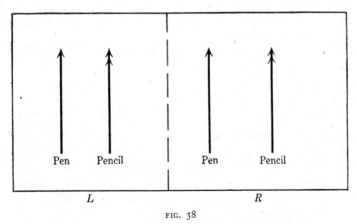

FIG. 38

STEREOSCOPIC SLIDE DRAWN TO GIVE PERCEPTION OF DISTANCE

look like Figure 38, in which the single-tufted arrow represents the pen and the double-tufted arrow the pencil. Be sure and separate the left-eye and right-eye pictures by about two and a half inches in your drawing. Now hold the completed picture out twelve to eighteen inches in front of the face. Focus the eyes as though you were looking at a far-distant point, and keeping this fixation steadily, move the figure in slowly until the right-hand and left-hand pictures fuse. and there is only one pen and one pencil. When this occurs, the pen will seem nearer than the pencil.

A simple explanation of this interesting phenomenon is derived from the fact that the distance between the left and right pencils is greater than the distance between the left and right pens (this can easily be verified from your picture). Hence, the eyes must converge more from the parallel position to make the pens combine than to make the pencils combine. The greater the convergence, the nearer the object, and so we see the pen as nearer than the pencil. It is a common experience that near objects require greater convergence to be brought to a focus than far objects; and so convergence is a direct cue to relative distances.

In Figure 39, the principle upon which the refracting stereoscope works is represented schematically. The picture seen by the left eye is placed at A, and the picture seen by the right eye at B. Owing to refraction of the light-rays by the prisms P and P', the two pictures are combined by the two eyes E and E' to be seen as a single fused image at X. The impression of distance and depth got from pictures combined stereoscopically is astonishingly real. In taking pictures for ordinary stereoscopic work, the camera first takes the right-eye picture; then it is moved about three inches to the left to take the left-eye picture. Two and one-half to three inches is approximately the interocular distance. Because of this separation, each eye, as we have said, sees around different sides of objects, the right eye around the right, the left eye around the left, and in this way cues to distance and depth are secured. If two pictures are taken, separated by more than three inches —by one foot, for example—striking and often ludicrous results will be obtained when they are combined stereoscopically. On such a slide we see objects as we would see them if our eyes were a foot apart. Seeing around corners, therefore, be-

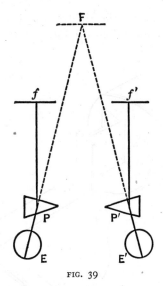

FIG. 39

THE PRINCIPLE OF THE REFRACTING STEREOSCOPE

(Brewster's Model)

The picture for the left eye is placed at f; that for the right eye at f'. Refraction of the light rays by the prisms at P and P' gives a single fused image at F.

comes highly exaggerated, and objects and people are stretched out in amusing proportions.*

An illustration of the ordinary Brewster stereoscope is shown in Figure 40. The hood serves to exclude from the eye nearly all of the light which does not come directly through

---

*Titchener's Stereoscopic Slides (Stoelting), forty-three in number, include several in which the interocular distance is much increased.

the prisms. The partition between the two prisms restricts each picture to the eye for which it is intended, while the extension slide permits adjustment for eyes of different focal lengths.

The part played by the right-eye and left-eye images in determining our perceptions of objects in three dimensions is

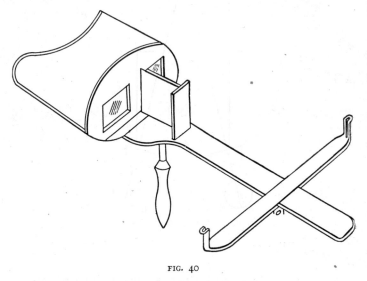

FIG. 40

BREWSTER'S HAND STEREOSCOPE

even more strikingly shown by the pseudoscope than by the stereoscope. In the pseudoscope, the pictures belonging to the right and left eyes are transposed, so that the right eye sees the left eye's picture, and vice versa. The net result of this is a complete reversal of perspective in the fused picture; near things seem far, and far things seem near. Go back for a moment to Figure 38. If this slide is cut vertically into two equal parts and the parts transposed, the pencil pictures will now be closer together than the pen pictures. Hence, when the right and left pictures are combined, more convergence is required to combine the pencils than the pens, and accordingly the pencil is judged to be nearer. In simple line drawings and geometrical figures, pseudoscopic effects (reversal of perspective) can usually be secured readily enough, either by transposing the right-eye and left-eye pictures, or by inverting the whole slide. With actual scenes, landscapes, objects, and people, for example, it is difficult to get pseudoscopic effects when the result would be meaningless, or contrary to experience. Few people, for instance, can see a human face pseudoscopically, i. e., concave, as the "central" or associative facts of experience are too well established. The reversal of lifetime habits is not readily achieved.

6. PHYSIOLOGICAL FACTORS UPON WHICH PERCEPTIONS OF DISTANCE AND DEPTH DEPEND

There are a number of factors upon which our perceptions of three dimensions depend besides this matter of the fusion of left-eye and right-eye pictures. These criteria may be divided conveniently into those primarily physiological and those primarily psychological. Under physiological factors should be included convergence, accommodation, muscular strain on the eye muscles, and double images.

1. *Convergence*. It is a familiar fact that in order to be brought into focus objects near at hand require greater convergence of the two eyes than objects some distance away. Sensations of strain resulting from convergence furnish cues to distance. Convergence, however, is not of much value except in the perception of objects fairly close at hand. When the eyes are focused on objects thirty feet or more away, the lines of sight are parallel and convergence is no longer a real factor.

2. *Accommodation* to distance is effected by the eye through

changes in the crystalline lens. The lens is a translucent prism-like structure which lies behind the pupil and between it and the retina. Light-rays coming through the pupil are refracted by the lens, and focused upon the retina. When a photographer wants to adjust his camera for distance, he lengthens or shortens the distance between the lens and the screen. The eye, on the other hand, adjusts to distances by increasing or decreasing the thickness (refractive power) of the lens. This pull, or release, of the muscles controlling the lens for different degrees of accommodation supplies us with cues to distance and depth. But since far objects require little accommodation, this factor, like convergence, is limited mainly to objects close by.

3. *Muscular strain* on the eye muscles. Each eye is moved by six little muscles arranged in pairs. When we compare the lengths of two lines, or gauge the width of a creek or the height of a building, the degree of strain on the eye muscles is a valuable factor in determining our judgment of distance.

4. *Double Images.* The doubling-of-images factor (though mainly physiological) is also of psychological interest because it is so seldom noticed in everyday life. In fact, Helmholtz remarked that the existence of double images "remains unknown to many people even in adult life." Their existence may readily be shown, however, in the following simple way. Focus on a point on the opposite wall some ten to fifteen feet away, and then (holding this fixation) bring a pencil up directly before the eyes and about twelve inches away. The pencil will appear double—unless your focus slips—and Figure 41 shows why this is true. When you focus upon F, the pencil images, since they fall upon non-corresponding retinal points (points which do not give single vision), appear as two pencils at P and P' in the plane of fixation. If you close the left eye, the pencil image (seen now by the right eye) is on the left side; and if you close the right eye, the pencil image

(seen by the left eye) is on the right side. That is, the images are crossed, and hence crossed images always mean an object *nearer* than the fixation point. If the focus is upon the near object, it is the far object that doubles, as you can readily demonstrate by focusing upon your pencil (twelve inches away) and doubling a picture on the wall in the same line of

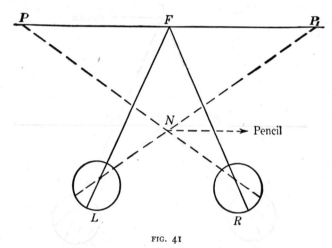

FIG. 41

THE DOUBLING OF "NEAR" OBJECTS IN FAR FIXATION

L, left eye; R, right eye; N, near point; F, far point. When the eyes are focused at F, the pencil at N is seen as two pencils, at P and P₁ respectively, in the plane of F.

vision. In this case the doubled images are not crossed, as Figure 42 shows, and hence uncrossed images always mean an object farther away than the fixation point.*

5. *Gestalt Effects.* The figure-ground distinction (p. 212)

---

* The essential facts in Figures 41 and 42 may be more easily recalled, perhaps, with the help of the couplet proposed by Titchener:

"Remote regard reverses
Nearer, notice not"

and the "good-figure" theory are considered by Gestalt psychologists to describe physiological or native factors in perception. According to Gestalt theory, the figure intrinsically has greater form than the ground; it has, too, more character of "thingness" and hence tends to stand out from the ground. The

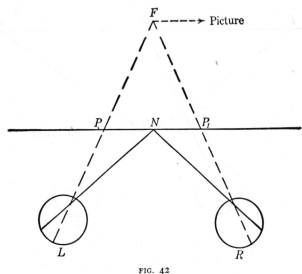

FIG. 42

THE DOUBLING OF "FAR" OBJECTS IN NEAR FIXATION

L, left eye; R, right eye; N, near point; F, far point. When the eyes are focused at N, the picture (or other object) at F is seen double, at P and at P₁, in the plane of N.

figure-ground relationship has relevance in auditory as well as in visual perception. The figure in music is higher in pitch than the ground, is louder and has different timbre. Thus a melody "stands out" as figure against its accompaniment as ground.

The geometric illusions have long been of interest to psychologists because they furnish clues to the perception process. Geometric illusions belong in the category of normal
false perceptions—false because they can be shown to be
erroneous, and normal because every one gets the illusory
effect to some degree. Figure 43 shows the famous Müller-
Lyer illusion; it is representative of a great many diagrams
of the same sort. The two horizontal lines are of the same

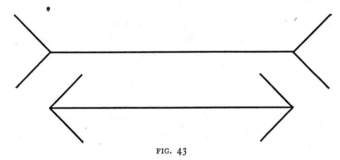

FIG. 43

THE MÜLLER-LYER ILLUSION

length, but the upper seems longer. This illusion has been
variously explained as owing to eye movements, to confusion
of the lines with the angles, to the relativity of all judgment,
and in other ways. The Gestalt psychologist considers the
geometric illusions to be instances of the "good-figure"
theory. A three-quarters circle tends to be seen as a complete
circle, and a broken triangle as a complete triangle (see
p. 214); that is, each figure expresses its essential characteristics as fully as it can—tends to be as good as possible.
The upper line in Figure 43 is extended (and hence is seen
as longer) and the lower contracted (and hence is seen as
shorter) to fit the configuration of the out-turning and the
in-turning angles.

7. PSYCHOLOGICAL FACTORS IN DISTANCE AND DEPTH PERCEPTION

More important, perhaps, than the physiological factors in space perception are the so-called psychological factors. These depend upon learning and are the result of everyday contacts with near and far objects. Among such determiners may be mentioned superposition, clearness of outline (aërial perspective), shade and shadows, relative movement, size of image on the retina, and some of the Gestalt effects.

1. *Superposition.* This factor is of value in relative distance judgments. When a tree, for instance, partially obstructs our view of a house, the immediate inference is that the tree stands *between* us and the house, and hence must be nearer.

2. *Clearness of outline* generally means nearness; dimness and blurring, distance. On a very clear day we are often astonished by the apparent nearness of distant objects, while individuals accustomed to fog and an obscured sky are often completely misled by distances at a high altitude where the moisture content of the atmosphere is very low.

3. *Differences in lighting, shadows and shade,* are especially valuable cues in the perception of depth. Brightly lighted objects in the visual field are generally higher than those dimly lighted, since light usually comes from above; again, on a plane surface depressions or concavities are darker, while protrusions or convexities are brighter. Artists depend to a considerable degree upon light and shade to represent distances and depth. Near objects seem "down" in the foreground, and far objects "up" closer to the horizon, and these facts are regularly employed in pictures to give the proper perspective.

4. *Relative movement* is an important factor in space perception. Objects move toward us and away from us, before

and behind other objects, and in this way give us cues as to relative position and relative distance. We are all familiar with the fact that when we are moving, on a train for instance, far objects move along with us and near objects seem to speed backward in the direction opposite to our movement.

5. *Size of Retinal Image.* From Figure 37 it is obvious that at the same distance from the eye a large object will subtend a greater visual angle than a small object, and that the retinal images will vary proportionally. Also it is clear that the farther away an object is from the eyes, the smaller its retinal images will be. Retinal images, then, furnish valuable data as to distance and size, provided, of course, the actual dimensions of some of the physical objects are known through other means. The man a block away takes up much less retinal space in your eyes than the ink-bottle on your desk, but the two objects are interpreted as being at different distances from the eyes, each its natural and customary size. Since the retinal images vary both for size and distance, this factor is only a partial cue until supplemented by other sense data.

8. THE RETINAL IMAGE IN PERCEPTION

If reference is made again to Figure 37, it will be noted that, with reference to the physical object, the retinal image is inverted. This inversion is due to the refractive mechanism of the lens. How is it that we see objects right side up when their retinal images are upside down? This question, which has often been proposed as a philosophical enigma, is puzzling only if we fail to appreciate properly the enormous rôle of experience and learning in perception. What we see is not the inverted retinal image, but the object in the field from which light-rays are reflected. The image on the retina is, part of the total physiological process involved in getting the perception; but we are no more conscious of it than of the

sensory impulse traversing the optic nerve. It must be remembered, too, that the retinal image is spatially correct
with reference to its various parts, even though inverted, so
that objects are perceived in their right relations. Up-ness
and down-ness, right and left, what we see and how we see
it, depend upon all of the factors which we have mentioned
plus hundreds of associated tactual and muscular experiences and contacts. We see things, feel them, fall over and
walk to them, in this way coming to know them.

An exceedingly interesting experiment carried out by Stratton has a direct bearing upon this question of the relation of
retinal images to our perceptions of space. Stratton fastened
before his right eye a tube containing two convex lenses. This
instrument, of course, gave a retinal image which was right
side up, and hence an inversion of objects appeared in the
visual field. The left eye was covered over by a hood which
excluded light, but allowed free ocular movements. Over a
period of eight days (a total of eighty-seven hours), Stratton wore this instrument, meanwhile observing carefully any
changes and new arrangements in the visual field. To prevent, as far as possible, conflicts between the new and the
old (normal) perceptions, at night when the instrument was
removed the eyes were carefully bandaged. On the first day,
as might have been predicted, everything was topsy-turvy;
things on the right were reached for on the left and things
lying on the floor were reached for toward the ceiling. This
confusion gradually abated, however, and by the end of the
third day little was left of the nervous conflict so clearly
apparent at first. By the eighth day the confusion in the
visual field had almost disappeared; things could be reached
for in their correct positions, and objects appeared normal
(right side up) again. Stratton notes that even then, however,
there were sudden slips or inversions, which could usually be
corrected by reaching for the object or moving toward it.

This experiment is valuable in showing that the retinal image, although absolutely necessary to vision, is but one cue in the total process whereby we perceive objects in space. It demonstrates, furthermore, how flexible are the connections between hand and eye and how readily modifiable and adaptable our various sensory experiences are. Ordinary everyday experiences demonstrate the same thing. We learn to shave in a mirror, although right and left are reversed, and to operate a microscope, although the field is inverted. To repeat, it is clear that the retina simply gives us the image in its proper relations; how we place these relations in space depends upon myriad associated tactual and muscular impressions.

9. THE NATURE OF EYE MOVEMENTS

In describing briefly on pp. 359 to 365 the various factors which contribute to our knowledge of position in space, we did not deal directly with the rôle of eye movements in visual perception. It is readily recognized, however, that this must be a valuable factor, for our knowledge of objects and their structures is not obtained by steady fixation upon them, but by a series of short "views" as the eyes flit over the object and its surroundings. Careful studies by psychologists have shown that eye movements fall into two main classes, "jump" movements and "pursuit" movements. Jump (or saccadic) movements occur when the eyes are moved voluntarily over an object; pursuit movements, when the eyes are controlled, so to speak, by the moving objects upon which they are fixated and move along with them.

Dodge has made probably the most careful studies of angular eye movements of the jump type, using the method of photography. Earlier investigators, for example Huey, had attempted to register eye movements by mechanical means. A small disk was glued to the cornea of the subject's eye, and a fine thread led from this to a delicate writing point. When the eye moved, its excursion was recorded by the writing point on a smoked drum. Besides obvious objections to this procedure from the standpoint of the subject, there was inaccuracy and lag in the recording by this system. The tracings, too, tended to blur at the beginning and end of the movement, thus making measurement unreliable. Photography of the eyes in motion eliminates most of these difficulties. With his subject seated in a dark room, and position of the head kept constant by means of a head rest, Dodge reflected a beam of light from the cornea upon a moving sensitive plate. As the plate moved downward vertically between two grooves, the subject was instructed to move his eyes from a given point to another in the same horizontal line. Focus, or rest points, showed up as bright spots on the film, intermediate movements as white lines, or streaks.

The time required to shift the focus from point A to point B was measured by photographing an oscillating spring pendulum along the edge of the moving plate. The vibrations of this time marker showed up as a series of teethlike indentations which could easily be counted. Since the pendulum rate of vibration was known, it was possible to measure the time intervening between the fixation at A and then at B. As might be expected, the time of an angular movement of the eyes depends largely upon the extent of the excursion. Dodge found that the time required for the eyes to move through an angle of five degrees is about .03 second, the time for twenty degrees is about .06 second, and the time for forty degrees is .1 second. These results are based upon the records of three subjects. The reaction time of the eye to a beam of light cast upon the retina—i. e., the time intervening between the stimulus and the eye's movement—was determined by Dodge to be around .165 second.

The jerky character of eye movements in ordinary seeing has been clearly shown by Stratton, who also employed the photographic method. Contrary to casual opinion, the eye does not move in a smooth sweep, unless the movement is of the pursuit variety. In such movements, as previously noted, the eye simply follows the moving object, and is not

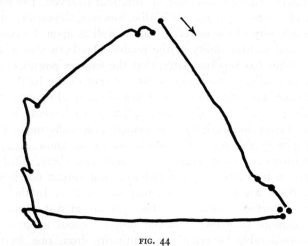

FIG. 44

PHOTOGRAPHIC RECORD OF THE EYE'S MOVEMENT IN TRACING THE OUTLINE
OF A CIRCLE

(After Stratton.)

controlled by the observer. In looking at an object or a picture, however, Stratton found that the eye moves in a series of jerks or jumps, even though the subject thinks he is moving his eyes smoothly. Like Dodge, Stratton placed his subject in a dark room and photographed the eye movements by reflecting light from the cornea upon a sensitive plate. The way in which the eye moves in looking around a circle is shown in Figure 44. The dots represent pauses.

10. EYE MOVEMENTS IN READING

One of the most careful studies of eye movements in reading was made by Dearborn, who also used the method of photographic registration employed by Dodge and Stratton. Dearborn found that the number of fixations per line for ordinary printed matter varied from four to seven. The number of "stops" in a line is variable, however, depending upon the difficulty of the material read as well as upon the education and mental ability of the reader. Dearborn also found, as Tinker has reported later, that the *fixation pauses* of the eye in reading consume 90 to 95 per cent of the total reading time. The utilization of so much of the total reading time in fixation, and the high speed of "jump" movements, makes clear perception during eye movement practically impossible. In spite of this our visual world, as we all know, is not a patchwork of clear visual spots here and there, filled in between by blurs, but is continuous and spread out before us. There are many reasons why this is true. In the first place, the visual field, when the eyes are at rest, embraces much more than the particular object focused upon; there is considerable "overlap" or continuity from one fixation pause to another. There is clear vision, too, of moving objects in pursuit movements, although in following rapidly moving objects the background is blurred. More important than these is the continuous "filling-in" by data got from the other senses. This background of information and learned material in terms of which our immediate perceptions are "sized up" and made meaningful is sometimes called our "apperceptive mass." A familiar example is the speed with which educated adults read easy or familiar prose. The eye sweeps along over the page, hitting important or "key" words here and there, the gaps being filled in by the context and by associated information.

Early in the chapter we referred briefly to the two theories of visual space perception, the nativistic and the empiristic. Perhaps most of the facts here presented have seemed to favor the empirical theory, although the physiological factors of accommodation, convergence, and muscular strain weigh heavily. No one, of course, can say definitely just where the influence of native factors leaves off and the influence of learned factors begins. Here again we are faced with the same dilemma encountered in the familiar controversies of instinct versus learning, heredity versus environment. Certainly learning could do nothing without the native equipment of a spatially correct retinal image and the physiological factors which furnish cues to movement. Nor could the eye alone build up visual space as we know it unless aided by associated observations from the other senses. Both sets of factors are important and necessary, and we could dispense with neither.

Chapter 14

CATTELL'S STUDIES IN THE MEASUREMENT OF REACTION TIME

I. REACTION TIME AND PSYCHOLOGICAL RESEARCH

One of the most direct ways in which the processes of perception, discrimination, and choice may be subjected to quantitative study is to measure the *time* it takes an individual to perceive and report upon the likenesses or differences among several stimuli. Various experiments in the psychological laboratory have been concerned with the measurement of time of response, or *reaction time,* i. e., with the accurate recording of the time intervening between the application of a stimulus, the sound of a buzzer, say, and the motor response of the subject, e. g., lifting the finger from an electric key. The primary interest of many experimenters has been in the establishment of reaction time *norms for various kinds of stimuli,* viz., lights, sounds, and touches; and in studying individual differences in reaction to such stimuli. Other workers have studied the effect of different stimulus conditions—the subject meanwhile being kept relatively "constant"—by changing the quality, intensity, or duration of the stimulus. Or different parts of the body have been stimulated and, in the case of light, the effects compared of activating the retina at the fovea, and at varying distances from this central point. Still other researchers have investigated the effect of varying the *condition of the subject,* meanwhile keeping the task relatively constant. In this way it is possible to measure the effect of drugs, fatigue, practice, incentive and punishment, and other factors upon the reaction time of the individual.

In America much of the interest in reaction time in psychology may be traced to the work and influence of James McKeen Cattell. Cattell was one of the first American students to take his doctor's degree in Wundt's laboratory at the University of Leipzig. Wundt's laboratory was established in 1879, and was the first psychological laboratory in the world. Cattell's dissertation was printed in English in 1886 under the title *The Time Taken Up by Cerebral Operations*, and was immediately followed by other important reaction time studies. During his thirty years as Professor of Psychology at Columbia University, Cattell and his students published many investigations on the measurement of the mental processes. Some of these studies will be described later on in this chapter. For the present, let us consider the influences which prepared the way for the interest of psychologists in the time measurements of mental phenomena.

2. THE HISTORY OF THE REACTION TIME EXPERIMENT

The reaction time experiment has a long and interesting history. A story which dates back to 1796 tells of an unlucky assistant in the astronomical observatory at Greenwich, England, who lost his job because he persistently recorded the instant when a star passed across the meridian with too large an error—his reaction time or "personal equation" was abnormally long. The first publication of the results of comparative tests showing fairly large and persistent individual differences in recording the transits of stars was made by the German astronomer, Bessel, in 1822; too late, unfortunately, to save the slow-reacting assistant mentioned above. In 1850 Helmholtz, the great physiologist, used the reaction time method to measure the speed of nerve conduction. Working with the motor nerve of the frog, Helmholtz stimulated a nerve attached to a muscle at a point some distance from the reacting muscle. The time intervening between the application of this stimulus and the movement in the muscle was recorded, as was also the shorter time-interval elapsing between the application of a stimulus nearer the muscle and the appearance of movement. The difference between these two reaction times gives the time taken by the impulse in traveling along the nerve between the two points of stimulation. For the frog, Helmholtz reported the speed of motor nerve conduction to be 27 meters (about 89 feet) per second; in man he calculated the speed of motor nerve conduction by the same method to be about twice as great.

Helmholtz also applied his method to the measurement of sensory nerve conduction. He assumed that if two points on the same sensory nerve, one, say, on the foot, and one on the upper leg, were stimulated in successive experiments, the subject's response in both cases being the same, the difference in reaction time would be a measure of the time taken by the impulse in traversing the nerve length between the two stimulated points. Unfortunately, the results of these experiments were so variable that Helmholtz's determinations were highly uncertain. Probably the main reasons for this variability are the many influences, both facilitating and inhibiting, which the impulse must undergo in passing through the nerve centers in the brain and spinal cord.

The many investigations which followed those of Helmholtz gave results for the most part widely divergent from his results and from each other. Finally, in 1895 Cattell and Dolley published the most thorough investigation into the problem of nervous conduction in man by the reaction time method. Cattell and Dolley applied electrical stimuli at two points on the median nerve of the arm thirty centimeters apart, and at two points on the posterior tibial nerve of the

JAMES MC KEEN CATTELL
(Born 1860)

leg fifty centimeters apart. The reaction movement was the same for all stimuli. Large variations were found in the velocities of the sensory impulse as so measured, the times being 31 meters per second for one observer, and 65 meters per second for another. Considerable variability, as well, was encountered in each observer. These results led Cattell and Dolley to suggest that the differences in reaction time found must be due, not to differences in the speed of the nervous impulse, but to the variability of the central connections involved, as well as to qualitative differences in the sensations aroused at the different points of stimulation. This explanation was substantiated by the interesting finding that either hand will react more quickly when it, rather than the other hand, is stimulated. According to these authors, this obviously means that some sensori-motor connections, owing possibly to innate linkages and more probably to practice, are more closely knit than others, so that the reaction time varies even when the *same* length of nerve fiber is traversed. Because of these complications in the central connections, Cattell and Dolley concluded that the velocity of the nervous impulse cannot be adequately measured by reaction time methods. It should be added in ending this section that physiologists using other and improved methods have determined the speed of the nerve impulse in man to be around 70 meters (about 225 feet) per second. This is much faster than the times found by the early investigators who used reaction time methods. The speed of the sensory nerve process is probably about the same as that of the motor.

3. EARLY STUDIES OF REACTION TIME

The first studies of the psychological factors influencing simple as well as complex reactions were those of the Dutch scientists Donders and De Jaeger in 1865. In the simple reaction experiment as now set up in the laboratory, the subject knows beforehand what stimulus he will receive, as for example, a flash of light or a sound. Usually his instructions are to make a single prescribed movement, such as lifting the finger from an electric telegraph key (which is being held down) as quickly as possible when the stimulus is given. After practice, the *simple reaction* becomes highly automatic and almost reflexive. In the *discrimination reaction* experiment, as devised by Donders, two stimuli (e. g., two notes of different pitch or two differently colored lights) are employed, and the subject is instructed to react to the one and remain quiet to the other. When, in addition to the two stimuli, the subject is given *two* reaction keys, and is instructed to react with the *right hand* if one stimulus appears and with the *left* if the other stimulus appears, we have what is called a *choice reaction.*

Donders, as well as other early workers, believed that by *subtracting* the simple from the discriminative reaction time, "discrimination times" could be obtained. Donders also held that by subtracting discrimination reaction time from discrimination *plus* choice, "will" or "choice" times could be obtained. This procedure is called *elimination by subtraction.* It assumes that a complex response is in reality a simple response plus certain added central processes, and that the time taken by these processes may be determined by subtracting the time of the simple reaction.

Cattell, as early as 1885, criticized the view that a discriminative reaction may be analyzed into a simple reaction plus some more or less constant "will time" or "perception time." Subtracted times, he held, were simply measures of the increased complexity of the total process, or of the increased difficulty of the task. Other investigators who questioned elimination by subtraction as a method were Erdmann and Dodge (1898), and Ach (1905). The latter, especially, argued that the different preparation of the subject for a simple and a discriminative reaction made the two very different psychologically. When faced by several stimuli, or given the choice of several responses, the *situation,* said Ach, is very different from that in the simple reaction time experiment. As a result a different attitude is set up in the subject, so that the whole process is different, not merely the *central* part of it. Moreover, as was urged by other experimenters, there is no introspective evidence that, when one mental process is added to another, the first retains its identity unchanged.

Cattell's view of what happens in reaction time experiments is very different from that of Donders, and also from the explanation advanced by Wundt. At the ready signal, he said, the subject, in making a simple reaction, concentrates his attention upon the stimulus which is to appear, e. g., a red light, or an electric shock, and upon the finger which is to react. Hence, the nervous pathways between the eye or skin→brain→finger are especially well prepared or open when the stimulus comes. In the discriminative or choice experiment, naturally more "switches" and more pathways must be "set" because of the increased complexity of the situation. This introduces an element of suspense or indecision which in turn necessitates greater preparation and makes for a longer reaction time. Wundt had regarded the whole reaction process as analyzable psychologically into (a) perception of the stimulus, (b) apperception (Wundt's term for the recognition or comprehension of the stimulus), and (c) will, or the release of the impulse to react. This analysis, said Cattell, is not psychologically accurate. Apperception, or the clear recognition of the stimulus, comes if at all *after* the reaction has been made, while will exists simply in the preparation for movement and becomes less and less a factor as the reactions grow more and more automatic.

In justice to Wundt it should be said that, while his analysis was probably more elaborate than is necessary to describe the somewhat simplified laboratory experiments on reaction time, it does fit quite well the unprepared reactions of everyday life. Suppose, for instance, that a child runs in front of an oncoming street-car, and that the motorman cuts off his current and applies his brakes just in time to prevent an accident. Here, in Wundt's terms we have perception of the child on the tracks, apperception of the danger in the situation, and will, or the release of impulses which stop the car. But these psychological processes cannot be analyzed out in any such clear-cut fashion in the simple laboratory situation of lifting a finger from an electric key as soon as one hears a sound or sees a light; nor do they appear as separate and distinct processes when reactions become habitual and automatic as they are for experienced street-car motormen.

4. APPARATUS USED IN MEASURING REACTION TIME

We have seen that the simple reaction time experiment measures the time-interval between a single and oft-repeated stimulus and a prescribed and constant response. In the usual laboratory set-up, the subject sits with his forefinger depressing an electric key; and at the appearance of the stimulus he reacts by lifting his finger from the key as quickly as possible. Various methods have been employed in the laboratory for measuring the time-intervals between stimulus and response. All of these make use of a chronoscope or some other time-measuring device. The Hipp chronoscope, an instrument which measures in units of .001 second * has perhaps been most widely used in the past by

---

* .001 sec. has usually been represented by 1σ in psychological literature. Thus, 100σ and .1 sec. are the same. Unfortunately, the sign σ is a bad choice, because of its widespread use in statistics to denote the standard deviation. A better time-unit, now coming into use, is milliseconds, or ms.; 1 ms. $= .001$ sec., and 100 ms. $= .100$ sec.

psychologists (see Figure 45). Apparatus for checking the accuracy of the Hipp chronoscope, as well as many improve-

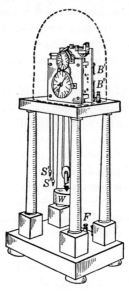

FIG. 45

THE HIPP CHRONOSCOPE

The clockwork of this chronoscope is driven by the weight, W, which is raised by a key fitting in the center of the lower dial. The chronoscope is started by pulling S' and stopped by pulling S". The two recording dials are divided into hundredth parts. The hand on the upper dial revolves ten times every second, each division on the dial corresponding to a thousandth part of a second or 1σ. The hand on the lower dial revolves once every ten seconds, each division on the dial corresponding to one-tenth of a second or 100σ. Reaction time is calculated from both dials, the units and tens from the lower and the hundredths and thousandths from the upper dial. The speed of the dial hands is controlled by a small steel tongue which is accurately tuned to vibrate 1,000 times per second. B' and B" are electromagnets which control the starting and stopping of the dial hands. F is a binding-post. Various control instruments have been devised to check the accuracy of the readings given by this chronoscope.

ments in the instrument itself, were made by Cattell and his students. The Bergstrom chronoscope, and the Dunlap chronoscope, a more recently devised instrument, are also used. In addition to instrumental measurements, graphic records of reaction time may be secured by using an electrically driven tuning-fork and a smoked drum apparatus. A tuning-fork which vibrates 100 times a second, say, is set to mark off a time-line on a revolving drum. Beneath this time-line the appearance of the stimulus and the subject's response are recorded by means of electric markers. The graphic method is accurate and is often used as a check on other methods; but it is too slow for most practical work.

All of the apparatus described above may be used in the measurement of complex as well as simple reactions. Experiments in complex reaction time may be set up either through the addition of extra stimuli, or through the employment of more than one response. In the Donders discrimination reaction experiment previously described, either of two stimuli was presented, to only one of which the subject was instructed to react. The obvious disadvantage of this set-up is that records are obtained in only about one-half of the trials. In Donders' discrimination and choice experiment, two stimuli were employed and two responses, the subject reacting with the right hand if the one stimulus appeared, and with the left hand if the other appeared. Henmon, one of Cattell's early students, simplified and improved this procedure by an arrangement in which the two stimuli were always presented side by side. The subject was instructed to react to a previously designated stimulus with his *right* hand if it appeared to the right of the other stimulus, and with his *left* hand if it appeared to the left of the other stimulus. As will be readily surmised, reaction time is considerably slower when the conditions are complicated than when only one stimulus and one response are utilized.

Reaction time is still longer in the *associative* type of response. Here the stimuli may be words (or lists of words) to which the subject is to react with the first word which comes to mind (free association); or, the subject may be instructed to give the opposites of the stimulus words, or responses bearing some other designated relation, e. g., part-whole, adjective-noun, verb-object (controlled association). The color-naming and form-naming tests illustrate other varieties of controlled association. The usual method in associative reaction is to take the total time required by the subject to give the correct responses to a list of words and then determine his average reaction time for each word. The one-fifth second stop-watch is usually considered to be accurate enough for reactions of this kind; for finer work, a one-hundredth second electric stop-clock may be employed.

5. FACTORS INFLUENCING SIMPLE REACTION TIME

There are many conditions which influence directly the speed of reaction besides the complexity of the stimulus-response situation. Most of these factors have been studied at one time or another by Cattell and his students, as well as by many others, and some of the more important findings will be considered in this section.

1. *Sense Organ.* In the first place, reaction time varies with the particular sense organ stimulated. Cattell reported the simple reaction time to light to be about 150 ms., with some variability (8–10 ms.), and the simple reaction time to sound to be about 120 ms. The simple reaction times to stimuli applied to the different sense organs, as determined by many investigators, may be summarized as follows:

Type of Stimulation	Reaction Time
Visual	150 ms. – 200 ms.
Auditory	120 – 160
Tactual	110 – 160
Olfactory	200 – 800
Gustatory	300 – 1000
Pain	400 – 1000
Temperature:	
Cold about	150 ms.
Warmth about	180

Probably the slow reaction time to taste and smell is owing to the chemical nature of these senses and to the difficulty in getting stimuli directly to them. The "free nerve endings" of the pain sense are fairly close to the surface, but are relatively slow to react. The fact that hot and cold stimuli must act by conducting heat or cold into the skin to the sensory end organs will obviously slow up the reaction time to such stimuli.

The part of the sense organ stimulated makes a difference in reaction time. Poffenberger, a student of Cattell, found that when the retina is stimulated with a light beam at points to the right and left of the fovea, the reaction time is longer than it is when the fovea itself is excited. Moreover, reaction time becomes longer and longer as the stimulus is moved out from the central point to the periphery. Reaction time is faster to stimuli applied to the hand than to stimuli applied to the forehead or foot, as a result probably of closer nerve center connections in the first instance.

2. *Intensity, Size, and Duration of the Stimulus.* Cattell studied the influence of all three of these factors upon reaction time as early as 1886. More accurate work was done later by Froeberg, under Cattell's direction. Working with graded light intensities (light reflected from gray and white paper), Froeberg found that the reaction time increased, but

very slowly, as the intensity of the light decreased. When reaction time to a given medium intensity, for example, was 191 ms., the reaction to a stimulus one-half as bright was increased by only 3 ms.; while the reaction to a stimulus one-tenth as bright was increased by 17 ms. The same general result was found when the *size* (area of a square surface reflecting light) and the *duration* of the stimuli were decreased. The reaction time increased in both cases, but somewhat more slowly for duration changes than for size changes. Froeberg found also that the reaction time to sound increased fairly rapidly when the intensity of the sound was diminished.

3. *The Foreperiod and the Reacting Movement.* The foreperiod, that is, the time-interval between the signal "Ready" and the presentation of the stimulus, is quite important in reaction time work. During the foreperiod, the subject "gets set," so to speak, to react to the expected stimulus as quickly as possible. If the foreperiod is short, i. e., less than one second, the subject may be caught before he is entirely ready, and in consequence react more slowly than usual; if the foreperiod is long, say ten seconds or more, the subject is likely to lose his "edge" and hence react too slowly. Cattell placed the optimum foreperiod close to one second. This interval, he said, is about as long as the nerve centers can be kept in a state of preparedness; longer times (up to fifteen seconds) were found to increase the reaction time as well as the variability of response. Other investigators placed the best foreperiod at from two to three seconds. Breitwieser, working in Cattell's laboratory with improved technique and more subjects, found the optimum foreperiod to be between two and four seconds, with, however, some individual differences. This determination has been verified by Woodrow, who also found two seconds to be the most favorable foreperiod.

The influence of the reacting movement upon time of response has already been touched upon. Either hand, for instance, responds more quickly to a stimulus applied to it than to one applied to the other hand. It has been shown, too, that releasing rather than depressing the reaction key gives a less variable response. In a careful study of the movements of the hand in reacting to a stimulus, carried out in the Yale laboratory in 1905 by Judd, McAllister, and Steele, it was discovered that the hand does not maintain a steady pressure on the reacting key during the foreperiod. On the contrary, there is a fluctuation from stronger to weaker pressure, the key sometimes being completely released to give a "premature" reaction. Whenever degree of readiness to react has reached a high point, the response may easily be premature, as when a runner springs from his mark before the signal is given. The Yale experimenters found, too, that often the first reactions of unpractised subjects show a quick depression of the key before it is released. This counter-movement takes time and consequently slows up the reaction. With practice it tends to be inhibited in favor of the correct release movement.

4. *Practice, Attention, Distraction, and Fatigue.* Practice, according to Cattell, has little effect upon time of response after the first few trials—in which the subject's reactions often vary markedly. The effect of distractions, such as the beating of a metronome, or the performance of mental addition during the experiment are also relatively slight provided the subjects are highly practised. For the first type of distraction the reaction time may increase from 2 to 10 ms., for the second from about 20 to 30 ms. Woodrow has investigated with great thoroughness the rôle of attention and practice in reaction time. He found that reaction time varies considerably with the amount of attention given the task. Degree of attention was measured by the prolongation in reaction time brought about by introducing foreperiods of

varying lengths. For stimuli of "moderate" intensity, Woodrow reports the subject's attention to be less affected for touch than for sound or light. J. E. Evans, using flashing lights, noises, and touch stimuli as distractions, found that these extraneous factors increased the reaction time markedly at first, but that their influence was much lessened with training. Both trained and untrained observers were affected by the distractions, however, the greatest disturbance occurring when both the distraction and the stimulus to which the subject was instructed to respond affected the *same* sense organ. Cassel and Dallenbach found also that distractions tend to lengthen reaction time, the increase for two observers ranging from 3 ms. to 37 ms. Fatigue, strangely enough, has an almost negligible effect upon reaction time. In his own case, Cattell found his reaction time to decrease very slightly even after a day of continuous reacting.

5. *Incentives, Punishment, Drugs, and Age.* The effect of incentive—encouragement or mild praise—upon reaction time is to increase it about 8 ms. Negative incentive, or punishment, as for example giving the subject an electric shock if he fails to react within a given time, speeds up the reaction time 20 ms. or more. Drugs have a variable effect upon reaction time. Coffee and tea appear to shorten it; small doses of alcohol first shorten and then lengthen it; morphine, ether, and chloroform usually lengthen it. As might be surmised, time of response is slower and more variable in childhood and in old age.

6. THE EFFECT OF ATTITUDE UPON REACTION TIME

In addition to the factors discussed in the last section, there is still another determinant in reaction time experiments which has excited much controversy, and which is important enough to be considered at some length. This has to do with the *direction* of the subject's attention, or preparatory set during the foreperiod. Several early workers on reaction time in Germany, notably Lange, in 1888, observed that when the subject in a simple reaction time experiment directed his attention specifically toward the awaited stimulus, his time of response was considerably *longer* than when he fixed his attention upon the movement to be made. Lange called the first kind of reaction "sensorial," and the second "muscular," or "motor." The first type of response, he said, is always longer than the second, the difference being as much as 100 ms. The distinction between sensorial responses and motor responses was accepted by most contemporaries of Lange as valid, although the differences found were not always as great as those he had reported.

Lange's Attention Theory, as this view was called, was challenged by Baldwin's (1895) and Flournoy's (1896) Type Theory. These two workers found among their subjects some whose motor reactions were faster than their sensory reactions and others who gave quicker sensory reactions than motor reactions. They suggested, accordingly, that individuals are natively sensory, motor, or indifferent in type, and that each type reacts at his best when allowed to follow his natural inclination. Thus, while accepting the distinction between sensory and motor responses, Baldwin and Flournoy reached a very different conclusion with regard to the differences in speed between the two types from that of Lange and his group.

Still a third explanation of the difference between sensory and motor responses has been given in terms of practice and habituation. This was the view advanced by Cattell in 1892 and by Angell and Moore in 1896. Cattell had found no reliable differences between the sensory and motor types of reaction in the case of practised observers. Whether a new subject is sensory or motor at the start, he said, is largely a matter of the instructions given, accidental direction of attention, and previous training; after practice, there is little or no difference between the two attitudes. Later work, done by Breitwieser, under Cattell's direction, tended to confirm this view. Breitwieser first took a long series of reactions in some of which his subjects were verbally instructed to give sensory, and in others motor, responses. Following these experiments, Breitwieser forced the attitude of his subjects into the sensory or motor category by means of the following ingenious arrangement. To insure a sensory attitude, he presented sometimes the one and sometimes the other of two closely similar stimuli, and required his subjects, after reacting, to report which of the two had been given. This necessitated close attention to the stimulus. To make sure that the reaction was of the motor type, Breitwieser used a reaction key which varied somewhat in the resistance which it offered to the subject's reacting finger. The subject was instructed, after responding, to tell which of the two resistances (the greater or less) had been employed. Here, clearly enough, it was the reacting movement which needed special attention. Finally, in order to guarantee a neutral, or indifferent attitude, the subject was instructed to identify after each reaction *both* the key pressure *and* the stimulus presented.

Breitwieser's results indicated in general a very slight advantage—averaging about 20 ms.—for the verbally instructed motor over the verbally instructed sensory reactions. He found little difference between those sensory responses in which the subject was verbally instructed to attend to the stimulus, or forced to attend. However, the verbally instructed motor responses were much faster (in fact, the fastest of all) than those motor reactions in which the subject was required to report upon the key pressure. When the subject was instructed to report *both* upon key pressure and stimulus difference, his reaction time was the slowest of all, the time being almost as great as that in a discriminative reaction.

The upshot of the whole controversy would seem to be (1) that there is a real distinction between the sensory and motor attitudes; (2) that untrained subjects are probably for the most part sensory at the start, becoming motor as the novelty wears off and the need for close attention to the stimulus becomes less; and (3) that the motor, being the more highly practised attitude, is the faster type of response.

7. ASSOCIATIVE REACTIONS

While Cattell was interested in the study and analysis of the factors influencing simple reaction time, he was also interested in the more elaborate discriminative and associative reactions. He found, for example, wide variations in the time it takes persons to multiply two numbers presented at the same time, and that a subject can name objects or pictures in his own language more readily than in a foreign tongue. All this seems fairly obvious, and is probably no more than one might expect. But many other findings are by no means so evident. Thus, Cattell found that when a word indicating a *part* of an object is the stimulus, e. g., *roof,* it takes longer to give the name of the *whole* object, e. g., *house,* than to give the part when the whole is presented, e. g., *pencil—point.* Also, it is easier to go from a special to a more general class, e. g., *cat—animal,* than in the reverse direction. Opposites are given with the quickest reaction times, but these times vary greatly, the differences here, as in the other cases, being due largely to familiarity, training, and frequency of usage.

In other experiments with words and language, Cattell found that while the reaction time to a single word exposed alone is about 360 ms., this time is reduced to 200 ms. per word when a series of words is exposed together. He found also that a higher speed of reading per word is secured when two words instead of one are presented; three instead of two, and so on up to four or five. These results, taken together with experiments made using the tachistoscope in which it has been demonstrated that one can group as many as two or three words together in an instant of exposure, indicate quite clearly the great importance of *overlapping* in efficient verbal response. They show, too, that an individual's reaction to a phrase or sentence composed of several words is not simply the sum total of his time reactions to the *separate* words, but is rather the response to a group of words taken as a *larger unit*. This suggests clearly that growth in reading ability, as well as in many other highly skilled performances, must be due to the fact that reactions are made to larger and larger groups of discrete impressions as wholes. Responses in larger units enter into the performance of the highly trained musician playing from score. For his experiments with language, Cattell devised a lip key and a voice key, both of which were distinct improvements on similar devices used by others in recording oral responses.

Cattell's experiments have had an interesting effect upon methods of teaching reading. On the theory that learning should proceed from the simple to the complex, for years children had been laboriously taught their *a, b, c*'s. These elements learned, pupils were then taught how to put letters into words, words into phrases, and phrases into sentences. This is a logical rather than a psychological method of learning. As Cattell's experiments showed, words are perceived and reacted to as *wholes,* not as clusters of letters; in fact, one may fail to see errors in a printed page because he is not looking for letters but reading words. In most modern schools children are now being taught to read words from the start, and letters are learned afterward. This more "natural" method is often employed, too, with adults who wish to acquire a rapid reading knowledge of a foreign language. The utilization of reaction time experiments in pedagogy is a good illustration of how a somewhat restricted laboratory result may have widespread practical outcomes.

8. THE DISCRIMINATION TIME METHOD

The last series of experiments which we shall describe is that in which a new psychophysical method, the "discrimination time method," was employed. This method was reported by Cattell in 1902, and is based upon the assumption that differences in sensation are equal when it takes the same time to perceive them, since, in general, the smaller the difference, the longer the time necessary to perceive and react to it. The most important study by the discrimination time method is that of Henmon. Henmon's method (see p. 376) was to present two stimuli simultaneously. Two keys were used for response, the subject being instructed to react to one of the two stimuli (which one was previously designated) with the right hand if it appeared on the right, and with the left hand if it appeared on the left. For example, suppose red and blue are the two stimuli, and the subject has been instructed to react to red. Under these conditions, when the stimuli are presented the subject must react with his right hand when the red is to the right of the blue, and with his left hand when the red is to the left of the blue. Some of Henmon's results with colors appear below.

Colors to Be Discriminated	*Discrimination Time*
White and black	197 ms.
Red and green	203
Red and blue	212
Red and yellow	217
Red and orange (mixed with 25% red) ..	252
Red and orange (mixed with 75% red) ..	271

It is clear that the smaller the *qualitative* differences between the two colors, the longer the reaction time. Using small differences in pitch Henmon obtained much the same results:

Differences in Pitch (in Vibrations)	Reaction Time
16	290 ms.
12	299
8	311
4	334

When the subject was instructed to react to the *shorter* of two lines, shown side by side, the following reaction times were obtained:

Differences in length of line (in mms.)		Reaction Time
From 10 to 13		296 ms.
10	12	305
10	11½	313
10	11	334
10	10½	345

These results show that the smaller the difference between the two stimuli, whether in vibration rate or in millimeters, the longer the reaction time to the difference.

Henmon's findings may be interpreted to mean (1) that the mental processes of apprehension and discrimination need more elaboration—and hence more time—when differences are decreased; and (2) that the preliminary adjustment for the movement is less and less adequate as the difference between the two stimuli becomes smaller and smaller. Both of these conditions serve to explain the lengthened reaction time. If we are justified in the assumption that differences are equal, for perception, when the times required to discriminate them are equal, it appears from Henmon's results that tones eight vibrations apart differ *perceptually* to about the same degree as lines differing by one and one-half millimeters (ten and eleven and a half millimeters).

9. SOME PRACTICAL APPLICATIONS OF REACTION TIME STUDIES

It should now be evident that the study of reaction time has passed through many phases and has excited many and various interests. Reaction time is measured to-day not so much for the purpose of analyzing its determinants or of finding "choice" or "will" times, but rather as a means of attacking practical problems of behavior. For example, the reaction time experiment may be employed (1) for measuring the *difficulty* of a task in an objective way, or (2) as an index of an individual's *efficiency* under different conditions. Or, it may be taken as a means (3) of *comparing* individuals under the *same* conditions, or (4) the same individual under *different* conditions; that is to say, the establishment of individual differences may be the primary interest. Again, the speed of a person's simple or discriminative responses may be compared with his quickness in solving problems or in performing other intellectual tasks to see whether a given individual may be characterized as generally quick or generally slow intellectually. In one study of this kind, memory for words, numbers and the like, was found to be related to speed of simple reaction, while the learning of verbal and other abstract relations was correlated with quickness of discriminative reaction. However, few persons can be fairly described as possessing a definite speed-level at which they habitually work. Differences in familiarity with the tasks to be done, degree of previous practice, interest, and incentive play too large a rôle. For these reasons a bookkeeper who is ordinarily very slow may, after long practice, or with sufficient incentive, surpass in mental calculation—addition, say—an individual much faster in other respects.

In vocational selection, as well as in the diagnosis of aptitudes, the reaction time of the individual is often an important factor. It is apparent, for instance, that knowledge of the time required by a chauffeur or a motorman to apply his brakes at a given signal, or to react quickly in an emergency is of the greatest practical value. Ingenious devices for testing the reaction time of prospective drivers of automobiles or of street-cars have been devised by psychologists. Wechsler, for instance, constructed a dummy automobile, with steering-wheel, brakes, clutch, and so on, which he used in testing prospective taxi drivers. The candidate was instructed to depress his clutch and apply his brakes at the flash of a yellow light on the board placed before him; at the appearance of other colored lights to react in various ways with appropriate hand and foot movements. Time of reaction and errors (wrong responses) were carefully recorded. After actual road experience it was found that, while men with the slowest reaction times had the most accidents, the fastest reacting men also had a large number of accidents. The failure of the very fast men to avoid accidents is attributed by Wechsler to the fact that very quick men are liable to take chances through overconfidence and hence risk mishap. It is significant that the number of errors, or wrong responses, proved to be a better criterion than simple speed of response in separating the frequent-accident men from those who have few accidents. All men, for instance, who made four or more errors in a fifteen minute test were rated as careless drivers. Frequent-accident men consistently made more errors than few or no-accident men.

The increasing death rate from automobile accidents has directed much study to the problem of locating the accident-prone driver. The method used in picking out the potentially dangerous driver has been to analyze driving skill and construct tests to measure important phases of this complex activity. It is well recognized that a number of factors enter into safe driving. Tests have been developed for measuring the factor of vision—color vision, effects of glare, accuracy in perception of depth, and so on. Also tests are available for measuring hand-eye coördination and other abilities. We have described above one test of reaction time under driving conditions. The attempt—as here—to simulate actual road conditions by means of a miniature situation illustrates a method widely used in vocational psychology. Driving tests are coming more and more into use. It is not unreasonable to hope that—when strictly applied—such tests will have a decided influence in decreasing the accident rate.

A study in which reaction time was employed in tests of prospective motormen may be cited briefly as an example of the work in this field. Shellow measured the time required by street-car motormen to react with the appropriate movements upon the appearance of a light signal. Time of reaction and errors, wrong responses and omissions (failure to react to signals), were recorded. Two groups of men were found to make the best operators, those who react very quickly but who have a fairly high error score (mostly omissions) and those who react slowly but make practically no errors. If a man reacts slowly and also makes errors, he is a poor prospect as a motorman.

It will be recognized that many of these problems have arisen since the early reaction time work of Cattell, and are the product of new conditions and of an attempt to satisfy new demands. The attack upon them, however, was stimulated by the early interest of psychologists in general, and of Cattell in particular, in the objective study of the time relations of human performance.

Chapter 15

WEBER'S AND FECHNER'S LAWS AND THE DEVELOPMENT OF PSYCHOPHYSICS

I. THE PROBLEMS OF PSYCHOPHYSICS

All of us have noticed that our impressions of the differences in the *magnitude, extent,* and *amount* of the things we perceive around us do not vary directly with the changes in the objects themselves. Every one would agree, for example, that a faint tone does not need to be increased as much as a loud tone for the *change* to be noticed; and that a four-year-old boy does not have to grow as much as his sixteen-year-old brother for the increase in height to be perceived. Furthermore, most of us recognize at once the fact that one pound added to a ten-pound load is more clearly felt as an *increased* weight than one pound added to a fifty-pound load; and that an error of one inch in measuring one foot is far cruder work than an error of one inch in measuring one mile. But few who note these facts have given much thought to the question of how our *perception of a difference,* and the *actual difference itself,* are related, other than to speculate, perhaps somewhat vaguely, that the relationship is clearly not one of simple correspondence.

It so happens that one of the very earliest attempts to employ experimental method in psychology was directed toward solving this problem of the relation of stimulus changes to sensation changes. There were several reasons for this. For one thing the early psychologists were mostly philosophers, and hence were concerned with the problem of how knowledge of the world and of ourselves is obtained through the senses. Moreover, there already existed a respectable body of fact concerning the chief sense-organs, the ear, the eye, the skin—which furnished a convenient starting-point for investigation. Whatever other less tangible reasons there were, the fact remains that the topic of sensation-stimulus dependence bulks large in the history of experimental psychology and has stimulated an enormous amount of research. A whole literature, in fact, has grown up around the subject of *psychophysics,* as this branch of psychology is called; and the purpose of this chapter is to outline the development of psychophysics and to evaluate in brief space its place in modern psychology.

2. WEBER'S LAW

Psychophysics really began with the work of Ernst Heinrich Weber (1795–1878), although as a separate branch of psychology it did not originate with him. During the years from 1829 to 1834, Weber, who was professor of anatomy in the University of Leipzig, published in Latin a long series of experiments on cutaneous and kinesthetic (or muscular) sensation under the title *De Tactu.* Weber was interested in discovering how accurately small differences in weight can be sensed when the weights are lifted by hand or are allowed to rest freely on the surface of the skin. He was interested also in how small a difference between two lines can be ascertained or perceived by the eye. In a series of experiments with weights held between the fingers and lifted by hand, Weber discovered that a weight of thirty ounces could just barely be distinguished as lighter than a weight of thirty-one ounces, and as heavier than one of twenty-nine ounces. This proportion he found to hold closely for drams * as well as for

* A dram = $\frac{1}{16}$ ounce avoirdupois.

GUSTAV THEODOR FECHNER

(1801–1887)

ounces, i. e., thirty drams could just be felt as lighter than thirty-one and heavier than twenty-nine drams. With practised subjects, the same proportion held for lighter weights— 14.5 ounces or 14.5 drams, for instance, could just be distinguished from 15 ounces or 15 drams, respectively. Smaller differences than these, said Weber, are very rarely "sensed," while greater differences are too readily discriminated to be considered just noticeable. In experiments concerned with judging the length of lines, Weber discovered that a different but consistent principle of proportion held good. A line of 101 millimeters could just be discriminated as longer than one of 100 millimeters, while a line of 51 millimeters was judged to be just observably longer than one of 50.5 millimeters.

On the basis of these results, Weber formulated the famous generalization known subsequently as Weber's Law. In comparing objects, he says, it is clear that we perceive not the *actual difference* between the two objects, but the *ratio* of this difference to the magnitudes of the two objects compared. To put it in other words, the observed difference between two objects is not absolute and completely independent of the objects themselves, but is relative to the *size* of the stimuli and is a *constant fraction* of one of them, the so-called "standard stimulus." The constant fraction must be discovered by experiment, and is called the "difference limen," or D L. For weights lifted by hand, the D L was determined by Weber to be $\frac{1}{30}$ to $\frac{1}{40}$, and for lines approximately $\frac{1}{100}$. To illustrate the meaning of the D L more concretely, if thirty ounces can just be discriminated from thirty-one ($\frac{1}{30}$ x 30 = 1), then sixty ounces should be just distinguishable from sixty-two ($\frac{1}{30}$ x 60 = 2), and ninety from ninety-three ($\frac{1}{30}$ x 90 = 3). In each case the just-noticeably-different stimulus differs from the standard stimulus by a certain frac-tional amount of the standard, and this fraction or D L remains substantially constant no matter what the actual size of the objects compared.

Weber's law may be expressed more concisely in mathematical form as follows: let R stand for the standard stimulus,* i. e., that object or thing with which other objects or things are to be compared. Then if dR is the *increment* by which R must be increased in order to produce a just noticeable change in the sensation—for example, a judgment of just barely heavier, or just observably longer—Weber's law may be summed up in the following equation:

$$\frac{dR}{R} = C \ (a \ constant)$$

As we have already seen, Weber put the constant for lifted weights at $\frac{1}{30}$, and the D L for lines at $\frac{1}{100}$.

Unfortunately, Weber's conclusion that the just noticeable increase in a stimulus is a constant fraction of that stimulus is not as clear-cut as it appears at first glance. The trouble lies in the expression "just noticeable." This term is decidedly ambiguous, as it is often necessary to specify exactly how often a stimulus-increase must be correctly noted in order to be called just noticeable. One method has been to take that difference which is judged correctly 75 per cent of the time as just noticeable. Though other percentages would serve, the 75 per cent point is usually chosen because it lies midway between 50 per cent correct (a "chance" difference), and 100 per cent correct (a difference so large as always to be correctly perceived). To illustrate, if a 102 millimeter line is called longer than a standard line of 100 millimeters seventy-five times in 100 comparisons, then according to Weber's Law fifty-one millimeters should be called longer than fifty millimeters, 204 millimeters longer than 200, and 510 milli-

---

* R = *Reiz*, the German word for "stimulus," and is regularly used in psychophysics.

meters longer than 500, in 75 out of 100 trials. All of these ratios, $1/50$, $2/100$, $4/200$, and $10/500$, are of course equal, and the "75 per cent threshold" or D L is $1/50$. We may now state Weber's Law more clearly and less ambiguously as follows: the increase in any given stimulus which is correctly perceived in 75 per cent (or other designated per cent) of the trials is a constant fraction of the size of the stimulus.

3. FECHNER'S CONTRIBUTIONS TO PSYCHOPHYSICS: THE WEBER-FECHNER LAW

The equation $\dfrac{dR}{R} = C$ was Weber's final statement of his law, and constitutes his chief contribution to the study of the relation between sensory judgments and stimulus intensities. It remained for Gustav Theodor Fechner (1801–1887) to take up where Weber left off and, building upon Weber's Law, to erect the intricate and highly complex structure called psychophysics. Fechner, besides being Professor of Physics at Leipzig was also a philosopher and something of a mystic. In Weber's generalization he saw a means of studying quantitatively the relation between the physical and mental worlds. In his *Elements of Psychophysics,* first published in 1860, Fechner defined psychophysics as "an exact science of the functional relation or relations of dependency between body and mind." The physical world for Fechner was represented by the physical stimuli, and the psychical world by the sensations within the organism aroused by these stimuli.

Fechner laid down two principles which enabled him to amplify and extend Weber's Law. First, he assumed that a large sensation may be thought of as the *sum* of a number of small sensations; and secondly he assumed that just noticeable differences (*j.n.d.*'s) in sensation are equal, and hence are suitable units for measuring sensation changes. Accepting Weber's equation $\dfrac{dR}{R} = C$ as fundamentally correct, Fechner on the basis of experiments extending over many years,[*] reformulated Weber's Law to read as follows: *When stimuli increase by a constant ratio, the sensations aroused by them increase by equal increments or steps.* What Fechner

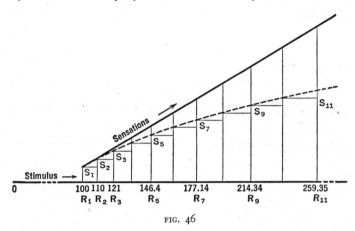

FIG. 46

GRAPHIC REPRESENTATION OF THE RELATION BETWEEN INCREASES IN THE
INTENSITY OF THE STIMULUS AND INCREASES IN THE INTENSITY
OF THE SENSATION

meant by this statement, and how it depends upon his assumptions may be seen most clearly, perhaps, in Figure 46.

In the diagram we begin with *two* stimuli, a standard and a variable comparison-stimulus, each designated by the value 100 on the horizontal scale. These two stimuli may be thought of as two lights of brightness value 100, or two lines each 100 mms. long, or two tones each of an absolute intensity designated by 100. To represent these values on the

[*] During the years from 1855 to 1859, Fechner alone made 67,072 weight comparisons, acting both as experimenter and as subject.

stimulus scale (the horizontal line), we lay off an arbitrary distance from zero to the point marked 100. Then on the vertical line above 100 (R_1) we lay off an arbitrary distance to represent the strength of the sensation (S_1) produced by stimulus 100. Suppose now that we increase very slowly the comparison stimulus 100, and that when this stimulus reaches the value 110 (R_2) it is judged to be *just noticeably greater* than the standard stimulus, which remains, of course, at 100 or R_1. The sensation value S_2 (on the vertical line) corresponding to stimulus 110 (R_2) will now equal the sensation S_1 (corresponding to stimulus 100) *plus* one *j.n.d.* unit—on Fechner's assumption that the *j.n.d.* may be taken as the unit of sensation-change. In Figure 46 the *j.n.d.* is taken as a small and arbitrary increment which when added to S_1 gives S_2.

Now let us begin with our two stimuli, the standard and comparison, both at the value 110 on the scale, and increase the comparison stimulus slowly until it is again just noticeably greater than the constant standard, still at 110. This point should be reached theoretically at 121 ($110 + {}^{110}\!/_{10}$), since in the previous trial our D L was found to be $\frac{1}{10}$. The sensation S_3 corresponding to the stimulus 121 (R_3) is S_2 plus one *j.n.d.*, or S_1 plus two *j.n.d.*'s and accordingly the distance S_1 plus two *j.n.d.* units is laid off above stimulus 121 (R_3). The other stimuli in Figure 46, viz., 133.1 (R_4), 146.4 (R_5), 161.04 (R_6), have all been calculated in the same manner as 121 and 110:—in each case *one tenth* of the preceding stimulus magnitude has been added on to the stimulus scale to give a just noticeable increase on the sensation scale and to accord with Weber's Law. The sensation (vertical distance) corresponding to the stimulus on the baseline is in every instance equal to the sensation aroused by the preceding stimulus plus one *j.n.d.* unit.

It should be noted that the stimuli in Figure 46 increase

in *geometrical progression* as we go from 100 to 161.04, while the sensations, the psychical series, increase in *arithmetic progression*.* Whenever we have two series which correspond point by point, the one increasing geometrically, the other arithmetically, we know from mathematics that the relation between the two variables must be logarithmic. Hence the sensation values (A P) may be here thought of as the logarithms of their corresponding stimulus-values (G P). The logarithmic relationship between a geometric and an arithmetic series may be simply illustrated by the common logarithms of 10 and its multiples. From any table of logarithms we find that

$$\log 1 = 0$$
$$\log 10 = 1$$
$$\log 100 = 2$$
$$\log 1,000 = 3$$
$$\log 10,000 = 4$$

On the *left-hand* side the numbers increase by a constant multiple (10), while on the *right-hand* side the logarithms increase by a constant increment (1). The first series is a geometric, the second an arithmetic, progression. If we let our numbers represent stimuli and our logs represent their corresponding sensations, we have the situation pictured in Figure 46. If the sensation values had increased in *direct proportion* to the increase in the stimuli (rather than by equal steps), we should have obtained the *linear* relationship

---

*A geometric progression (G P) is a series in which each term (except the first) is derived from the preceding one by multiplying by a constant number or *ratio:* e. g., 4, 12 (4 × 3), 36 (12 × 3), 108 (36 × 3). In the present case we have 100, 110 (100 × $1\frac{1}{10}$), 121 (110 × $1\frac{1}{10}$), 133.1 (121 × $1\frac{1}{10}$), 146.4 (133.1 × $1\frac{1}{10}$). An arithmetic progression (A P) is a series in which each term (except the first) is derived from the preceding by the *addition* of a constant number: e. g., 3, 7 (3 + 4), 11 (7 + 4), 15 (11 + 4), 19 (15 + 4). In Figure 46 we have S_1, S_2 (S_1 + 1 *j.n.d.*), S_3 (S_2 + 1 *j.n.d.*), S_4 (S_3 + 1 *j.n.d.*), S_5 (S_4 + 1 *j.n.d.*), S_6 (S_5 + 1 *j.n.d.*).

represented by the rapidly rising oblique line instead of the more slowly rising logarithmic curve shown in the diagram.

The discovery of the logarithmic relationship between stimuli and their sensations led Fechner to restate Weber's Law in mathematical terms as follows: *Sensations are proportional to the logarithms of their exciting stimuli, or, in the form of an equation:*

$$S = C \log R$$

wherein S is the sensation, R the stimulus, and C a constant to be determined from the experiment. This equation is generally known as the Weber-Fechner Law or simply as Fechner's Law. The first two quantities, of course, are variables, the third, C, is fixed for a given series of stimuli, e. g., weights, lines, or brightnesses, but varies from one sense modality to another. C's value depends partly upon the sense modality, the precision of measurement, and partly upon the choice of the zero point for sensation intensities.

Fechner's logarithmic law is regarded by many psychologists as one of the most important generalizations yet made in psychology. This principle, to be sure, is an extension and modification of Weber's Law, but it is also much more than this. Weber's equation, $\frac{dR}{R} = C$, said nothing about sensation intensities; it stated simply that, for a given proportion of correct judgments, the ratio of the stimuli is constant, no matter what the absolute magnitudes of the objects compared. Fechner's equation, on the other hand, expresses a *functional* relationship between physical stimuli and their corresponding sensation intensities—a relationship which Fechner, at least, believed to hold true over the whole range of perceptible stimuli.

4. LIMITATIONS OF WEBER'S AND FECHNER'S LAWS

As an expression of the general law of the relativity of all judgments, or the dependence of our perceptions of change upon the magnitude of the thing changed, Weber's Law serves to describe quite well many facts of everyday perception. Familiar examples (see also p. 395) readily come to mind: An inch is more perceptible when added to a man's finger than when added to his height; a room lighted by an electric light is scarcely brightened at all by the addition of a candle, but when lighted by a single candle the room's illumination is markedly increased by the addition of another candle; to hear a pin drop the room must be very quiet; five pounds added to a baby's weight is a much greater increase than five pounds added to a man's weight. These illustrations show the soundness of Weber's principle, but there are distinct limitations to the law which must be recognized in trying to evaluate it. In the first place, Weber's Law holds only approximately within *any* field. This is true whether we are concerned with the perception of linear magnitudes (e. g., lengths of lines), the perception of weights by passive pressure on the skin or by active lifting, the intensity of lights and sounds, the judgment of duration and movement, or the perception of pitch differences. Secondly, Weber's Law holds only in the *middle range* of stimulus intensities within a given sense modality. It breaks down with very weak or very strong stimuli. Expressed differently, the ratio $\dfrac{dR}{R}$ remains fairly constant over the middle range of stimuli, but increases markedly when the stimuli become very strong or very weak.

A series of careful experiments which show this phenomenon clearly were performed by König and Brodhun in 1888–1889. These investigators found the D L for light intensities varying from very faint to very bright to be a constant fraction (.017 to .018) of the stimulus over a wide range of medium brightnesses. The difference limens were considerably larger, however, for very faint and for very intense lights. This may be seen in König and Brodhun's data, some of which are reproduced in Table XXX below.

TABLE XXX

The stimuli are given in an arbitrary unit. The *ratios* give the fraction which the just-noticeable difference is of the absolute stimulus. Note that from about 400 to 100,000 the ratios are approximately equal. (After König and Brodhun)

Stimulus:	1	2	4	10	20	40	100	200	400	1,000
Ratio:	.256	.175	.120	.070	.048	.037	.030	.025	.022	.020

Stimulus:	2,000	4,000	10,000	20,000	40,000	100,000	200,000	400,000
Ratio:	.018	.017	.016	.017	.018	.021	.029	.038

These variations in D L are attributable in some degree to adaptation and various slight disturbances. But such factors are not sufficient, in a careful experiment, to account for the wide discrepancy in D L throughout the range of intensities. We are forced to conclude therefore that Weber's Law breaks down at the extremes of the stimulus scale.

Does Fechner's Law fare any better than Weber's as a universal principle? Again the answer is not a simple yes or no. In the first place, Fechner's Law, like Weber's, holds only approximately; and furthermore, like Weber's, it holds only for the middle range of stimuli. In the second place, Fechner's two assumptions have not stood the test of later experiment, nor of adverse criticism. Psychologists have not been slow to point out that a large sensation is not, psychologically at least, the sum of many elementary sensations, but is a new experience, just as water is not simply the sum of oxygen and hydrogen, but is essentially a new product. Moreover, the *j.n.d.* is by no means a fixed unit. The just noticeable difference between two lights or two tone intensities will vary from one observer to another, and for the same observer from time to time. Theoretically, there is no such thing as *a* "just noticeable difference," since even very small differences will occasionally be recorded, while large differences will sometimes not be perceived. The third objection to the universality of Fechner's Law is based upon the difficulty of fixing definitely the point of zero sensation. We know from mathematics that the logarithm of 1 is zero. Fechner fitted this into his formula, $S = C \log R$, by assigning the value 1 to that stimulus which arouses a just barely perceptible (zero) sensation. But the eye, the ear, and the skin rapidly become adapted to faint lights, faint sounds, and faint touches; and this adaptation, plus fatigue, slight distractions, and lapses of attention, shift and distort the zero point of sensation. Thus it would seem that the variability and instability inherent in the sensory receptors themselves must limit the universality of Fechner's Law.

These objections to Fechner's Law limit the range of its applicability. Nevertheless the principle of logarithmic relationship between stimulus changes and our perceptions of these changes has been found useful in many problems of biology, physics, and engineering. Several illustrations may be given. The relation of visual acuity to the brightness of the field is logarithmic. If absolute acuity (A) "is the reciprocal of the smallest visual angle for which neighboring contrasted portions of the field can be separated," and if B is the brightness of the field, then $A = c + k \log B$ (ref. 11). The constants c and k are dependent upon the units employed, the character of the field, and the eye itself. This equation is Fechner's Law, $S = C \log R$; it holds over the middle range of intensities. In the field of biophysics, it has been shown in certain organisms that the relationship between the reciprocal of the *latent time* of response (e. g., reaction time to light) and the *intensity* of stimulation is logarithmic, for a constant exposure time. If we let $X = 1/$latent time, and $I =$ intensity, then—over the middle range of intensities—$X = k \log I$, which again is Fechner's Law.

Telephone engineers have made good use of Fechner's principle. Experiments in audition have shown that the relation between "loudness" as sensed by the ear and the physical intensity (vibration amplitude) of the sounding body is logarithmic. Fletcher has put this relation in the form of an equation, $a = \log J$, wherein $a =$ loudness measured in "bels" and J is the physical intensity of the sound in microwatts. A bel (so-called after Alexander Graham Bell) equals ten decibels, the decibel being the smallest change in loudness which the ear can detect. A decibel or "sensation unit" is thus clearly analogous to the Fechnerian *j.n.d.* or to the D L for intensity of sound. The decibel is the unit most often used by audition experts in this country.

From these illustrations it would appear that Fechner's Law is by no means a dead issue, although it is a limited principle rather than the universal law Fechner proclaimed it to be. As far as psychology is concerned, the present worth of both Weber's Law and Fechner's Law would seem to lie in the fact that they do subsume quantitatively a large group of facts within the middle range of stimulus intensities.

5. INTERPRETATIONS OF THE WEBER AND FECHNER LAWS

The interpretation of Fechner's Law has led to much discussion and many theories. Fechner, as we have seen, regarded his law, $S = C \log R$, as essentially an equation expressing the fundamental relationship between the physical world and the mental world. Sensations, or mental states, he said, do not change as rapidly as do their physical stimuli; instead they lag more and more behind to give finally the logarithmic relationship which we have discussed above. According to Fechner's view, the fundamental relationship between "body" and "mind" is logarithmic.

Few psychologists have agreed with Fechner in this somewhat mystical interpretation of his experimental data. A far more common explanation has been in physiological terms. The lag between stimulus and sensation which Fechner noted is frequently interpreted as a kind of physiological inertia which causes the bodily effect to lag behind the exciting stimulus which aroused it. Physiologists have found, for instance, in working with isolated muscle groups, that as the stimuli increase in intensity, the muscular responses also increase, but by relatively smaller and smaller amounts. An analogous relation may well exist between changes in the external stimulus and changes in sense-organ (plus nerve and brain) processes.

Still other explanations of the lag which appears between stimulus and body response have been given in terms of (1) variability of response, and (2) relativity of judgment. The first explanation stresses the increase in variability of a large bodily response over that of a small one. With the physical increase in the stimulus, both the sensory stimulation and the body response involve more and more sensory elements and muscle groups. The more of these elements involved in a given response, the greater the probable over-lapping with other responses, and the less distinct each becomes. Hence a large or intense stimulus must needs be increased to a greater degree than a small and weak one in order for the change to be perceived. This is essentially what occurs in Weber's Law and Fechner's Law. The other explanation, that in terms of relativity, was first advanced by the German psychologist Wundt and is a purely psychological interpretation. All judgments, Wundt says, are governed by the general principle of relativity: changes are estimated always in terms of the thing which has been changed, and derive their importance from our common-sense evaluation of this relation. Several illustrations of the general principle of relativity have been given on p. 404. Relativity of judgment serves to describe what actually happens in a sensible way; but it does not explain in any precise fashion the mathematical relationships implied in Weber's and Fechner's Laws.

6. THE PSYCHOPHYSICAL METHODS

In previous sections we have pointed out that both Weber's Law and Fechner's Law grew out of an effort to generalize and quantify the relationship existing between stimulus changes and their corresponding sensory effects. In the study of this relationship, which Fechner called psychophysics, two chief questions arise: (1) What is the *least* difference that can be perceived between two given stimuli, i. e., what is the D L, or difference threshold? (2) What is the *least* amount of a given stimulus that will just produce a sensation at all (the absolute threshold)? * It is clear, of course, that we must first find our thresholds—our *j.n.d.*'s—before we can generalize or establish a principle of relationship between stimuli and sensations. Heretofore we have assumed tacitly that D L's can be found without telling exactly how this is done. We shall now consider the question of technique, or the psychophysical methods, as they are called, which were developed in the attempt to answer these two questions.

The history of the psychophysical methods goes back to Weber's experimental work on lifted weights in 1829, but the elaboration and development of these methods is linked up chiefly with Fechner. Many investigators have introduced modifications in the psychophysical methods since Fechner's time, among whom should be mentioned Müller, Urban,

---

* This second question grows out of the first and is concerned particularly with the location of the lowest limit of sensitivity in the sense organ.

Fullerton and Cattell, and Jastrow. Although developed primarily for the purpose of studying psychophysical relationships, these methods fortunately have much wider usefulness as practical techniques for the study of acuity of perception or efficiency of judgment under various conditions.

There are, in general, three psychophysical methods: the *method of minimal change,* the *method of constant stimuli,* and the *method of average error.* These will be considered in order.

1. *The Method of Minimal Change.* This method was developed from the earlier method of *just noticeable differences,* and is, as its name implies, concerned with determining the smallest change in a given stimulus or between two stimuli which can be just perceived or sensed. It can best be made clear by an illustration. Let L be a standard light intensity (e. g., four, eight, or sixteen candle-power) which illuminates equally the two ground-glass windows P and Q of a photometer.* (See Fig. 47.) In determining the just-noticeable difference in brightness or the threshold of sensitivity, there are four stages. (1) We begin with the two windows P and Q of equal brightness, and slowly increase the brightness of Q until it is judged to be just perceptibly brighter than P. Call this point A. (2) Next, with Q much brighter than P, we decrease the brightness of Q (the vari-

---

* The photometer is an instrument for measuring an observer's sensitivity to changes or differences in light intensity. A simple photometer much used in the laboratory consists of a rectangular box containing a light which is reflected equally upon two small white surfaces. These surfaces are viewed by the observer through two ground-glass windows in the side of the box. Movement of the light-source within the box, either to the left or to the right, changes the relative illumination of the two windows; as the one becomes lighter, the other becomes darker, and vice-versa. The distance which the light must be moved in order to make the difference in the illumination of the two windows just noticeable can be read from a scale on the outside of the box.

able) until it is judged to be of *equal* brightness with (or not perceptibly different from) P. Call this second determination B. (3) As in (1) above, we begin again with the windows P and Q of the same brightness, but this time we decrease Q's brightness very slowly until the observer judges it to be just less bright (darker) than P. This is point C. (4) Finally, following (2) above, we begin with Q much darker than P and increase its brightness until the two stimuli are judged to be equal. This is point D. From the average of these four points, A, B, C, and D, we can obtain the "general threshold," i. e., the brightness-difference which is just capable of being perceived. Needless to say, observations must be repeated again and again to insure reliable results.

Table XXXI illustrates the method of minimal change in an experiment similar to the one outlined above. Note that the ten trials taken under the four different sets of conditions have been averaged separately, and that they show considerable variation the one from the other. If we average the four determinations, A, B, C, and D, the result, 4.2, gives the general threshold, the average just observable difference, or the average D L. This value is a measure of the observer's keenness of discrimination under the given conditions. Other interesting comparisons may be made. By averaging A and C, for instance, and then B and D, we can compare the accuracy of perception when the change is from equality to difference with that when the change is from difference toward equality. When we do this, it is evident that judgment was more accurate when the difference between the standard and the comparison was *decreasing* than when it was *increasing*. The upper threshold, i. e., $\frac{A + B}{2}$, is determined from those settings in which the comparison stimulus is *brighter* than the standard; and the lower threshold, i. e., $\frac{C + D}{2}$, is determined from those settings in which the comparison is *darker* than the standard. It is clear from Table XXXI that the upper threshold was considerably smaller than the lower threshold, and hence perception of brightness changes was more accurate under the first set of conditions than under the second.

TABLE XXXI

DETERMINATION OF THE JUST NOTICEABLE DIFFERENCE IN LIGHT INTENSITY BY THE METHOD OF MINIMAL CHANGE

The standard was a four candle-power lamp, and ten trials were taken at each of four stages. In one half of the trials at each stage the standard was on the right, and in one half, on the left. (Data adapted with some changes from the original by the writer.)

Average Setting

(A) From equality upward, i. e., the comparison stimulus becomes brighter 4.6

(B) Toward equality downward, i. e., the comparison stimulus becomes darker 2.7

(C) From equality downward, i. e., comparison becomes darker 5.6

(D) Toward equality upward, i. e., comparison becomes brighter 3.9

General threshold $\dfrac{(A + B + C + D)}{4}$ 4.2

Average increasing difference $\dfrac{(A + C)}{2}$ 5.1

Average decreasing difference $\dfrac{(B + D)}{2}$ 3.3

Upper threshold $\dfrac{(A + B)}{2}$ 3.7

Lower threshold $\dfrac{(C + D)}{2}$ 4.8

2. *The Method of Constant Stimuli.* Like the method of minimal change, this method was also developed from an earlier procedure, the *method of right and wrong cases.* Though it may be employed with other stimuli, as for example, linear extents (lines), this method has most often been used to measure tactual and kinesthetic sensitivity through the lifting of weights, and hence we shall illustrate it with lifted weights data. (See Table XXXII.) Suppose that we have selected a standard weight of 100 grams, and comparison weights of 88, 92, 96, 104, 108, and 112 grams. The problem is to determine the amount by which the 100 gram standard must be increased or decreased for the change to be just observable. But instead of changing the standard by small amounts we compare it over and over again, first with the lighter and then with the heavier weights, noting in each case the number of correct judgments. Judgments may be recorded as heavier, as lighter, or as equal. To illustrate, in comparing 100 grams and 108 grams, the judgment "heavier" might be given 80 per cent of the time, "equal" 12 per cent, and "lighter" 8 per cent of the time; and such results as these will be secured with each weight pair, 100–88, 100–104, 100–112, and so on. When there are an equal number of heavier and lighter comparison stimuli, the standard weight is usually lifted first and the comparison weight second, the judgment of heavier, lighter, or equal expressing the subject's opinion of the relation between the variable (the second) weight and the standard (the first) weight. That weight above 100 grams which gives just 50 per cent "heavier" judgments determines the *upper threshold,* or the just-perceptibly-heavier difference; while that weight below 100 grams which gives just 50 per cent "lighter" judgments determines the *lower threshold,* or the just-perceptibly-lighter difference. The average of these two values is the *general threshold,* or

the average difference limen. It is seldom that a weight difference will be found experimentally which gives exactly 50
per cent "heavier" or 50 per cent "lighter" judgments, so
that interpolation is nearly always necessary. The two 50 per
cent points may be determined fairly accurately from graphs,
and somewhat more precisely from formulas for interpolation
between the percentages actually found.

The procedure for the method of constant stimuli above
outlined is the older, or classical, form in which the method
was developed by Fechner, Müller, and Urban. It is an accurate and precise method when used with highly trained subjects. But with those less well trained it is open to considerable objection, because of the allowance of equal judgments.
We have no way of controlling the number of judgments
which a subject will call "equal," and therefore if he is extremely cautious, a large part of his data will be so classified,
and hence not directly usable.

In 1892 Fullerton and Cattell showed in a series of experiments that if a subject will *guess* when inclined to say equal,
he is more often right than wrong, as there is usually present
some slight basis for a judgment, although it may be too
small to be very convincing. These investigators simplified
the method of constant stimuli, permitting only *two* judgments—"heavier" or "lighter." They made it up, in a sense,
to the subject for thus forcing his answer by allowing him
to qualify each judgment by expressing his degree of confidence as "sure," "fairly sure," "a guess."

In some recent experiments, Kellogg has found that the
variability of his subjects' responses differed little whether a
two or three category judgment was allowed. Hence the two-
answer scheme seems justified by experimental results. In
this simpler form of the method of constant stimuli, that
weight difference which gives 75 per cent "heavier" judgments determines the upper threshold, while that difference

giving 75 per cent "lighter" judgments fixes the lower threshold. Of course, the 75 per cent threshold is arbitrary, but it is, perhaps, the most reasonable value, since it lies midway between 50 per cent (chance) and 100 per cent (certainty). The average of the upper and lower thresholds gives the general threshold, or average D L. This D L, it will be noted, cannot properly be called a *j.n.d.* unless we assume that the difference which is perceived correctly in 75 per cent of the trials is in fact "just noticeable." As this is certainly questionable it is more accurate to call such a D L the "75 per cent threshold."

Certain data selected from an experiment on weight-lifting are given in Table XXXII to illustrate the method of constant stimuli in its simpler form. Since 300 comparisons were made of each weight-pair, e. g., 100–96, 100–112, and so on, the percentages of correct judgments are quite reliably determined. From the table it is seen at once that the lower threshold is eight grams, since the comparison 100–92 gave exactly 75 per cent correct judgments. Unfortunately the upper threshold cannot be obtained so readily. It is clear, however, that it must lie between four and eight grams, since the weight-pair 100–104 gave 66 per cent correct judgments and the pair 100–108, 85.3 per cent correct judgments. The value most likely to give 75 per cent correct would seem by simple proportion to lie approximately at 106 grams, half-way between 104 and 108. This 75 per cent point can be more accurately determined from tables prepared for the purpose or by graphical methods. If we put the lower threshold at eight grams and the upper threshold at six grams, the general threshold is the arithmetic mean of these two values, or seven grams. This indicates that, in many trials, the difference between 100 grams and 107, or 100 grams and 93, should be correctly perceived 75 per cent of the time. In order to verify Weber's Law for these data, it would be necessary to show that for a standard of 200 grams, the 75 per cent threshold is *fourteen* grams; for a standard of 500 grams, it is *thirty-five* grams, and so on. That is, the D L in each case must be a constant fraction of the standard stimulus.

Table XXXII

Discrimination of Lifted Weights: Method of Constant Stimuli

The combined records for six observers, each of whom made fifty comparisons of each weight-pair, giving 300 comparisons for each pair and 1,800 for all six weight-pairs.

Weights compared	Percentage of Right Judgments
100–88	84.3
100–92	75.0
100–96	56.3
100–104	66.0
100–108	85.3
100–112	90.7
Lower threshold (75%)	8 gms.
Upper threshold (75%)	6 gms. (approx.)
General threshold	7 gms. "

3. *The Method of Average Error.* This method is based on the assumption that measurements of just noticeable differences are essentially measurements of observational errors, i. e., of the limitations or lack of sensitivity of the subject's sensory and nervous mechanism. Ordinarily a subject is given a fixed standard stimulus and an adjustable or variable one which he is instructed to make equal to the standard. The amount by which the observer misses this standard is a measure of his "error of observation."

We may illustrate this method with the Galton bar, which is often used in the measurement of just non-perceptible differences between linear magnitudes. The Galton bar consists of a strip of flat enameled wood about 2.5 centimeters in height and 100 centimeters in length. It is divided in the center by a small wedge, and on the reverse side contains a graduated scale, by means of which the length of each half can be measured. Two sliding sleeves of metal permit varying distances to be set off from the center or o-point. The whole

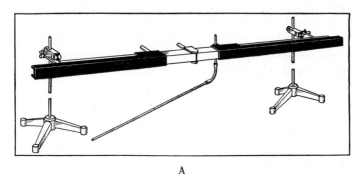

A

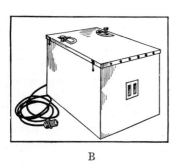

B

C

FIG. 47

SOME APPARATUS USED IN PSYCHOPHYSICAL EXPERIMENTS

A. Galton bar used in studying the accuracy of estimates of visually perceived lengths.

B. A photometer often used in measuring brightness discrimination.

C. Weights used in experiments on discrimination, or in studies of the kinesthetic sense.

apparatus is mounted against a black background. (See Fig. 47.) Now suppose a standard length of twenty centimeters is set off on the right-hand half of the bar and the subject is instructed to adjust the slide on the left-hand half from a much smaller setting than twenty centimeters up to apparent equality with this standard. Twenty trials at least should be made, and the average amount of error (overestimation or underestimation) calculated. A second series of trials is then taken from a too-large setting (greater than twenty centimeters) down to equality with the standard, and the average error again found. The whole procedure must be repeated with the standard set off on the left and the variable on the right half of the bar. The amount of variation or fluctuation in the subject's settings, the amount by which he misses the standard, gives a measure of his *average error*. The tendency of the subject repeatedly to overestimate or underestimate the standard is called his *constant error*.

Table XXXIII illustrates the method of average error with data for eighty trials on the Galton bar, the standard length being twenty centimeters. Note that one half of the trials were taken with the standard on the right and one half with the standard on the left to avoid any "place error." Each set of forty trials is equally divided between settings which are, on the one hand, too small and on the other too large; viz., one half of the time the variable was set shorter and one half of the time longer than the twenty-centimeter standard. The average of all eighty trials is 19.05 centimeters, which indicates a *constant error* of .95 centimeter (20 — 19.05). This is the amount by which, on the average, the observer fell short of the standard, or the amount by which he *overestimated* his settings. The extent to which the observer, on the average, missed the standard is given by his *average error* of 1.04 centimeters. To calculate the A E (average error), we sum up all of the deviations made in the eighty trials from the twenty-centimeter standard and divide by the number of trials. The calculation of the A E is not shown in the table, but can easily be made from the original data. To verify Weber's Law, the A E found for a ten-centimeter standard should be one half as large as the A E for our twenty-centimeter standard.

When the observer made his settings from the too-small position (average 18.6), he fell short of the standard to a greater degree than when he made his adjustments from a too-large position (average 19.5). Obviously in both cases he overestimated his settings, however, since both averages are less than the twenty-centimeter standard.

TABLE XXXIII

DATA FOR EIGHTY TRIALS ON THE GALTON BAR, FORTY WITH STANDARD ON THE LEFT AND FORTY WITH STANDARD ON THE RIGHT

(Adapted by writer with several small changes)

Standard left—forty trials cms.		*Standard right—forty trials* cms.	
From too small	18.5	From too small	18.7
From too large	19.2	From too large	19.8
General average	19.05		
Average (from too-small settings)	18.6		
Average (from too-large settings)	19.5	Constant error	.95
		Average error	1.04

7. THE PRESENT STATUS OF PSYCHOPHYSICS

The evaluation of Fechner's work is not an easy task. Many and various opinions have been expressed regarding it, from the enthusiastic commendation of Titchener, who regarded Fechner as the father of mental measurement, to the caustic remarks of William James, who wrote: "Fechner's book was the starting point of a new department of literature, which it would be perhaps impossible to match for qualities of thoroughness and subtlety, but of which, in the humble opinion of the present writer, the proper psychological outcome is just *nothing.*" As is usually the case, the truth is somewhere between these two rather extreme views, but the judgment of time inclines toward Titchener's rather than James's view.

It must be admitted at the outset that much of Fechner's psychophysics has not stood the test of research. His concept of a large sensation as the sum of many smaller sensations, as well as his idea that *j.n.d.*'s are equal over the scale of intensities, have both been rejected by present-day psychologists. Also his psychophysical law has been found to have a limited instead of, as he thought, a universal application. Modern psychology is interested more in the larger aspects of behavior than in the study of sensation and small sensory changes. The development of mental tests with their emphasis upon individual differences has, no doubt, had much to do with this shift in orientation, while the increasing emphasis upon the *wholeness* of the organism's activities, has played a not unimportant rôle. The psychologist of to-day is interested in the psychophysical methods as tools to be used in the study of problems involving the determination of sensory acuity, sensory efficiency, and the accuracy and precision of movement. Or he may be interested in the possibility of adapting these techniques more directly to problems of mental measurement. Rarely is he interested in Weber's or Fechner's principles as such, or in the measurement of the stimulus-sensation relation. To illustrate, in 1910 E. L. Thorndike devised his Handwriting Scale, the first scale for the measurement of an educational product, proceeding on the assumption that equally often noticed differences between specimens of handwriting are equal. According to this principle, if the difference in excellence between handwriting specimens A and B is noted by competent judges as often as the difference between specimens X and Y, then the difference between A and B is, in effect, equal to the difference between X and Y. Thorndike's assumption, as well as his technique, are direct outgrowths from the psychophysical methods. More recently, Thurstone has adapted and extended the psychophysical concepts on the theoretical side and has applied them to the problem of scale-making and to the study of attitudes and preferences.

In spite of the trend away from Fechner's psychophysics, as one reads through the experimental work in psychology since Fechner's time (and since James's, too) he cannot help being impressed with the influence exerted by psychophysics and the psychophysical methods. Fechner's work was important because it showed conclusively that problems in psychology can be subjected to quantitative methods and are amenable to exact mathematical treatment. The far-reaching result of this point of view is seen to-day in the development of mental, educational, and achievement tests and scales, and in the increasing use of statistical method in the study of human variability. Perhaps it is not too much to say that, beginning with Fechner, psychology ceased to be a branch of philosophy and began to be an experimental science.

Index

NOTE.—Proper names are not included unless indispensable in tracing a fact or theory. Instead of Pavlov, see Conditioned reflex, for detailed references.

A

Adrenin, in emotions, 323

Age, and intelligence, 40-43; loss in reaction time in, 385; *see* Mental age

Allport, and Vernon, studies in expressive movements, 118-119

Alpert, A., experiment of, 227-228

Alpines, intelligence of, 50-51

Ambiguous figures, in Gestalt psychology, 212-216

American Council on Education Psychological Examination, 56

American immigrants, apparent decline in intelligence of, 51-52; reasons for, 52

Anger, *see* Rage

Animal learning, and C R, 144-145; experiments in, 178-186, 217-223; interpretations of, 186-196; reasoning in, 186-191; insight in, 191-193; imitation in, 192-196

Apes, insight in, 222-225

Aphasia, brain injury in, 160-162

Areas of brain, in learning, 154-162

Army Alpha, description of, 31-36; distribution of soldiers' scores on, 38-42; limitations of, 40; scores of occupational groups on, 43-46; scores of arms of service on, 45-46; Negro and White scores on, 46-49; foreign-born men compared on, 49-52; immigrants'

scores on, 51; effect of schooling on, 52-55; college success and, 55-57

Army Beta, 32, 46-47

Ascendance-submission, studies of, 113

Association, laws of, 127-128; free, 336-340

Associative reaction time, 381, 388-389

Attitude, in reaction time, 385-388

Attitudes, studies of, 113-114

Auditory apparatus, description of, 346-348

Autonomic nervous system, divisions of, 322; rôle in emotions of, 323-329

Average error, method of, 416-419

B

Backward association, 284

Behaviorism, 292-293

Betts, G. H., 62

Binet, A., 1-2; his concept of intelligence, 2-3

Binet-Simon Scale, construction of, 2-4; 1908 edition, 3; 1911 scale reproduced, 4-6; revisions of, 6-10; training necessary for giving, 10; criticisms of, 16-19; limitations of, 16-20; value of, 30

Binocular vision, 359-363

Blatz, W. E., experiment of, 325-327

423

BIBLIOGRAPHY

Chapter 1

1. Asher, E. J. The inadequacy of current intelligence tests for testing Kentucky mountain children. J. genet. Psychol., 1935, 46, 480–486.
2. Binet, A., & Simon, Th. L'intelligence des imbéciles. L'Année Psychologique, 1909, 15, 1–147.
3. Binet, A., & Simon, Th. The development of intelligence in children. Translated by E. S. Kite, Baltimore: The Williams and Wilkins Company, 1916.
4. Brown, R. R. Time-interval and constancy of I Q. J. educ. Psychol., 1933, 24, 81–96.
5. Burks, B. S. Twenty-seventh Yearbook of the National Society for the Study of Education, 1928, Part I, 219–316.
6. Burt, C. Mental and scholastic tests. London County Council, 1921, 190–198.
7. Cattell, P. Constant changes in the Stanford-Binet I Q. J. educ. Psychol., 1931, 22, 544–550.
8. Cox, C. M. The early mental traits of three hundred geniuses. In Terman, L. M., Genetic studies of genius. Stanford University Press, 1926, Vol. II.
9. Downey, J. E. The will-temperament and its testing. Yonkers: World Book Company, 1922.
10. Garrett, H. E., & Schneck, M. R. Psychological tests, methods, and results. New York: Harper & Brothers, 1933, Part I.
11. Goddard, H. H. The Kallikak family. New York: The Macmillan Company, 1912.
12. Hollingworth, L. S. The psychology of subnormal children. New York: The Macmillan Company, 1920.
13. Hollingworth, L. S. Gifted children, their nature and nurture. New York: The Macmillan Company, 1926.
14. Intelligence: Its nature and nurture. Thirty-ninth Year-

book of the National Society for the Study of Education, 1940, Parts I and II.

15. Jones, H. E., & Conrad, H. S. The growth and decline of intelligence. Genet. Psychol. Monog., 1933, 13, 223–298.

16. Kelley, T. L., Ruch, G. M., & Terman, L. M. New standard achievement test; advanced examination, directions for scoring. 1931, 7–9.

17. Leahy, A. M. Nature-nurture and intelligence. Genet. Psychol. Monog., 1935, 17, 236–308.

18. Louttit, C. M. Clinical psychology. New York: Harper & Brothers, 1936, especially chaps. 4, 5, 6.

19. McNemar, Q. A critical examination of the University of Iowa studies of environmental influences upon the I Q. Psychol. Bull., 1940, 37, 63–92.

20. Merrill, M. A. The significance of I Q's on the revised Stanford-Binet scales. J. educ. Psychol., 1938, 29, 641–651.

21. Miles, W. R. Psychological aspects of ageing. Chap. 20 in Problems of ageing, edited by E. V. Cowdry. Baltimore: The Williams & Wilkins Company, 1939.

22. Penrose, L. S. Mental defect. London: Sidgwick & Jackson, 1933.

23. Pintner, R. Intelligence testing, methods, and results. New York: Henry Holt and Company, 1931, Chaps. I, II, III.

24. Rogers, C. R. The clinical treatment of the problem child. Boston: Houghton Mifflin Company, 1939.

25. Sandiford, P. Foundations of educational psychology. New York: Longmans, Green & Co., 1938.

26. Seashore, C. E. Psychology of music. New York: McGraw-Hill Book Company, Inc., 1938.

27. Terman, L. M. The measurement of intelligence. Boston: Houghton Mifflin Company, 1916.

28. Terman, L. M. The intelligence quotient of Francis Galton in childhood. Amer. J. Psychol., 1917, 28, 209–215.

29. Terman, L. M., et al. Genetic studies of genius. Stanford University Press, 1925, Vol. I.

30. Terman, L. M., & Merrill, M. A. Measuring intelligence. Boston: Houghton Mifflin Company, 1937.

31. Thorndike, E. L., et al. The measurement of intelligence.

New York: Teachers College, Columbia University, 1927.

32. Thorndike, E. L., et al. Adult learning. New York: The Macmillan Company, 1928.

33. Tredgold, A. F. Mental deficiency. New York: William Wood and Co., 1929.*

34. Weisenberg, T., Roe, A., & McBride, K. E. Adult intelligence. New York: Commonwealth Fund, 1936, 15–32.

35. Wellman, B. L., Skeels, H. M., & Skodak, M. Review of McNemar's critical examination of the Iowa studies, Psychol. Bull., 1940, 37, 93–111.

Chapter 2

1. Brigham, C. C. A study of American intelligence. Princeton: Princeton University Press, 1923.

2. Franzblau, R. N. Race differences in mental and physical traits. Arch. Psychol., New York, 1935, 26, No. 177.

3. Hirsch, N. D. M. A study of natio-racial mental differences. Genet. Psychol. Monog., 1926, 1, 231–406.

4. Intelligence: its nature and nurture. Thirty-ninth Yearbook of the National Society for the Study of Education, 1940, Parts I & II.

5. Jones, H. E., & Conrad, H. S. The growth and decline of intelligence: a study of a homogeneous group between the ages of ten and sixty. Genet. Psychol. Monog., 1933, 13, 223–298.

6. Klineberg, O. A study of psychological differences between "racial" and national groups in Europe. Arch. Psychol., New York, 1931, 20, No. 132.

7. Klineberg, O. Negro intelligence and selective migration. New York: Columbia University Press, 1935.

8. Miles, C. C. & W. R. The correlation of intelligence scores and chronological age from early to late maturity. Amer. J. Psychol., 1932, 44, 44–78.

9. Miles, W. R. Age and human ability. Psychol. Rev., 1933, 40, 99–123.

10. Noble, E. L., & Arps, G. F. University students' intelli-

---

* Now published in a sixth edition (1937) by The Williams and Wilkins Company, Baltimore.

gence ratings according to the Army Alpha test. Sch. & Soc., 1920, 11, 233–237.

11. Terman, L. M., & Merrill, M. A. Measuring intelligence. Boston: Houghton Mifflin Company, 1937.

12. Yerkes, R. M. (Editor). Psychological examining in the United States army. Memoirs National Academy of Sciences, 1921, XV. Washington: Government Printing Office. Pp. 162, 422, 764, 766, 767, 768, 770, 779, 800, 814, 824, 836, 848.

13. Yoakum, C. S., & Yerkes, R. M. Army mental tests. New York: Henry Holt and Company, 1920.

Chapter 3

1. Anastasi, A. Differential psychology. New York: The Macmillan Company, 1937.

2. Arlitt, A. H. On the need for caution in establishing race norms. J. appl. Psychol., 1921, 5, 179–183.

3. Betts, G. H. The distribution and functions of mental imagery. Teachers Coll. Contrib. Educ., 1909, No. 26.

4. Burks, B. S. The relative influence of nature and nurture upon mental development. Twenty-seventh Yearbook of the National Society for the Study of Education, 1928, 219–316.

5. Cattell, J. McK., & Farrand, L. Physical and mental measurements of the students of Columbia University. Psychol. Rev., 1896, 3, 618–648.

6. Crane, A. L. Race differences in inhibition. Arch. Psychol., New York, 1923, 9, No. 23.

7. Ferguson, G. O. The psychology of the negro. Arch. Psychol., New York, 1916, 5, No. 36.

8. Freeman, F. N., Holzinger, K. J., & Mitchell, B. C. The influence of environment on the intelligence, school achievement, and conduct of foster children. Twenty-seventh Yearbook of the National Society for the Study of Education, 1928, 103–216.

9. Galton, F. Hereditary genius. London: Macmillan, 1925. First published in 1869.

10. Galton, F. Inquiries into human faculty and its development. London: Macmillan, 1883.

11. Galton, F. Natural inheritance. London: Macmillan & Co., Ltd., 1889.

12. Gansl, I. Vocabulary; its measurement and growth. Arch. Psychol., New York, 1939, 33, No. 236.

13. Gilbert, J. A. Researches on the mental and physical development of school children. Yale Psychol. Lab. Studies, 1893, 40–100.

14. Griffitts, C. H. Fundamentals of vocational psychology. New York: The Macmillan Company, 1924, chapters 2, 3, 4, 13.

15. Hildreth, G. H. The resemblance of siblings in intelligence and achievement. Teachers Coll. Contrib. Educ., 1925, No. 186.

16. Hirsch, N. D. M. A study of natio-racial mental differences. Genet. Psychol. Monog., 1926, 1, 231–406.

17. Hunter, W. S., & Sommermier, E. The relation of degree of Indian blood to score on the Otis intelligence test. J. comp. Psychol., 1922, 2, 257–277.

18. Intelligence: its nature and nurture. Thirty-ninth Yearbook of the National Society for the Study of Education, 1940, Parts I & II.

19. Jones, H. E. A first study of parent-child resemblance in intelligence. Twenty-seventh Yearbook of the National Society for the Study of Education, 1928, 61–72.

20. Klineberg, O. An experimental study of speed and other factors in racial differences. Arch. Psychol., New York, 1928, 15, No. 93.

21. Klineberg, O. A study of psychological differences between "racial" and national groups in Europe. Arch. Psychol., New York, 1931, 20, No. 132.

22. Kraepelin, A. Clinical psychiatry. Abstracted and adapted by A. R. Diefendorf. New York: The Macmillan Company, 1918.

23. Lauterbach, C. E. Studies in twin resemblances. Genetics, 1925, 10, 528–568.

24. Leahy, A. M. Nature-nurture and intelligence. Genet. Psychol. Monog., 1935, 17, 235–308.

25. Lincoln, E. A. Sex differences in the growth of American school children. Baltimore: Warwick & York, 1927.

26. Mayo, M. J. The mental capacity of the American Negro. Arch. Psychol., New York, 1913, 4, No. 28.

436   Bibliography

27. McFadden, J. H., & Dashiell, J. F. Racial differences as measured by the Downey Will-Temperament test. J. appl. Psychol., 1923, 7, 30–53.
28. McGraw, M. B. A comparative study of a group of southern white and negro infants. Genet. Psychol. Monog., 1931, 10, 1–105.
29. McNemar, Q. Twin resemblances in motor skills, and the effect of practice thereon. J. genet. Psychol., 1933, 42, 70–99.
30. Merriman, C. The intellectual resemblance of twins. Psychol. Monog., 1924, 33, No. 5.
31. Pearl, R. Medical biometry and statistics. New York: W. B. Saunders Company, 1930.
32. Pearson, K. On the laws of inheritance in man. II. On the inheritance of the mental and moral characters in man, and its comparison with the inheritance of the physical characters. Biometrika, 1904, 3, 131–190.
33. Rugg, H. Is the rating of human character practicable? J. educ. Psychol., 1921, 12, 425–438, 485–501; 1922, 13, 30–42, 81–93.
34. Stern, W. Die differentielle Psychologie. Leipzig: J. A. Barth, 1921.
35. Sunne, D. Comparison of white and negro children in verbal and non-verbal tests. Sch. & Soc., 1924, 19, 469–472.
36. Terman, L. M. Genetic studies of genius. Stanford University Press, 1925, Vol. I.
37. Thompson, H. B. The mental traits of sex. Chicago: University of Chicago Press, 1903.
38. Thorndike, E. L. Measurements of twins. Arch. Phil. Psychol. & Sci. Metho., 1905, No. 1.
39. Thorndike, E. L. Educational psychology. New York: Teachers College, Columbia University, 1925, Vol. III, 220–221.
40. Thorndike, E. L. The resemblance of siblings in intelligence. Twenty-seventh Yearbook of the National Society for the Study of Education, 1928, 40–53.
41. Thorndike, E. L., Lay, W., & Dean, P. R. The relation of accuracy in sensory discrimination to general intelligence. Amer. J. Psychol., 1909, 20, 364–369.

42. Woodworth, R. S. Race differences in mental traits. Science, 1910, 31, 171–186.

43. Woodworth, R. S. Experimental psychology. New York: Henry Holt and Company, 1938, 39–47.

Chapter 4

1. Allport, G. W. A test for ascendance-submission. J. abnorm. (soc.) Psychol., 1928, 23, 118–136.
2. Allport, G. W., & Vernon, P. E. Studies in expressive movement. New York: The Macmillan Company, 1933, chapters 9, 10, 11.
3. Beck, S. J. Introduction to the Rohrschach method. New York: American Orthopsychiatric Association, 1937.
4. Blackford, K. M., & Newcomb, A. The job, the man, the boss. Garden City, New York: Doubleday, Page & Co., 1924.
5. Bradshaw, F. F. The American council on education rating scale. Arch. Psychol., 1930, 18, No. 119.
6. Downey, J. E. The will-temperament and its testing. Yonkers, New York: World Book Company, 1923.
7. Fryer, D. The measurement of interests in relation to human adjustment. New York: Henry Holt and Company, 1931, chapters 3, 4.
8. Garvey, C. R. Comparative body build of manic-depressive and schizophrenic patients. Psychol. Bull., 1933, 30, 567–568.
9. Gilliland, A. R. A revision and some results with the Moore-Gilliland aggressiveness test. J. appl. Psychol., 1926, 10, 143–150.
10. Griffitts, C. H. Fundamentals of vocational psychology. New York: The Macmillan Company, 1924, chapters 3–4.
11. Hartshorne, H., & May, M. A. Studies in deceit. New York: The Macmillan Company, 1928.
12. Heidbreder, E. Measuring introversion and extroversion. J. abnorm. (soc.) Psychol., 1926, 21, 120–134.
13. Hoskins, R. G. The tides of life. New York: W. W. Norton and Company, 1933.

14. Hull, C. L. Aptitude testing. Yonkers, New York: World Book Company, 1928, chapter 4.

15. Hull, C. L., & Montgomery, R. B. An experimental investigation of certain alleged relations between character and handwriting. Psychol. Rev., 1919, 26, 63–74.

16. Hunt, T. The measurement of social intelligence. J. appl. Psychol., 1928, 12, 317–334.

17. Klineberg, O., Asch, S. E., & Block, H. An experimental study of constitutional types. Genet. Psychol. Monog., 1934, 16, 139–221.

18. Kretschmer, E. Physique and character. New York: Harcourt, Brace and Company, 1925.

19. Moore, H. T., & Gilliland, A. R. The measurement of aggressiveness. J. appl. Psychol., 1921, 5, 97–118.

20. Moreno, J. L. Who shall survive? Washington, D. C., Nervous and Mental Disease Monograph Series, No. 58, 1934.

21. Murphy, L. B. Social behavior and child personality. New York: Columbia University Press, 1937.

22. Murray, H. A., et al. Explorations in personality. London: Oxford University Press, 1938.

23. Paterson, D. G. Physique and intellect. New York: The Century Co., 1930.*

24. Rohrschach, H. Psychodiagnostik. Berlin: Hans Huber, 1932.

25. Symonds, P. M. Diagnosing personality and conduct. New York: The Century Co., 1931,* chapter 5.

26. Terman, L. M., & Miles, C. C. Sex and personality. New York: McGraw-Hill Book Company, Inc., 1936.

27. Terman, L. M., & Oden, M. Correlates of adult achievement in the California gifted group. Thirty-ninth Yearbook, National Society for the Study of Education, 1940, 74–84.

28. Thurstone, L. L. A scale for measuring attitude toward the movies. J. educ. Res., 1930, 22, 89–94.

29. Thurstone, L. L., & Chave, E. J. The measurement of attitude. Chicago: University of Chicago Press, 1929.

* Now published by D. Appleton-Century Company, Inc., New York.

Chapter 5

1. Allport, F. H. Social psychology. Boston: Houghton Mifflin Company, 1924.
2. Anderson, O. D., & Liddell, H. S. Observations on experimental neurosis in sheep. Arch. Neurol. Psychiat., 1935, 34, 330–354.
3. Anrep, G. V. Pitch discrimination in the dog. J. Physiol., 1920, 53, 367–385.
4. Bull, H. O. Studies on conditioned responses in fishes. Part I. J. Marine Biol. Ass. United Kingdom, 1928, 15, 485–533.
5. Cason, H. The conditioned pupillary reaction. J. exp. Psychol., 1922, 5, 108–146.
6. Dashiell, J. F. Fundamentals of general psychology. Boston: Houghton Mifflin Company, 1937.
7. Dodge, R. Problems of human variability. Science, 1924, 59, 263–270.
8. Frolov, J. P. Pavlov and his school: the theory of conditioned reflexes. New York: Oxford University Press, 1937.
9. Guthrie, E. R. The psychology of learning. New York: Harper & Brothers, 1935.
10. Hilgard, E. R. The relationship between the conditioned response and conventional learning experiments. Psychol. Bull., 1937, 34, 61–102.
11. Hilgard, E. R., & Marquis, D. G. Conditioning and learning. New York: D. Appleton-Century Company, Inc., 1940.
12. Hilgard, E. R., & Marquis, D. G. Acquisition, extinction, and retention of conditioned lid responses to light in dogs. J. comp. Psychol., 1935, 19, 29–58.
13. Hollingworth, H. L. Abnormal psychology. New York: The Ronald Press Company, 1930.
14. Humphrey, G. Extinction and negative adaptation. Psychol. Rev., 1930, 37, 361–363.
15. James, W. Principles of psychology. New York: Henry Holt and Company, 1890. Two volumes.
16. Lashley, K. S. Nervous mechanisms in learning. Chap. 10 in Handbook of general experimental psychology.

Worcester, Massachusetts: Clark University Press, 1934.

17. Maier, N. R. F. Studies of abnormal behavior in the rat. New York: Harper & Brothers, 1939.

18. Pavlov, I. P. Conditioned reflexes. London: Oxford University Press, 1927.

19. Pavlov, I. P. Lectures on conditioned reflexes. New York: International Publishers, 1928.

20. Razran, G. H. S. Conditioned responses in children. Arch. Psychol., New York, 1933, 23, No. 148.

21. Razran, G. H. S. Conditioned responses; a classified bibliography. Psychol. Bull., 1937, 34, 191–256.

22. Shaffer, L. F. The psychology of adjustment. Boston: Houghton Mifflin Company, 1936.

23. Skinner, B. F. On the rate of extinction of a conditioned reflex. J. gen. Psychol., 1933, 8, 114–129.

24. Thompson, E. L. An analysis of the learning process in the snail, Physa gyrina Say. Behav. Monog., 1916, 3, No. 14.

25. Thorndike, E. L. The fundamentals of learning. New York: Teachers College, Columbia University, 1932.

26. Watson, J. B. The place of the conditioned reflex in psychology. Psychol. Bull., 1916, 23, 89–116.

27. Wendt, G. R. Auditory acuity of monkeys. Comp. Psychol. Monog., 1934, 10, No. 3.

28. Wolfle, H. M. Conditioning as a function of the interval between the conditioned and the original stimulus. J. gen. Psychol., 1932, 7, 80–103.

29. Woodworth, R. S. Psychology. New York: Henry Holt and Company, 1940.

30. Woodworth, R. S. Experimental psychology. New York: Henry Holt and Company, 1938.

31. Yerkes, R. M., & Morgulis, S. The method of Pavlov in animal psychology. Psychol. Bull., 1909, 6, 257–273.

Chapter 6

1. Brickner, R. M. The intellectual functions of the frontal lobes. New York: The Macmillan Company, 1936.

2. Brown, C. W., & Ghiselli, E. E. Subcortical mechanisms

in learning. II. The maze. J. comp. Psychol., 1938, 26, 27–44.

3. Franz, S. I. On the functions of the cerebrum: the frontal lobes. Arch. Psychol., New York: 1907, 1, No. 2.

4. Franz, S. I. Nervous and mental re-education. New York: The Macmillan Company, 1923.

5. Harlow, J. M. Passage of an iron rod through the head. Boston Med. & Surg. J., 1848, 39, 389–393.

6. Jacobsen, C. F. Functions of frontal association area in primates. Arch. Neurol. Psychiat., 1935, 33, 558–569.

7. Jacobsen, C. F., & Taylor, F. V. Behavioral changes associated with lesions of the frontal lobes in monkeys. Psychol. Bull., 1937, 34, 767.

8. Jasper, H. H. Electrical signs of cortical activity. Psychol. Bull., 1937, 34, 411–481.

9. Klüver, H. Behavior mechanisms in monkeys. Chicago: University of Chicago Press, 1933.

10. Kreezer, G. The electro-encephalogram and its use in psychology. Amer. J. Psychol., 1938, 51, 737–759.

11. Lashley, K. S. Studies of cerebral fnuction in learning. Psychobiol., 1920, 2, 55–135.

12. Lashley, K. S. Nervous mechanisms in learning. In Murchison, C. (Ed.), Handbook of general experimental psychology. Worcester, Massachusetts: Clark University Press, 1934, chapter 10.

13. Lashley, K. S. Factors limiting recovery after central nervous lesions. J. nerv. ment. Dis., 1938, 88, 733–755.

14. Pike, F. H., & Chappell, M. N. On the recovery following lesions in the cerebral cortex. Science, 1930, 71, p. 76.

15. Williams, A. C. Some psychological correlates of the electroencephalogram. Arch. Psychol., New York, 1939, 34, No. 240.

Chapter 7

1. Adams, D. K. Experimental studies of adaptive behavior in cats. Comp. Psychol. Monog., 1929, 6, No. 1.

2. Allen, C. N. Individual differences in delayed reaction of infants. Arch. Psychol., New York, 1931, 19, No. 127.

3. Guthrie, E. R., & Horton, G. P. A study of the cat in the puzzle box. Psychol. Bull., 1937, 34, 774.

4. Hunter, W. S. The delayed reaction in animals and children. Behav. Monog., 1913, 2, No. 1.
5. Koffka, K. The growth of the mind. New York: Harcourt, Brace and Company, 1928, 180–193.
6. Köhler, W. The mentality of apes. New York: Harcourt, Brace and Company, 1925, pp. 256–259.
7. Maier, N. R. F. Reasoning in white rats. Comp. Psychol. Monog., 1929, 6, No. 3.
8. Maier, N. R. F., & Schneirla, T. C. Principles of animal psychology. New York: McGraw-Hill Book Company, Inc., 1935, p. 449.
9. Ruger, H. A. An experimental study of the processes involved in the solution of mechanical puzzles. Arch. Psychol., New York, 1910, 2, No. 15.
10. Shellow, S. M. Individual differences in incidental memory. Arch. Psychol., New York, 1923, 10, No. 64.
11. Thorndike, E. L. Animal intelligence. New York: The Macmillan Company, 1911.
12. Thorndike, E. L. Human learning. New York: The Century Co., 1931,* 3–29.
13. Warden, C. J. A short outline of comparative psychology. New York: W. W. Norton and Company, 1927.
14. Warden, C. J., & Warner, L. H. The sensory capacities and intelligence of dogs. Quart. Rev. Biol., 1928, 3, 1–28.
15. Warden, C. J., & Jackson, T. A. Imitative behavior in the rhesus monkey. J. genet. Psychol., 1935, 46, 103–125.
16. Washburn, M. F. The animal mind. New York: The Macmillan Company, 1936, 370–372.
17. Yerkes, R. M. Modes of behavioral adaptation in chimpanzee to multiple-choice problems. Comp. Psychol. Monog., 1934, 10, No. 1.

Chapter 8

1. Alpert, A. The solving of problem situations by pre-school children: an analysis. Teachers Coll. Contrib. to Educ., 1928, No. 323.
2. Dashiell, J. F. A survey and synthesis of learning theories. Psychol. Bull., 1935, 32, 261–305.

* Now published by D. Appleton-Century Company, Inc., New York.

3. DeSilva, H. R. An experimental investigation of the determinants of apparent visual movement. Amer. J. Psychol., 1926, 37, 469–501.
4. Ellis, W. D. A source book of Gestalt psychology. New York: Harcourt, Brace and Company, 1938.
5. Guilford, J. P., & Helson, H. Eye-movements and the phi-phenomenon. Amer. J. Psychol., 1929, 41, 595–606.
6. Hartmann, G. W. Gestalt psychology. New York: The Ronald Press Company, 1935.
7. Hulin, W. S. An experimental study of apparent tactual movement. J. exper. Psychol., 1927, 10, 293–320.
8. Hunter, W. S. Experimental studies of learning. In Murchison, C. (Ed.), Handbook of general experimental psychology. Worcester, Massachusetts: Clark University Press, 1934, 509–514.
9. Koffka, K. Perception: an introduction to the Gestalt-theorie. Psychol. Bull., 1922, 19, 531–585.
10. Koffka, K. The growth of the mind. New York: Harcourt, Brace and Company, 1928, 108–111.
11. Köhler, W. The mentality of apes. New York: Harcourt, Brace and Company, 1927.
12. Köhler, W. Gestalt psychology. New York: Horace Liveright, 1929.
13. Lewin, K. A dynamic theory of personality. New York: McGraw-Hill Book Company, Inc., 1935.
14. Taylor, H. A study of configurational learning. J. comp. Psychol., 1932, 13, 19–26.
15. Titchener, E. B. A text-book of psychology. New York: The Macmillan Company, 1928, p. 37.
16. Watson, J. B. Behaviorism. New York: W. W. Norton and Company, 1925, p. 6.
17. Wheeler, R. H. The science of psychology. New York: Thomas Y. Crowell Company, 1929, p. 317.

Chapter 9

1. Allport, G. W. Personality: a psychological interpretation. New York: Henry Holt and Company, 1937.
2. Brolyer, C. R., Thorndike, E. L., & Woodyard, E. A sec-

ond study of mental discipline in high school studies. J. educ. Psychol., 1927, 18, 377–404.

3. Davis, R. A. Psychology of learning. New York: McGraw-Hill Book Company, Inc., 1935, chapter 10.

4. Dearborn, W. F. Experiments in learning. J. exp. Psychol., 1910, 1, 373–388.

5. Gates, A. I., & Taylor, G. A. An experimental study of the nature of improvement resulting from practice in a mental function. J. educ. Psychol., 1925, 16, 583–592.

6. James, W. The principles of psychology. New York: Henry Holt and Company, 1890. Two volumes.

7. Judd, C. H. The relation of special training and general intelligence. Educ. Rev., 1908, 36, 28–42.

8. Morgan, B. Q. The place of modern foreign languages in the American high school. Sch. & Soc., 1928, 27, 185–193.

9. Orata, P. T. The theory of identical elements. Columbus, Ohio: Ohio State University Press, 1928.

10. Pressey, S. L. Psychology and the new education. New York: Harper & Brothers, 1933, chapter 15.

11. Starch, D. Educational psychology. New York: The Macmillan Company, 1919, 201–202.

12. Symonds, P. M., & Penney, E. M. The increasing of English vocabulary in the English class. J. educ. Res., 1927, 15, 93–103.

13. Thorndike, E. L. Mental discipline in high school studies. J. educ. Psychol., 1924, 15, 1–22, 83–98.

14. Thorndike, E. L., & Ruger, G. J. The effect of first year Latin upon knowledge of English words of Latin derivation. Sch. & Soc., 1923, 18, 260–270, 417–418.

15. Thorndike, E. L., & Woodworth, R. S. The influence of improvement in one mental function upon efficiency of other functions. Psychol. Rev., 1901, 8, 247–261, 384–395, 553–564.

16. Webb, L. W. Transfer of training. Psychol. Monog., 1917, 24, No. 3.

17. Wilson, Woodrow. Princeton for the nation's service. Science, 1902, 16, 721–731.

18. Wiltbank, R. T. Transfer of training in white rats upon various series of mazes. Behav. Monog., 1919, 4, No. 1.

19. Woodworth, R. S. Experimental psychology. New York: Henry Holt and Company, 1938.

Chapter 10

1. Britt, S. H. Theories of retroactive inhibition. Psychol. Rev., 1936, 43, 207–216.
2. Ebbinghaus, H. Memory, a contribution to experimental psychology, 1885. Translated by H. A. Ruger and C. E. Bussenius. New York: Teachers College, Columbia University, 1913.
3. English, H. B., Welborn, E. L., & Killian, C. D. Studies in substance memorization, J. gen. Psychol., 1934, 11, 233–260.
4. Gillette, A. L. Learning and retention. Arch. Psychol., New York, 1936, 28, No. 198.
5. Irmina, M. The effects of summer vacation upon the retention of the elementary school subjects. Cath. Univ. Amer. Educ. Res. Bull., 1928, 3.
6. James, W. Talks to teachers on psychology. New York: Henry Holt and Company, 1939 (reprint), 89–90.
7. Jones, H. E. Experimental studies of college teaching: the effect of examination on permanence of learning. Arch. Psychol., New York, 1923, 10, No. 68.
8. Krueger, W. C. F. The effect of overlearning on retention. J. exp. Psychol., 1929, 12, 71–78.
9. Ladd, G. T., & Woodworth, R. S. Elements of physiological psychology. New York: Charles Scribner's Sons, 1911.
10. Luh, C. W. The conditions of retention. Psychol. Monog., 1922, 31, 1–87.
11. McGeoch, J. A., & McDonald, W. T. Meaningful relation and retroactive inhibition. Amer. J. Psychol., 1931, 43, 579–588.
12. Pressey, S. L. Psychology and the new education. New York: Harper & Brothers, 1933, chapter 11.
13. Pyle, W. H., & Snyder, J. C. The most economical unit for committing to memory. J. educ. Psychol., 1911, 2, 133–142.

14. Radosavljevich, P. R. Das Behalten und Vergessen bei Kindern und Erwachsenen nach experimentellen Untersuchungen. Leipzig: Otto Nemnich, 1907. (Pädagogische Monographien).
15. Robinson, E. S. The relative efficiencies of distributed and concentrated study in memorizing. J. exp. Psychol., 1921, 4, 327–343.
16. Steffens, L. Experimentelle Beiträge zur Lehre vom ökonomischen Lernen. Z. Psychol., 1900, 22, 321–382.
17. Strong, E. K. Effect of the time interval upon recognitive memory. Psychol. Rev., 1913, 20, 339–372.
18. Titchener, E. B. A text-book of psychology. New York: The Macmillan Company, 1928, 380–381.

Chapter 11

1. Blanton, M. G. The behavior of the human infant during the first thirty days of life. Psychol. Rev., 1917, 24, 456–483.
2. Bühler, C. The first year of life. New York: The John Day Company, 1930.
3. Darwin, C. A biographical sketch of an infant. Mind, 1877, 2, 285–294.
4. Furfey, P. H., & Muehlenbein, J. The validity of infant intelligence tests. J. genet. Psychol., 1932, 40, 219–223.
5. Gesell, A. The mental growth of the pre-school child. New York: The Macmillan Company, 1928.
6. Gesell, A. Infancy and human growth. New York: The Macmillan Company, 1928.
7. Goodenough, F. L. Anger in young children. Minneapolis: University of Minnesota Press, 1931.
8. Goodenough, F. L., Foster, J. C., & Van Wagenen, M. J. Minnesota pre-school tests. Minneapolis: Educational Test Bureau, 1932.
9. Guthrie, E. R. The psychology of learning. New York: Harper & Brothers, 1935, chapters 5 and 9.
10. Jersild, A. T. Child psychology. New York: Prentice-Hall, Inc., 1936, chapter 5.
11. Jones, M. C. The elimination of children's fears. J. exp. Psychol., 1924, 7, 382–390.

12. Jones, M. C. The development of early behavior patterns in young children. J. genet. Psychol., 1926, 33, 537–585.

13. Kuhlmann, F. Tests of mental development. Minneapolis: Educational Test Bureau, 1939.

14. Lederer, R. K. An exploratory investigation of handed status in the first two years of life. University of Iowa Studies in Child Welfare, 1939, 16, No. 2.

15. Murphy, L. B. Social behavior and child personality. New York: Columbia University Press, 1937.

16. Pintner, R., & Paterson, D. G. A scale of performance tests. New York: D. Appleton-Century Company, Inc., 1917.

17. Pratt, K. C., Nelson, A. K., & Sun, K. H. The behavior of the newborn infant. Ohio State University Series: Contributions in Psychology, 1930, No. 10.

18. Sherman, M. The differentiation of emotional responses in infants. J. comp. Psychol., 1927, 7, 265–284.

19. Sherman, M. & I. C. Sensori-motor responses in infants. J. comp. Psychol., 1925, 5, 53–68.

20. Shinn, M. W. The biography of a baby. Boston: Houghton Mifflin Company, 1900.

21. Staples, R. The responses of infants to color. J. exp. Psychol., 1932, 15, 119–141.

22. Stutsman, R. Mental measurement of pre-school children. Yonkers, New York: World Book Company, 1931.

23. Travis, L. E. Speech pathology. In Murchison, C. (Editor), Handbook of child psychology. Worcester, Massachusetts: Clark University Press, 1933, 650–698 (see esp. pp. 689–695).

24. Watson, J. B., & Morgan, J. J. B. Emotional reactions and psychological experimentation. Amer. J. Psychol., 1917, 28, 163–174.

25. Watson, J. B., & Rayner, R. Conditioned emotional reactions. J. exp. Psychol., 1920, 3, 1–14.

26. Whipple, G. M. (Ed.) Child development and the curriculum. Thirty-eighth Yearbook of the National Society for the Study of Education, 1939, Part I.

27. Wile, I. S. Handedness, right and left. Boston: Lothrop, Lee & Shepard Co., 1934.

Chapter 12

1. Bard, P. The neuro-humoral basis of emotional reactions. Chapter 6 in Murchison, C. (Ed.). A handbook of general experimental psychology. Worcester, Massachusetts: Clark University Press, 1934 (esp. pp. 290–296).
2. Blatz, W. E. The cardiac, respiratory, and electrical phenomena involved in the emotion of fear. J. exp. Psychol., 1925, 8, 109–132.
3. Cannon, W. B. The James-Lange theory of emotions: a critical examination and an alternative theory. Amer. J. Psychol., 1927, 39, 106–124.
4. Cannon, W. B. Bodily changes in pain, hunger, fear and rage. New York: D. Appleton and Company, 1929.*
5. Chappell, M. N. Blood pressure changes in deception. Arch. Psychol., New York, 1929, 17, No. 105.
6. Crosland, H. R. The psychological methods of word association and reaction time as tests of deception. University of Oregon Publications, Psychol. Series, 1929, 1, No. 1.
7. Dana, C. S. The autonomic seat of the emotions: a discussion of the James-Lange theory. Arch. Neurol. Psychiat., Chicago, 1921, 6, 634–639.
8. Feleky, A. M. The expression of the emotions. Psychol. Rev., 1914, 21, 33–41.
9. Gates, G. S. An experimental study of the growth of social perception. J. educ. Psychol., 1923, 14, 449–461.
10. Hull, C. L., & Lugoff, L. S. Complex signs in diagnostic free association. J. exper. Psychol., 1921, 4, 111–136.
11. Jung, C. G. The association method. Amer. J. Psychol., 1910, 21, 219–269.
12. Jung, C. G. Studies in word-association. New York: Moffat, Yard & Company, Inc., 1919, chapters 2, 5, 7, 10.
13. Kent, G. H., & Rosanoff, A. J. A study of association in insanity. Amer. J. Insanity, 1910–11, 67, 37–96, 317–390.
14. Landis, C. Studies of emotional reactions. II. General be-

* Now published by D. Appleton-Century Company, Inc., New York.

havior and facial expression. J. comp. Psychol., 1924, 4, 447–509.

15. Landis, C. Psychology and the psychogalvanic reflex. Psychol. Rev., 1930, 37, 381–398.

16. Landis, C. Studies of emotional reactions. V. Severe emotional upset. J. comp. Psychol., 1926, 6, 221–242.

17. Landis, C., & Hunt, W. A. The conscious correlates of the galvanic skin response. J. exp. Psychol., 1935, 18, 505–529.

18. Landis, C., & Hunt, W. A. The startle pattern. New York: Farrar & Rinehart, 1939.

19. Larson, J. A. The cardio-pneumo-psychogram in deception. J. exp. Psychol., 1923, 6, 420–454.

20. Marston, W. M. Systolic blood pressure symptoms of deception. J. exp. Psychol., 1917, 2, 117–163.

21. Patterson, E. A qualitative and quantitative study of the emotion of surprise. Psychol. Monog., 1930, 40, No. 181.

22. Sherrington, C. S. The integrative action of the nervous system. New Haven, Connecticut: Yale University Press, 1906, 259–262.

23. Wechsler, D. The measurement of emotional reactions: researches on the psychogalvanic reflex. Arch. Psychol., New York, 1925, 12, No. 76.

24. Woodrow, H., & Lowell, F. Children's association frequency tables. Psychol. Monog., 1916, 22, No. 97.

25. Woodworth, R. S. Psychology. New York: Henry Holt and Company, 1940, 417–439.

Chapter 13

1. Dearborn, W. F. The psychology of reading: an experimental study of the reading pauses and movements of the eye. Arch. Phil. Psychol. & Sci. Method, 1906, 4.

2. Dodge, R., & Cline, T. S. The angle velocity of eye movements. Psychol. Rev., 1901, 8, 145–157.

3. Huey, E. B. On the psychology and physiology of reading. Amer. J. Psychol., 1900, 11, 283–302; 12, 292–312.

4. Myers, C. S. A textbook of experimental psychology. New York: Longmans, Green & Co., 1925, chapters 3, 4, 6, 7.

5. Seashore, C. E. The psychology of musical talent. New York: Silver, Burdett and Company, 1919.

6. Starch, D. Perimetry of the localization of sound. Psychol. Monog., 1905, 6, No. 28, 1–45; 1908, 9, No. 38, 1–55.
7. Stevens, S. S., & Newman, E. B. The localization of actual sources of sound. Amer. J. Psychol., 1936, 48, 297–306.
8. Stratton, G. M. Vision without inversion of the retinal image. Psychol. Rev., 1897, 4, 341–360, 463–481.
9. Stratton, G. M. Symmetry, linear illusions and the movements of the eye. Psychol. Rev., 1906, 13, 82–96.
10. Tinker, M. A. Time taken by eye movements in reading. J. genet. Psychol., 1936, 48, 468–471.
11. Wever, E. G., & Bray, C. W. The nature of acoustic response: the relation between sound frequency and frequency of impulses in the auditory nerve. J. exp. Psychol., 1930, 13, 373–387.
12. Wever, E. G., & Bray, C. W. Present possibilities for auditory theory. Psychol. Rev., 1930, 37, 365–380.
13. Woodworth, R. S. Experimental psychology. New York: Henry Holt and Company, 1938, chapters 21, 22, 23, 26.
14. Young, P. T. Auditory localization with acoustical transposition of the ears. J. exp. Psychol., 1928, 11, 399–429.

Chapter 14

1. Bingham, W. V., & Freyd, M. Procedures in employment psychology. Chicago: A. W. Shaw Company, 1926.
2. Boring, E. G. A history of experimental psychology. New York: The Century Co., 1929,* chapter 8.
3. Breitwieser, J. V. Attention and movement in reaction time. Arch. Psychol., New York, 1911, 2, No. 18.
4. Cassel, E. E., & Dallenbach, K. M. The effect of auditory distractions upon the sensory reaction. Amer. J. Psychol., 1918, 29, 129–143.
5. Cattell, J. McK. The time taken up by cerebral operations. Mind, 1886, 11, 220–242, 377–392, 524–538.
6. Dolley, C. S., & Cattell, J. McK. On reaction-times and the velocity of the nervous impulse. Nat'l Acad. Science, Memoirs, 1895, 7, 391–415: also Psychol. Rev., 1894, 1, 159–168.

* Now published by D. Appleton-Century Company, Inc., New York.

7. Evans, J. E. The effect of distraction on reaction time. Arch. Psychol., New York, 1916, 5, No. 37.

8. Froeberg, S. The relation between the magnitude of stimulus and the time of reaction. Arch. Psychol., New York, 1907, 1, No. 8.

9. Griffith, C. R. An introduction to applied psychology. New York: The Macmillan Company, 1937, chapter 1.

10. Henmon, V. A. C. The time of perception as a measure of differences in sensations. Arch. Phil. Psychol. & Sci. Meth., 1906, No. 8.

11. Henmon, V. A. C. Professor Cattell's work on reaction time. In The psychological researches of James McKeen Cattell. Arch. Psychol., New York, 1914, 4, No. 30, 1.-33.

12. Johanson, A. M. The influence of incentive and punishment upon reaction-time. Arch. Psychol., New York, 1922, 8, No. 54.

13. Judd, C. H., McAllister, C. N., & Steele, W. M. Analysis of reaction movements. Psychol. Monog., 1905, 7, No. 29, 141–184.

14. Lauer, A. R. Fact and fancy regarding driver testing procedures. J. appl. Psychol., 1937, 21, 173–184.

15. Lauer, A. R., & Kotvis, H. L. Automotive manipulation in relation to vision. J. appl. Psychol., 1934, 18, 422–431.

16. Lemmon, V. W. The relation of reaction time to measures of intelligence, memory, and learning. Arch. Psychol., New York, 1927, 15, No. 94.

17. Lickley, J. D. The nervous system. New York: Longmans, Green & Co., 1931, 15.

18. Poffenberger, A. T. Reaction time to retinal stimulation. Arch. Psychol., New York, 1912, 3, No. 23.

19. Shellow, S. M. Selection of motormen: further data on value of tests in Milwaukee. J. pers. Res., 1926, 5, 183–188.

20. Toops, H. A., & Haven, S. E. Viewing the traffic problem. J. appl. Psychol., 1937, 21, 185–197.

21. Wechsler, D. Tests for taxicab drivers. J. pers. Res., 1926, 5, 24–30.

22. Woodrow, H. The measurement of attention. Psychol. Monog., 1914, 17, No. 76.

23. Woodrow, H. The faculty of attention. J. exp. Psychol., 1916, 1, 285–318.
24. Woodworth, R. S. Experimental psychology. New York: Henry Holt and Company, 1938, chapter 14.

Chapter 15

1. Boring, E. G. A history of experimental psychology. New York: The Century Co., 1929,* chapter 13.
2. Fletcher, H. Speech and hearing. New York: D. Van Nostrand Company, Inc., 1929, 68–70.
3. Fullerton, G. S., & Cattell, J. McK. On the perception of small differences. University of Pennsylvania Philosophical Series, 1892, No. 2.
4. Hecht, S. The nature of the photoreceptor process. In Murchison (Ed.), A handbook of general experimental psychology. Worcester, Massachusetts: Clark University Press, 1934, chapter 14.
5. James, W. Principles of psychology. New York: Henry Holt and Company, 1890, I, 534.
6. Kellogg, W. N. An experimental evaluation of equality judgments in psychophysics. Arch. Psychol., New York, 1930, 17, No. 112.
7. Thorndike, E. L. Handwriting. Teach. Coll. Rec., 1910, 11, 1–81.
8. Thurstone, L. L. A method of scaling psychological and educational tests. J. educ. Psychol., 1925, 16, 433–451.
9. Titchener, E. B. Experimental psychology. Instructor's Manual, Quantitative. New York: The Macmillan Company, 1923.
10. Woodworth, R. S. Professor Cattell's psychological contributions. In The psychological researches of James McKeen Cattell. Arch. Psychol., New York, 1914, 4, No. 30, 60–74.
11. Woodworth, R. S. Psychological data pertaining to errors of observation. International Critical Tables. New York: McGraw-Hill Book Company, Inc., 1926, I, 92–95.
12. Woodworth, R. S. Experimental psychology. New York: Henry Holt and Company, 1938, chapter 18.

* Now published by D. Appleton-Century Company, Inc., New York.

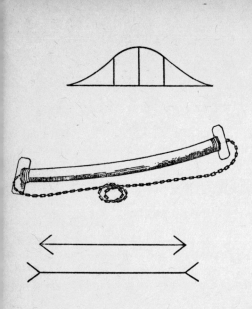

$$r = \frac{\Sigma \times y}{N \sigma_x \ \sigma_y}$$

tropics is in the produced rubber_ _ _ _ _true-fals

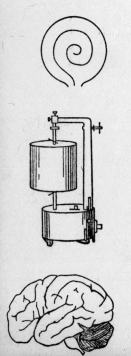

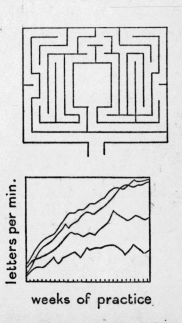